HOW LOCAL ART MADE AUSTRALIA'S NATIONAL CAPITAL

HOW LOCAL ART MADE AUSTRALIA'S NATIONAL CAPITAL

ANNI DOYLE WAWRZYŃCZAK

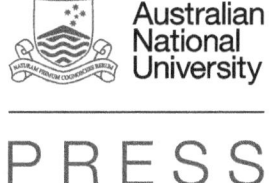

PRESS

For my daughter Callie with love

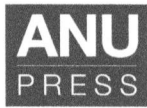

Published by ANU Press
The Australian National University
Acton ACT 2601, Australia
Email: anupress@anu.edu.au

Available to download for free at press.anu.edu.au

ISBN (print): 9781760463403
ISBN (online): 9781760463410

WorldCat (print): 1164067633
WorldCat (online): 1164067426

DOI: 10.22459/HLAMANC.2020

This title is published under a Creative Commons Attribution-NonCommercial-NoDerivatives 4.0 International (CC BY-NC-ND 4.0).

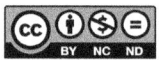

The full licence terms are available at
creativecommons.org/licenses/by-nc-nd/4.0/legalcode

This publication was awarded a College of Arts and Social Sciences PhD Publication Prize in 2017. The prize contributes to the cost of professional copyediting.

Cover design and layout by ANU Press.

Cover photograph: Patricia Piccinini, Skywhale, 2013 by Martin Ollman.

This edition © 2020 ANU Press

CONTENTS

Acknowledgements ix
List of illustrations xi
List of abbreviations and acronyms xv
Introduction 1
1. The national capital space and arts practice: 1913–1978 19
2. The rapid growth of local arts and culture: 1978–1989 47
3. Self-government and the arts 89
4. Bitumen River Gallery – evolution and early years 105
5. Transition: BRG to CCAS 163
6. Transformation: Transcending the local 185
Conclusion 245
References 253
Index 269

ACKNOWLEDGEMENTS

Canberra's arts community has extended much kindness and moral support to me over the last decade. During those years, I have had the privilege of working across visual arts, dance, theatre and music, and within community arts and the multicultural communities as a writer, curator, stage manager, mentor and facilitator. Thank you, to all of you – you are our city's beating heart.

Thanks, also, to Canberra Contemporary Art Space staff, Annika Harding, Sabrina Baker and Alexander Boynes, and particularly David Broker for support and friendship; my daughter Callie, my Canberra family and Anna Pafitis, Anne Chung, Helen Musa, Deborah Clark, Gordon Bull, Robyn Craig, Helene Halliday and Robert Wellington; Professor Helen Ennis, who steered me through the final year and a half of my PhD candidature from which this history arises – her own exceptional scholarship is inspiring; the ANU School of Art and Design community and the School of Art History and Art Theory, led by Professor Denise Ferris, for their support; and Raewyn Arthur, who was there from the beginning.

My grateful thanks to all those who, in person, by phone and via email, shared their experiences and memories with me with such generosity of spirit.

I acknowledge the incomparable Jan Wawrzyńczak whose moral, emotional and physical support afforded me the luxury of study, and whose life, spent as it was in the cultural service of the minoritised and dispossessed, continues to give me courage and inspiration.

I pay my respects to the Ngunnawal people, on whose land we live and make our work, and to their elders, past and present. May your many thousand years of meeting and cultural sharing, with the Gundungurra to the north, the Ngarigo to the south, the Yuin on the coast, and the Wiradjuri inland, continue to enrich our arts and cultural communities.

LIST OF ILLUSTRATIONS

Figure 1. Canberra School of Art building, circa 1980s 8

Figure 2. Group exhibition, *Bad girls: twenty witness 1000*, 8 February – 16 March 2013. Installation photograph, detail 14

Figure 3. Opening of Canberra Mothercraft Society, 1927 23

Figure 4. One of many posters made at Megalo for Jobless Action. Artist unknown 44

Figure 5. Memorial advertisement submitted by S Brown. 69

Figure 6. *Bill posters appreciated*, BRG opening exhibition poster, printed at Megalo, April 1981 113

Figure 7. David Morrow, *Well I've never heard of YOU either*, screen print, postcard, BRG opening invitation for 4 April 1981 114

Figure 8. Alison Alder, *Share the shitwork: even a man can do it*, 1981, brown paper bag, screen print, 25 x 20 cm, Bill posters appreciated, BRG opening exhibition. 115

Figure 9. Collective members 'doing it for themselves', BRG Gallery 119

Figure 10. Collective members 'doing it for themselves', BRG Gallery 119

Figure 11. Alison Alder and Gaida Serilus, Trevor Nickolls, *From Dreamtime to machinetime*, exhibition poster, 1–17 May 1981 . . 121

Figure 12. Alison Alder and Julia Church, *True bird grit*, book cover 134

Figure 13. *Women against rape march*, poster, April 1982 141

Figure 14. Collective members in costume for *Off the beach*, 27 February – 17 March 1985, 23 February 1985 145

Figure 15. Collective members in costume for *Off the beach*, 27 February – 17 March 1985, 23 February 1985 145

Figure 16. Julia Church, *Super Doreen*, 1982, poster, 102 x 76 cm . . 147

Figure 17. Catriona Holyoake, *I won't see you in paradise (slut)*, 1983, screen print, 100 x 80 cm. 151

Figure 18. *Post-atomic card!: Working art!*, colour postcard 154

Figure 19. BRG group exhibition, *Salon coda: the making of history*, 10 June – 5 July 1987, installation photograph, detail 177

Figure 20. Exterior, BRG renamed CCAS Gallery 3 177

Figure 21. Arthur Wicks, *Mobile observatory*, wooden machine (working), main blades 4 m, total length 2 x 1.3 m, installed in gallery in *Site specific city*, CCAS group exhibition, 10 July – 2 August 1987 178

Figure 22. Artist and policeman, preparing tyre tower; tyre tower detritus installed in gallery in *Site specific city*, CCAS group exhibition, 10 July – 2 August 1987. 178

Figure 23. Dale Frank, *Satellite of love*, CCAS, 11 December 1994 – 29 January 1995, installation photograph 197

Figure 24. Left to right: Hawk McLean, Renald Navilly (formerly Navarro) and eX de Medici, 'Inside out', performance art season, 26 September – 24 October 1998, CCAS Gorman House 205

Figure 25. Cristy Gilbert and Anna Simic, *Edible art*, 'Inside out', performance art season, 26 September – 24 October 1998, CCAS Gorman House 205

Figure 26. Poster advertising 'Up till now … a season of films by independent filmmaker Tony Ayres', 'Inside out', curated by Jane Barney, 25 September – 3 October 1998, CCAS Gorman House 206

Figure 27. Bronwyn Sandland and Paull McKee, *Beautiful home: just what is it that makes today's home so different, so appealing?*, CCAS, 11 July – 8 August 1998, installation photograph 207

Figure 28. Poster, The Foundry, printed at Megalo, artists unknown 218

LIST OF ILLUSTRATIONS

Figure 29. *Nowhere utopia*. BRG touring group exhibition at THAT Space, Brisbane, 3–14 March 1987, installation photograph. Far right: eX de Medici's *Pistol*, 1985, gridded black-and-white laser-copied image, 1200 x 1600 cm, printed on Canon's first prototype laser photocopier as a 16-piece gridded image 223

Figure 30. eX de Medici, *United colours*, gridded colour laser-copied image, in Goethe-Institut's international travelling exhibition, *I am you: artists against violence, art for tolerance*, CCAS, 12 October – 6 November 1994, installation photograph 227

Figure 31. eX de Medici, *60 heads*, exhibition detail, laminated inkjet prints, 59.4 x 84.1 cm, CCAS travelling exhibition, ACCA, Melbourne, 24 January – 2 March 1997, installation photograph 230

Figure 32. eX de Medici, *60 heads*, laminated inkjet prints, 59.4 x 84.1 cm, CCAS travelling exhibition, ACCA, Melbourne, 24 January – 2 March 1997, installation photograph 230

Figure 33. *Naii Ngarrambai Wanggirali Burrangiri Nangi Dyannai Ngurui (the lay of the land is how you know your country; when you look behind you, you can always see your tracks)*, installation photograph, detail 236

Figure 34. *Naii Ngarrambai Wanggirali Burrangiri Nangi Dyannai Ngurui (the lay of the land is how you know your country; when you look behind you, you can always see your tracks)*, artists: Neville O'Neill, Kalara Gilbert, Megan Elliot, Gail Harradine, Michael Kennedy, Gordon Hookey, Arnold Williams, Jim 'Boza' Williams, Johnno Johnson, Aunty Matilda House, Joan Wingfield; exterior CCAS, Gorman House, April 1995 ... 237

Figure 35. Shane Breynard and Marta Penner, *Canberra Brasilia*, CCAS artist exchange and travelling exhibition at CCAS, 8 September – 20 October 2001, installation photograph 241

Figure 36. Shane Breynard and Marta Penner, *Canberra Brasilia*, CCAS artist exchange and travelling exhibition at CCAS, 8 September – 20 October 2001, installation photograph of hammocks strung between apartments in the Currong apartments, Canberra................................. 243

Figure 37. Patricia Piccinini, *Skywhale*, 2013 246

LIST OF ABBREVIATIONS AND ACRONYMS

ABS	Australian Bureau of Statistics
ACA	Arts Council of Australia
ACG	Arts Council Gallery
ACP	Australian Centre for Photography
ACT	Australian Capital Territory
ADB	ACT Arts Development Board
AETT	Australian Elizabethan Theatre Trust
AGNSW	Art Gallery of New South Wales
aGOG	australian Girls Own Gallery
ANCA	Australian National Capital Artists
ANG	Australian National Gallery
ANU	The Australian National University
ANU SOA	Australian National University School of Art
APW	Australian Print Workshop
ASOC	Artists' Society of Canberra
AWM	Australian War Memorial
BRG	Bitumen River Gallery
CAM	Canberra Arts Marketing
Canberra Rep	Canberra Repertory Society
CAOA	Contemporary Art Organisations Australia
CAPO	Capital Art Patrons' Organisation
CAS	Contemporary Art Society (Australia)

CAST	Contemporary Art Space Tasmania
CCAE	Canberra College of Advanced Education
CCAF	Canberra Community Arts Front
CCAS	Canberra Contemporary Art Space
CDF	ACT Community Development Fund
CDP	Community Development Program
CEMA	Council for the Encouragement of Music and the Arts
CEP	Community Employment Program
CIT	Canberra Institute of Technology
CMAG	Canberra Museum and Gallery
CPAML	Communist Party of Australia Marxist Leninist
CPI	Consumer Price Index
CSA	Canberra School of Art
CSIRO	Commonwealth Science and Industrial Research Organisation
CSO	Canberra Symphony Orchestra
CTC	Canberra Theatre Centre
CWL	Canberra Women's Liberation
CYSS	Community Youth Support Scheme
CYT	Canberra Youth Theatre
DCT	Department of the Capital Territory
DTLG	Department of Territories and Local Government
EAF	Experimental Art Foundation
EASS	Emerging Artist Support Scheme
FCAC	Federal Capital Advisory Committee
FCC	Federal Capital Commission
IMA	Institute of Modern Art
NATEX	National Exhibition Centre
NCA	National Capital Authority
NCDC	National Capital Development Commission
NCPA	National Capital Planning Authority

NETS	National Exhibitions Touring Support
NFSA	National Film and Sound Archive
NGA	National Gallery of Australia
NGV	National Gallery of Victoria
NLA	National Library of Australia
NMA	National Museum of Australia
NPG	National Portrait Gallery
NSW	New South Wales
NT	Northern Territory
P&A	Pastoral and Agricultural Association
PAM	Progressive Art Movement
PLO	Palestine Liberation Organisation
SA SOA	South Australian School of Art
SofA	ANU School of Art
SRC	Student Representative Council
TAU	Through Art Unity
VAB	Visual Arts Board
VBU	Vehicle Builders Union
WEL ACT	Women's Electoral Lobby ACT

INTRODUCTION

How local art made Australia's national capital considers Canberra from a perspective that pays homage to art and culture as a generative force in the city's development, unfolding the complex circumstances that gave rise to a distinctive citywide arts practice.

Canberra's contemporary arts sphere is the result of junctures between two distinct iterations of space: national capital space and local space. The arts community that emerged is unique – the product of a complex set of circumstances as the ideals of the national capital butted up against the realities of local life. This pre-eminent iteration of place – the national political centre of a young but advanced democracy – ensured fertile tensions arose that directly impacted on the genesis and development of the city's contemporary arts practice in ways not seen elsewhere in the country.

This history of two contemporary art galleries is set within the broader narrative of the development of arts and culture from the 1920s to the 2000s. The rise of Bitumen River Gallery (BRG), which was established in Australia's national capital in 1981, and Canberra Contemporary Art Space (CCAS), which followed in 1987, illustrates the triumph of local arts practice and community over the cultural imperatives of nation-building.

During 20 years in Canberra I have experienced, and seen extended to many others, particularly warm and useful interactions within CCAS and across the broad spectrum of local arts and cultural practices. In a city primarily constructed to accommodate the business of federal politics, the arts scene is, by contrast, marked by a distinct lack of political correctness. I determined to find out why this was so.

From the earliest days of the formation of arts societies and the activities of The Australian National University (ANU) in the 1940s, to a broad array of community endeavours, there is much evidence of Canberra's arts community's commitment to expanding a local cultural agenda from within the confines of Commonwealth-controlled funding and political ideology. As the 1970s and 1980s progressed, social activism became a forceful expression of this community strength. Political engagement was evidentially hardwired into Canberra life, itself a product of the continuing tussle between national and local politics. Social activism emerged as a powerful force in the early 1970s, resulting in a raft of desperately needed social initiatives, including the 1973 establishment in Canberra of Beryl, Australia's second women's refuge. By 1978 social activism was instrumental in the birth of contemporary arts practice as fledgling local print and poster makers began responding to local, national and international social concerns.[1] Throughout the 1980s, activists became increasingly insistent in Canberra, alerting federal government and local representatives to rapidly growing needs in local arts and culture. They ensured that, by the time the Australian Capital Territory (ACT) achieved self-government in 1992, members of the territory's Legislative Assembly were fully aware of the community's desires and needs and were determined to fulfil them.

The Commonwealth Government's uncertain commitment to Canberra over the first half of the twentieth century, which was transformed under Liberal Prime Minister Robert Menzies in 1958, provided fertile ground for emerging tensions. From the late 1960s, based on the arts funding models of the United Kingdom, Canada and the United States, the Commonwealth sought to develop nationally recognised, flagship performing arts companies in Canberra, which was entirely at odds with the realities of local need and desire, and Canberra's small population.[2] During this period, the emphasis on performing arts came at the expense

---

1   Megalo Print Studio and Gallery (Megalo) and the National Gallery of Australia (NGA) have a large collection of prints and posters by Canberra artists. The majority of early works remain unattributed and, more than 40 years on from 1978, there is an urgent need for resources to be allocated to attribution while there are still living artists who may remember the particular circumstances under which these posters were made. For posters evidencing the work of Jobless Action (the Commonwealth-funded, local job-creation organisation established in 1976) see for example: Paul Ford, *Unemployment: a creative alternative – Jobless Action* (1981–82) and David Morrow, *May Day '81: march for full employment* (1981). Both examples are held in the Megalo Poster Archives.

2   There are distinct similarities between the development of national arts policy in Australia from 1967 and the policies of the United Kingdom and United States, which were developed in 1964 and 1965. Indications of similarities in language and policy development can be found as follows:

of the visual arts. The 1970s and 1980s were marked by increasing tensions between the Commonwealth and the local community as the latter sought to control local arts and the cultural trajectory from within this focus on national identity. In the visual arts, the drive for national excellence promulgated by the Commonwealth led arts consultant Timothy Pascoe to erroneously conclude, in 1985, that local artists enjoyed higher investment and outcomes in comparison to their colleagues in other Australian cities, because of the presence of the National Gallery of Australia (NGA), which opened in 1982.[3]

The transition to self-government, which commenced in 1989, was of fundamental importance to Canberra's maturing art scene. Foremost among the positive benefits flowing from the release from Commonwealth control that followed self-government from 1992, was the ability of successive local governments to drive a coherent and bipartisan local arts and cultural agenda.[4]

Throughout the latter half of the century, women exerted a profound influence over the development of Canberra's arts milieu. In the 1960s and 1970s, they set up creative women's groups to combat the loneliness and lack of extended support groups that were a feature of Canberra

---

Australia: Harold Holt, 'Australian cultural activities', Ministerial statement, House of Representatives, 1 November 1967, historichansard.net/senate/1967/19671107_senate_26_s36/#subdebate-17-0-s0, accessed 22 May 2013; *Canberra Times*, 'Council grants to arts', 12 December 1968, p 33.

United States: National Council on the Arts policy statement in National Council on the Arts, *The first annual report on the National Council on the Arts*, 1964–65, Washington DC, 1965, www.arts.gov/sites/default/files/NEA-Annual-Report-1964-1965.pdf, accessed 23 May 2013. See especially 'Foreword' and 'Policy statement', pp 1–2.

United Kingdom: Jennie Lee, *A policy for the arts – the first steps*, London, HMSO, 15 February 1965, p 6, action.labour.org.uk/page/-/blog%20images/policy_for_the_arts.pdf, accessed 26 May 2013; Lawrence Black, 'Not only a source of expenditure but a source of income', in Christiane Eisenberg, Rita Gerlach and Christian Handke (eds), *Cultural industries: the British experience in international perspective*, Berlin, Humboldt University, 2006, p 120, edoc.hu-berlin.de/conferences/culturalindustries/proc/culturalindustries.pdf, accessed 22 May 2013.

The companies nominated as flagship companies, pre-1985, were Canberra Theatre Trust, Human Veins Dance Theatre, Opera ACT, and Canberra Symphony Orchestra.

3   See Timothy Pascoe, *Arts in the ACT: funding priorities and grant administration*, Canberra, ACT Arts Development Board, Commonwealth of Australia, 1985, p 57. Pascoe Report recommendations for flagship performing arts companies from 1985: Theatre ACT, Human Veins Dance Theatre, Crafts Council of the ACT Canberra Symphony Orchestra. See Chapter 2 for a close reading of this ACT Arts Development Board–commissioned report into the state of the arts in the ACT.

4   See Australian Capital Territory, Parliamentary debates, Legislative Assembly, Hansard, 26 August 2004: 4323; Select Committee on Cultural Activities and Facilities, *Final report*, Canberra, ACT Legislative Assembly, June 1991; Standing Committee on Planning, Development and Infrastructure, *Report no. 9*, Canberra, ACT Legislative Assembly, December 1992.

life because of the small and transient population, and they established the first commercial galleries. Their critical influence, in contrast to the trend of a male-dominated art scene in the rest of late twentieth-century Australia, is felt throughout the history of BRG/CCAS: as teachers and mentors; as students and activists who went on to establish printmaking workshops and exhibition venues; and as coordinators, curators and artists who collectively influenced the development of local practice.

Histories of Canberra

Studies of Canberra's history are increasing in number and breadth as writers respond to the inherent complexities of national capital development. Recent publications have covered Canberra's Indigenous history;[5] the city's conception, planning and execution as a national centre;[6] the relationship of Canberra to its national cultural institutions;[7] notable Canberra buildings and general architecture;[8] its citizens;[9] and its broad history.[10] It has been the custom for some of the national cultural institutions to publish widely in their areas, from the single sheets outlining aspects of Canberra's development issued by the National Archives of Australia to

---

5   See, for example, Ann Jackson-Nakano, *The Kamberri: a history from the records of Aboriginal families in the Canberra–Queanbeyan district and surrounds 1820–1927 and historical overview 1928–2001* (Weerawa History Series, Canberra, 2001). Also see ACT Government Genealogy Project, *Our kin our country* (Canberra, ACT Government, August 2012, www.communityservices.act.gov.au/__data/assets/pdf_file/0005/394385/CSD_GSR_web.pdf, accessed 7 November 2015).
6   See, for example, six booklets published by the Chief Minister's Department to mark the centenary of Canberra: Greg Wood, *Maps and makers* and *The community that was* (2009); David Headon, *Crystal palace to golden trowels* and *Those other Americans* (2009) and *Beyond the boundaries* (2012); Ian Warden, *Think of it! Dream of it! In six snapshots* (2009).
7   Chris Beer, 'The production of Canberra and its national cultural institutions: imagination and practice of national capital space, national leadership and transnational and national museum practice, and Commonwealth managerial space', conference paper, Australasian Political Studies Association, Newcastle, NSW, 25–27 September 2006.
8   For specific buildings, see, for example, principally Lenore Coltheart, *Albert Hall: the heart of Canberra* (Sydney, UNSW Press, 2014); Sarah Rood and Belinda Ensor, *Olims Hotel Canberra: through the ages* (Sydney, CL Creations, 2007). For general architecture, see, for example, Ken Charlton, *Federal capital architecture: Canberra, 1911–1939* (Canberra, National Trust of Australia, 1984); Andrew Metcalfe, *Canberra architecture* (Watermark Architectural Guides, Boorowa, NSW, Watermark, 2006); Tim Reeves and Alan Roberts, *100 Canberra houses: a century of capital architecture* (Canberra, Halstead Press, 2013); Ken Charlton, Paola Favaro and Bronwen Jones, *The contribution of Enrico Taglietti to Canberra's architecture* (Canberra, Royal Australian Institute of Architects, ACT Chapter, 2007).
9   See, for example, Brian Smith and Heide Smith, *A portrait of Canberra and of Canberrans 1979–2012* (Narooma, NSW, Hobbs Point Publishing, 2012); 'From Lady Denman to Katy Gallagher: a century of women's contributions to Canberra' (www.womenaustralia.info/exhib/ldkg/, accessed 15 August 2014).
10 See principally Nicholas Brown, *A history of Canberra* (Cambridge University Press, 2014); also see Paul Daley, *Canberra* (City Series, Sydney, NewSouth Publishing, 2012).

that institution's ambitious centenary research guide *Government records about the Australian Capital Territory*, to the wealth of material held by the National Library of Australia (NLA) and made available online.[11]

The Centenary of Canberra in 2013 provided further impetus for projects such as the Australian Women's archive project *From Lady Denman to Katy Gallagher: a century of women's contributions to Canberra*.[12] Recently, small booklets produced by those involved in social initiatives, such as the women's refuge Beryl, Toora Women Inc (established in the early 1980s) and Majura Women's Group (founded in 1981),[13] have all contributed to a fuller picture of Canberra's development.

Studies of important Canberra art institutions have appeared in recent years. Michael Agostino's *The Australian National University School of Art: a history of the first 65 years* (2009) gathers together rich archival material relating to the development of that institution from the Canberra Technical College to the workshops and lecturers, visiting artists and arts initiatives of the Canberra School of Art (CSA). To coincide with the centenary, Megalo Print Studio and Gallery (Megalo) published *Megalomania: 33 years of posters made at Megalo Print Studio 1980–2013*, an abridged history comprising an introduction, a selection of hundreds of prints produced by artists working with that organisation over 30 years, and interviews.[14] Another centenary publication, a short history of the Australian National Capital Artists (ANCA) studios and gallery, *Intensity of purpose: 21 years of ANCA*, was published to coincide with an exhibition of the same name at the Canberra Museum and Gallery (CMAG – established 1998).[15] As well, former NGA director Betty Churcher,

---

11   For example, National Library of Australia, 'Griffin and early Canberra collection', Selected Library Collections (www.nla.gov.au/selected-library-collections/griffin-and-early-canberra-collection), and 'Focus: Canberra', Research Guides and Subject Listings (www.nla.gov.au/research-guides/federation/focus-canberra, accessed 10 August 2014); Ted Ling, *Government records about the Australian Capital Territory* (Canberra, National Archives of Australia, 2013, www.archives.act.gov.au/__data/assets/pdf_file/0008/562544/Canberra_Research_Guide.pdf, accessed 3 April 2012).
12   Henningham, 2013.
13   Farzana Choudhury (ed), *Opening a new door: the herstory of Beryl Women Inc. 1975–2015*, Canberra, Beryl Women Inc, 2015; Elena Roseman, *Talking like a Toora woman*, Canberra, Toora Women Inc, 2004. See also Helen Skeat (ed), *Majura Women's Group celebrating 25 years: a selection of recollections, reflections, images and quotations* (Canberra, Majura Women's Group Inc, 2006). This commemorative booklet accompanied an exhibition at CMAG.
14   Chris Wallace with Robyn Archer, Kathryn Ross and Emily Sykes, *Megalomania: 33 years of posters made at Megalo Print Studio 1980–2013*, Canberra, Megalo Print Studio + Gallery, 2013. The publication coincided with an exhibition of the same name at Megalo.
15   Alison Bell (ed), *Intensity of purpose: 21 years of ANCA*, exhibition catalogue, Canberra, Australian National Capital Artists, 2013.

assisted by Lucy Quinn, produced *Treasures of Canberra*, a book of selected artworks from Canberra's national cultural institutions.[16] Particularly relevant to Canberra's contemporary visual arts have been the exhibitions and catalogues produced by CMAG, such as *Something in the air: collage and assemblage in Canberra region art* and *Imitation of life: memory and mimicry in Canberra region art*.[17]

Ideas regarding the formal beginnings of Canberra as an art centre go back to the 1940s. In 1941, Charles Bean, chair of the Australian War Memorial (AWM – opened 1943), proposed that Canberra should be developed as a cultural centre and establish its own art school. Taking up the idea in 1965, Richard 'Dick' Kingsland, secretary of the Department of the Interior, with the support of HC 'Nugget' Coombs, governor of the Reserve Bank, invited art educator Donald Brook to Canberra to discuss establishing a serious art school at Canberra Technical College.[18]

To that end, Brook assumed leadership of the college, which, since 1933, was housed in a series of repurposed timber and fibro huts, built in 1911 for Canberra's Royal Military College, Duntroon, and relocated to the inner south suburb of Kingston as 'temporary' accommodation.

The journey from the college's first part-time art classes in 1942, to the eventual establishment of the CSA as the sole inhabitant of its own premises in 1976, exemplifies the principal struggle that daunted Canberra's arts community until the 1990s. That is, the resourcing of and control over appropriate spaces where the *idea* of Canberra as an arts centre, and local desire to affect this, was matched with suitable physical spaces.[19] Despite many submissions, editorials, enquiries, committees and reports over more than 30 years, from the 1930s through to the beginning

---

16   Betty Churcher and Lucy Quinn, *Treasures of Canberra*, Canberra, Halstead Press, 2013.
17   Deborah Clark and Mark Van Veen (eds), *Something in the air: collage and assemblage in Canberra region art*, exhibition catalogue, Canberra, CMAG, 2010; Deborah Clark (ed), *Imitation of life: memory and mimicry in Canberra region art*, exhibition catalogue, Canberra, CMAG, 2011.
18   *Artlink*'s editor Stephanie Britton described Brook, who is currently emeritus professor of art history at South Australia's Flinders University, as 'Australia's most revered art theorist', in an editor's note to Brook's essay, 'The art school way back when' (*Artlink* 31, 3, 2011, p 80). Brook was a seminal figure in the development of Australia's contemporary art spaces. In Adelaide in the mid-1970s, he spearheaded the campaign for a small gallery run on a collective basis by artists, for artists. His work led to the founding of Adelaide's Experimental Art Foundation (EAF) in 1974.
19   At the time, and until 1977, the NSW Department of Education had responsibility for technical education in the ACT with regard to full-time staffing (through the National Art School in Sydney) and curricula. The Department of the Interior, representing the Commonwealth, took responsibility for support staff, policy and the provision of buildings.

of the 1970s, technical trade students and the growing contingent of art and craft students largely continued to be housed in the entirely unsatisfactory, repurposed huts and demountables.

From the 1950s, 'hobbyist' art classes accounted for an increasing percentage of overall technical college enrolments, testifying to the increasing hunger for art education within the population; colloquially, those enrolled were referred to as attending the School of Arts or the School of Arts and Crafts. Through the 1960s, under full-time teacher Henri le Grand in ceramics and part-time teachers including Beverley Batt, Jan Brown, Tom Cleghorn, Lola de Mar, Lyndon Dadswell and Robin Wallace-Crabbe, enrolments and course offerings continued to increase.[20] By 1966 a full-time introductory art course was established, at what by now was referred to as the 'School of Art', Canberra Technical College.

Although Brook resigned, unhappily, less than 12 months into his tenure, his further reports on the condition of the buildings, which made them unsuitable as a post-secondary art college, and the difficulties associated with external control, assisted in increasing community determination to find new premises and to establish a standalone art school.[21]

In 1969, the school began transitioning to the old Canberra High School in Acton, the site of The Australian National University (ANU). Although some renovations in 1974 transformed the art deco building into a structure more suited to an art school, a $3 million building program between 1979 and 1981 resulted in Canberra finally being able to claim a fully resourced School of Art.

In 1977, CSA was greatly expanded to be a Bauhaus-inspired group of art and craft workshops under inaugural director Udo Sellbach. From that time onwards, the school attracted lecturers and produced artists of national and international importance, becoming a central player in the development of the city's unique arts practice.

---

20   Agostino (pp 6–20) comprehensively details the period from 1942/43 to 1976, when the teaching of art was separated from technical education. Michael Agostino, *The Australian National University School of Art: a history of the first 65 years*, Canberra, ANU School of Art, 2009.
21   Brook's employment at Canberra Technical College foundered on the obduracy of NSW Education Department officials, in spite of the overt support of Kingsland and Coombs (who was soon to be the proponent and chair of the Australian Council for the Arts and chancellor of ANU), and of students and staff at Canberra Technical College.

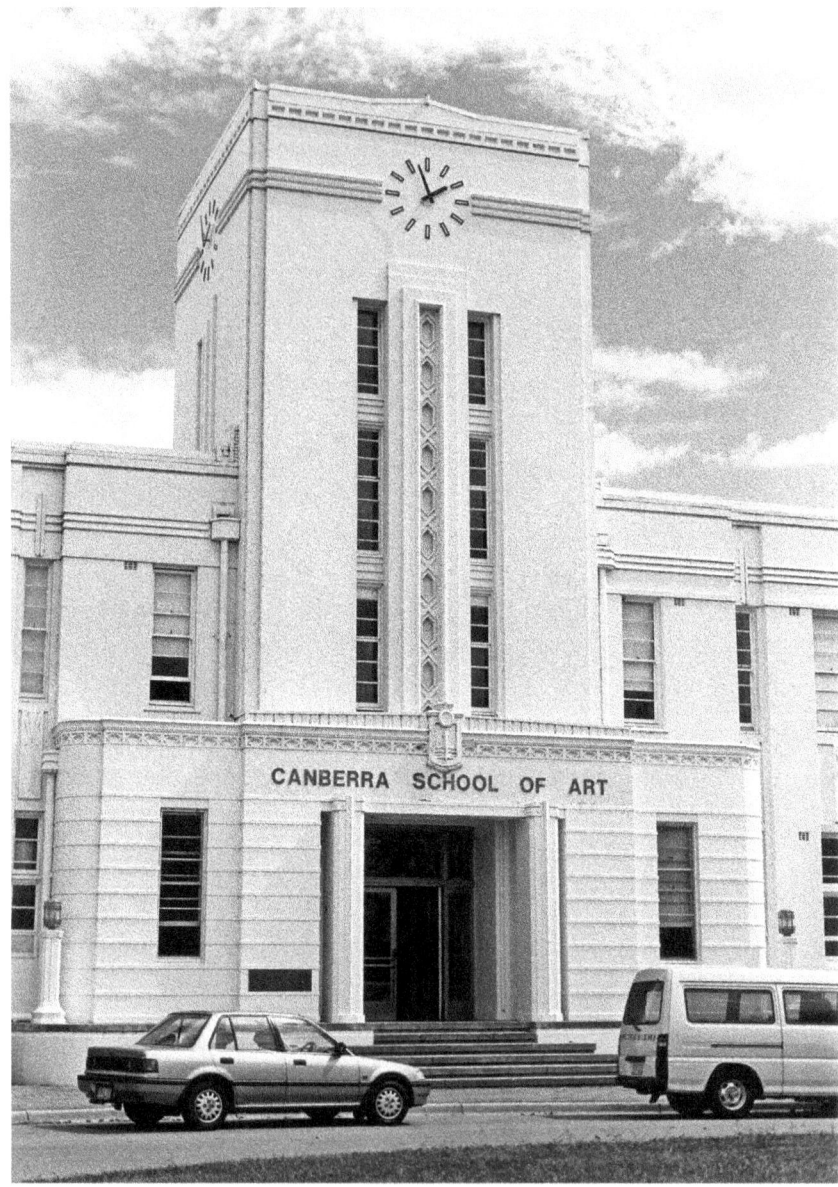

Figure 1. Canberra School of Art building, circa 1980s
Source. Australian National University Archives, photographer Julie Macklin, ANU Photographic Services, reproduced with permission

INTRODUCTION

Contemporary arts organisations

Part two of this history explores the development and activities of Bitumen River Gallery/Canberra Contemporary Art Space. Predicated on the local, the organisation displayed both local and national relevance from its inception and, in the 1990s, it developed an increasingly international outlook.

The context within which BRG evolved stemmed from meetings held in Canberra in 1980 to canvas the idea of a collective gallery. In the absence of government funding alternatives, the Commonwealth-funded, local job-creation organisation Jobless Action provided initial support for the establishment of Megalo in 1980, and then BRG 12 months later. By 1986, of Australia's six states and territories, only the ACT, where Canberra is sited, and the Northern Territory (NT) lacked a contemporary art space. Between the opening of BRG in 1981, and 1986, when the first public meeting was held seeking interest in forming a contemporary arts space in the NT's capital city, Darwin, the Visual Arts Board (VAB) of the Australia Council for the Arts (Australia Council) committed to supporting contemporary art spaces in all Australian states and territories.[22] During the 1986 meeting, the VAB outlined its willingness to provide 'in-principle support and potential funding'.[23] CCAS was then established, with some Australia Council assistance, through a merger of BRG with the Arts Council Gallery (ACG) in 1987, continuing BRG's important foundational work. By the end of the 1980s, CCAS was one of 12 contemporary art spaces in Australia that united under the national support organisation Contemporary Art Organisations Australia (CAOA). Funded by state and federal government arts bodies, they supported and presented work by living artists across a range of media. With the exception of the Contemporary Art Centre of South Australia (CACSA), which opened in 1942, most of these spaces were founded in the 1970s and 1980s.

Of the CAOA member organisations, seven have produced partial histories in various formats that review or examine periods in their development, including the Institute of Modern Art (IMA, Brisbane, founded 1975), Performance Space (Sydney, 1983), Contemporary Art Tasmania

---

22 Malcolm McKinnon, *The hottest gallery in the world: 10 years at 24HR Art – Northern Territory Centre for Contemporary Art (1990–2000)*, Darwin, 24HR Art, 2001, p 6.
23 McKinnon, 2001.

(CAT, Hobart (previously Chameleon/Arthouse/NETS/CAST), 1983), Northern Centre for Contemporary Art (NCCA, Darwin (previously 24HR Art), 1989), Experimental Art Foundation (EAF, 1974), Gertrude Contemporary (Melbourne, 1985) and CACSA.[24] Perth Institute of Contemporary Arts (PICA (from Praxis), 1974), Artspace Visual Arts Centre (Sydney, 1983), the Centre for Contemporary Photography (CCP, Melbourne, 1986) and the Australian Centre for Photography (ACP, Sydney, 1973) have no published histories, although the latter's publication, *Photofile*, first published in 1983, provides a comprehensive history of contemporary photography practice in Australia.[25]

While BRG began in response to particular local social, political and cultural factors, it was also in line with national developments of the 1980s regarding the exhibition and development of contemporary art. While this history does not compare BRG/CCAS with the other 11 CAOA members, it is useful to compare the beginnings of Canberra's

---

24   For South Australia, see Stephanie Britton (ed), *A decade at the EAF: a history of the Experimental Art Foundation 1974–1984* (Adelaide, Australian Experimental Art Foundation, 1984). This publication gathers together images and recollections of exhibitions and events, and includes essays from Donald Brook that speak eloquently of the pace of change in 1970s art practice in Australia. Subsequently to this, in various years, the EAF has produced small booklets covering its exhibitions. See also Dean Bruton (ed), *The contemporary art society of South Australia 1942–86: recollections* (Adelaide, The Contemporary Art Society of South Australia, 1986). For Queensland, see Bob Lingard and Sue Cramer (eds), *Institute of Modern Art: a documentary history 1975–1989* (Brisbane, Institute of Modern Art, 1989), which documents the first 15 years of the organisation through the eyes of its directors. Former director David Broker wrote 'Quo vadis: 1994 to 2004: the Snelling years' (Brisbane, Institute of Modern Art, 2005, web.archive.org/web/20140306081944/http://www.ima.org.au/pages/history/1994E280932004-the-snelling-years.php, last captured 6 March 2014, accessed 2 August 2012). The IMA is compiling an exhibitions list that currently runs from 1975 to 2000, and includes a qualifier as to its non-completeness and accuracy. For Tasmania, see Victoria Hammond (ed), *Chameleon: a decade (1983–1993)* (Hobart, Contemporary Art Space Tasmania, 1983). This publication and exhibition considered Chameleon over its 10-year history and was produced by CAST (now CAT) following the amalgamation between Chameleon in Hobart and Arthouse in Launceston. For the Northern Territory, see McKinnon, 2001. CAST and 24HR Art (now NCCA) publications use voices from a variety of ex- and current members whose stories privilege place and whose writing is lively and compelling. For New South Wales, see *21 years of hybrid arts practice* (Sydney, Performance Space, 2004). Released to mark Performance Space's 21st birthday celebrations, this publication includes a list of works based on the organisation's incomplete archive. In addition, Mike Mullins, who founded Performance Space and devised the inaugural show *Long, long time ago (aka New blood two)* in 1983, presented his Masters thesis in the form of a two-hour video at COFA on aspects of the organisation's history. For Victoria, see Charlotte Day (ed), *A short ride in a fast machine: Gertrude Contemporary Art Spaces 1985–2005* (Melbourne, Gertrude Contemporary, 2006). This 280-page, full-colour book marked the organisation's 20-year anniversary.

25   In addition to the above organisations, the George Paton Gallery at the University of Melbourne was important as the first experimental art space to be supported by an institution. From 1973–80, under the visionary direction of Kiffy Rubbo, the gallery provided a home for the Women's Art Register and the Women's Art Movement and championed women's and political art, performance and video, photography and sculpture.

contemporary arts space with Darwin's NCCA and Hobart's CAT. This is because of important similarities, despite the emergence of these three groups over a decade, and the vast differences between the three cities in which they are located.

The ACT, Tasmania and the NT are home to Australia's smallest populations. The NT has the nation's highest non-urban population of Aboriginal people. Both the NT and Tasmania are geographically isolated from major Australian cities, while the ACT covers the smallest geographical area. Of the three capital cities, Darwin, which is geographically close to Asia, is the most culturally diverse, although Canberra's cultural ecology benefits from more than 80 international embassies based in the city. The ACT and the NT face similar arts funding challenges as a result of restricted legislative agency. Of course, Tasmania, the ACT and the NT are separated by thousands of kilometres and, despite similarities in population numbers, are vastly different in make-up. Yet the published histories of both NCCA and CAT highlight key concerns shared by arts communities in Canberra, Darwin and Hobart[26] at a time when none of these cities offered art school graduates or emerging artists continuing exhibition opportunities outside the art school paradigm. Artists in all three locations were therefore compelled to create their own galleries.

Inaugural BRG coordinator Alison Alder reflected on the need for a gallery to promote the work of local artists in a national forum in 1983:

> The Art School was the pivot of art activity which was closed to artists outside of that system. There were no collective studios, although a number of people had tried to set up artists' studios which had failed, mainly, I think, because of the small number of graduates remaining in Canberra and also from the lack of space due to the artificial nature of the city.[27]

Alder's comments about the founding of BRG to support local Canberra artists with opportunities to develop their practice and further their careers is echoed in statements by the founders of spaces in Tasmania and the NT. Bo Jones, founding member of Chameleon in Hobart, recalled that 'the Art School wore the responsibility for the whole visual art scene'.[28] Once the idea for a local contemporary artist-run collective was established in

---

26 McKinnon, 2001; Hammond, 1983.
27 Alison Alder, 'Serving the needs of artists', conference paper, *Open sandwich conference*, ANZART, Hobart, May 1983.
28 Jones, quoted in Hammond, 1983, p 8.

Hobart, 'the idea took off like wildfire'.[29] Likewise, the inaugural director of 24HR Art, Chris Downie, remembered the period directly prior to its establishment in 1989: 'There's been nowhere for graduates from art school to go, most of them leave the Territory the minute they graduate.'[30]

Similarities can also be found in the ways that the three collectives developed their exhibition spaces. All reclaimed sites, BRG occupied a derelict shelter shed attached to the grounds of a church and primary school; 24HR Art was established in a decaying petrol station earmarked for demolition; and Chameleon opened in the abandoned Blundstone boot factory. The sites of these galleries inspired their names: Alder remembers BRG as being named for the evocative sighing of the wind through the trees edging the large bitumen car park adjacent to the gallery building; 24HR Art referenced the 24-hour-a-day trading of the former Go-Lo petrol station it occupied; and Chameleon encapsulated art's ability to transform place. The buildings were reclaimed for the display of contemporary arts practice, and the names given to them reflect the 'do-it-yourself' mentality with which these organisations were formed.

Unlike other states and territories, however, the ACT is the site of the nation's capital and home to its premier art, cultural and educational institutions. These mark Canberra as national capital space. Within a small population, this has given rise to citizens who are, broadly speaking, politically and culturally literate and who extended support, in unique ways, for the growth of a local arts practice during the final two decades of the twentieth century.

Canberra women and contemporary art

An exceptional aspect of the contemporary art community in Canberra is the profound influence exerted by women on its development. As drivers of social change in the 1970s, women were responsible for instigating much-needed social reform within Canberra's unusual population demographic that, by the 1960s, saw a majority of women and children

---

29 Jones, quoted in Hammond, 1983, p 8.
30 Chris Downie, '*Eyeline Magazine*, 1991', in McKinnon, 2001, p 7.

within the population.³¹ These statistics created unique circumstances for active community engagement with women's social problems, including isolation, housing, domestic violence and public safety issues. Women's political activism went hand-in-hand with international and national social and political movements, including women's liberation, opposition to the Vietnam War, the countercultural movement, the fight for Indigenous rights and the campaign for nuclear disarmament. This led to poster making that was practised largely, though not exclusively, by women as an instrument to champion social change and cohesion, shaping the beginnings of a local contemporary arts practice.

Poster making was an ideal tool for communication and agitation. While the printing process was physically arduous, the production process was cheap and accessible. It was, therefore, an ideal collective endeavour. Its ability to be rapidly deployed throughout an urban environment made it unparalleled as a public message machine.

The influence of women in the history of Canberra's arts is usefully illustrated by a statistical anomaly: BRG/CCAS is distinguished as the only contemporary art space in Australia that has continuously exhibited a higher percentage of female artists than male. This was revealed by a compilation statistics of exhibitors at BRG/CCAS from 1981 to 2012 in preparation for the exhibition *Bad girls: twenty witness 1000*, which I curated in February 2013.³² The exhibition comprised 28 artworks from 20 female artists who had exhibited at BRG/CCAS from April 1981 to December 2012 and reflected the tremendous diversity of ideas addressed over the period and the local, national and global frames of reference in which the artists couched their practice (see Figure 2). The artists in the exhibition were representative of the more than 1,000 women who had shown at the gallery over the preceding 32 years. For a relatively small regional contemporary art space, this is an extraordinary record.

---

31 In 1961, in a total population of 58,856, there were 10,885 women aged from 20–44 and 20,651 children under 14 years old. By 1966, in a total population of 96,013, there were 22,206 women between 20–44 and 31,708 children under 14 years old. Except where otherwise footnoted, all population data throughout this study is extrapolated from Table 2.17 Population (a) (b), age and sex, ACT (b), 30 June, 2011 (Australian Bureau of Statistics, Australia Historical Population Statistics (cat no 3105.0.65.001), 2014).
32 *Bad girls: twenty witness 1000*. Curator: Anni Doyle Wawrzyńczak. Artists: Alison Alder, Jane Barney, Vivienne Binns, Rachel Bowak, Jacqueline Bradley, Julie Bradley, Julia Church, Fiona Davies, eX de Medici, Mariana del Castillo, Anna Eggert, Cherylynn Holmes, Catriona Holyoake, Stephanie Jones, Deborah Kelly, Mandy Martin, Brenda Runnegar, Bronwen Sandland, Erica Secombe, Ruth Waller. CCAS, 8 February – 16 March 2013.

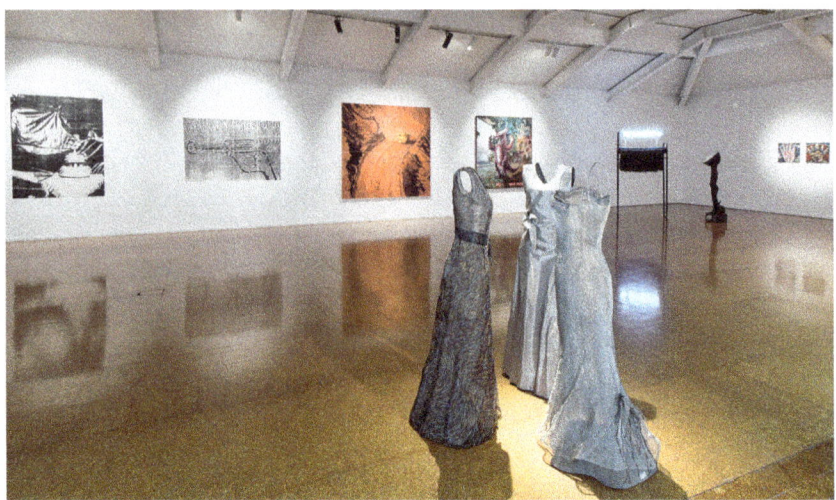

Figure 2. Group exhibition, *Bad girls: twenty witness 1000*, 8 February – 16 March 2013. Installation photograph, detail
Source. Photographer: Brenton McGeachie. CCAS image archive, reproduced with permission

This is borne out by recent research by artist and academic Elvis Richardson who since 2008, under the pseudonym 'the CoUNTess', has been recording gender bias in the art world.[33] Her research confirms that the number of enrolled female students is significantly higher than that of male students in all art schools, including CSA/ANU School of Art (ANU SOA).[34] An examination of graduating student lists from CSA since 1977 confirms that this statistic holds true across all years.[35] With a national and occasionally international focus, Richardson has compared graduating numbers with women artists represented in exhibitions. For 2011 she compiled statistics from the six state CAOA member organisations and the NT, with the exception of CCAS.[36] In contrast to art school enrolment statistics, Richardson's data reveals a significantly

---

33 CoUNTess, countesses.blogspot.com.au, accessed 12 January 2013.
34 'Educating and exhibiting artists', *CoUNTess*, 2 December 2012, countesses.blogspot.ca/2012/12/educating-and-exhibiting-artists.html, accessed 12 January 2013.
35 'Appendix J: Graduates 1978–2008', in Agostino, 2009, pp 237–53.
36 *CoUNTess*, 2 December 2012. CCAS exhibition data is not represented in these figures as the CCAS website was inaccessible during the period that 2011 figures were being compiled (CoUNTess [Elvis Richardson], email to the author, 21 February 2013).

higher number of male exhibitors across the country. Only 24HR Art during 2011 exhibited more female artists,[37] with these higher figures accounted for by the prevalence of Indigenous women exhibiting.[38]

That more female artists have exhibited at BRG/CCAS might be explained by the leading role of women in its administration. Indeed, of the eight coordinators/directors over 32 years, six have been women.[39] In the main, men hold directorial positions at art galleries, including at contemporary art spaces. Of the two male directors of BRG/CCAS, however, Trevor Smith was joined in his second and final year by Jane Barney in the role of curator. Nevertheless, incumbent director David Broker's tenure since 2006 has also been characterised annually by a greater proportion of female to male exhibitors, which suggests other important factors at work. In short, women artists, lecturers and gallerists played an unusually dominant role in the founding of the contemporary arts community in Canberra. This can be seen in the influence of female print and poster makers; the example of women artists/lecturers at Canberra School of Art (CSA); the presence of Helen Maxwell's australian[40] Girls Own Gallery (aGOG 1989–2000); and Canberra's position as a political fulcrum for concerns impacting on women.

The global and the local

The growth of international biennales and triennials over the last two decades is evidence of an increasingly globalised art world. A commensurate flattening of discourse across international boundaries has cast an opaque film around the representation and value of local

---

37   *CoUNTess*, 2 December 2012. In four of the eight years from 2005–12, 24HR Art showed more female than male artists, with 14 more female artists showing overall for the period (24HR Art, email to the author, 26 February 2013).
38   The NT has the highest concentration of Indigenous Australians and, therefore, the greatest number of Indigenous artists. The largest number of Indigenous artists are women. If the anomaly was due, say, to a smaller population base, then CAST in Hobart would also be expected to reflect a greater number of female exhibitors, whereas its greater ratio of male exhibitors is in keeping with national and international trends.
39   Alison Alder, Anne Virgo, Erica Green, Brenda Runnegar, Jane Barney and Lisa Byrne.
40   Note that 'australian' is rendered all in lowercase. In using the lower case 'a', Maxwell was overtly choosing to foreground the women artists she was representing. It was, in a way, a diminution of the importance of the word 'National', considered in this case to be somewhat patriarchal.

practices.[41] The production of local histories of art provides an important antidote to this. Australian art historian Terry Smith, who gave one of the first public lectures at BRG in 1984, in 2010 called for:

> a variety of kinds of critical practice, each of them alert to the demands, limits and potentialities of both local worlds and distant worlds, as well as actual and possible connections between locality and distance. In practice, translocality amounts to a focus on local artistic manifestations, and on actual existing connections between them and art and ideas elsewhere.[42]

This study answers Smith's call with a deeply local history, rife with paradox and rich in narrative; an inspiring story of local endeavour pitted against national imperatives. It is, in many ways, a David and Goliath story that, until the handover to self-government was completed in 1992, saw emerging local expressions of art and culture struggle against the Commonwealth's implementation of its national cultural agenda. This dichotomy, between the local and the national, lay at the heart of the immense difficulties surrounding the early understanding and funding of a local practice that manifested broadly through community, amateur and professional practitioners, firstly in the performing arts and then in the visual arts. Despite this essential locality, Canberra's position as national capital meant that the ideas that influenced the community assumed national and international importance, ensuring that the development of practice was not parochial and was evidentially informed by international and national viewpoints – translocality in practice.

How local art made Australia's national capital

This history comprises two parts. Beginning in the 1920s, it traces the origins of what has proven to be an exceptionally active and unique local arts community. The first part reveals and analyses the defining factors, and their complex intersections over the twentieth century, that led to this. The second part tracks the development of contemporary visual

---

41   For example: *55th Venice biennale 2013*, 'Universes in universe – worlds of art'; *56th Venice biennale 2015*, 'All the world's futures'; *20th biennale of Sydney 2016*, 'The future is already here: it's just not evenly distributed'; *Sharjah biennial 12*, 2015, 'The past, the present, the possible'; *10th Taipei biennial 2016*, 'Gestures and archives of the present, genealogies of the future'.
42   Terry Smith, 'The state of art history: contemporary art', *The Art Bulletin*, December 2010, p 380.

INTRODUCTION

arts practice from 1978 to 2000 through the case study of BRG/CCAS. It investigates the changing roles and impacts of coordinators/directors Alison Alder, Anne Virgo, Trevor Smith and Jane Barney, and it also examines the role and impact of other key players, especially the CSA Print Workshop's first tutor – artist Mandy Martin – and Canberra artist eX de Medici. Martin's journey to Canberra encapsulates the political/artistic focus that inspired the founding members of BRG. De Medici's career exemplifies the trajectory from local to international focus that charted the maturing of Canberra's contemporary arts community.

Chapter 1 examines the years from the 1920s to 1978 and the events and proclivities that laid the groundwork for the emergence of contemporary visual arts practice from 1978. It examines Canberra's unique sociopolitical duality as federal/national capital and as the site of a burgeoning regional/local community, the background to and rise of women as agents of social change, the trajectory and impacts of federal arts funding nationally and locally, the growth of commercial galleries and other exhibition spaces, and the historic and physical make-up of Canberra's suburbs.

Chapter 2 continues this broad exploration of the city's wider arts and cultural manifestations. It proposes the 1980s as the decade of the genesis of local contemporary visual arts practice and examines formative issues of the 1980s that influenced its development. With the ACT under the control of the Commonwealth, and local government therefore hampered by restricted legislative agency, the chapter reveals unique local solutions to rapidly growing needs in the broad arts sector. These included a lack of studio and exhibition spaces for visual artists, a continued unsuccessful focus on funding performing arts as flagship companies, and inadequate funding and forward planning for the entire arts sector. The chapter is anchored by a close reading of the 1985 Pascoe Report into arts funding in the ACT. This report, which considered local arts as an expression of national capital space culture, was entirely at odds with the growing needs and desires of local arts and culture practitioners. In response to the report's delivery, the chapter charts the robust community reactions that assisted in alerting the incoming, self-governing ACT Legislative Assembly to the power and relevance of local contemporary arts.

Chapter 3, in considering the 1990s, examines the path to self-government and the impacts of successive local governments on arts development during the decade. The 1990s saw a powerful confluence of local support mechanisms delivered via an intelligent, bipartisan approach to arts and cultural development and funding. Although national public and federal government perceptions remained bound up with Canberra's position as national capital space and a federal power base, in the 1990s local arts and culture conclusively claimed its own space. Nowhere was this more evident than in the visual arts. An analysis of two major committees established by the ACT Legislative Assembly, which enabled rapid sector-wide growth, reveals an unprecedented depth of government engagement with the arts community.

Beginning part two of this history, Chapters 4 and 5 continue the examination of Canberra's unique social/political duality, focusing on the case study of BRG/CCAS. Chapter 4 begins in 1978 with an investigation of the factors leading up to BRG's founding, and concludes at the end of 1983 with Virgo's arrival at BRG as co-coordinator. Chapter 5 examines the process and impacts of BRG's amalgamation with the ACG to form CCAS in 1987. Together, the chapters reveal that the process from unfunded collective to fully funded contemporary art space was marked by circumstances unique to Canberra. The chapters examine the impact of these circumstances on the growth of contemporary art practice, as tracked by several case studies of groups and individuals. These trace the growing maturity of Canberra as an art centre, from the youthful dynamism that characterised BRG to the progressing of national relationships and capacity-building through CCAS.

The history concludes in Chapter 6 with a focused investigation of expressions of arts practice through BRG/CCAS. It analyses the gallery's history under the two directors, Smith and Barney, who steered the organisation through the 1990s. The chapter charts the paradigmatic changes in the roles of curators and directors during this decade, and examines the gallery's declining preoccupation with the local. This is followed by an examination of minorities in exhibition through the 1980s and 1990s and a comparative analysis of travelling exhibitions mounted during these decades. A close reading of exhibitions, including *Satellite of love* (Dale Frank), curated by Smith and Christopher Chapman, and exhibitions curated by Barney including *Beautiful home* (Bronwen Sandland and Paull McKee), *60 heads* (eX de Medici), *Canberra/Brasilia* and *Black books*, reveal the narrative arc that moved the organisation from its earlier preoccupation with establishing a local space to a mature engagement with international themes and markets. The chapter as a whole places CCAS within its national and international contexts through examinations of personnel, exhibitions and artists.

1

THE NATIONAL CAPITAL SPACE AND ARTS PRACTICE: 1913–1978

The population of the Australian Capital Territory (ACT) during the broader period covered in this history was marked by rapid growth and a degree of transience unprecedented in other Australian cities. This resulted in a lack of historical continuity, and the majority of Canberrans, including contemporary arts practitioners, are largely unaware of the rich history of arts and cultural development in Canberra. If we are to critically examine who we are now, it is essential to understand where we have come from.

Capital constructs

Canberra's two distinct iterations of space – that is, as federal/national capital and as a regional/local community – comprise a unique sociopolitical duality.

The pre-eminent construct of Canberra as Australia's national capital, 'the centre of our national ideas',[1] is both symbolic and actual. As a federal capital city, Canberra provides the physical site for Australia's governing institutions. Principal among these are: the federal parliament located in Australia's Parliament House; the federal administrative departments clustered in the Parliamentary Triangle; and the nation's supreme judiciary body, the High Court of Australia.

---

1   *Canberra Times*, 'Canberra's population', 19 July 1927, p 4.

Canberra is also home to national institutions that provide actual services to national and local users but which carry the symbolism in their naming as 'National' or 'Australian', and in the national ceremonies and commemorative functions that they coordinate. The first of the national cultural institutions, the Australian War Memorial (AWM), opened in 1943. This was followed by the opening of the National Library of Australia (NLA, 1968), the National Gallery of Australia (NGA, 1982)[2], the National Portrait Gallery (NPG, 1998, initially sited in Old Parliament House) and the National Museum of Australia (NMA, 2001). The foundation stone of the National Archives of Australia was laid in 1920, and the predecessor to the National Film and Sound Archive (NFSA) was established in 1935. The latter became an independent cultural organisation in 1984. The Australian National University (ANU) was ratified by a bill of parliament in 1946. From 1992, Canberra School of Art (CSA), which opened on 1 January 1976, became part of the ANU. Additionally more than 80 foreign embassies contribute to the city's national cultural landscape.

The carving out of a functioning local space within this overarching idea of a national capital is complex because the nature of a national capital is, primarily, *national* in focus and in actualisation. While the federal capital city has been identified as encompassing both 'good physical environments where people live out ordinary lives, as well as symbolically rich [environments] that capture the qualities a state wishes to portray to the larger world',[3] it has also conversely been identified as more likely than state capitals to become a contested site. This is because a federal government seeks:

> to control and develop the capital in the interests of the nation as a whole, while the people of the capital naturally wish to govern themselves to the greatest extent possible.[4]

The national capital is, therefore, a unique and dynamic city construct that allows the possibility for multiple tensions to arise along the boundaries where the symbolic and actual national capital meet the functioning local. These dynamic interplays, which heralded the birth of Canberra as a modern city, began to manifest in the late 1960s.

---

2   Francis Kelly, 'A national gallery but when?', *Canberra Times*, 15 February 1969, p 11.
3   Beth Moore Milroy, 'Commentary: what is a capital?', in John Taylor, Jean G Lengellé and Caroline Andrew (eds), *Capital cities/les capitales: international perspectives/perspectives internationales*, Montreal, McGill-Queens University Press, 1993, p 86.
4   Donald C Rowat (ed), 'Introduction', *The government of federal capitals*, University of Toronto Press, 1973, pp xi–xii, quoted in Enid Slack and Rupak Chattopadhyay, *Finance and governance of capital cities in federal systems*, vol 1, *Thematic issues in federalism*, Montreal, McGill-Queen's University Press, 2009, p 4.

Prior to this – from the city's establishment in 1913 within the newly excised land named as the Australian Federal Territory, and then from 1927, when the federal government relocated from Melbourne to the newly constructed Parliament House – Canberra existed, first symbolically and then actually, as Australia's federal capital. In 1938, the Federal Capital Territory was renamed the Australian Capital Territory suggesting 'changing views … to a national centre rather than [simply] a federal meeting place'.[5] The idea of Canberra as a national centre arguably attained its initial concrete form in 1943 when, with a population of less than 15,000, the AWM, opened its doors.

Population growth and social impacts to 1978

Population numbers remained low in Canberra in the 1940s with slow growth experienced until the late 1950s. Although the city was imagined as the seat of federal government from the beginning and inchoately as a national centre, funding and the political will to develop the city was fraught, as factionalism in successive federal governments, and cataclysmic world affairs – World War I, the Great Depression, World War II – constantly intervened to prevent any smooth fulfilment of the capital's promise. In the late 1950s, the Liberal government, led by Prime Minister Robert Menzies, renewed its commitment to Canberra and the city began to experience dynamic growth,[6] largely driven by Menzies' desire to make Canberra 'a worthy capital'.[7] To this end, the federal government committed to further transfers of public servants to Canberra and, in 1958, it instituted the National Capital Development Commission (NCDC) to oversee the government's renewed commitment to planned development. The impact of these decisions on growth was profound: the population of Canberra trebled over 12 years; from a base of 30,356 in 1954, numbers rose rapidly to 58,856 in 1961 and then to 96,013 by 1966. The population grew to 217,981 by 1978.

---

5   Brown, 2014, p 94.
6   It is possible that this rapid upwards population trajectory is unique among federal capitals. Brasilia, the capital of Brazil, is the only other national capital to have been purpose-built. This similarity provided fertile curatorial ground for Jane Barney's exhibition *Canberra Brasilia* at CCAS in 1998. See Chapter 6.
7   Peter Freeman, 'Building Canberra to 1958', National Capital Authority fact sheets, www.nca.gov.au/factsheet/building-canberra-1958-0, accessed 16 June 2014.

The brunt of the negative social impacts that resulted from this rapid growth was borne by the large numbers of women who, as new residents of the national capital, had to carve out a functioning local space from within a national capital city construct that was ill-equipped to serve their growing social welfare needs or the needs of their young families.

An historical precedent to the social activism practised by women in the 1970s occurred in 1927. In March of that year, when federal parliament was officially welcomed into the provisional Parliament House, the Federal Capital Commission (FCC) – the forerunner of the NCDC – estimated Canberra's population at 7,384 people.[8] This included the housing of parliamentarians in the newly built Hotel Canberra and Kurrajong Hotel, public servants in hostels and houses in the northern and southern inner city suburbs of Ainslie, Reid, Forrest, Kingston and Yarralumla, and workers under canvas in construction camps.[9] This small but socially varied population included many young families who shared a need for child and maternal welfare services – services not yet provided by government.

Early local engagement with women's welfare needs was evidenced when the Women and Children's Committee established the Canberra Mothercraft Society, with the support of Dr Beatrice Holt, Canberra's first female general practitioner (see Figure 3). 'One of the most active and useful of the many [social] organisations in Canberra',[10] the society adopted 'innovative approaches to child and maternal welfare'[11] that sought to provide services across Canberra's early and diverse social divides. Reports presented at its third annual general meeting on 24 July 1929 indicate that, over the previous year, 'the sister-in-charge had paid 897 visits to homes, and that there had been 2,155 attendants at the society's clinics'.[12] The preponderance of women of childbearing age and young families that this statistic implies, reached unprecedented levels from 1961 to 1978.[13]

---

8   *Canberra Times*, 'Canberra's population', 19 July 1927, p 4.
9   See, for example, Brown (2014, p 77). The Ainslie Hostel became Gorman House Arts Centre in 1981.
10 *Sydney Morning Herald*, 'Canberra Mothercraft Society', 26 July 1929.
11 Brown, 2014, p 83.
12 *Sydney Morning Herald*, 1929. The society was subsidised by the FCC. Transport for the sister-in-charge was provided by 'Mr and Mrs Barton'.
13 In 1961, in a total population of 58,856, there were 10,885 women aged 20–44 and 20,651 children aged under 14. By 1966, in a total population of 96,013, there were 22,206 women aged 20–44 and 31,708 children aged under 14. In 1973, in a total population of 173,306, there were 45,703 women aged 20–44 and 55,387 children aged under 14. In 1978, in a total population of 217,961, there were 46,049 women aged 20–44 and 65,856 children aged under 14.

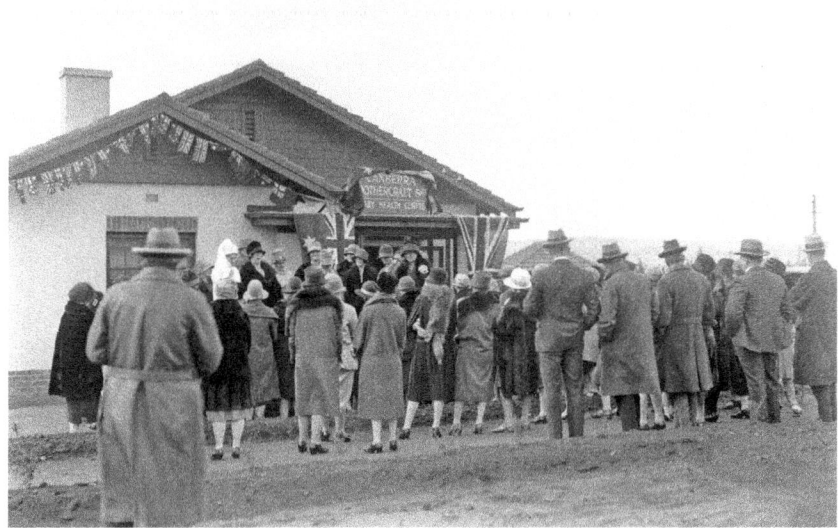

Figure 3. Opening of Canberra Mothercraft Society, 1927
Source. The Canberra Mothercraft Society, reproduced with permission

The continuous rapid increases in population over consecutive census dates[14] directly contributed to the rise of women as radical, social activists during the late 1960s and the 1970s, because it was women, particularly those with young families, who were most negatively impacted by the unique circumstances of life in the national capital. Statistical data indicates that, over 17 years, Canberra's population almost quadrupled from 58,828 in 1961 to 217,981 in 1978. Negative impacts included the effects of transience and isolation on residents, both inbuilt factors in a population largely dedicated to realising the government's renewed commitment to consolidating Canberra as the national space. A large percentage of Canberra's population during this period comprised public servants, who, whether single or in family groups, were posted to the city for periods of two years. The isolating effects of transience were compounded by the loss of extended familial and friendship support mechanisms, which were left behind in other cities and towns.[15] Additionally, within the overwhelmingly young demographic, there were

---

14   Total populations over the period: 1961 – 58,828; 1966 – 96,013; 1973 – 173,306; 1978 – 217,981.
15   'Women in Canberra frequently lacked any of the traditional supports to women at home, they often lacked family and old friends. They had a strong need to create a new community to build up supportive networks' (Paula Simcocks, *Majura Women's Group Newsletter*, 2005, quoted in Skeat, 2006, p 2).

few older woman who might otherwise have extended support to young mothers.[16] The emphases throughout this period were on physically building the national capital, governing the nation, and providing services that supported these endeavours and those engaged in them. Through these decades, the provision of social services for local women and children was the nominal responsibility of the federal government, but with the renewed, principal focus on establishing Canberra as a 'worthy' national capital, government agencies were slow to recognise growing social needs.

By the early 1970s the number of women and children requiring a broad range of social services reached a critical mass. In 1973, in a total population of 173,306, the combined number of women aged 20–44 and children aged under 14 reached 100,190 or 57.81 per cent of the total population. Transience and isolation led to increasing levels of domestic violence and other family dysfunction, and the need for support services became acute.[17]

The resulting sociopolitical effects of this dramatic rise in population over the period 1961–78, coupled with the politics of feminism and the wider women's movement from the beginning of the 1970s, stimulated the contribution made by young, progressive, social-activist women. It was these women, in the absence of government-funded support mechanisms, who conceived and enacted service solutions to Canberra's emerging social problems during the 1970s. These included in 1970, Sexual Health and Family Planning ACT; in 1971, Canberra's first family planning clinic; in 1972, the Joint Women's Action group; in 1973, Canberra's Incest Support Centre, known from 1976 as the Rape Crisis Centre and operated as a feminist collective; in 1975, Beryl was established, as was the Women's House in O'Connor, which housed the headquarters of Canberra Women's Liberation (CWL); and, in 1978, the Women's Information and Referral Centre opened as a shopfront service in the city centre.

This emergence of women as social activists also occurred during the rise of the Canberra women's liberation movement, which was active in the capital from 1970.[18] The various impacts of the women's liberation

---

16   In 1961, for example, there were only 1,667 women aged 50–60 in a total population of 58,856.
17   Domestic violence and family dysfunction in general were not recognised as social problems and, therefore, statistics indicating rates of incidence were not gathered at this time. Oral histories recorded from women who lived in Canberra and brought up their families at this time, and the fact of the provision of these services from the beginning of the 1970s, is evidence of need.
18   See Chapter 4, 'Feminist politics and art: intersections', for further information on women's liberation in Canberra.

movement were felt, to a greater or lesser degree and at different times, in other Australian cities. However, Canberra women were well-educated and often administratively skilled and were uniquely positioned, living in the national capital with access to political decision-makers, to respond to need and then to effect community change with government support.[19] At this time, they were also directly supported by the progressive social policies of the Labor government under Gough Whitlam, elected on 2 December 1972. Whitlam was three times dux of Canberra Grammar and had attended Telopea Park High School, a period he credits with '[strengthening his] … convictions about the role of the national Government in the nation's affairs'.[20] Arguably, this period in Whitlam's life may also have inculcated a belief in Canberra as a vibrantly local, as well as national, centre.

Beryl, run by the Canberra Women's Refuge Collective, was opened on International Women's Day in 1975 by then 78-year-old Canberran Beryl Henderson. Henderson's involvement in first-wave feminism in Australia provided inspiration and impetus to second-wave feminists agitating for social change. Beryl was the second of around 50 women's refuges established in Australia by the end of the 1970s. The first was Elsie, which began as a squat in the Sydney suburb of Glebe in 1972. Inspired by, but in contrast to this, Beryl was established after successful submissions to the federal government in a three-bedroom house on the northern edge of Canberra in Adams Place, Watson.[21] A grant of $4,000 from the Department of the Capital Territory (DCT) was allocated to run the refuge. Julia Ryan was a founding member of CWL in 1970. She recalled:

> Being Canberra people … we thought we would ask the government for a house … [I]t was the Whitlam government and we thought we could talk them into it, which we did.[22]

---

19 Historic examples of organisations that supported educated women were the National Council of Women (ACT) (1939) and the Australian Federation of University Women (ACT) (1944). Canberra's small female demographic around this time is evidenced by an extrapolation of Australian Bureau of Statistics (ABS) population data available for 1933 and 1947. In 1933 the number of females over 20 years old in the ACT was 2,445; in 1947 they numbered 4,807.
20 Brown, 2014, p 88. Telopea School opened in 1923 and was 'one of the earliest public buildings undertaken by the [Federal Capital Advisory Committee] and the first school completed by the Commonwealth' (Brown, 2014, p 87).
21 'We were very aware of what was happening in Sydney around the formation of Elsie, and that was our inspiration' (Julia Ryan, quoted in Choudhury, 2015, p 23).
22 Choudhury, 2015, p 24.

Developing arts and culture to 1978

From 1927 art was considered integral to establishing a national perception of Canberra as culturally literate.[23] In these early days this was imagined as community-based:

> As a centre of culture Canberra will be dependent in the early stage on the establishment of its University, but meanwhile art societies and the like may accomplish useful endeavour.[24]

The earliest of these societies was the Artists' Society of Canberra (ASOC), active from 28 June 1927.[25] In recess from July 1934, it re-emerged in August 1945. Also founded in 1945 was the Canberra Photographic Society,[26] followed in 1948 by the Canberra Art Club.[27]

Art classes began at Canberra Technical College in 1942. Agostino reveals that in 1941, Charles Bean, then chair of the AWM, proposed to the leader of the Opposition, Joseph Collings, 'that Canberra be developed as an art centre, and that an art course be established at Canberra Technical College'.[28] The first classes offered were in freehand and model drawing and landscape painting. By 1952, the ACT Pastoral and Agricultural Association (P&A) began inviting Technical College staff to assist in an expanded arts and craft section at the P&A's annual show – held in the far

---

23   Brown relates what is arguably the first instance of a local artist presenting work that is particularly identifiable as Canberran when, in 1927, the artist Eirene Mort offered a book of her drawings to the FCC to mark celebrations of the opening of the federal parliament: 'She evoked,' writes Brown, 'an agrarian landscape of nostalgic decline, as if to set it against the coming city, and to confer its own legitimacy on the growing city' (Brown, 2014, p 90). In 2017, CMAG staged a comprehensive exhibition of Mort's work and life titled *Eirene Mort: a livelihood*, 30 September 2017 – 25 February 2018, curated by Dale Middleby.
24   *Canberra Times*, 19 July 1927.
25   From 1952 to c 1966, ASOC met at Riverside Centre, Barton; 2004–06, Canberra Technology Park, Watson; 2007 – July 2010, Unit 2, Geils Court, Deakin West; August 2010–, Blaxland Centre, 25 Blaxland Crescent, Griffith. Data collated from ACT Heritage Library visual arts ephemera collection.
26   Established 11 September 1945, the Canberra Photographic Society met from 1945–51 at 2CA Theatrette, Mort Street, Civic; 1951–52, Institute of Anatomy, Acton; 1952–66, Riverside Centre; 1966–2005, Griffin Centre, Bunda Street, Civic; 2005–, PhotoAccess, Manuka. In the mid-1980s, the society was incorporated as Monaro Camera Club. Data collated from ACT Heritage Library visual arts ephemera collection.
27   The Canberra Art Club was incorporated as Canberra Art Workshop Group in 1975. The club met until 1982 at 8 Riverside Centre and then at B Block, Kingsley Street, Turner; 1982–84, ANU Arts Centre; 1984–2002, Studio 13, Kingston Art Space (later Leichhardt Street Studios), 71 Leichhardt Street, Kingston; 2002–09 M16, 16 Mildura Street, Fyshwick; 2010–, Blaxland Centre. Data collated from ACT Heritage Library visual arts ephemera collection.
28   Agostino, 2009, p 3.

northern suburb of Hall – envisaging that the 'increased competition' this would encourage would add to 'cultural relations between rural and city sections of the population'.[29]

The developments in the cultural scene accelerated in the 1960s and 1970s, evident in the fast-growing numbers of informal and formal groups and associations. Among the informal initiatives was the 1960s Wednesday Group, comprising women who, in the absence of extended families, came together in meetings that, while nominally social, provided a focus for creative initiatives. In the 1970s, the Thursday Group, which comprised around 15 women potters associated with the Craft Association of the ACT (formed in 1970), continued this example, as did the Majura Women's Group (convened in 1981). Throughout the 1960s, 1970s and 1980s, these groups acted in much the same way as art societies, providing a sense of social cohesion and opportunities for creative community expression.

A key formal development was the growth of craft-based activities.[30] The Craft Association was established at the Canberra Theatre Centre (CTC) and, from the beginning, it displayed a high degree of activity, coordinating weekend workshops, discussions, slide and film evenings and an annual members' exhibition.[31] Professionalism was foregrounded, with members admitted after an assessment process requiring that work be of a 'consistent high standard and … [an] original design'.[32] By October 1977, when the organisation held its inaugural annual exhibition at its new premises in Watson, a large contingent of 37 craft workers exhibited 170 works, marking 'an important stage in the growth of the crafts in Canberra'.[33] This dynamic and enduring community organisation changed its name in 1973 to the Craft Council of the ACT and again in 1998 to Craft ACT: Craft and Design Centre.[34] By the mid-1980s, the demonstrated strength

---

29   *Canberra Times*, 'Art and craft prizes at Hall', 16 February 1952, p 2.
30   The Craft Association of Australia (NSW) was formed in 1964, signalling the beginning of a national focus for the many craft groups operating throughout the country. The peak body, the Craft Council of Australia, was convened in 1971 following the emergence of craft associations in all states and the ACT.
31   John Scollay, the ACT chapter's inaugural president, opened the first members' exhibition at Narek Galleries on Saturday 15 May 1971. See *Canberra Times*, 'Diary dates', 14 May 1971, p 9.
32   *Canberra Times*, 'Tour of craft studios', 8 August 1974, p 14.
33   Sasha Grishin, 'A festival-like atmosphere', *Canberra Times*, 8 October 1977, p 18.
34   The organisation was initially housed at 1 Aspinall Street, Watson. On 13 October 2000, it re-opened in North Building, Civic Square, London Circuit, Canberra City, in the same building as CMAG. Directors: 1973–74, Derek Wrigley (vice-president); 1974–78, Margaret Vanduren; 1978–86, Meredith Hinchliffe; 1986–88, Jane de Stoop; 1988–94, Joy Grove; c 1994–2000, Jenny Deves; 2000–03, Catrina Vignando; 2003–09, Barbara McConchie; March 2010 – end March 2016, Avi Amesbury. Data collated from ACT Heritage Library visual arts ephemera collection.

of the work by the organisation's members led arts consultant Timothy Pascoe to conclude that the crafts constituted the pre-eminent plastic arts form in Canberra.[35]

Another sign of growing civic maturity was the increasingly broad range of employment on offer in the national capital. It therefore followed that many who accepted postings to Canberra from larger Australian cities and from overseas countries were educated and visually and culturally literate. Art societies had indeed 'accomplished useful endeavour' from the 1920s and, from the 1940s, the New South Wales (NSW) Council for the Encouragement of Music and the Arts (CEMA), along with its national successor the Arts Council of Australia (ACA), provided local access to travelling visual arts exhibitions. Missing from the visual arts landscape, however, were local commercial galleries and the opportunity they provided to view and purchase contemporary Australian visual art. By 1962, with the city's population at around 60,000,[36] Hendrieka (Riek) Le Grand judged the national capital ready for such an endeavour and established Canberra's first commercial art gallery, Studio Nundah, at her home on Macarthur Avenue, O'Connor.

The mother of Canberra sculptor Michael Le Grand, Riek Le Grand settled in Canberra in 1955 with her husband Henri, who had accepted a position in the early 1950s at Canberra Technical College. The couple were partners in a pottery business in Holland and immigrated to Sydney in 1950. Studio Nundah was renovated in 1965 by modernist architect and Canberra resident Theo Bischoff, and renamed Nundah Gallery. Bischoff's architectural features – which included cypress pine floors, matte-black ceilings and hidden lighting tracks – provided the young Michael Le Grand with 'an education in sophistication and taste' and memories of '"artists tramping through the house" during his school years'.[37] Nundah Gallery, which closed in 1975, remained Canberra's only commercial gallery for 11 years, until Joyce (Joy) Warren founded Solander Gallery in 1973.

Joy Warren (1923–2015) settled in Canberra in 1952, with her architect husband Robert (Bob) Warren (1920–2002). Bob was 'enticed by the possibilities the relatively fledgling city offered' to design and build

---

35   See Pascoe, 1985, p 57.
36   1961 population: 58,828.
37   Helen Musa, 'Michael le Grand: sculptor or "boy racer"?', *World of Antiques and Art*, 81, August 2011 – February 2012, p 78.

'good quality housing at affordable prices'.[38] Joy was a performer for 15 years with Canberra Repertory Society (Canberra Rep) (for which Robert designed many sets), and opened an eponymous public relations company. By 1973, when she established her gallery at 2 Solander Court, Yarralumla,[39] Canberra's population had reached 173,306. Warren's background in business and public relations helped to ensure the gallery's success and, in June 2013, Solander Gallery celebrated 40 years of continuous operation. A talented self-promoter, Warren recalled on this 40th anniversary that:

> we had absolutely nothing to look at, not from the government, no National Gallery, no National Portrait Gallery, nothing like that. If you wanted to see art, you had to come to Joy's place … It has been my aim and privilege to bring top Australian painters from all over Australia to the capital.[40]

This talent for self-promotion resulted in the promulgation of the erroneous fact, oft-repeated in Warren's obituaries, that Solander Gallery, as opposed to Studio Nundah/Nundah Gallery, was the first commercial gallery in Canberra.

It was a testament to the large segment of Canberra's population who could be considered wealthy, established and visually literate, that Warren was able to show and sell Indigenous art as it contemporaneously emerged from Australia's Western Desert, as well as continuously show the majority of Australia's mid-career and established artists. In addition, she exhibited 'Papua New Guinean, Indonesian, African, Eskimo, Turkish, Mexican, Peruvian, Indian and Japanese art … some of the earliest exhibitions of such art to be held in the nation's capital'.[41]

Ruth Prowse's Gallery Huntley joined Nundah and Solander galleries in 1974. Prowse (1920–2005) settled in Canberra in 1959 with her husband, Keith, who accepted a job with the Department of Primary Industry.

---

38 John Farquharson, 'Warren, Robert George (Bob) (1920–2002)', *Obituaries Australia*, oa.anu.edu.au/obituary/warren-robert–george-bob-1002, accessed 2 April 2012.
39 From August 1986 – 1997, Solander Gallery was located at 36 Grey Street, Deakin; May 1997 – closure in 2014, 10 Schlich Street, Yarralumla.
40 Joy Warren, quoted in Sally Pryor, '40 years since the day art came to town', *Canberra Times*, 29 June 2013, www.canberratimes.com.au/act-news/40-years-since-the-day-art-came-to-town-2013 0628-2p33h.html, accessed 2 July 2014.
41 Sasha Grishin, quoted in Sally Pryor, 'Canberra farewells Joy Warren, doyenne of the local art scene', *Canberra Times*, 5 January 2015, www.canberratimes.com.au/act-news/canberra-life/canberra-farewells-joy-warren-doyenne-of-the-local-art-scene-20150105-12i598.html, accessed 8 November 2015.

She worked variously as a nurse at the Canberra Hospital, a secretary at the British High Commission and at ANU. A degree in zoology and cell biology at that institution was followed by her enrolment as a PhD candidate. In 1974, the year after Warren opened Solander Gallery, Prowse left her PhD and established Gallery Huntley at her home in Savige Street, Campbell, where, for the next 30 years, she exhibited and sold Australian and international art and built 'an extensive private collection'.[42] Gallery Huntley closed in 2005. Prowse had a lasting influence on the development of a local contemporary arts practice; she often travelled to Europe where she met printmaker Jorg Schmeisser (1942–2012), and Gallery Huntley represented both Schmeisser and printmaker Petr Herel before their respective appointments to CSA as head of the Printmaking Workshop (in 1977) and head of the Graphic Investigation Workshop (in 1979). According to Sasha Grishin, the inaugural head of the ANU Department of Fine Art (established 1977), Prowse 'played an important role as conduit' in encouraging both artists to settle in Canberra.[43]

Abraxas Gallery also opened in 1974 (mid-1974–end 1978), in La Perouse Street, Manuka. Founded by Susan Stanton and Lindsay Moloney, it was considered 'more radical'[44] than other Canberra galleries, providing the only opportunity, at that time in the city, to view conceptual, post-object art contemporaneously with galleries in southern capitals. Many Australian artists, including Gary Shead, Jenny Watson, Keith Looby and Richard Larter, held exhibitions there early in their careers. Stanton and Moloney also held monthly meetings at the gallery from 1976 to discuss issues such as 'art and art criticism', 'radicalism and art' and 'sociology and the arts'.[45] In 1975, Ron and Betty Beaver established their eponymous Beaver Galleries at their home in Red Hill, specialising mainly in three-dimensional craft works. During the 1980s, Beaver Galleries moved into its current location comprising four galleries under one roof, designed by the Beavers' architect son, Ross. Since 1991, under the second-generation ownership of son Martin and his wife Susie, Beaver Galleries has exhibited a broad range of Australian artists working in various media and at various stages of their careers.

---

42 Deborah Clark, 'The legacy of Ruth Prowse', *Canberra Museum and Gallery*, www.liveguide.com.au/Events/736280/Ruth_Prowse/The_Legacy_of_Ruth_Prowse_2012, accessed 10 November 2015.
43 Sasha Grishin, 'A gift our city can savour', *Sydney Morning Herald*, 13 March 2012, www.smh.com.au/entertainment/a-gift-our-city-can-savour-20120312-1uubu.html, accessed 11 November 2015.
44 Sonja Kaleski, 'City's private galleries versus keeping art for the people', *Canberra Times*, 3 December 1981, p 29.
45 Peter George, 'For art's sake', *Canberra Times*, 29 April 1976, p 3.

The last of the important commercial galleries to open in Canberra during this period was Judith Behan's Chapman Gallery in 1976. Behan (1934–2008) moved to Canberra with her husband Ron, who was posted to the Royal Military College, Duntroon, in the early 1970s. When Ron was promoted to colonel and transferred to Melbourne, Behan chose to stay in Canberra with their two young children. Chapman Gallery opened in their home in Chapman, where she 'pioneered' the 'ethical and professional display' of Indigenous art.[46] She brought elements of taste and discrimination to exhibitions and became close to the artists she supported. The gallery remained open under her directorship until 2007 and for a further seven years under Behan's chosen successor, Kristian Pithie.

Between 1962 and 1976, therefore, six commercial art galleries opened in the city, five of these in the 1970s, and five of them initiated and run by women. Four of these women, arriving with husbands who were posted to or who chose to relocate to the national capital, came from various careers in other centres and in Canberra. In addition, three of the women – Warren, Prowse and Behan – enrolled, after establishing their galleries, in art history courses at ANU under Grishin. Until the 1980s, they dominated the commercial art market in the nation's capital.

As well as these important commercial galleries, a number of smaller galleries opened and closed during the period. The first of these, the Centre Gallery, was operated by Dr Darcy Williams from 1958 to 1961.[47] This was the first instance of Canberra's penchant for home-based galleries, a predisposition that in 1984 would lead the NCDC to release a draft proposal concerning the location of art galleries in residential areas.[48] Anna Simons Gallery was registered from the early 1960s until c 1977 and active prior to 1967 and from 1975 to 1977.[49] Gallery A (Canberra) opened in the Town House Motel in 1964 and closed after 1966, and Macquarie

---

46   From c 1984 to 2006, Chapman Gallery was located at 15 Beaumont Close, Chapman; 1976 – c 1984, 31 Captain Cook Crescent, Griffith; 2007, re-opened at 1/11 Murray Crescent, Griffith. Directors: 1976–2006 Judith Behan; 2007 – 31 October 2013, Kristian Pithie. Sasha Grishin, 'Canberra's visual arts landscape: an art critic's view', *Art Monthly Australia*, 259, May 2013, p 28.
47   Centre Gallery was located at 33 Ainslie Avenue, Civic, just off London Circuit.
48   See Chapter 2.
49   The Anna Simons Gallery was initially located at Simon's home in Campbell, then at CTC Playhouse, where Simons also managed Macquarie Galleries Canberra. In 1969 the gallery moved as Macquarie Galleries to 23 Furneaux Street, Forrest, and remained there when Macquarie Galleries withdrew in 1972; it closed c 1977 (deregistered 21 February 1977). Data extrapolated from ACT Heritage Library visual arts ephemera collection.

Galleries Canberra was established in 1965 and closed after 1978.[50] Macquarie Galleries hosted Canberra artist Rosalie Gascoigne's inaugural exhibition in 1974 and was closely associated with both Anna Simons, who directed Macquarie Galleries from 1965 to 1975, and Macquarie Galleries Sydney. Further dedicated gallery spaces included the Australian Sculpture Centre, which opened on 5 June 1966 (Donald Brook exhibited there that year);[51] Narek Galleries (from 1972);[52] and Fantasia Galleries[53] (established in 1973), which hosted Australia's foremost feminist artist Vivienne Binns' first Canberra exhibition, *Experiments in vitreous enamel – silkscreened portraits of women*, in May 1977.[54] Arunta Galleries was active from 1973,[55] as was ceramicist Hiroe Swen's Pastoral Gallery,[56] with Lasseters Gallery (from 1975),[57] Griffith Gallery[58] and La Perouse Gallery (active between 1976 and the end of 1980).[59]

The Canberra exhibition scene was extremely diverse during the 1960s and 1970s. As well as the six important commercial galleries and the fluctuating numbers of smaller galleries, a variety of non-dedicated exhibition venues arose prior to and during these decades. Prior to 1960, occasional venues included the 2CA Theatrette (established in 1943), the Riverside Gallery (active from the 1950s to 1966) and Wesley Uniting Church (Wesley Centre – founded in 1955). Canberra's large civic buildings provided important exhibition spaces in the 1960s, including the Albert Hall, the ANU (from 1963) and the CTC (from its opening on 24 June 1965). Within CTC were the Playhouse Gallery,

---

50   From 1965–67, Macquarie Galleries Canberra exhibited at Canberra Theatre; 1969–72, Macquarie House, 23 Furneaux Street, Forrest; 1976–77, 35 Murray Crescent, Manuka. Director: 1965 – c 1972, Anna Simons.
51   The Australian Sculpture Centre was located at 83 Dominion Circuit, Deakin. Director: Lesta O'Brien.
52   Narek Galleries was originally located at Old Tanja Church, 1140 Bermagui Road, Tanja, via Tathra, NSW. Until June 1977, 23 Grey Street, Deakin; 16 July 1977 – c 1996, 'Cuppacumbalong', Naas Road, Tharwa; 1996 – c 2001, Pialligo Plant Farm. Closed December 2004, reopened at Tanja.
53   Fantasia Galleries was firstly located in Scullin and then in Manuka, specialising in prints. Proprietor: Susan Gillespie.
54   As advertised in the *Canberra Times*, Saturday 8 May 1977, p 12. This exhibition was initially presented at the George Paton Gallery, under curator Kiffy Rubbo, in 1976. See Chapter 4 for an extrapolation of Binns' importance to Canberra's emerging artists.
55   Arunta Galleries was located on Limestone Avenue, Ainslie.
56   Pastoral Gallery was located at Bimbimbi, Old Cooma Road, via Queanbeyan. In 1974, Hiroe Swen started Bimbimbi Potters in the same location.
57   Lasseters Gallery was located at Rudd Street, Canberra City.
58   Griffith Gallery was located at 14 Bremer Street, Griffith.
59   La Perouse Gallery was located at 57 La Perouse Street, Manuka.

Canberra Theatre Gallery and Link Gallery.[60] In the 1970s, venues used for occasional exhibitions included the David Jones department store in the city centre (from 1971); Yarralumla Marine Centre (active from 1972 to c 1991); YMCA (for a brief period from 1971); Albert Hall; Deakin High School (from 1975); Tuffin's Music Studios (active from 1976); and John Curtin House and the National Jewish Centre (in 1978). Exhibitions held in these venues included those from local community groups, schoolchildren, special interest groups and travelling exhibitions.

In considering Canberra's galleries during the 1970s, it is important to note the role played by the opening of the National Gallery of Australia (NGA, then known as the Australian National Gallery), first mooted for 1974. The Commonwealth's commitment to building Australia's pre-eminent manifestation of the visual arts in Canberra compounded the difficulty of discerning the needs of local emerging visual artists within the national capital paradigm. The erroneous perception that local visual artists would be the best resourced in the country once the NGA opened gained currency as the 1970s progressed.

Another focus for emerging visual arts practice was the annual Civic Permanent Art Award created in 1971. In 1976, the award was won by Indigenous artist Trevor Nickolls. Nickolls' significance to the early exhibition calendar at BRG and to the trajectory of Urban Indigenous art in Australia is described in Chapter 4.[61] A further indication of the growing health of the ACT as a locus for emerging contemporary arts and activism occurred in March 1975 when the Festival of Creative Arts and Sciences, which became known as the Down to Earth ConFest, was held at the Cotter River. This public expression of the countercultural movement brought many interstate activists and artists to Canberra, some of whom, such as BRG member Cherylynn Holmes, would return in the early 1980s to study at CSA.[62]

---

60 CTC opened on 24 June 1965 in Civic Square, Canberra City. The Playhouse opened on 18 August 1965 and was rebuilt in 1998; Canberra Theatre Gallery was established in June 1966 and closed after 1978; Playhouse Gallery was established on 1 May 1969; the Link building opened in October 2006. Data collated from ACT Heritage Library visual arts ephemera collection.
61 See Chapter 6 for further information on Trevor Nickolls and *Dreamtime machinetime*.
62 See Chapter 4 for a fuller account of this period and the role played by Cherylynn Holmes.

Federal government commitment to public art from 1960

The NCDC was responsible for activation of the federal government's commitment to an ambitious public art program in the national capital. In 1961, with Canberra's population at 58,928, the commission unveiled the first major civic sculpture: a totemic 4-metre-high bronze titled *Ethos*, by Australian sculptor Tom Bass, centrally located in Civic Square. Its commission and placement can be seen as a symbolic articulation of Canberra as a future centre of enlightenment and culture.[63] Sponsored by the Chamber of Commerce, *Ethos* was one of only a handful of public artworks present in Canberra in 1961. Other works swiftly followed at ANU, including bronze and iron screens and 'an abstract piece of sculpture in the courtyard of the Physics building'.[64]

Menzies took a direct interest in the ACT's proposed public sculpture program. In September 1963, he requested information from Gordon Freeth, minister for the interior, about some 'proposals the NCDC had in mind for pieces of sculpture to be placed in Canberra'.[65] Freeth's reply enclosed notes from NCDC Commissioner Sir John Overall that detailed the commission's progress and thinking to date. Acknowledging a 'growing public interest in this and other arts', Overall explained that 'so far the Commission has done very little due principally to the difficulty in obtaining work which is considered suitable'.[66] Overall advised that he had sought the opinions of senior administrators including eminent art historian Sir Kenneth Clark; Sir William Holford, professor of town planning at University College, London; and Sir Colin Anderson, who the Menzies government invited to advise on Canberra's planning and development. Following this, Overall appointed a 'small committee of experts' to advise on the selection and design of sculptural works. These experts included director of the National Gallery of Victoria (NGV) (1942–56) Sir Daryl Lindsay; deputy vice-chancellor ANU and

---

63 'Sculpture and artworks in the ACT, policies and practices prior to 1982', NC–76/00122, Archives ACT.
64 John Overall, Notes, 18 September 1963, Personal Papers of Prime Minister Menzies, NAA M2576, 44, Canberra, p 39. Lithuanian artist Vincas Jomantas' sculpture, *Pursuit of scientific knowledge*, is located in the courtyard of the Physics building at the ANU.
65 Gordon Freeth, Minister of the Interior, letter to Sir Robert Menzies, Prime Minister, 20 September 1963, NAA M2576, 44, p 37.
66 Overall, Notes, NAA M2576, 44, p 39.

master of University House Arthur Trendall; Herald chair of fine arts at the University of Melbourne (1947–78) Joseph Burke; and dean of the Faculty of Architecture and professor of town and country planning at University of Sydney Denis Winston. The calibre of Overall's initial advisers and subsequent committee members indicates that the NCDC and the government were serious in their approach to public sculpture in the ACT. Menzies confirmed his interest by responding 'Could I have a talk with Mr Overall on this subject at some convenient time?'[67]

In its sixth annual report of 1962/63, the NCDC explained that 'Sculpture, used with care and restraint, must add interest to buildings and landscape'.[68] The words 'care and restraint', and the careful selection of advisers, indicate a conservative, cautious but above all ambitious approach to public art in the national capital. Commissioner Overall would undoubtedly have felt great responsibility given the precedents the NCDC was setting and the personal interest of the prime minister.

From the end of the 1950s, commissioned artwork in all new ACT schools became 'a requirement stipulated in architectural design briefs'[69] – an enlightened innovation that showed the NCDC's commitment to widespread public art. The first of these, completed in September 1960, marked the entrance to Lyneham High School in Canberra's inner north. Painted by Sydney artist Cedric Flower, it comprised 24 square metres of murals 'depicting highlights of Australian history from first settlement', no doubt to encourage a national historical perspective among students.[70] The commitment to public art and sculpture was particularly important during the 1960s, both in service to the federal government's desire to build a worthy national capital and, in examples such as the commitment to art in schools, for the benefit of the local population. It was designed to encourage civic and national pride and arguably indicated that the government viewed the arts as integral to a balanced society.

67 RG Menzies to the Hon Gordon Freeth, note, 15 October 1963, NAA M2576, 44, p 36.
68 National Capital Development Commission, *Sixth annual report*, Canberra, 1962/63, p 17.
69 Ling, 2013.
70 *Canberra Times*, 'Artist finishes school murals', 13 September 1960, p 7.

Australia's Liberal governments have traditionally sought private investment in arts and cultural funding. Thus, the commission's hopeful – though unfounded – belief that the provision of public sculpture and art was among the 'opportunities for development open to private benefactors which the Commission hopes will be taken up in future'[71] aligned with the government's wishes. The NCDC retained responsibility for the placement of public art until the beginning of the handover to self-government in 1989, when this responsibility devolved to the Commonwealth (within the parliamentary zone only) and successive ACT governments through the ACT Legislative Assembly.

Funding arts and culture in Canberra during the 1960s and 1970s

The delivery of funding to arts and cultural programs in Australia has historically been problematic, given the vast distances between the country's population centres. In Canberra, the nexus between the city's status as national capital and the cultural needs of its small local population created additional difficulties. On one hand, for the local population, Canberra was predominantly an urban/suburban community and a regional centre. On the other hand, as national capital, it was the locus of national governmental, administrative and, increasingly, national cultural functions. Explicitly understood in these national cultural functions was that Canberra would begin to reflect a national identity of excellence in arts and culture, both to the rest of Australia and internationally.

The problem throughout the 1960s and 1970s was that the population was simply too small to sustain the national flagship companies that the federal government envisaged as appropriate for the national capital. From the establishment of the Australian Council for the Arts in 1967 until the advent of the Australia Council for the Arts in 1973 (Australia Council), the federal government's definition of 'the arts', almost without exception, was concerned entirely with the performing arts. In this, it closely followed the funding path previously set from 1954 by the Australian Elizabethan

---

71   NCDC, 1962/63, p 17.

Theatre Trust (AETT).[72] The focus on funding performing arts had an important bearing on the developing visual arts sector in Canberra from the 1970s through to the completion of the handover to self-government in 1992. This narrow definition of the arts, and the insistence on funding the development in Canberra of flagship companies seen as appropriate for a national capital, would result in extreme reactions among local arts and cultural practitioners by the mid-1980s, as Chapter 2 reveals.

The historic and important exception to this vision of the arts as performance-based was the setting up of the Commonwealth Art Advisory Board in 1912.[73] This Board constituted the first commitment to federal government funding of visual arts in Australia and was the first instance of an Australian federal government's awareness, under Labor Prime Minister Andrew Fisher, that the power of visual art could be harnessed to building the nation's cultural memory. The board comprised artists and those working in the arts, and its purpose was to advise the Historic Memorials Committee (also established in 1912) on the commission and collection of portraits, by Australian artists, of notable Australian Government figures. It was replaced in 1973 by the Acquisition Committee for the proposed national gallery in Canberra, when its increased responsibilities

---

72 This is recognised historically, in Bill Hayden's response, in the House of Representatives on 2 November 1967, to the government's announcement that HC 'Nugget' Coombs, chairman of the AETT and governor of the Reserve Bank, would be appointed chairman of Aboriginal Affairs and of the new Australian Council for the Arts: 'I wish,' said Hayden, 'in no way to detract from the qualities of Dr Coombs as a central banker and public servant and one of Australia's most able public administrators. What I want to do is to bring to the Government's attention the tremendous amount of criticism that is being voiced concerning the way in which the affairs of the Australian Elizabethan Theatre Trust have been handled and the concern of people involved in arts and letters.' Calling for a public enquiry into 'the state of arts and letters', Hayden concluded that '[t]he Government is virtually just establishing a body that will be manipulated by the same old brigade that has been running the Elizabethan Theatre Trust for too long. In addition, it is obvious that the Government's propositions in this field are related only to the performing arts. These are only one segment of the field of arts and letters in the Australian community' ('Aboriginals', House of Representatives, 26th Parliament, 2 November 1967, p 2629, *Historic Hansard*, built by Tim Sherratt, historichansard.net/hofreps/1967/19671102_reps_26_hor57/#debate-22, accessed 11 February 2015). For further examples of the continued emphasis on the performing arts see: John Gorton, 'Recommendations of the Australian Council for the Arts for 1969/1970', news release, PM No 85/1969, 3 December 1969, historichansard.net/hofreps/1967/19671102_reps_26_hor57/#debate-22, accessed 11 February 2015.
73 Ruth Bereson has written, in relation to the Commonwealth Art Advisory Board, that 'structures that were intended to link government's interests and the arts had been sewn into the fabric of government after Federation (1901)' ('Advance Australia – fair or foul? Observing Australian arts policies', *Journal of Arts Management, Law, and Society*, 35, 1, 2005 pp 49–59).

included 'advi[sing] the Commonwealth government, building a national collection, providing works for official buildings in Australian and overseas, and for touring exhibitions'.[74]

Historically, prior to the establishment of the Australian Council for the Arts in 1967, funding for the arts fell largely to two key organisations: the AETT, established in 1954, and the Arts Council of Australia (ACA) from 1966.[75] The first of these, the privately funded NSW-based AETT, can be usefully considered as the (only) forerunner to the Australian Council for the Arts, given its focus on excellence in the performing arts.[76] It was funded with £90,000 of private money (equal to $3,188,076 in 2019) and £30,000 pounds from the federal government (equal to $1,062,692.31 in 2019).[77] Nugget Coombs (from 1968 to 1974 inaugural chairman of the Australian Council for the Arts) was instrumental in raising the private funds that allowed the Trust to be convened as a non-profit public company limited by guarantee. Over the next 15 years, individuals and companies investing in the arts via the Trust were entitled to generous tax concessions.[78] Its funding provides an early example of the combination of government and private sector partnership funding for the arts that would become a foundational concept of arts funding from the 1975 Liberal government, under Malcolm Fraser, onward.

---

74 Margaret Seares, with assistance from John Gardiner-Garden, *Cultural policies in Australia*, Sydney, Australia Council, June 2011, p 8.
75 From 1943, when NSW adopted the British model of community arts delivery via the CEMA/Arts Council of Australia, through to the late 1960s when the federal government – after reviewing funding mechanisms in the United States, Canada and the United Kingdom – largely adopted the British model of professional arts funding delivery with the Australia Council, successive federal governments have looked to Australia's colonial forebear for arts funding models. Thus, broadly speaking, in Australia as in England, arts funding has been directed into these twin areas: firstly, what could be termed professional excellence, with a view to encouraging and supporting those art forms that would improve the national mindset and represent the country as broadly cultured and internationally educated; and, secondly, what could be termed domestic art and culture for the masses, or art and culture based in and run by and for communities. This latter model was exemplified through ACA.
76 The AETT was established following the visit to Australia of the British Queen Elizabeth and Prince Philip. Bereson writes that it was 'a de facto arts agency [that] had a considerable impact on what was considered to be artistic production for one and a half decades' (Bereson, 2005, n 4).
77 Reserve Bank of Australia pre-decimal inflation calculator.
78 In October 1955, the premiere performance of *Medea*, the first production of the AETT-formed Australia Drama Company, was held in Canberra's Albert Hall, arguably in a nod to the city's national capital status. The hall's history is revealed in historian Lenore Coltheart's *Albert Hall: the heart of Canberra* (2014), wherein Coltheart defines the building as Canberra's 'unofficial town hall' (p 126) and, for 37 years, as its 'theatre and concert hall for professional artists performing in Canberra' (p 129). Albert Hall relinquished that status in 1965 with the opening of CTC, the first federally initiated performing arts centre completed in Australia.

The influence of the AETT was vast and its reverberations continue today, despite its liquidation in March 1991. Although it provided 'significant financial support for performing arts organizations through tax breaks and through Musica Viva, a semi-autonomous agency still in existence', it continually garnered strong criticism, including the lack of arts practitioners on the Trust's board.[79] Labor parliamentarian Bill Hayden was aware of the AETT's domination of 'national arts and letters', referring to it 'as a sort of ruthless ogre'.[80] And yet, the AETT wrought profound changes in Australia's cultural landscape, providing funding that would otherwise not have been available to performing arts companies. Additionally, it was responsible, in part or in whole, for the establishment of a number of major organisations, many of which are now deeply embedded in Australian cultural life.[81]

In the history of arts funding and development in Canberra, the second key organisation, the ACA, played a crucial role from 1948 to the end of the 1980s.[82] It began in 1946 in NSW, and was modelled on the state's CEMA (established in 1943), the historical precursor of which was Britain's CEMA (established in 1940). It was comprised of various state and territory Arts Councils that, in 1966, became the ACA.[83] This national body received its first funding from the Australian Council for the Arts in 1969. The purview of the ACA was, as in United Kingdom, to provide artistic and cultural experiences for regional communities and schools. This was seen to be particularly important in Canberra because, although the federal government had renewed its commitment to developing the city as a national capital in 1958, its geographical location and small population confirmed it as a regional centre well beyond this date.

The ambitious idea of Canberra as a future national centre for the arts remained strong throughout the 1940s. This was indicated again when CEMA's president Sir Robert Garran changed the name of the ACT branch of the organisation to the Arts Council Australia (ACT Division) on

---

79   Bereson, 2005.
80   Hayden, 1967.
81   These included the Australian Opera Company in 1956, Trust Ballet Company in 1957, Young Elizabethan Theatre Players in 1958, Australian Ballet Foundation in 1961, Australian Ballet School in 1963 and, with the University of New South Wales (then the New South Wales University of Technology), the National Institute of Dramatic Arts (NIDA) in 1959.
82   The ACA lapsed between1953 and 1961 and was reconstituted in February 1962; it became the Arts Council (ACT) in 1993.
83   Britain's CEMA was established by the Pilgrim Trust, which was founded in 1930 with a £2 million endowment from American railroad entrepreneur Edward Harkness (see www.thepilgrimtrust.org.uk).

26 May 1948, at a time when Australia's state and territory Arts Councils were identified only by the name of their state or territory.[84] This also anticipated the Arts Council's national status by almost 20 years. Annual fees were modest: in 1948 an annual subscription increased to 5 shillings (approximately $14 today).[85] Planned events for that year included a Brahms and Schubert festival at Albert Hall in June and a Great Britain handicrafts exhibition, accompanied by a travelling curator, in October. Although it showed a loss for the year of 3 shillings 8 pence ($10.41), Garran explained that 'CEMA was not out to make money but to bring culture to the people'.[86]

The ACA (ACT) was pivotal in the development of Canberra's cultural landscape over the next 40 years, with the exception of an eight-year period from 1953 to 1961 when the organisation lapsed. Through its committees, the organisation delivered musical, theatrical, dance and literary events; hosted diverse community meetings; organised summer schools and festivals such as Canberra Day celebrations and Canberra youth and folk festivals; involved itself with education and the arts, including dance and theatre; hosted varied community workshops and ran a diverse schools program, including school holiday programs. From 1969, it also redistributed small amounts of funding to a broad range of community arts organisations from funds allocated to it by the two iterations of the federal funding body the Australian Council for the Arts/Australia Council for the Arts.[87] The organisation consistently lobbied at federal and local level for increased funding to the arts. From its earliest days it ran a program of visual arts exhibitions, mostly travelling exhibitions hosted in turn by each of the state and territory Arts Councils.

The ACA's (ACT) most egalitarian venture was Sunday in the Park. This ran from the mid-1970s through the 1980s in Commonwealth Park. Beginning in 1975 with a six-week season over summer, the following year it extended to 10 weeks from the first Sunday of December, finishing in late March. More than 100,000 Canberrans, out of a population of 230,000, enjoyed the 10 weeks of entertainment during the 1976 summer season.[88] Over the period, Sunday in the Park remained a multicultural

---

84 CEMA in the ACT was established in October 1945 as ACT Division of CEMA.
85 $55 using GDP (relative average income).
86 *Canberra Times*, 'Canberra division of Arts Council: new name for CEMA', 26 May 1948, p 2.
87 Records of the Arts Council of Australia, MS 4570, NLA (Canberra).
88 Mr Valentine McKelvie, administrator, ACT division of the Arts Council, quoted in *Canberra Times*, '"Sunday in the Park" praised', 26 October 1977, p 9.

affair with a cyclic array of various national dance troupes, plays, puppetry, folk music, jazz, circus, brass bands and stalls, and was at different times assisted with funding from the Department of the Capital Territory, the Apex Club of Ginninderra and the *Canberra Times*.[89]

More than any single event over the two decades, Sunday in the Park revealed residents as avid consumers of a broad range of community-focused, local cultural products. This citywide pull towards the local remained at odds with the insistent desire of funding bodies, particularly throughout the 1980s, to develop and fund one 'flagship' company in each of the four core areas of dance, music, theatre and opera, in line with federal arts funding policy nationally. This desire to reflect excellence in performing arts in Canberra was concerned with the city as national capital space, and therefore as the face of national excellence in the arts. Arguably, this intention was flagged in 1965 when the first federal government-initiated performing arts centre in Australia, the Canberra Theatre Centre, was completed. By the 1980s, as Chapter 2 reveals, this disjunct between federal funding of Canberra arts in service to the national agenda and the increasing needs of local arts and cultural initiatives would reach an eruptive head.

Federal funding through the Australia Council for the Arts from 1968

Canberra's performance-based cultural organisations began to receive small amounts of funding from the Australian Council for the Arts' initial grants round in 1968. With a population of around 100,000, the city's performance venues then included Albert Hall and the new CTC.[90] The allocations were announced on 11 December 1968 and included $3,200 to Canberra Rep, $7,000 to Canberra's Spring Music Festival; and $15,000 to the Canberra Theatre Trust to fund a visit from Sydney's flagship theatre company, the Old Tote Theatre. Canberra Rep's president, Ken Farnham, commented on the allocation to Canberra as 'welcome

---

89   In 1988, after an absence of two years, Sunday in the Park made a one-year return under the auspices of the Canberra Theatre Trust, funded with a grant from the Local Government Initiatives Grant Scheme as an Australian Bicentennial Authority project.
90   1966 population: 96,013.

only because it is more than Canberra has received previously'.[91] From these small beginnings, funding amounts rose modestly over the next four years.[92]

Funding also rose modestly immediately following the election of the Whitlam Labor in late 1972 when government announced allocations for 1973 that included $20,000 to the Canberra Theatre Trust and $6,000 to Canberra Rep. The press release announcing the grants is notable for Whitlam's inclusion of painting, craft work and sculpture as being among the 'diverse pleasures' that would ensure that 'the leisure time of all Australians will be enriched'. This intimated a changing federal focus from wholly performing arts–based funding to a broader, more holistic definition of arts and culture.[93]

While the ACA's state divisions continued to receive grants from their state governments, the ACA's federal division, which was based in Canberra until 1971, was funded by the Australian Council for the Arts from 1970.[94] Over a four-year period, the division's funding rose from $75,000 in 1970 to $175,000 in 1973, following Whitlam's decision to 'give increased assistance to bodies like the Arts Councils which cater for the needs of country people'.[95] The increased funding supported costs associated with national administration, as well as the delivery of touring programs and regional arts programs into Canberra and throughout Australia, in line with the Whitlam government's desire to 'foster this general community interest [in the arts]'.[96]

---

91 *Canberra Times*, 'Arts grants criticised', 13 December 1968, p 19.
92 Allocations for 1970 included $15,000 to the Canberra Theatre Trust and $3,500 to Canberra Rep, with the ACA's federal division, based in Canberra, receiving $40,000 for administration and country touring programs and a further $35,000 in reserve for future activities. In 1971, funding for the federal division increased to $110,000, while funding for Canberra Theatre Trust remained at $15,000 and Canberra Rep's funding increased to $5,500. By 1972, the Canberra Theatre Trust was able to announce: 'During the year, there was a further increase in the trust's activities as an entrepreneur. Fourteen ventures were undertaken alone or in partnership with interstate managements compared with eight in the previous year. These were supported by the trust's cultural activities fund, replenished in January by the Australian Council for the Arts and the development fund' (*Canberra Times*, 'Theatre's runs could be longer', 28 November 1972, p 3).
93 *Canberra Times*, 'Major grants for the arts announced', 12 December 1972, p 3.
94 In 1969, the ACA was funded through the AETT, which was itself funded in that year by the new Australian Council for the Arts.
95 Gough Whitlam, 'Major grants for the arts', media release, 11 December 1972, pmtranscripts. pmc.gov.au/release/transcript-2740, accessed 14 February 2015.
96 Whitlam, 11 December 1972.

In his election policy speech of 13 November 1972, Whitlam flagged his intention to comprehensively overhaul the Australian Council for the Arts.[97] The renamed Australia Council for the Arts was set up as a new statutory body, 'to provide the direct and specialised administration which the arts require'.[98] It comprised seven boards, including, for the first time, the Visual Arts Board (VAB). These promising forward moves towards increased national and ACT federal arts funding were adversely affected from 1975 as the incoming Fraser Liberal government instituted cost-cutting measures across all sectors. One of these measures, however, provided new opportunities in the development of community arts.

Arts organisations that could demonstrate strong community engagement in Canberra benefited from successive federal government job creation initiatives from late 1976 onwards. These included, most importantly, the Community Youth Support Scheme (CYSS) created in 1976. The scheme was a critical factor in the development of contemporary arts practice in Canberra because it signalled the rise of the job creation enterprise Jobless Action.

Established in 1976, Jobless Action was a homegrown, highly effective, direct action provider of skills to disadvantaged and unemployed persons. Initially funded through the CYSS, the organisation was enabled through all iterations of federal community job creation programs to deliver short-term jobs, including art and craft programs, to the Canberra community.[99] Jobless Action quickly became a locus for passionate, creative, young social justice advocates, and a pivotal catalyst for the rapid growth of grassroots, youth-led music and collective arts enterprises from the late 1970s. Among its founding workers were Julian Webb, Annie Kavanagh and Jill Lang.

---

97 'We believe that the existing Commonwealth agencies should be brought within a single council set up by statute. The Council will be based on a number of autonomous boards with authority to deal with their own budget allocation and staff. The following boards would be established: Theatre arts (opera, ballet, drama); Music; Literary arts; Visual and plastic arts; Crafts; Film and television; Aboriginal arts. These boards would have substantial independence and authority to make decisions. Indeed, in their own field of responsibility they would be the major sources of initiative in policy and in communication with those involved in the Arts' (Gough Whitlam, 'It's time', Labor Party election policy speech, Blacktown Civic Centre, Sydney, 13 November 1972, whitlamdismissal.com/1972/11/13/whitlam-1972-election-policy-speech.html, accessed 24 May 2013).
98 Whitlam, 11 December 1972.
99 Successive programs were the Fraser government's Wage Pause Program (agreement made 7 December 1982) and the Bob Hawke's Labor government's Community Employment Program (CEP) (legislated 19 May 1983, with the program launched in August 1983). These two programs aimed to pause wage rises among the Australian public service.

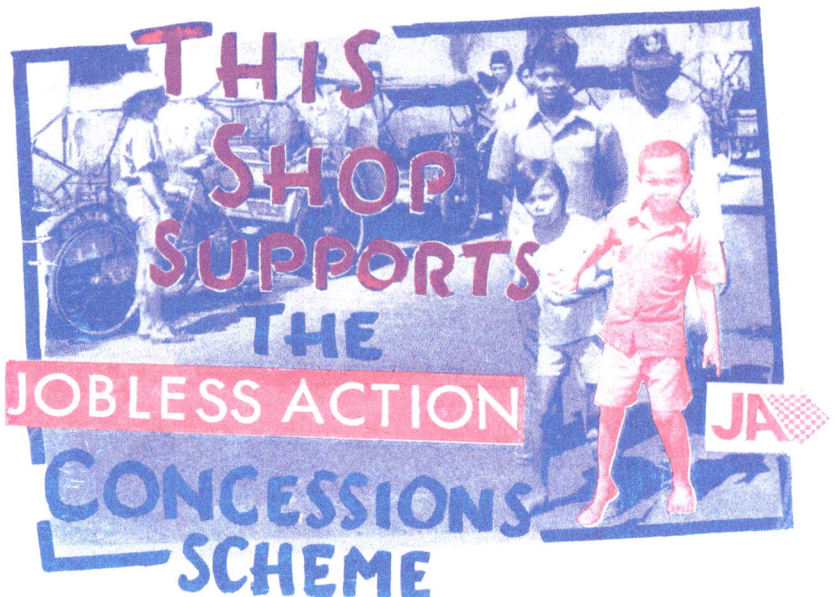

Figure 4. One of many posters made at Megalo for Jobless Action. Artist unknown
Source. Megalo poster archives, reprinted with permission

The organisation's initiatives included employing young activist printmakers to produce socially motivated prints, posters and T-shirts advertising Jobless Action programs. Many of these printmakers were Jobless Action members and students of the first intake, in 1978, of the new CSA Printmaking Workshop. Jobless Action reflected a particular, identifiably Canberran do-it-yourself ethos in its needs-driven response to disadvantage that encouraged the growth of Canberra's unique, northern suburbs–based, homogenised subculture. This subculture went on to actively carve out, through a contemporary printmaking culture, a local identity among the principal rhetoric of federal government and national capital space. As described in Chapter 4, Jobless Action's significance was ongoing in the respective geneses of Megalo and BRG in 1980 and 1981.

Lines of difference

In considering the broad factors that laid the groundwork for the growth of contemporary arts practice, one more crucial element was in play: the physical nature of Canberra. It was no coincidence that the new community-oriented arts/activists practices centred on the inner-north suburbs of Ainslie and Braddon.

The city's physical structure was set down in 1921, when WM Hughes' Nationalist Party government created the forerunner to the FCC, the Federal Capital Advisory Committee (FCAC). The FCAC's allocation of housing blocks led to the creation of artificial economic and social difference in the settlements to the north and south of the nominal city centre. Ainslie and Braddon, deemed workers' suburbs, were located to the north of the vast empty space that would, by 1963, contain the man-made Lake Burley Griffin. Building costs were set at £700 per quarter-acre (at that time the standard Australian house block) and an all-timber construction was allowed. In the suburb of Reid, still in the north but closer to the proposed Parliament House that hugged the inner southern perimeter, building costs for houses to accommodate skilled workers and mid-level public servants were set at the significantly higher rate of £1,000 and brick construction was mandated. Further to the south at Mugga Heights, where it was envisaged senior public servants would live, building sites increased to 3 acres with a rise in permissible building costs set at £3,500.[100] Manual labourers were housed under canvas in a number of small settlements south and north of the centre. Though these were conceived of as temporary structures, in reality they continued to house labourers and then a growing number of unemployed workers well into the 1950s.

The legacy of the initial land release may not have been deliberately intended but it was profound. By the late 1970s, the entrenched geographic, social and economic divide was inextricably linked to the growth of an homogenised subculture in the northern suburbs, and the consequent birth of a politicised, contemporary arts practice, foregrounded through poster and printmaking.

---

100 I am indebted to Nicholas Brown, who details these codes and costs on p 70 of his marvellous book *A history of Canberra* (2014).

2
THE RAPID GROWTH OF LOCAL ARTS AND CULTURE: 1978–1989

The 1980s was marked by increasing activism within the broad Canberra arts community as the need for funding and infrastructure support began to rapidly outstrip meagre available resources. The community's focus as the decade unfolded became how to develop, manage and fund local practice from within Canberra's increasingly visible construct of national capital space.

Community concerns were met with genuine but largely ineffectual attempts from government agencies to respond to the rapidly changing milieu from within an increasingly complex governance scenario. In fact, the complexities of three-tier governance in the Australian Capital Territory (ACT), although not new, became more difficult to navigate as the demand for services increased with the growing population. Canberra's population reached 227,581 by 1981 and, despite the economic downturn that occurred in the early part of the decade, it swelled to 282,211 by the end of the 1980s. Although the increased population progressively demonstrated their desire to claim and manage that strand of arts and culture in the national capital that could be considered local, the pressing question, in the face of decreasing federal commitment, became how to fund developing need.

The Commonwealth's political commitment to the ACT as a local community waned during the decade and remained focused on delivering national arts and cultural outcomes of excellence. During this period, under-resourced local advisory bodies struggled to respond to increasing demands and to provide adequate support structures. Within the dominant national capital paradigm and without the legislative freedoms and arts-infrastructure development that self-government would bring in the 1990s, local arts practitioners felt themselves to be unheard and largely invisible. The way forward during the 1980s, although it proved exceptionally difficult to navigate, was forged by an intelligent and politicised community for whom activism was a familiar mode.

The visual arts demonstrated growing relevance and importance as the 1980s progressed. This was anchored by the Canberra School of Art (CSA), which from 1978 onwards attracted some of the finest art teachers in the country to its Bauhaus-inspired workshops and enrolled an annually expanding student body. CSA graduates bore a peculiar burden. As they were often reminded by federal funding bodies, particularly from the mid-1980s as the number of national cultural institutions increased, Canberrans enjoyed a city that was arguably the best culturally resourced in the country. And yet, outside CSA, young visual artists lived and worked in ad hoc and make-do conditions.

The concerns of the local arts community – expressed through a remarkable number of meetings and forums, held throughout the decade in Canberra and in the regional towns of Yass and Braidwood – centred on the lack of four critical support factors. These were, a suitably resourced local arts funding body, consultation with the federal funding body, a cohesive community arts plan, and an overarching cultural and arts development plan for the Territory. Additionally, major issues for visual artists were the lack of studio spaces and exhibition venues for contemporary visual art, and the continued primacy of performing arts within the arts funding debate.

During 1983 and 1984, activity around these concerns began to coalesce and this section charts the intersections of concurrent community and government actions. The eventual denouement was the release of the 1985 Pascoe Report into the funding of arts and cultural development in the ACT, commissioned by the ACT Arts Development Board (ADB) and authored by Timothy Pascoe.

The rise and funding of community arts

Performance and visual artists were most often conflated with community arts, particularly during the first half of the 1980s. This was particularly the case with the emerging contemporary visual arts. As this naming characterised funding and debate during the 1980s, the following discussion deals with matters relating to community arts in the ACT over the period.

The ADB was created in 1981 as the principal instrument of local arts administration in the ACT. It replaced the ACT Advisory Committee on the Arts, which was itself preceded by the ACT Committee on Cultural Development, established in 1949 by Labor Prime Minister Ben Chifley (1945–49). The ADB – as were its antecedents – was responsible for advising the federal minister responsible for the ACT on grant allocations for the arts and on arts development policy in the Territory.

The locus of Canberra's community arts organisations from the 1970s to 1980 was Reid House. (It was demolished in 1980, after being partially destroyed by fire, to make way for the National Convention Centre.)[1] Reid House was home to a number of performing arts initiatives that were modestly supported, most often by the ACT Community Development Fund (CDF), which itself was funded through gambling revenues accrued from licensed ACT clubs. (This use of gambling revenue for arts development provided a precedent for the application of a $19 million casino premium to arts infrastructure in 1992.) Reid House tenants included Canberra Youth Theatre (CYT), which was formed in 1972 by Carol Woodrow; Jigsaw Theatre Company, which was established out of CYT in 1976 as a cooperative providing theatre for schools and community venues locally and in Adelaide, Sydney, Brisbane, Melbourne and country centres; and Oops Multiarts, running school holiday drama/multiarts programs for children, led by CYT members. Woodrow formed Fools Gallery Theatre Co, a full-time experimental ensemble performance group, in 1979 with a director's grant of $10,000 from the Australia Council.[2] In the same year, Camilla Blunden and Robyn Alewood

---

1 The federal government closed Reid House, which was moved to Canberra from Victoria to serve as a low-cost hostel, in 1972. With little low-cost housing available in the city, squatters began moving into the accommodation wings in 1974 (*Woroni*, 'The story of Reid House', 4 March 1974, p 5).
2 Canberra, as evidenced in Chapter 4, provided a focal point for legislative gains for women during the height of second-wave feminism. Fools Gallery Theatre Co spent two years developing a series of four plays concerning the history of patriarchy and the liberation of rejecting sexist philosophy.

founded the Women's Theatre Workshop, making work concerned with women's issues and women in the arts. The workshop attracted a small amount of funding from the Department of the Capital Territory (DCT) towards its 1979 productions of Sylvia Plath's *Three women*, directed by Alewood, and David Selbourne's *Alison Mary Fagan*, directed by Blunden.[3] Also at Reid House was the Canberra Community Arts Front (CCAF), initiated by Peter Sutherland. This collective of independent community artists formed to develop community arts in Canberra and to offer an administrative and supportive base for its members. CCAF coordinated children's activities for Sunday in the Park and presented the program *Good goose – a proper gander at the arts* on Canberra's arts radio station 2xx. (This program was a forerunner to *A hitchhiker's guide to the galleries*, which was initiated by Bitumen River Gallery (BRG) in the 1980s.)

Most of the groups at Reid House were later relocated to the Gorman House Arts Centre, which was remodelled for the purpose of providing spaces for community groups and the Arts Council Gallery (ACG).[4] Also, from 1979, Strathnairn homestead provided a base for the Blue Folk Community Arts Association, led by Domenic Mico, which provided community engagement opportunities for schools and groups.

These early examples of community arts practice provided the base for the formation, post self-government in the 1990s, of standalone community arts infrastructure and personnel in Canberra's growing town centres of Tuggeranong and Belconnen. The arts community's desire to extend Canberra into the regions became evident for the first time in May 1983. This logical progression built from the powerful sense of community that was evidenced in Canberra through Sunday in the Park during the 1970s and through the formation of the small organisations that were based first at Reid House and then at Gorman House Arts Centre from 1981. The sense of community was also established by the growth of women's groups, which moved from social gatherings into art and craft practices – as seen with the Majura Women's Group from 1981 – and through the cross-fertilisation of young artists (particularly print and poster makers), students, activists and musicians as the 1980s continued. The first industry-led moves towards acknowledgement of Canberra's regional arts status would culminate in the opening of the Canberra Museum and Gallery in 1998.

---

3   Blunden recalls that *Alison Mary Fagan* was written for one woman but that she staged the play with several women performing the role (Camilla Blunden, email to the author, 5 July 2016).
4   *Woroni*, 'Reid House: innovative theatre', 18 September 1980, pp 26–27.

The possibility of forming a regional community arts network was canvassed in 1983 during a day-long meeting in Yass, involving members of the Canberra, Yass, Goulburn, Queanbeyan and Cooma districts. Following this meeting, Ben Grady, then director of the ACG, wrote to Alison Alder at BRG in June, asking the collective to consider becoming part of the proposed network, to contribute to 'the process of exploring the relationship between arts and the community'.[5] This sequence of events was in line with the growth of the community arts sector internationally and in Australia. The international rise of community arts began with the alternative arts movement in Britain in the 1960s. In Australia, community arts networks began operating in New South Wales (NSW) and Victoria in the early 1970s as support organisations for artists working in the community, developing opportunities for community engagement. Their national growth was assisted through the Australia Council's Community Arts Board from 1973. Vivienne Binns, whose relationship with Canberra is expanded in Chapter 4, was among Australia's foremost early exponents of community arts practice.

A development in the evolution of local government agencies responsible to the arts and cultural sector occurred at the end of 1981, when the ACT Advisory Committee on the Arts was replaced by the ADB with Sir Richard Kingsland as chair.[6] Although the change of name flagged an awareness of local arts as a growing sector, the previous eight members of the Advisory Committee comprised the new board's members. A change of name alone was not enough to guarantee forward development. Kingsland, a committed advocate for the arts, was a recently retired senior public servant who held the inaugural chair at the Canberra School of Music from 1972 to 1975 and chaired CSA from 1976. Canberra's status as national capital space and the performing arts as the signifier of culture were uppermost in his mind:

> As the physical focus of national self-awareness, Canberra must play a significant part in the development of all aspects of artistic performance and expressions and participation … Canberra is much more of a theatre and concert going public than any other comparable city. We are a participating group, a city with a soul.[7]

---

5   Ben Grady and Edwin Relf, letter to Alison Alder, 10 June 1983, Correspondence file, 1983, CCAS archives.
6   Kingsland was knighted in 1978.
7   Stephen Payne, 'Sir Richard named arts chairman', *Canberra Times*, 11 December 1981, p 7.

While this was a strong acknowledgement of Canberrans' broad cultural literacy, Kingsland's belief that young people were absent from these theatre-going audiences 'because they watch television or their parents cannot be bothered taking them to performances' indicated his lack of awareness of the growing cross-arts youth culture.[8]

Arts ventures in Canberra that could demonstrate links to the community continued to be assisted through the federal government's Wage Pause and Community Employment programs in the first half of the 1980s and by the ACT Community Development Fund (CDF) throughout the decade. However, funding requirements for the Community Employment Program (CEP) required clarification. In April 1984, CEP officers wrote to the Canberra Symphony Orchestra (CSO) general manager, Maeve Galloway, to clarify the rules under which community organisations could apply for job creation funding. The rules stipulated that CEP funding for the arts was not to be viewed simply as an alternative funding source, the program required that at least 70 per cent of the grant sought must be committed to the wages of previously unemployed people, CEP positions must be filled from priority unemployed groups, and jobs should require a low level of experience and skills.[9] This was a big ask for small arts organisations in which, logically, there are only a limited number of jobs requiring low-level skills.

Jobless Action took a leading role in advocating for changes to the CEP programs. Following the CEP's clarification of the funding rules, Jobless Action project officer Annie Kavanagh wrote to Canberra arts organisations, suggesting that both Wage Pause and CEP was previously inundated with requests for funding from individuals and organisations who fell outside the criteria. Additionally, unskilled applicants to job positions were rejected by community organisations due to the high degree of self-reliance, motivation and commitment required under Wage Pause and CEP requirements. Kavanagh successfully proposed that the CEP modify its requirements and approach community groups with a view to the training of unskilled workers rather than their immediate employment. In order to streamline information sharing and CEP funding application processes, Jobless Action's Julian Webb took on the additional role of community development officer and was tasked with assisting

---

8   Payne, 1981.
9   CEP, letter to Maeve Galloway, GM of the CSO, April 1984, Communication folder 1984/2, CCAS archives.

community groups to apply for CEP funding. As the CEP program evolved to include this funding for training unskilled workers, Jobless Action provided additional employment to young printmakers who were leading programs that developed printmaking skills among local groups of unemployed persons. This was to prove crucial for the growth of a strong printmaking community in Canberra.

Increasing need and diversity in local arts and culture was indicated when CEP provided more than $340,000 to arts organisations and projects in 1983/84. Of this, Megalo International Screenprint Collective received $80,000, supporting full-time employment for four persons and allowing the fledgling organisation to provide classes and services to the Canberra community, including through Jobless Action. Other arts organisation beneficiaries were able to offer full- and part-time positions through Wage Pause. In 1983/84, these were the Arts Council (ACT), Craft Council of the ACT, Australian National Eisteddfod Society, Blue Folk Community Arts Association, Café Boom Boom, CCAF, Capital Art Patrons' Organisation (CAPO), and Stagecoach Theatre School.

Arts community needs and government responses: 1981–1985

Revealing an awareness of the growing local visual arts sector within the national capital space, in June 1983 the National Capital Development Commission (NCDC), the federally appointed body responsible for Canberra's development, released the first draft land-use policy concerning art galleries on residential leases.[10] The policy's opening phrase, 'Properly conducted, art galleries on residential leases have cultural value',[11] implied a growing awareness of Canberra's lively home-based gallery scene (the first gallery opened in the late 1960s) and the activity generated since the 1981 opening of the BRG collective in the inner south suburb of Manuka, Canberra's premier residential, shopping and dining suburb. It also implied a growing understanding that the relationship between artists and the community, mediated by accessible artwork, had positive

---

10   As discussed in Chapter 1, the NCDC was responsible for development in Canberra insofar as it impacted on the original Griffin Plan.
11   NCDC, 'Draft land use policy concerning art galleries on residential leases', public notice, *Canberra Times*, 6 August 1983, p 10.

cultural resonance 'of benefit to both the community and the artist'.[12] The draft's end statement commenting on 'the generally low economic viability of galleries dedicated solely to the display of artworks'[13] reflects the number of smaller galleries that continued to open and close during the period. The difficulty in accessing affordable space was also recognised by the report's authors:

> Without this form of [home] gallery the bulk of the artwork might not be displayed at all, because of the severe limitations in Canberra on the availability of leasable public gallery space [and] the high rents demanded for commercial premises.[14]

There were already considerable strictures around the operation of galleries in private homes. *Canberra Times* art critic Sonja Kaleski reported in September 1981 that:

> Canberra gallery directors live under constant fear of closure by the Department of the Capital Territory. Each year the directors are presented with an official form and are obliged to supply details of their operations such as provisions for parking, number of visitors, number of cars and other pieces of administrivia. The DCT has the power to close galleries if the answers on the forms appear unsatisfactory, while gallery directors claim that the system is unduly authoritarian and exists nowhere else in Australia.[15]

Members of the fledgling BRG collective were understandably preoccupied with identifying and securing visual arts spaces. Their *Future directions forum*, in mid-1983, considered all potential ACT spaces beginning with 21 commercial galleries. Of these, they recorded, 15 dealt in 'the import/export trade of used consumables of "pre-loved art", such as Salvador Dali prints', while the other six were seen to deal with 'craft objects' produced outside the ACT.[16] These conclusions reflect the disjunct between BRG members and the local commercial gallery scene. Fourteen other possibilities included occasional spaces such as shopping centres, schools and colleges. These occasional spaces were an important avenue for community exhibitions during the 1960s and 1970s and potentially suitable for emerging artist exhibitions. Seven institutions

---

12 NCDC, 1983.
13 NCDC, 1983.
14 NCDC, 1983.
15 Kaleski, 1981.
16 Stephanie Radok, '*Future directions forum*', *Bitumen River Gallery Newsletter*, 5 ½, September 1983, p 2.

with gallery potential were The Australian National University (ANU) (four spaces in total), Canberra College of Advanced Education (CCAE), Australian War Memorial (AWM), National Library of Australia (NLA), Alliance Française, Goethe-Institut and St John the Baptist Church at Reid. The option offered by the Goethe-Institut was considered to be 'the most exciting while the others tended to be fairly conservative and have well drawn parameters'.[17] Indeed, none of the above was suitable for exhibitions for emerging artists. The National Gallery and the CSA were regarded as 'institutionalised Taj Mahals and hardly public art spaces where you can bring your own art object along'.[18] This last conclusion speaks eloquently to the change occurring locally and nationally in contemporary art communities. The purpose-built ACG at Gorman House was identified as a potential space for larger exhibitions organised by groups such as BRG.[19] This last venue suggestion was the forum's most prescient conclusion.

The developing needs of Canberra's arts community were discussed at a high level. On 6 July 1983, Minister for Territories and Local Government Tom Uren met with arts community representatives and Senator Susan Ryan, federal Labor senator for the ACT (December 1975 – January 1988).[20] At the meeting, the ADB, then chaired by Kingsland, with two minister-approved community representatives – Simon Dawkins (administrator of the Arts Council (ACT)) and George Whaley (the new general manager of the Canberra Theatre Centre (CTC)) – committed to formulating a discussion paper on arts development in the ACT. This was a most promising development. The paper's proposed ambit included mechanisms for policy formulation and grants allocations, a policy for arts development in the Territory, appropriate administrative arrangements, and the desired level of support for the arts from the CDF. In an interview the following day, Uren commented that 'the paper would meet a clear need, expressed at yesterday's meeting, to promote wide discussion concerning arts development in the ACT'.[21] The ADB committed to circulating the discussion paper for public comment in early August.

---

17   Sasha Grishin, quoted in Radok, 1983.
18   Radok, 1983.
19   Radok, 1983.
20   Ryan was both the ACT's first female senator and first Labor senator.
21   Tom Uren, Minister for Territories and Local Government, media statement, 7 July 1983, CCAS archives.

No such paper had appeared by October, however, and concerns grew over the lack of a cohesive vision around the development of local art activities. In that month, in the most significant meeting to date concerning the state of the arts in Canberra, executive officers from nine of Canberra's arts organisations met at Braidwood.[22] To contest Canberra's status as a planned city, attendees believed that opportunities existed to develop a unique cultural face for the city that was 'adventurous, eccentric and innovative'.[23]

Nine important recommendations were made. One was that the ADB should 'conduct discussions with the Canberra Development Board and the NCDC regarding the arts in the overall development strategy of Canberra', indicating attendees' understanding of the complexity of planning and decision-making at that time in Canberra.[24] Another was that the ADB 'should commission an appropriate organisation to gather statistical data on the patterns of involvement in the arts in the ACT', reflecting a belief that the ADB were not up to undertaking this task themselves.[25] A further recommendation was that the ADB:

> should investigate the placement of Arts Officers in the Belconnen and Tuggeranong areas to identify needs, facilitate networking and put the [ADB] in contact with grass roots demands.[26]

The latter would come to fruition after self-government in the 1990s. The meeting also recommended that, as the ACT was under-represented on the Australia Council with only two representatives out of 56 members, there needed to be 'closer consultation between the Australia Council and arts funding bodies in the ACT'.[27]

---

22   They included representatives from BRG, Blue Folk Community Arts Association, Arts Council (ACT), CSO, CYT, Canberra Opera, Jigsaw Theatre Company, CCAF and Theatre ACT.
23   *BRG Newsletter*, 'Braidwood seminar of Canberra's arts organisations', 6(b), November 1983, p 2.
24   *BRG Newsletter*, 1983.
25   *BRG Newsletter*, 1983.
26   *BRG Newsletter*, 1983, p 3.
27   *BRG Newsletter*, 1983. Further recommendations were that: the ADB should be requested to give direct and indirect employment impact statements in relation to its funding decisions; funding strategies should ensure that projects are funded to realistic levels and provide for appropriate remuneration for professional arts workers involved; supplementary to General Grant provisions to professional organisations, the Community Arts Program and Special Projects Grants, which in the past have provided valuable assistance and a flexible response to Canberra's needs, be maintained and appropriately serviced; the ADB is encouraged to consult with NSW and Victorian governments' arts funding authorities about funding for ACT groups touring to those states. The meeting further emphasised that any policy guidelines developed for the ACT will have to perform two basic functions: provide a perspective for the development of the arts in relation to total cultural programs and provide reliable information to arts groups on funding criteria.

Lack of provision for studio space was a crucial issue undermining the development of a vibrant local arts community. As the number of graduating students from CSA continued to increase, this became a driving factor for the loss of artists post-graduation to capital cities elsewhere in Australia. The warehouses and abandoned industrial sites that were repurposed as art spaces in Melbourne, Sydney and Adelaide since the 1970s were simply not in evidence in a young planned city.[28] There was some hope that the 1981 revamp of Gorman House Community Arts Centre, previously a hostel for single public servants, would provide some artist studios, but its spaces were quickly filled with the community organisations relocating from Reid House, and with the refurbished spaces of the new ACG.

In response to these pressing issues around lack of availability of studios, a 'Space for Artists' campaign was convened in 1983 by a group of art school graduates, students, musicians and activists. In July, they staged a multi-day mural paint-in of the public toilets in Garema Place, reported in the *Canberra Times* as a 'creative demonstration'.[29] Their action aimed to reverse the government's decision to allocate the centrally located Beauchamp House to the Academy of Science and, instead, to turn it over to artists. While this claim for studio space was unsuccessful, the tendency to conflate artists with community groups (which yielded funding benefits from both of the federal government's Wage Pause programs and the CDF) proved useful once again when a campaign for community space was run concurrently with the Space for Artists campaign. Members of the former succeeded in gaining access to the old motor registry in Mort Street, Braddon, and to spaces in the Griffin Centre in the city centre for community groups to carry out activities and hold meetings. The combined lobbying of both campaigns resulted in the allocation at the end of 1983 of the converted three-storey building, previously home to the Australian Archives in Leichardt Street, Kingston, as a community arts centre. This was a landmark victory.

The preceding three years brought tremendous changes to the local arts and cultural landscape. By the end of 1983 neither the federal minister, the NCDC nor local advisory bodies could doubt the presence

---

28   Chapter 4 discusses the reclamation of parts of Ainslie Village in 1980 by Megalo Screenprint International and the repurposing of the old bus shelter at St Christopher's School in Manuka by the BRG collective in 1981.
29   Michael Foster, 'Jobless paint a plea for artists' space', *Canberra Times*, 8 July 1983, p 1.

of a determined, effective and broad-based arts lobby that aggressively sought appropriate government support. Changes included the 1980 establishment of Megalo Screenprint International, the 1981 launch of BRG, the 1981 refurbishment and opening of Gorman House Community Arts Centre and the 1982 opening of the National Gallery. As well, the NCDC acknowledged the growth of visual art galleries, community groups and arts groups engaged in concerted joint activist actions, a number of meetings took place involving the wider arts community and government, and the first dedicated studios/gallery spaces for the visual arts were allocated. The increasingly politically savvy pressure for expansion applied by the arts community over the next three years was marked by rapid response to government-initiated discussion papers and reports.

The much-awaited *Arts development in the Australian Capital Territory: a discussion paper* was released by the ADB in January 1984, between the announcement of the allocation of the Kingston Art Centre at the end of 1983 and its opening in March. While acknowledging that the last five years saw a 'visible growth and diversification of the arts in Canberra',[30] Kingsland, the ADB's outgoing chair, remarked that achieving 'consensus', including among members of the ADB, 'on some aspects [of arts, administration] is a task of exquisite difficulty'.[31]

The statement is unsurprising. Peer assessment of grant applications and arms-length funding were foundational concepts of the federal funding body, the Australia Council for the Arts, established in 1973. Neither was evident in the make-up of the ADB, whose nine members included Kingsland, two non-arts senior public servants, one from the Department of Home Affairs and Environment and one from the Department of Territories and Local Government (DTLG), and arts bureaucrat Catherine Santamaria, who would shortly replace Kingsland as chair. Of the four remaining members, only poet Geoff Page and visual arts critic and ANU head of Art History Sasha Grishin were involved with contemporary arts practice. Eight board members filled the 16 positions on each of four art form committees comprising theatre, music, visual and community arts, thus sitting on a minimum of two committees each. Consensus was impossible.

---

30   Richard Kingsland, 'Overview', in ACT Arts Development Board, *Arts development in the Australian Capital Territory: a discussion paper*, Canberra, 1984, p 3.
31   ADB, 1984, p v.

2. THE RAPID GROWTH OF LOCAL ARTS AND CULTURE

The continuing primacy of performing arts, including music, and the treatment of visual arts as expressed through craft and community arts, is demonstrated in the discussion paper. Statements around performing arts, music, craft and community arts accounted for 17 of the 22 points in the overview. Four points were specifically allocated to the visual arts, the principal expression of which was considered to be the National Gallery. Importantly, however, the discussion paper directly recognised the gallery as 'a national institution with no formal responsibility to the ACT community'.[32] Growing calls for a regional art/heritage museum were addressed in the statement:

> The location of national institutions in Canberra seems to have led Government to overlook the need for cultural and other institutions – including art and heritage museums – at the Territory and municipal levels.[33]

CSA's wider involvement of staff and teachers in the local community was recognised. The discussion paper credits CSA, however, with the formation of BRG, ACME Silkscreen Workshop, the Artworkers Union and 'the current campaign for community space for artists'.[34] This reading indicated that there was no understanding of the critical role of Jobless Action and Canberra's young social activists not connected to CSA in the formation of all of the above, except for ACME.[35] Finally, the overview listed, among a number of writers and musicians, some 'less visible' individual artists, with a shortlist comprising painters Michael Taylor and Robin Wallace-Crabbe, sculptor Rosalie Gascoigne, ceramicists and CSA staff Alan Watt and Alan Peascod, and printmaker and CSA director Udo Sellbach. Again, this reading reveals only a superficial knowledge of what was occurring in the burgeoning visual arts scene.

The discussion paper called for general feedback on the wider arts milieu, as well as specific submissions around the management of the General Grants Scheme of the Arts Development Program. Having delivered a comprehensive series of recommendations in the preceding October,

---

32 ADB, 1984, p 5.
33 ADB, 1984, p 5.
34 ADB, 1984, p 6.
35 ACME's support from CSA's Print Workshop tutor Mandy Martin is discussed in the section 'Mandy Martin: background and impacts' in Chapter 4.

the arts communities' general frustration with the slow progress of response from the ADB was growing. Clearly the sector was now looking for concerted action rather than continued invitations for discussion.

Some relief for visual artists was provided by the opening of the Kingston Art Centre on 30 March 1984. The centre was funded by the ACT CDF and managed by the Arts Council ACT. The first facility of its kind in the city, it provided multiple artist studios, fee-free gallery hire and spaces for a number of commercial galleries. In opening the centre, Uren 'signalled the Government's intention to establish similar projects in other parts of Canberra'.[36] Dawkins, then administrator of the Arts Council (ACT) (no doubt additionally buoyed by the January release of the ADB's discussion paper), said the opening marked 'a new era in art'.[37] There is little doubt of Uren's awareness of the pressing need for space and his genuine intention to build infrastructure. At the press conference that followed the opening, he urged the successful lobbyists to 'campaign for other groups in other areas of Canberra'.[38] In spite of this, it was not until the advent of self-government in the 1990s that purpose-built community art centres and standalone artist studio complexes would adequately service arts and community cultural groups.

Lobbying for support continued apace throughout 1984. The timed release of grant monies was the focus of the CCAF's sector-wide letter sent to 17 Canberra arts organisations on 21 June.[39] The letter, evidencing growing frustration with the cycle of meetings and discussion papers, concluded:

> Finally, could we draw your attention to a discussion at your meeting with arts groups and the Arts Development Board on 4 July 1983 [11 months before]. Arts groups made representations of this nature to you, and the Departmental representative undertook to follow the matter through.[40]

---

36   Debbie Cameron, 'Kingston space launched for art', *Canberra Times*, 31 March 1984, p 9.
37   Cameron, 1984.
38   Cameron, 1984.
39   These were BRG, Arts Council (ACT), Blue Folk Community Arts Association, Canberra Stereo Public Radio, Craft Council of the ACT, Theatre ACT, CYT, Canberra Dance Ensemble, CTC, Canberra Opera, Human Veins Dance Theatre, CSO, Stagecoach, Canberra Rep, Megalo Screenprint Workshop and Gorman House Community Arts Centre.
40   CCAF Inc, letter to arts organisations, 21 June 1984, Correspondence file 1/1984, CCAS archives.

The letter sought written support to back up a request to Uren to change the payment of arts grants from quarterly instalments to bi-annual instalments payable in April and November.[41] Concerns regarding the efficacy of current arrangements included the working capital deficits sustained by 'almost all of the large professional arts organisations in Canberra'.[42] These were caused by 'the rapid expansion of these organisations, their full and effective usage of all grants received, and the lack of opportunity for them to build adequate working capital reserves',[43] and resulted in the use of overdraft facilities in November and December. The letter reflected the cyclic nature of performing arts in the city and the desire to reduce requests to the ADB for accelerated payment of grants, thereby reducing the growing administrative overload on under-resourced companies. In 1984, five companies including CCAF, Canberra Opera, CYT, Human Veins Dance Theatre and the Arts Council (ACT) found it necessary to apply for accelerated funding. The requested change sought to bring the ACT into line with Australia Council practices, which were already servicing clients with payments in two instalments.

In fact, by 1984, the wider process of developing an arts and cultural policy for the ACT seemed unlikely. Continuing population growth was matched by rising local unemployment and decreasing federal government commitment to Canberra. Numerous local advisory committees, with reporting and advisory responsibilities to federal government, operated across government departments, creating increasingly expensive and unwieldy overall management of the Territory.

Clearly the task of formulating a comprehensive Territory-wide arts and culture strategy was beyond the under-resourced ADB, now chaired by Santamaria who had replaced Kingsland at the beginning of the year. Additionally, the political and economic climate in which the ADB was attempting to devise a forward plan was not conducive to long-term planning. In response to the previously detailed persistent lobbying from an increasingly visible and vocal extended local arts community, the ADB decided to engage a consultant to undertake a review of the General Grants Scheme of the Arts Development program, alerting arts organisations to this decision on 31 October 1984. Issues the consultant was required to address included:

---

41   CCAF Inc, 21 June 1984.
42   CCAF Inc, 21 June 1984.
43   CCAF Inc, 21 June 1984.

The range and nature of arts activities which should be supported, the level of funding appropriate in the territory, the balance of support between professional, semi-professional and amateur organisations, the contribution of different activities to the cultural and community life of the ACT and the limitations on funds available under the Arts Development Program and from other sources.[44]

The consultant appointed was Timothy Pascoe.

The Pascoe Report

At the heart of the problem of developing funding that responded to existing local needs and provided opportunities for growth in local arts was the difficulty of separating the construct of Canberra as national capital space from the real and rapidly developing needs of Canberra's local arts community. The complexity of developing funding mechanisms that supported local arts within this national space was exemplified throughout the processes of commissioning, researching, final reporting and responses to Pascoe's report.

The ADB commissioned Pascoe in October 1984 to deliver in the following March a report titled *Arts in the ACT: funding priorities and grant administration*. Having completed a three-year term as executive chairman of the Australia Council (1982–84), Pascoe was previously based in Canberra as federal director of the Liberal Party of Australia in 1974/75. It is likely that the ADB concluded that these factors made Pascoe an appropriate choice to conduct a survey to enable the ADB to adjust their funding parameters to meet increasingly vocal concerns and needs around local funding.

Rather than confer a bias towards the local, however, Pascoe's Australia Council role and his political role in the mid-1970s were overtly linked to Canberra as national capital space and as the locus of federal politics. Additionally problematic was that he carried out his research over the summer of 1984/85. The following pages examine these three difficulties, beginning with Pascoe's connection to the Commonwealth arts funding body.

---

44   ACT ADB, letter to Canberra arts organisations, 31 October 1984, Correspondence file 1/1984, CCAS archives.

For almost 20 years, the two iterations of federal government funding for the arts, that is the Australian Council for the Arts and its successor, the Australia Council, had garnered significant criticisms. Among these was the ever-present charge of elitism. This stemmed from the core decision made by the Australia Council to fund major or 'flagship' performing arts companies as internal and external signifiers of a nation civilised by culture. So much money had been invested in these companies by the beginning of the 1980s that it was impossible to conceive of them failing, with the resulting widespread perception that they exerted undue influence over the Commonwealth funding body.

This entrenched tendency to continue funding performing arts companies regardless of economic or artistic justifications was increasingly obvious in Canberra during the period from the end of the 1970s to the onset of self-government in 1989, and it was one of the major contributing factors to growing unease among the arts community in the capital. This was particularly pertinent to the continued unsuccessful attempts to develop a professional theatre company in the capital.

Nationally, between 1983 and 1985, there emerged the possibility of a major policy shift in the way that Australia Council funding was allocated. In 1985, one quarter of all Australia Council funds went to the Australian Opera, the Australian Ballet and the two major orchestras. Debate centred around whether the council should continue to use limited Commonwealth funding to support these major companies – which it was felt should be able to attract corporate and private sponsorship – or whether funds should be directed away from these and other large dance and theatre companies, towards smaller companies making more experimental works.[45] Labor Party rhetoric appeared to support a change in funding focus and Pascoe was bipartisan in his support for this change. In the middle of his three-year term as executive chair, Pascoe urged the Council 'to support a shift in funding from assumed excellence to genuine creativity'.[46] This insider knowledge of Commonwealth funding mechanisms and politics and his public support for the funding of creative, community and regional art development provided compelling reasons in support of the ADB commissioning Pascoe to write an ACT arts funding report.

---

45 John Gardiner-Garden, *Commonwealth arts policy and administration*, Social Policy Section, Parliament of Australia, Canberra, Department of Parliamentary Services, 7 May 2009, p 9. The 1984 Australia Council–commissioned Throsby Report supported the change in policy 'to shift the emphasis of its overall financial policy towards individual artists'. See also *Age*, 'Australia shuns its artists: inquiry', 1 February 1984, p 3.
46 Internal Australia Council report, as quoted by Gardiner-Garden (2009, p 20).

And yet, the opposite of Pascoe's public views is evident in the finished report. It contains clear indicators that its author, though willing, struggled to distinguish between Canberra as national capital space and Canberra as home to a growing local arts community. This is not surprising. Pascoe's time as executive chair of the council coincided with the opening of the National Gallery in October 1982. The gallery's establishment was the ultimate cultural signifier of both national capital space and civilised nation that had been in train since Liberal Prime Minister Harold Holt simultaneously announced the formation of the Australian Council for the Arts and the commitment to a Canberra-based national gallery in November 1967. Since that time, successive federal governments variously approved, rescinded, re-proposed and completed various national cultural monuments in Canberra. Pascoe was thus surrounded by the rhetoric and problems of culturally funding Canberra as national capital space. Secondly, Pascoe's experience of Canberra, where he was based during 1974/75 in his capacity as federal director of the Liberal Party, was inexorably tied to the construct of Canberra as the seat of federal government. Federal politicians and federal party directors left Canberra, as they do today, on Thursday or Friday afternoons during sitting weeks and were absent from the capital during non-sitting weeks. During the working week, Pascoe may have attended events at the CTC. If so, he may have seen travelling performances from Old Tote Theatre Company, Nimrod Theatre, Hungarian State Symphony Orchestra, Marcel Marceau or Kamahl, Australian Opera, Melbourne Symphony Orchestra, Barry Humphries, Cleo Laine or Roy Orbison. Local offerings were diverse, including performances from Canberra Rep, Canberra Philharmonic Society, Canberra Theatre Trust, Tempo Theatre, CSO, Canberra Youth Orchestra, Canberra School of Music faculty in concert, the first and second Canberra Film Festival, Woden Valley Youth Choir and Canberra Opera.[47] It is unlikely, however, that Pascoe was a regular Canberra Theatre attendee; his business during those two years of sitting weeks was politics, not art and culture.

Finally, the research phase of the report was initiated in the lead up to and during the 1984/85 summer holiday, beginning on Wednesday 28 November. Research during this period was unlikely to foster a deep understanding of Canberra's cultural development needs. Pascoe understood the local scope of the report saying, 'I think the challenge of

---

47 'Canberra Theatre Centre ephemera at the ACT Heritage Library', www.library.act.gov.au/find/history/search/ephemera/performing_arts/canberra-theatre-centre-ephemera, accessed 16 March 2014, updated 6 July 2015.

the study is to do something about Canberra's needs'.[48] But then, as now, a large number of Canberrans left the Territory for extended summer holidays in southern NSW coastal towns and elsewhere. Not only were audiences absent but also the majority of galleries were closed. Students were absent from CSA and ANU, which regularly hosted local arts and culture events throughout the academic year, during the November to February period when Pascoe conducted his research. Pascoe admits that he sometimes had to make do 'with an external inspection and peering through windows'.[49] There were a number of wide-ranging events on at CTC, some of which he may have attended.[50] In November, December, January and February, he could have seen the Beverley Flanagan School of Classical Ballet, Queensland Ballet, Melbourne's Playbox Theatre Company, the Australian tour of the Oxford Revue group, Canberra's Philharmonic Society performing *The sentimental bloke*, Canberra theatre company Women on a Shoestring and Canberra Opera. In February, Theatre ACT performed the Kathy Lette–written, Carol Woodrow–directed *Perfect mismatch*, and Human Veins Dance Theatre presented a week of lunchtime dance.[51]

Both during Pascoe's 1974/75 period of flying in and out of Canberra and the 1984/85 summer months when he conducted research for the report, his impression of arts in Canberra would have been of performing arts as expressed locally and as imported as part of the national touring circuit. In terms of visual arts, it was the ANG that remained open over the summer period, where art was a cultural function of the national capital space. It was too much to expect that Pascoe would be able to view the city through local eyes or to conceive of a broader arts practice that was unequivocally local in expression and requirements. The imprimatur of the national capital space was powerful.

---

48   *Canberra Times*, 'Chairman appointed for arts review', 30 November 1984, p 13.
49   Pascoe, 1985, p 6.
50   'Canberra Theatre Centre ephemera'.
51   The Canberra-based touring company Human Veins Dance Theatre was founded by Don Asker in November 1979. It was envisaged as the flagship carrier of dance in the national capital, and funded by the Australia Council in this and continuing guises until 2006. It disbanded in 1988 when Asker took up a Churchill Fellowship, and it reformed as the Meryl Tankard Company. In 1992, it metamorphosed into Vis-a-Vis Dance Canberra under the directorship of Melbourne's Sue Healey, who left in 1995. A rethink saw the company change to the Choreographic Centre, directed from 1996 by Mark Gordon, and then expanded in 1999 under Ruth Osborne's Quantum Leap Youth Choreographic Ensemble, becoming the Australian Choreographic Centre in 2001. After triennial funding was not renewed in 2006, the centre closed in 2007 and re-launched as QL2 Youth Dance Ensemble in 2008 under Osborne as artistic director and continuing until the present day. The continued success of QL2 is due in no small part to the programs run by the centre over the period of Gordon's leadership.

The Pascoe Report was submitted to the ADB in mid-March 1985. 'As an input to the debate that will follow', Pascoe, positing several scenarios for discussion, concluded, 'There is no right answer',[52] Arguably the ADB was looking for clarity in the way forward and a funding model that had a higher possibility of success and consensus. On both counts they would have been disappointed.

The bias towards national capital space is clear in Pascoe's comments in the introduction that characterise Canberra as the city best served by arts funding nationally. Central to this argument was the presence of the National Gallery, but surely it was the nation in whose service this gallery functioned. From the late 1970s, Roger Butler, the gallery's inaugural curator of Australian Prints, Posters and Illustrated Books, vigorously collected the work of Canberra-based printmakers – along with nationally produced prints and posters – for the national collection. The gallery was, however, inextricably tied to the conception of Canberra as national capital space. Many of Pascoe's recommendations were likewise tied to the development of professional, performing arts organisations whose success in the national capital space would reflect well on Australia. This in spite of the fact that he was writing his report in the middle of a funding debate that proposed the benefits of moving away from flagship companies towards more experimental arts ventures, a move he publicly supported.

In opposition to ACT arts community desires and in apparent opposition to his public calls for increased funding of experimental art forms, but in line with historical funding trajectories, Pascoe recommended funds go to four core areas with only one company in each area being selected for funding. Additionally, he recommended that these companies be funded with the proviso that they attain a level of excellence reflecting their position as national flag bearers resident in the capital. Given that Canberra's small population of 220,000 citizens displayed an immensely diverse arts and cultural practice, it is clear that Pascoe's recommendations centred on funding the national capital space and not the local community.

Pascoe summarised his recommendations under three headings: core strategy, supplementary strategy, and administration. Under core strategy he wrote: '[T]he ADB should provide ongoing, operating funding to achieve a small core of world-class, full-time, fully professional activity

---

52   Pascoe, 1985, p 17.

in a limited number of areas'.⁵³ These were: classical and contemporary drama, through Theatre ACT; contemporary dance, through Human Veins Dance Theatre; craft, through extending the role and facilities of the Crafts Council of the ACT; and community arts, by building on the Arts Council (ACT). In the report's introduction he wrote: 'As a final note, I should point out that my study has not covered the delegated Community Arts Program. However it does get a passing mention towards the end of the report.'⁵⁴ This omission, given that Canberra's community arts scene was such an integral component of its arts and cultural landscape, reveals his low-level engagement with and understanding of the realities of the community's arts and cultural needs.

The report's core strategy did not mention individual artists, innovative and experimental artists and art forms, musical theatre or education in the arts, on which Pascoe, shifting responsibility away from arts funding, wrote that 'the ADB should work assiduously to have [education in the arts] funded within the education budget'.⁵⁵ The supplementary strategy recommended upgrading studio and exhibition facilities for visual arts and craft, sustaining some non-core areas of professional endeavour and reserving some funds for other art forms. Administration recommendations included three grant categories: professional development, professional assistance and facilities, and special projects and equipment.

The omission of the visual arts from the report's core strategy is further evidence of a disconnect from the realities of developing arts practice. Pascoe reported that 'this art-form is not particularly strong in Canberra'. For this reason, he continued:

> [A]n injection of funds to create a professional infrastructure might have been attractive. However, I came to the contrary view for three reasons – galleries tend to be the major professional and institutional structures supported by governments and their funding agencies. In the ACT, the Australian National Gallery fulfils most of the roles of a State gallery; compared with craft there is not the same foundation on which to build; nor is the strength of the School of Art so distinctive; there does not appear to be the same opportunity for uniqueness.⁵⁶

---

53   Pascoe, 1985, p 57.
54   Pascoe, 1985, p 6.
55   Pascoe, 1985, p 58.
56   Pascoe, 1985, p 57.

In between the release of the report to the community for comment on 27 March 1985 and prior to 11 November that year, when the ACT arts community was advised of grant decisions for the 1986 calendar year, the ADB held three meetings with arts community members[57] and accepted 32 written submissions.[58] Continued funding for the major recipients, Theatre ACT and Canberra Opera, were of particular concern; their time was widely felt to be over.[59] Participants reported feeling that their concerns and suggestions, principal among which was for a diversification of resources, had not been heard.

On 24 May the chair, Cathy Santamaria, reported that the ADB:

> would not implement the Pascoe report in 1986 except where it was agreed that the report's approach was appropriate … Even where there is agreement the Board sees 1986 as an interim year with the full effects of any substantial change in approach not being implemented until at least 1987.

The *Canberra Times* additionally reported on the widespread misgivings surrounding the report's implementation, writing that:

> much concern [was] expressed by the arts community that the recommendations would be accepted before there had been enough time for their implications to be considered.[60]

Therefore, on 11 November, when the ADB released funding allocations for the 1986 year that closely shadowed the recommendations of the report, the response from the arts community was swift and outraged. Quite rightly, they felt that both the carefully considered recommendations from meetings held in the first half of the decade, and the feedback given and apparently accepted prior to the release of the 1986 grants, had fallen on deaf ears.

On 16 November 1985, five days after the 1986 grants were announced, members of the ACT arts community placed an advertisement in the *Canberra Times* to draw attention to their profound disappointment (see Figure 5 below).

---

57 The meetings ran on 9 April (advertised in the *Canberra Times* on 3 April 1986) and 11 May (*Canberra Times*, 8 May 1986).
58 Ken Healey, 'Practical Pascoe sheds light on art wars', *Canberra Times*, 12 May 1985, p 12.
59 Funding for both organisations was withdrawn by 1987.
60 *Canberra Times*, 'Timing of arts funding decision', 25 May 1985, p 7.

2. THE RAPID GROWTH OF LOCAL ARTS AND CULTURE

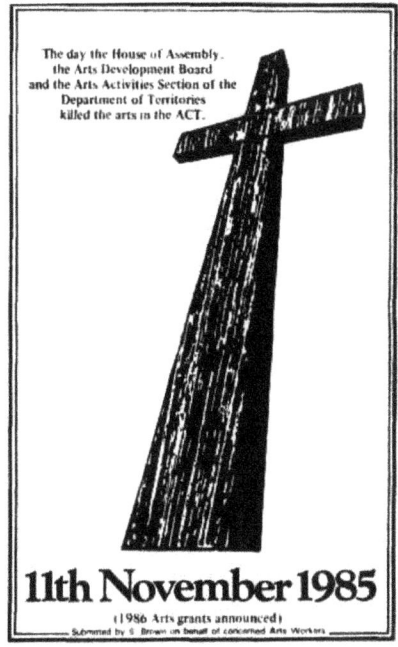

Figure 5. Memorial advertisement submitted by S Brown
Source. *Canberra Times*, 16 November 1985, p 9s, reproduced with permission

At the heart of the powerful negative response that swept through the local arts community was the report's primary recommendation that grants to core groups be increased by decreasing available funding to smaller groups. This was exceptionally bad news for the lively local theatre scene, which included five active theatre companies in addition to Theatre ACT, the Territory's nominated flagship company. Theatre ACT received the majority of total arts funding – $170,000 for the 1986 year from the overall $210,000 allocated to theatre. Of the remaining $40,000, Human Veins Dance Theatre received $10,000. Pascoe's recommendation was out of step with the concerns of local arts workers who deeply desired:

> enlightenment under the present system … [T]hat institutional model, with four flagship companies, has failed in the ACT. Institutionalisation is the last thing a developing industry like ours needs.[61]

With no response to the memorial advertisement forthcoming from the ADB by 30 November, a number of ACT arts workers took the radical step of submitting their resignations. They included, among others: Steve Brown, administrator and artistic director of the Arts Council (ACT), who had arrived from Adelaide in mid-1984, 'where there is respect for the professional arts worker as well as support and understanding'[62] and who had submitted the memorial advertisement; Wendy Taubman,

---

61 Wendy Taubman, quoted in Ken Healey, 'Disheartened arts workers leave their jobs: 1986 grants meet silence of the defeated', *Canberra Times*, 30 November 1985, p 18.
62 Steve Brown, quoted in Healey, 30 November 1985.

administrator of Through Art Unity Theatre (TAU)[63]; Jim Koehne, music coordinator at the Arts Council (ACT); and Gail Kelly, director of CYT. Pascoe recommended the latter organisation not receive increased funding, because he felt the success of CYT was wholly dependent on its current director. 'The predominant feeling,' remarked Brown, 'is one of despondency rather than anger.'[64]

The provision of hidden subsidies from arts workers in the form of unremunerated working hours was of great concern. The Arts Council (ACT), which had demonstrated broad relevance across the arts sector for decades in Canberra, including – though not recognised in Pascoe's report – as the instigator and driver of community arts projects, received $105,000 in funding for the 1985 year with a grant of a further $105,000 for 1986. Brown maintained that he had given around half of his working hours for no remuneration since arriving from Adelaide and taking up the job in 1984, a situation common then and now in the arts industry.[65] Taubman felt strongly that '[b]y continuing to provide such large hidden subsidies we are only continuing to cover up the ADB's inadequacies'.[66]

The final sally in the sector's response to the release of arts grants for 1986 revealed extreme distress from the growing sector over the lack of direction and clear, appropriate policy from the overworked and understaffed Arts Activities section of the DTLG. On Thursday 5 December, arts workers published an open letter to the ACT community, the House of Assembly, and Gordon Scholes, the new Minister for Territories, demanding that all positions on the ADB be declared vacant and the Arts Activities section of the DTLG be restructured.[67] The meeting that developed the wording of the letter was organised by Anne Virgo, then coordinator of BRG, and BRG member Mark Ferguson.[68]

The *Canberra Times*' interpretation of the memorial advertisement as a 'theatrical statement' by arts workers masks a much more pervasive exhaustion felt throughout the community, not just in the arts sector. By the end of 1985, economic hardships were biting deep in Canberra.

---

63 Through Art Unity Theatre (1984–94). Founder: Dominic Mico. TAU – renamed UP Front Theatre in 1991 – was one of the success stories of the CEP program, continuing as it did beyond the initial six months of CEP funding.
64 Healey, 30 November 1985.
65 Healey, 30 November 1985.
66 Taubman, quoted in Healey, 30 November 1985.
67 *Canberra Times*, 'Call for change for arts sake', 5 December 1985, p 8.
68 Ken Healey, 'FOI adds material to arts funding debate', *Canberra Times*, 13 December 1985, p 21.

The slowing economy was matched by a growing paralysis around local decision-making as increasing population numbers and need were met by a decline in federal commitment to local endeavours in the national capital.

The passionate local response to the Pascoe Report in the mid-1980s marks an important moment in the development of contemporary arts. The ACT arts landscape had undergone dramatic change between 1978 and the release of the report in 1985, with local performing arts companies, community arts organisations and Commonwealth-funded cultural institutions being joined by an increasingly vocal contemporary visual arts sector that had gained considerable momentum. The commissioning of the report marked a chance to radically alter the funding landscape in response to local needs, but, in the end, inertia prevailed and a bold leap into a better future for arts funding and development eluded the advisory bodies.

Comprehensive change in the sector would not occur until 1991, after the introduction of self-government. That year saw the handing down of the recommendations of the Select Committee on Cultural Activities and Facilities. The first recommendation adopted was the formation of the peak arts body the Cultural Council, which replaced the ADB. Most critical to forward development was the handover of the $19 million casino premium to the ACT Government and the decision to allocate the premium to the provision of arts and cultural infrastructure. As a result, the ACT entered an extended era of rapid and inspired growth in local arts with a trajectory that was managed and directed by Canberrans themselves and a legacy that would transform the face of the city up until the present day.

Unique local solutions

Now I turn my attention to three significant local communication and funding solutions: the establishment of the arts magazine *Muse*, the creation of the fundraising group CAPO, and the Emerging Artist Support Scheme (EASS).

As previously noted, the Commonwealth continued to grapple unsuccessfully throughout the 1980s with funding art forms in Canberra that were not related to developing identified flagship companies.

Additionally, the ADB, which was responsible for advising the federal minister for territories on funding needs, was extremely under-resourced. Conversely, however, the national capital paradigm allowed the rise of unique solutions to the challenge of carving out the local from within the primary rhetoric of national capital space. Within Canberra's highly educated and politicised population were passionate arts practitioners and supporters and experienced teachers, administrators and negotiators. The continued success of these local solutions indicates that there were also community members with resources available to support the growing sector as consumers and buyers of locally created artworks.

Three innovative solutions were developed, two of which continue to the present day. The first was the arts magazine *Muse*, which from 1980 to 1998 provided a focal point for the rapidly developing arts community. The second was CAPO's unique arts funding model that, from 1983 to the present, has provided an alternative non-government funding source for local arts practitioners. The third, the EASS, emerged from CSA and, from 1988 until now, it has extended funding and exhibition opportunities to CSA graduates.

Muse provided an alternative voice for local arts in a city in which media coverage was dominated by the *Canberra Times*. It was deeply embedded in the local community from its inception and demonstrated lively topicality, relevance and commitment to Canberra's arts and cultural practitioners for 18 years. During this time it remained true to its founding statement that as '[t]he arts and entertainment provide a vital means of expression for the whole community ... *Muse* will concentrate on the work of Canberra artists and groups'.[69] *Muse* was launched in June 1980, assisted by a $1,000 grant from the DCT, and initially operated as a collective, coordinated by Robert Garran and staffed by volunteers. The free arts magazine, initially published every six weeks, included features and reviews, drawings, photographs and cartoons, stories and poetry, arts news and an arts and entertainment diary. Until 1987, *Muse* was published collectively by CCAF. In 1987, following protracted negotiations with the CCAF over paperwork that – curiously for a volunteer arts organisation that attracted a level of government funding – implied ownership rather than custodianship of *Muse*, the Arts Council (ACT) assumed the role of publisher. Following this, *Muse* was awarded a grant of $20,000 from the

---

69   *Muse*, 'Statement and call out for contributors', advertisement, *Canberra Times*, 23 May 1980, p 22.

ADB. By its 10th anniversary in 1990, funding had increased to $25,000 and *Muse* was additionally able to raise another $19,000 from advertising and sponsorship, conclusively demonstrating its relevance within and for the community. At the end of 1990, with the Arts Council (ACT) coming to an end, *Muse* became an incorporated association and, in August 1991, the magazine celebrated its 100th issue with a party at Gorman House.

By employing local writers from its first issue, *Muse* was instrumental in developing arts writing and criticism in Canberra. Arts journalist Helen Musa (who was arts editor of the *Canberra Times* from 1995 to 2007) wrote for *Muse* from 1985 and was its editor from 1990 to 1996. During her editorship, the magazine was published on the first of each month. Musa encouraged robust journalism, and 'invited conflicts of interest and bias'[70] by encouraging writer/practitioners in visual and performing arts to write and review within their disciplines. Among these, from 1984 to 1986, was Tim Ferguson, whose comedy trio the Doug Anthony All Stars learnt its craft busking on Canberra streets; and Australian author Cate Kennedy, a graduate of the University of Canberra. Long-time *Canberra Times* visual arts reviewer Sonia Barron first wrote for *Muse* before moving on to the *Canberra Times*, as did senior visual arts critic Kerry-Anne Cousins. Musa herself employed Canberra artist Stephen Harrison, whose cartoons featured in every issue. Importantly, Musa presided over an expanded program that, in addition to providing local arts content, hosted regular arts-focused events including political forums, public meetings with arts practitioners and, under the umbrella of the Canberra Critics Circle (itself founded by Musa in 1991), regular arts writing workshops.

The founding of *Muse*, its focus on the work of Canberra artists and groups, and its continued strong presence in the Canberra community over 18 years are testament to a growing awareness of the importance of local arts as the glue binding a strong local community and as a central marker of place. That it survived during economically difficult periods is proof of its relevance. Importantly, its longevity also indicates continuing and growing capacity within the local sector over the period.

The second unique local endeavour arose at the end of 1983. On Saturday 12 November, CAPO held its inaugural gala banquet auction at the Lakeside International Hotel, at which '500 people paid $60 each for

---

70   Helen Musa, interview with the author, 18 September 2015.

a bidding stick'.[71] CAPO was modelled on the Seattle, Washington State, organisation PONCHO,[72] whose president travelled to Canberra to act as auctioneer for the gala. The evening's proceedings were managed by Richard Thorp, architect of Australia's new Parliament House. The cost of the bidding stick covered the gala banquet's considerable expenses and the monies raised through auction were distributed via a committee to arts groups and individuals who had successfully applied for funding.

It is unlikely that any other Australian jurisdiction would have been able to raise the level of interest in such an event or the kind of rewards available to bidders in early CAPO auctions. An extraordinary 182 gifts were donated for the inaugural event. Among them was a chestnut yearling colt called Gulliver, a carcass of venison, the opportunity to conduct an orchestra, local Olympian Robert de Castella's running shorts, a skiing holiday in Aspen, Senator Flo Bjelke-Petersen's pumpkin scone recipe printed for the occasion on Senate notepaper, an autographed copy of Labor Prime Minister Bob Hawke's inaugural parliamentary speech, and a 'commemorative banner of the opening of Parliament House on May 9, 1927 … presented on parchment and extremely rare'.[73]

Canberra provided a unique environment for CAPO's success. The quality and number of donations says a great deal about the nature of its community at that time. On one hand, the nationwide period of economic decline that had followed the dismissal of the Whitlam Labor government and the rise of the Liberal Fraser government in 1975 was acutely felt in the national capital. By 1981, Canberra registered a net 'out' migration of 262.[74] Unemployment rose sharply with concomitant flow-on effects throughout the city, particularly among young job seekers. The public service, which in 1975 had accounted for 60 per cent of the workforce, had contracted by almost 10 per cent by the early 1980s. By 1983, homelessness and emergency housing issues affected 2,396 adults and 276 children in a population of just over 238,983. By 1984, 'an inquiry into welfare services in the ACT declared that the political will to develop Canberra had evaporated'.[75]

---

71 Edna Boling, 'Auctioneer has sociable way to raise money', *Canberra Times*, 10 November 1983, p 8.
72 Between 1978 and 1983, PONCHO raised $4.4 million for the arts.
73 Ross Andrews, 'From pasture to gala dinner', *Canberra Times*, 23 October 1983, p 11.
74 Brown, 2014, p 198.
75 Brown, 2014, p 202.

In spite of the economic downturn, the city's position as the seat of federal government and the Commonwealth public service and as home to the majority of embassies resulted in a culturally literate and educated population with high disposable income. The gala banquet auction format infused the concept of support for the broader arts in the ACT with pleasure. Philanthropy as practised in this model was unique within Australia and allowed supporters to experience close engagement with contemporary cultural life.

One individual and 23 Canberra-based arts organisations submitted 43 projects to CAPO for consideration in 1983. Ten were awarded funding. Most useful in supporting the growth of visual arts were 'several thousand dollars' granted to Studio One to enable the provision of printing services to assist young artists; $1,160 to the Crafts Council of the ACT to support tours of visual arts collections within Canberra; and $1,000 to the CCAF to enable it to pay small fees to *Muse* contributors. The largest grant, of $11,440, went to the oft-funded Theatre ACT, to employ a full-time actor for 1984. The CSO, Canberra Opera, Jigsaw Theatre Company and the Canberra Children's Choir represented performing arts. A proposed scheme from the Arts Council (ACT) to circulate the work of young artists among potential purchasers was funded at $5,500, but it did not come to fruition. A prescient grant of $6,540 was awarded to Canberra Stereo Public Radio to purchase digital recording equipment and to cover costs involved in an application, if successful, for a broadcasting licence. Although the first application for a broadcast licence was unsuccessful, this grant provided vital early support for the station that would become ArtSound FM, and that continues to inform and add cohesiveness to the broader Canberra arts and cultural community.[76]

The *Canberra Times* reported a combined total of $150,000 raised over the first two CAPO auctions, with just over $100,000 distributed to practitioners: $46,694 in 1983 and $54,435 in 1984. The balance of around $50,000, raised from ticket sales, covered the costs of the gala evenings. The third gala ball in 1985 was advertised as *An affair of the arts*

---

76 The remaining grants were: $5,904 to CSO to fund a two-day rehearsal and performance with Japanese conductor Hiroyuki Iwaki; $3,000 to Jigsaw Theatre Company for designer fees and set construction for *The dream circle*, a play about Marion Mahony, who worked hand in glove with her architect husband Walter Burley Griffin on the design of Canberra; $900 to Canberra Children's Choir to buy a sound system; and $3,500 to Canberra Opera to hire a principal singer. The *Canberra Times* reported that CAPO had reserved $4,000 of auction monies for auction expenses, with a balance of $11,000 retained for further future allocations to the arts ('Auction to benefit arts organisations', 30 November 1983, p 9).

and auction items on offer included a return trip to Europe, fine furs, jewellery, antiques, and a day at the races with Queensland politician, the Hon Russ Hinze.[77]

CAPO's relevance extended into the period post self-government. By 1990, CAPO's raison d'être addressed successive federal governments' desire for partnership funding of the arts with non-government organisations. CAPO was good news also for the fledgling ACT Government, which demonstrated a growing awareness of the importance of local arts to the wider community but with a budget, one year into the three-year handover to self-government, that was constrained.[78] ACT Liberal Minister for Health, Education and the Arts Gary Humphries, calling on the Canberra business community to support the 1990 auction, identified CAPO as being 'unique in Australia' as it raised funds from local businesses and individuals and dispersed those back to the local arts community. Humphries acknowledged the $500,000 raised since 1983 as an 'extraordinary amount of money for a city the size of Canberra' and encouraged the continued flow of private monies to the sector:

> Last year, the statistics showed that the arts are good business. Vigorous arts activity helps to create business for a number of different industries ... [B]y supporting CAPO, those industries are helping to support themselves ... The Alliance Government will continue to assist the arts in Canberra. However, arts organisations will increasingly require additional assistance.[79]

As the national capital experienced the slowing of business that gripped the rest of Australia by the mid-1990s, the rewards available to bidders became more moderate. In the mid-2000s the board elected to change the evening's format from the expensive gala banquets to a smaller cocktail party and auction. Reflecting the ascendancy of visual art within the Canberra community, the bulk of items available at auction by then comprised artworks donated by the region's senior and emerging artists,

---

77 *Canberra Times*, 'Bid for your own star', 26 April 1985, p 7.
78 Reminiscing on the first years of self-government on his last sitting day in 2004, Bill Wood asserted, 'Self-government is a success, not without a large number of bumps, bruises and broken limbs along the way. Richard Madden was the first Under Treasurer. Wayne Berry, and I think Bill Stefaniak – not in the same cabinets – would remember the downward graph that he presented at budget time. "This is where we are folks," he would say. "This is where we have to get to." The only cabinet decisions in those times were where we would cut' (Parliamentary Debates, Legislative Assembly, Australian Capital Territory, 26 August 2004, 4323).
79 Gary Humphries, 'Message from the minister', *Canberra Times*, 19 July 1990, p 24.

many of whom attended the auctions. The evening became an opportunity for collectors and art enthusiasts to mingle with and to buy the work of local artists at a reasonable cost.

By 2013, CAPO had dispersed more than $2 million of non-government funding to the ACT arts sector over 30 years. Although the awards are, as they have always been, open to the broader arts community, the largest group of funding recipients since the 2000s have been visual artists. In this way, CAPO has become a not-for-profit funding entity auctioning donated visual artworks to visual arts consumers and returning the majority of funds raised back to visual arts practitioners. Whether it is sustainable for visual artists to continue to support their own in this way remains to be seen.

The third unique concept, EASS, emerged from CSA. It was envisaged by the school's second director, David Williams, as a 1988 bicentennial project designed to 'complement the landmark International Master Workshops and Symposia' held at the school that year.[80] As the advent of both self-government and Australia's bicentenary approached, CSA was graduating in excess of 70 students annually, a cohort that was increasing each year, across 10 workshops.[81] The growing number of contemporary visual arts graduates and others not associated with CSA required more support than federal or local government could provide. Concern over the lack of appropriate artist studio space and the small number of suitable contemporary art exhibition venues was exacerbated by uncertainty due to the expected tightening of Commonwealth funds in a time of economic downturn and the unknown effects of impending self-government.

That Williams was able to attract support from individuals, businesses, art organisations and institutions indicated that, by 1988, CSA was deeply embedded in the Canberra community. As Canberra's population continued to grow and local arts infrastructure continued to expand rapidly from the early 1990s, EASS grew along with it. EASS extended opportunities to CSA graduates in the form of acquisition awards, cash endowments, materials grants and many exhibition opportunities, and provided concrete examples of widespread community support for

---

80   David Williams, foreword to Agostino, 2009, p ix.
81   In 1986, the first year that CSA offered bachelor's degrees, 74 students graduated. In 1987, 79 students graduated. In 1988, 62 students graduated, marking the only decline in numbers since 1978; and, in 1989, 81 students graduated. The 10 workshops were: printmaking, graphic investigation, painting, sculpture, textiles, wood, leather, gold and silver, glass and ceramics (Agostino, 2009, p ix).

emerging artists and the school. Then, as now, awards were conferred during the annual end-of-year graduate exhibition/open studios celebration, which is a highlight for the broad arts community of practitioners and workers, and the extended community of the national capital. The efforts of EASS to make staying in Canberra more viable and to continue a valued and supported arts practice played a vital role in reversing the flow of young artists to other cities.

Canberra music and theatre commentator Ken Healey opined in 1985 that, given the size of Canberra's community, 'innovation and experimentation [should] not be funded at the expense of emerging professional activity in established areas'.[82] In fact, Canberra's unique environment required that funding address both the innovative and experimental as well as the emerging professional; these two categories often overlapped. Clearly more money to support the growing sector was urgently required, and EASS and CAPO played critical roles in extending non-government opportunities for funding.

The Brickworks, Studio One and aGOG

The lack of studio space continued to be a problem for the annually increasing numbers of graduates from CSA. Waiting lists for studios within the Kingston Art Centre were long, and with no other suitable studio space available in the city, some local artists devised an ad hoc solution. From 1913 to 1976 the Yarralumla Brickworks, the first industrial complex built in Canberra, produced the bricks from which many of the city's homes were constructed. From the early 1980s, as the brickworks' buildings deteriorated, the site provided a number of visual artists with quasi-official studio space, available on weekly leases.

Four of these artists were recognised as leaders in their field in Australia and had some profile in Europe and the United States. From 2–26 October 1986, works from these four, together with works from three emerging artists who benefited from the support of their more experienced fellows, were exhibited in *Prime cultural estate*, at the ACG. The exhibition comprised Jay Arthur's paper works, Helen Wadlington's bookbinding, James Whitehead's photography, Gaynor Cardew's feminist cartoons (printed on fabric at Megalo Screenprint), Brigitte Ender's ceramics, Churchill

---

82   Healey, 12 May 1985, p 12.

Fellowship recipient Morgyn Phillips' silk and paper works, and glass works from CSA's head of Glass Workshop, Klaus Moje. Meredith Hinchliffe, in reviewing the exhibition, concluded that it 'shows how important artists are to the Canberra community. The work is exceptional in every case'.[83]

The exhibition's title reflected the ongoing tussle between the local government's interest in developing the prime real estate that the brickworks represented, and the belief of the cultural practitioners using the site that studio spaces could be developed there with minimal expense. The development impasse remained unsolved until April 2019, when the ACT Government announced Canberra Developer DOMA as preferred tenderer for the renamed Canberra Brickworks Precinct. On 26 September 2019 contracts were signed. The redevelopment will include conservation of heritage values and comprise 380 mixed dwellings, a museum and recreational facilities. It is expected to be completed by 2024. The last artist to occupy the site, Canberra sculptor Peter Vandermark, who moved into a reclaimed studio space in 1989, left the site in mid-2019. Vandermark's national and international profile were forged over that 30 years within those historic kilns and tunnels.[84]

Among the many smaller commercial galleries and art enterprises that opened and closed in the city during the decade were two that had lasting influence on the Canberra and wider Australian art scenes. Both initially opened in the Kingston Art Centre: Studio One (1983–2001), which was founded by Meg Buchanen and Dianne Fogwell, and Helen Maxwell's aGOG, which opened on 16 March 1989.

Studio One was an independent printmaking workshop servicing CSA graduates and providing printmaking facilities to the wider community. As evidenced in Chapter 4, the Printmaking Workshop at CSA encompassed two disparate printmaking cultures during the early years: head of the workshop and master printmaker Jorg Schmeisser's European and Japanese aesthetic and workshop tutor Mandy Martin's politically

---

83 Meredith Hinchliffe, 'Fragile tenancy but exceptional art', *Canberra Times*, 18 October 1986, p 7s.
84 Despite growing safety concerns around the site's deterioration, a handful of artists continued to make work there over the ensuing decades. These included furniture designers Tom Harrington and Mark Spain, sculptors Stuart Vaskess and Peter Vandermark, painter Marie Hagerty, furniture designer Thor's Hammer and Geoff Farquhar-Still's collaborative art/design studio Artillion. As well, Canberra's radical theatre collective Splinters used the brickwork's spaces for set construction, rehearsals and performances from 1989 to 1996 and an exhibition space, Gallery Fred, was also in use for a period of time. For more on Splinters see Gavin Findlay and Jose Robertson (eds), *Splinters Theatre of Spectacle: massive love of risk* (exhibition catalogue, Canberra Museum and Gallery, 2013).

charged poster aesthetic, which was fostered in Adelaide. These differing, though not exclusively oppositional, practices continued to play out post-graduation at Megalo International Screenprint and at Studio One, which coexisted for 18 years. Megalo, arising from progressive social activism and housed in the grungy surrounds of Ainslie Village, was broadly concerned with the poster as a voice for social cohesion and change. Studio One, initially specialising in intaglio and relief processes, was concerned with printing as fine art. Studio One, incorporated in 1987 as Studio One Inc, is regarded as having been extremely influential in Australian printmaking and, with the appointment of master printmaker Theo Tremblay in 1993, it became nationally respected for its work with many of Australia's best-known Indigenous artists.

Maxwell's aGOG was established to redress the historical and contemporary gender imbalance that consistently saw more male than female artists in exhibition. Maxwell recalls that, when she decided to launch a gallery devoted to the work of women artists, '[a] number of people objected … and said it was sexist'.[85] aGOG exhibited the work of Australian women artists, including Indigenous artists, from March 1989 to the end of 1998. The great success of the gallery over 10 years speaks to the breadth and timeliness of Maxwell's vision, with increased national research occurring over this time into the previously unwritten histories of Australian women artists of the twentieth century. Maxwell also required that works expressed each artist's personal politics, evidencing 'a stance that they are taking in their life' and, further, that '[the artist has] to know how to use their medium to successfully express their views'.[86] These requirements lent tremendous depth to aGOG's exhibition calendar. Additionally, Maxwell's experience as an assistant curator in Australian art at the National Gallery meant that her unique vision was underpinned with professionalism.

It is no surprise that Canberra was home to aGOG. Maxwell's requirement for work that expressed personal politics was apt in a city where social activism was demonstrated from the 1920s. As examined in Chapter 4, the national capital attracted feminists from around the country who participated in political lobbying, activism, forums and festivals. Art and politics were deeply entwined from the late 1970s. Additionally, BRG/

---

85   Roslyn Russell, 'Helen Maxwell', *The Australian Women's Register*, www.womenaustralia.info/biogs/AWE2104b.htm, accessed 17 July 2014.
86   Russell, 'Helen Maxwell'.

CCAS, since its 1981 opening and in every year since, has consistently – against national and international trends – shown more female than male artists in exhibition. Women artists were highly visible in the city, and Maxwell and aGOG contributed enormously to their growing profile. After closing aGOG in late 1998, Maxwell re-entered the Canberra commercial gallery scene in 2000 with her eponymous Helen Maxwell Gallery (the gallery closed at the end of 2009) in the inner-city suburb of Braddon, exhibiting the works of both female and male artists, including many Indigenous artists.

The campaign for free admission

The campaign for free admission to the soon-to-be-opened National Gallery was a unique local campaign that highlighted the growing strength of the contemporary arts community in the capital. Launched by BRG members in mid-1982 in response to a decision to impose a $2 entrance fee to the gallery, the campaign indicated the strength of political awareness and the commitment to political cultural causes among emerging arts practitioners in the capital.

The federal government's decision to establish a national gallery in Canberra was initiated by Prime Minister Robert Menzies in 1965, on the urging of the Commonwealth Art Advisory Board; it was formalised by Liberal Prime Minister Harold Holt in 1967.[87] In the second week of June 1971, the design – by architect Colin Madigan from the Sydney firm Edwards Madigan Torzillo and Partners – was publicly released.

---

87   'I turn now to the second important decision the Government has taken to encourage the arts in Australia. The House will recall that my predecessor Sir Robert Menzies and his Administration decided that a national art gallery should be established in Canberra and in 1965 appointed a committee of inquiry to consider what form it should take, what its function should be and how it should be controlled. This committee, under the distinguished chairmanship of Sir Daryl Lindsay, completed its work last year and I would like to acknowledge here how comprehensive the report is and how valuable it has been to the Government. It has contributed significantly to the Government's latest decision on the art gallery and is tabled in this Parliament for the information of honourable members. The Government has decided that work on the establishment of this national gallery will begin immediately. The National Capital Development Commission expects the planning, design and costing stage to take about 2 years. A site for the gallery is being considered. The gallery will house the national collection which at present consists of nearly 2,000 works of art. Future acquisitions will include Australian art past and present, art of the Asian and Pacific areas and art on a world-wide basis, beginning with the 20th century' (Harold Holt, Ministerial statement, House of Representatives, Procedural Text, 1 November 1967, 'Australian cultural activities', parlinfo.aph.gov.au/parlInfo/genpdf/hansard80/hansardr80/1967-11-01/0077/hansard_frag.pdf;fileType=application%2Fpdf, accessed 22 May 2013).

James Mollison was appointed as acting director in October 1971 and as director in 1977. The gallery opened to the public in October 1982, eight years after its originally mooted 1974 completion date.[88]

When the gallery opened, almost 235,000 people called the national capital home. The burgeoning visual arts landscape then uniquely included the nation's new national gallery and the nation's newest artist-run space, BRG, separated by a physical distance of just 2 kilometres. Though widely divergent in intent, Canberra was small enough to ensure that each was easily accessible to the other. Senior gallery staff were early and significant supporters of BRG including Mollison; the inaugural head of Australian Art, Daniel Thomas; and the inaugural curator of Australian Prints, Posters, and Illustrated Books, Roger Butler.

In the lead-up to the opening, Press Gallery reporter Warwick Costin published a story in the *Sunday Telegraph* on 19 August, informing readers of a Cabinet decision to charge an admission fee. Cabinet was responding to the gallery council's recommendation to charge a $2 entrance fee to all members of the public, excepting the unemployed, pensioners, full-time students, children under 15 and 'the handicapped'.[89] Canberra's socially progressive young arts practitioners were outraged and swiftly mounted the campaign for free admission that rallied the nation and galvanised the arts community. The campaign was initiated and managed by BRG member and part-time administrator Karilyn Brown (who was Noel Sheridan's assistant during the latter part of 1975 at Adelaide's Experimental Art Foundation (EAF)), and BRG members Dan Coward – the pseudonym of Megalo printmaker Raymond Arnold – and Toni Robertson. Robertson, a leading figure in Australian political printmaking, who exhibited in BRG's first exhibition in April 1981 as a member of the Earthworks Poster Collective, was at that time lecturing in printmaking and photo-media at CSA.[90] Although BRG was not mentioned by name in any of the materials concerned with the campaign, the return address for all such materials and for further contact was the BRG post office box. The campaign's leaflet pertinently asked:

---

88   For further information on the path to opening, see: Frances Kelly, 'ALP man says gallery delay "an insult"', *Canberra Times*, 13 May 1970, p 8.
89   Australian Government, 'National Gallery regulations 1982', Federal Register of Legislation, www.legislation.gov.au/Details/C2004H02339, accessed 2 May 2014.
90   Based at University of Sydney's Tin Sheds in Sydney.

> Should anyone be charged to enter what is a national institution, containing the National Collection, belonging to the people of Australia and paid for with our taxes?[91]

Brown wrote a letter to the editor of the *Canberra Times* on 14 September, beginning a campaign of letters from locals that continued until November of that year. Her letter reads in part:

> The visual arts are an integral part of our cultural identity and the creation of the Australian National Gallery can contribute to promoting a more broadly based awareness, development and support for the visual arts in Australia, a process which will be greatly hindered if members of the public are to be charged for what should be freely accessible to them.[92]

A deputation, including Brown, Robertson, Coward and Schmeisser – who 'inscribed his personal plea to the Prime Minister to reconsider the decision to impose the $2 fee on one of his large etchings of the Canberra garden-city landscape'[93] – met first with the Minister for the Capital Territory Michael Hodgman on 22 September. On 23 September, the deputation met with Tom McVeigh, minister for home affairs and the environment, who 'refused to take their representation to Cabinet'.[94]

Canberra commentators Ian Warden and Grishin joined the discursive fray in the *Canberra Times*. Grishin pointed out that, as opposed to those international galleries privately bequeathed to nations and sustained thenceforward partly by entrance fees, the National Gallery was built from taxes paid by the people who could not now be reasonably expected to pay additionally for its upkeep. Grishin also declared that he was opposed to an entry charge on three grounds: philosophically, because 'art is an integral part of life and not something for viewing on special occasions'; economically, where, citing the short-lived introduction of entry fees at the National Gallery in London, he revealed that 'administering the fees was more expensive than the revenue they brought in'; and thirdly because

---

91 'Campaign for free admission to the Australian National Gallery', leaflet, CCAS archives.
92 Karilyn Brown, letter to the editor, *Canberra Times*, 14 September 1982, p 3.
93 'Campaign for free admission to the Australian National Gallery', press release, 22 September 1982. This artwork, the press release reported, was left with Hodgman to pass on to the prime minister.
94 *Canberra Times*, 'Gallery fee discussed', 24 September 1982, p 7.

'it seems a peculiar act of discrimination against the National Gallery' when art displays in other national institutions such as the National Library of Australia or Australian War Memorial were free.[95]

Warden commented that, as the $2 collected was to be used to develop the collection, the public might be more amenable to the plan if it was known for sure that 'one's two dollars had paid for the left nipple of the fifth nude bather from the right in a Renoir fleshscape' and that, while acknowledging there were those who were fee-exempt:

> Mr McVeigh might also exempt another tiny, oppressed minority, the citizens of Canberra, on the grounds that they should be able to treat the Gallery as a local amenity to pop into on impulse at lunch time or of a weekend when they have no adultery or gardening lined up.[96]

The campaign rapidly gained a national following. On 27 October 1982, Geoffrey Brown, president of the Contemporary Art Society (Australia) (CAS) wrote, 'for and on behalf of the Council, Administrative Staff and 350 members of the CAS':

> The Contemporary Art Society supports the Campaign for Free Admission and is in complete agreement with their stand that the Australian National Gallery belongs to the people of Australia, their taxes having been used to pay for the Gallery ... Together the art community, voices united, may help reverse the Government's decision.[97]

Letters of support arrived from, among others, local schoolteachers, the University of Queensland Department of Fine Arts, and Nancy Underhill – then head of the Art Museums Association of Australia, who wrote, 'I have sent telegrams to both the Prime Minister and Tom McVeigh deploring the imposition of charging at the ANG'[98] – and from the Artworkers Union (NSW), which stated that they were 'collectively surprised and disturbed'.[99] Blacktown City Council, a leader in Australian community arts practice, wrote:

---

95   Sasha Grishin, 'Visiting the National Gallery: should owners pay twice?', *Canberra Times*, 19 September 1982, p 7.
96   Ian Warden, 'Getting our $2 worth', *Canberra Times*, 22 September 1982, p 21.
97   Geoffrey Brown, letter to Campaign for Free Admission (BRG Post Office Box), 27 October 1982, 'Campaign for Free Admission', CCAS archives.
98   Nancy Underhill, letter to Campaign for Free Admission, undated, CCAS archives.
99   Artworkers Union (NSW), letter to Campaign for Free Admission, undated, CCAS archives.

> The arts are by the people for the people, and it is the right of every Australian to have admission to these works, free of charge, to view our heritage.[100]

BRG members were aware that their campaign had an international precedent. A user-pays pricing approach in visual arts was trialled previously in Britain with a similar response from museum professionals and the public. In early 1971, director of the Art Gallery of South Australia John Bailey wrote to the art critic of the South Australian *Sunday Mail*, Ivor Francis, enclosing a photostat of a December 1970 statement from the eight trustees of the Tate Gallery and the gallery's chairman, Robert Sainsbury. The statement was delivered to British Prime Minister Edward Heath, MP Lord Eccles and the Chancellor of the Exchequer Anthony Barber, following their decision to impose admission charges to national museums and galleries, a decision the trustees viewed 'with dismay':

> We believe that this decision is entirely contrary to the spirit which has guided these great institutions for generations. Once the principle of free entry has been over-ridden a unique and precious attribute of our national lives will have been destroyed for small return.

'I am,' wrote Bailey to Francis, 'naturally concerned about the principles involved in the enclosed discussion.'[101]

In spite of a concerted nationwide effort, the campaign did not succeed in changing Cabinet's decision. It was not until 1997 that the gallery's third director, Brian Kennedy, introduced free admission to the National Gallery, with the exception of entry to major exhibitions.

The members of BRG were active in the community and were therefore more aware than most of the impact that an entry fee would have on the wider Australian population. Additionally, the imposition of charges for that which should have been freely available to all Australians for study, inspiration and relaxation, was antithetical to the spirit of open access to arts and culture that was envisaged by prime ministers Holt, Gorton and Whitlam in relation to the ANG. Although many BRG members,

---

100 Patricia Parker, Community Arts Officer, Blacktown City Council, letter to Campaign for Free Admission, 12 October 1982, CCAS archives.
101 John Bailey, letter to Ivor Francis, undated, CCAS archives. See also 'Arts Workers' Coalition: statement of demands' (in Charles Harrison and Paul Wood (eds), *Art in theory – 1900–2000: an anthology of changing ideas*, Malden MA, Blackwell Publishing, 2003, p 926): 'Admission to all museums should be free at all times and they should be open evenings to accommodate working people'.

by virtue of their status as students, or as poor, unemployed, Canberra-based artists, were exempt under the regulation, they knew that those affected by the charges would be ordinary Canberrans.[102] That BRG began as an alternative to established spaces, and that members then fought for the rights of Australians to be able to freely enter the newly established space, successfully galvanising a national population, was a powerful marker of the growing relevance of the emerging contemporary art sector in the capital.

The Drill Hall Gallery

In concluding this chapter, it is important to recognise the critical role played by the National Gallery between 1985 and 1991 in bringing the best contemporary art exhibitions to Canberra audiences. As inaugural director, Mollison determined to add a temporary exhibitions gallery, dedicated to showing contemporary Australian and international art, to complement the permanent collection spaces of the National Gallery. The Drill Hall, on the ANU campus, was built in 1940 as a World War II training hub for soldiers and provided the solution to this need for an alternative space.[103] In 1985, in an arrangement with the ANU and after an extensive renovation program that yielded four discrete exhibition spaces, The Drill Hall Gallery opened, with Michael Desmond as curator.[104] During the period it played host to an average of 10 exhibitions a year, which was around a third of the National Gallery's overall exhibition program.

Generally acknowledged as providing a string of groundbreaking exhibitions, its proximity to the CSA made it particularly accessible and useful to students. Amongst the memorable exhibitions were those drawn from the National Gallery's permanent collection including, from 4 December 1985 to 23 February 1986, *Lightworks: works of art using*

---

102 By June 2011, six months after the opening of MONA, his private museum in Hobart, David Walsh realised that he would need to charge admission fees to assist with covering costs. Importantly, he exempted Tasmanian residents from that charge.
103 For more on the history of the Drill Hall, see Gary Estcourt and James Collet, 'The Australian National University: Heritage Management Plan: Drill Hall Gallery: Australian Capital Territory', services.anu.edu.au/files/document-collection/drill_hall_gallery_hmp.pdf.
104 Desmond is an independent curator and writer who, after six years as curator of the Drill Hall Gallery, was appointed senior curator of International Paintings and Sculpture at the National Gallery, then manager of collection development and research at the Powerhouse Museum and, then, at the National Portrait Gallery, senior curator and then deputy director until 2012.

light as a medium,[105] which included works from American artists Dan Flavin, Bruce Nauman, Joseph Kosuth, Edward Keinholz and Robert Rauschenberg.[106] Grishin reviewed *A first look: Philip Morris Arts Grant purchases 1983–1986*, for the *Canberra Times*, marking it as 'the most important exhibition of contemporary Australian art to be held in recent times … succeeding where the Sydney Perspecta have failed'.[107] Artists from Brisbane and Adelaide, and Melbourne artists including Susan Rankine, Jon Cattapan, Andrew Ferguson and Sarah Faulkner, 'displayed a hedonistic joy in the use of materials', with the show as a whole 'suggesting a powerful resurgence presently taking place in Australian art that is quickly overtaking the relative barrenness of the 1970s'.[108]

In 1991, the National Gallery's second director, Betty Churcher, facing staffing cuts, and under increasing budgetary pressures from the federal government, released the Drill Hall Gallery to the ANU. The Drill Hall's final exhibition, from 6 July – 22 September 1991 was a 20-year retrospective of costumes, furniture, posters and jewellery from Australian artist Peter Tully. Tully's work overtly referenced popular culture and *Urban tribalwear and beyond* utilised everyday items and unexpected elements including holograms. For Desmond, the exhibition was a 'conscious choice as the gallery's final … an eye-dazzler … we wanted to end on a spectacular note'.[109] In commenting that 'Visitors to Canberra tend to have a limited amount of time, so the Drill Hall really had a local audience', Desmond succinctly foregrounded the gallery's important contribution to the local scene.[110]

---

105 Sonia Barron, 'Light as the medium', *Canberra Times*, 1 February 1986, p 6.
106 The exhibition was advertised as 'Presenting ten very bright ideas … a very exciting, very different exhibition of work using artificial light as an important component' (*Canberra Times*, 18 January 1986, p 6).
107 Sasha Grishin, '*First look* of high quality', *Canberra Times*, 14 October 1986, p 14.
108 Grishin, 1986.
109 Jodie Brough, 'Gallery goes out in spectacular style – the Tully style', *Canberra Times*, 7 July 1991, p 1.
110 Brough, 1991. Since that time, the renamed ANU Drill Hall Gallery, under consecutive curators Nancy Sever and Terence Maloon, has exhibited works from the extensive ANU collection. As well, and paired with scholarly publications, the gallery stages exceptionally fine retrospectives and exhibitions of new works in photography, painting, the decorative arts and printmaking from Australian and international artists.

3

SELF-GOVERNMENT AND THE ARTS

The changes wrought by self-government on Canberra's developing arts community, beginning in mid-1989 when the Australian Capital Territory (ACT) Legislative Assembly convened the first of two select committees, were extraordinary. The transfer from national control to emancipation over three years transformed Canberra's culture and yielded a new spirit of connectedness. Infrastructure that was enabled by the visionary decision to allocate the one-off $19 million casino premium to the arts also transformed the city's landscape and enabled a decade of unparalleled growth, particularly in local visual arts.

In this chapter I make a close analysis of the major enquiries tasked with investigating and reporting on the capacity and desires of the arts and culture communities in the ACT: the Select Committee on Cultural Activities and Facilities (final report delivered June 1991); and the Standing Committee on Planning, Development and Infrastructure (*Inquiry into the possible use of the $19 million casino premium*, delivered December 1992). Their ambits and recommendations reflect a greatly changed perception of the position of local arts and culture in Canberra and a powerful commitment to privileging its development.

My analysis allows a comparison of two extraordinarily different decades. The methodologically flawed Pascoe Report of 1985 was intrinsically connected to the idea of local arts and culture in Canberra as a representation of national capital space; its recommendations proved entirely out of step with the reality of local needs. By contrast, the final committee reports of the early 1990s resulted from an intense period of community consultation. Their focus and recommendations acknowledged local arts and culture as an increasingly dominant feature of Canberra life.

The ACT Legislative Assembly's commitment to the arts came at a time when demand for resources outstripped current models of funding and other support. By 1989 the arts funding model in the ACT was broken. During the 1980s, the sector's escalating demand for scarce resources was met by responses from a local government with limited self-determination. While increasingly willing, local government was simply unable to meet and effectively manage growing demand. As the decade came to an end, of most concern was the lack of a model to ensure sustainable future planning. Providing for generational growth was uppermost in the minds of assembly members.

Steps to self-government

The first request for self-government – a 'right [that] has long been recognised as an inherent part of British citizenship'[1] – was made in the Federal Capital Territory Representation League's pre-petition to parliament in November 1927 'praying for representation in the House of Representatives and on the Federal Capital Commission'.[2] Self-determination remained on the agenda, with debate varying in intensity as the Territory's fortunes seesawed through cataclysmic world affairs and changes in federal governments and Commonwealth administrative bodies. By 1978, however, with the national capital's 218,000 citizens enjoying some of the lowest costs of living in Australia, 63.75 per cent[3] of the eligible population voted in a plebiscite for a continuation of the Commonwealth's 'benign dictatorship'.[4]

In spite of this, the Commonwealth determined to divest itself of the financial responsibility for local services and commenced the task of bringing together the various departments responsible for managing the

---

1   *Canberra Times*, 'Petitions to parliament: voice in local affairs: seat in parliament', 1 November 1927, p 4.
2   *Canberra Times*, 1 November 1927.
3   When calculated as a proportion of the eligible voting population, 63.75 per cent equalled 69,893 persons voting against self-government and 30.54 per cent, or 33,480, voting in favour of self-government.
4   Bill Wood, Hansard, Parliamentary Debates, Legislative Assembly, Australian Capital Territory, 26 August 2004, p 4323.

ACT, in order to ascertain the costs of its maintenance. By the late 1980s, with the population approaching 280,000, preparations were complete. On 6 December 1988, the Governor-General of Australia signed off on bills that began a three-year transfer from full federal control and funding to standalone local self-government under an ACT Legislative Assembly.

The first elections for the ACT Legislative Assembly were held on 4 March 1989. Residents elected a minority Labor government under Chief Minister Rosemary Follett, with the Assembly's first meeting held on 11 May. The National Capital Development Commission (NCDC) was dismantled and planning responsibilities were divided between the NCDC's replacement, the National Capital Planning Authority (NCPA to 1996; National Capital Authority (NCA) thereafter), and the ACT Legislative Assembly. The former retained control over planning and continued funding those areas of Canberra the Griffin Plan categorised as national capital space; the ACT Legislative Assembly assumed planning and funding control of the remainder, including of local arts and cultural endeavours.

Self-government brought hope and a sense of cohesion to the Canberra arts community. From the earliest days the community – led by Canberra School of Art's head David Williams and the Labor Assembly member Bill Wood – was intent on refocusing the debate from its previously narrow focus on grant funding to the broad holistic development, including generational development, of arts and cultural planning, and the building of arts and community cultural infrastructure. Although Wood recalled that 'the first years … were marked by an Assembly whose members were, in the early days, not in favour of self-government',[5] there were, from the beginning, strong indications of bipartisan support for local arts.

Committees played a central part in the next three years of intense research and planning around arts and cultural development. Among the many that were established by the Legislative Assembly from the end of 1989 onwards were the Select Committee on the Establishment of a Casino, the Select Committee on Cultural Activities and Facilities and the Standing Committee on Planning, Development and Infrastructure. The work of these committees specifically affected forward planning for arts and culture.

---

5   Wood, 2004, p 4328.

The decision to allocate funding revenue via the casino premium radically altered the face of arts infrastructure in the city for the benefit of local practitioners and consumers, and the pleasure of national and international visitors. There was a modest precedent. Throughout the 1980s, taxes accrued from gambling in the ACT had allowed funding, via the ACT Community Development Fund (CDF), of modest equipment and employment needs for arts and cultural projects, and community and sporting organisations. This new initiative, however, was unparalleled in terms of the amount of funding it made available to the local arts sector. Successive ACT governments committed to allocating $19 million, payable as a one-off premium from the successful bidder for the proposed Canberra casino, to fund community cultural infrastructure projects. These projects conclusively altered Canberra's landscape and raised expectations about the importance of culture in a modern city.

The Select Committee on the Establishment of a Casino

The inaugural ACT Legislative Assembly convened the Select Committee on the Establishment of a Casino in its first sitting month. This was a strong indication of the government's commitment to swift action and decision-making. It was the first of a number of select committees addressing arts and culture and the casino premium. It commenced in May 1989 and reported to the Assembly in July 1989. The ACT's first government (Labor; May–December 1989) provided a submission to the committee in which it confirmed the government's commitment to using the one-off premium obtained from the commercial site for the 'funding of facilities which could include a Theatre complex, Territorial Library and other community and cultural facilities'.[6] Subsequently, the Alliance government (December 1989 – June 1991) affirmed, in May 1991, the use of the casino premium for community facilities.[7] The second Labor government – with Bill Wood as the minister for education and the arts – reiterated the government's commitment in December 1991 and, again,

---

6 Quoted in *Select Committee on the Establishment of a Casino*, Canberra, Legislative Assembly for the ACT, July 1989, p 3.
7 Quoted in Standing Committee on Planning Development and Infrastructure, *Inquiry into the possible use of the $19 million casino premium, report no 9*, Legislative Assembly for the ACT, December 1992, p 6.

on re-election in April, and a further time in October 1992, when Chief Minister Follett assured the Assembly that the casino premium would be 'applied to community facilities in the ACT, specifically cultural and heritage facilities'.[8]

The proposed casino was intended for the area known as Section 19, Civic, which housed the Canberra Theatre Centre (CTC). The committee recommended that, along with the proposed casino, community facilities be enabled on the site, writing that, 'an idealised community facility would include a lyric theatre (2,000 seats), play house, performance studio, library, regional art gallery, heritage centre, civic square upgrade, infrastructure and car parking'.[9]

The Select Committee on Cultural Activities and Facilities

With these basic recommendations in place, the government determined to enter into an extended period of research. The Select Committee on Cultural Activities and Facilities was convened on 23 August 1989, with Wood, whom the arts community already 'regarded as one of their own', as chair.[10]

Over 22 months of intense community consultation, the committee received 58 submissions from groups and individuals; heard evidence from 66 witnesses over nine days of public hearings; inspected and met arts administrators and the directors of various state libraries, art galleries, museums and theatre complexes in Brisbane, Melbourne and Hobart; and investigated theatre complexes in Geelong and Adelaide, regional galleries in Orange and Wollongong, and municipal libraries and regional galleries in Bathurst and Goulburn. The committee convened a public seminar on 8 September 1990, held 'in the interests of widening the debate on the need for a State art gallery',[11] which brought government

---

8   Reply to question put on notice, 21 October 1992 (quoted in Standing Committee on Planning Development and Infrastructure, 1992, p 6).
9   Quoted in Select Committee on the Establishment of a Casino, 1989, p 16.
10 Robert Macklin, 'Cultural scene transformed under council', *Canberra Times*, 21 November 1991, p 5. The committee's other two members included Hector Kinloch and William (Bill) Stefaniak.
11 Select Committee on Cultural Activities and Facilities, *Final report*, Legislative Assembly for the ACT, June 1991, p 5.

officials, major arts groups and private gallery owners together. By the end of this exhaustive process, Wood was able to claim that 'there is not an Arts group or a related group in Canberra ... that we did not approach'.[12]

This unprecedented engagement with the community across every sector, organisation and many individuals was followed up with informed, intelligent analysis. Wood's driving passion for the arts in the ACT, his ability to effect government decisions and his desire to understand the sector's present needs and to engage in visionary planning enabled insightful conclusions. Delivered to the Assembly in June 1991, the committee's final report provided, as he recalled it, 'the basis for a lot of later activity'.[13] More than this, it marked the beginning of long-term, locally managed, broad arts and cultural planning, the benefits of which extended across subsequent decades.

The final report comprised 74 recommendations across 10 areas. The first related to overall arts funding, where the committee recommended 'that funding increase in real terms by 10% per annum'[14] over the period from 1992 to 1997. This proved impossible to implement then or at any time since.

Of particular importance were recommendations 2–35 that concerned the establishment of a Territorial library, museum and art gallery in a purpose-built facility in Section 19. The report proposed that this lead to the repurposing of Civic Square as a cultural precinct comprising cultural and commercial undertakings.

The literary arts were dealt with in recommendations 36–41.[15] The performing arts were covered in recommendations 42–59, with a caveat stressing the need for 'a new model of consultation ... for the effective development of the performing arts in the ACT'.[16] Recommendations 60 and 61 concerned community art, with 62–68 encompassing education and youth arts, and 69–74 covering advocacy,

---

12 Bill Wood, Hansard, Parliamentary Debates, Legislative Assembly, Australian Capital Territory, 22 October 1992, p 2874.
13 Wood, 1992, p 4328.
14 Select Committee on Cultural Activities and Facilities, 1991, p xiii.
15 Specific recommendations involved a significant increase in overall funding for literature, the establishment of the ACT Writers Centre in the Civic Square redevelopment, the establishment of funding and support for writers-in-residence programs, the funding of a community literature coordinator, and increased support for the Australian National Word Festival.
16 Select Committee on Cultural Activities and Facilities, 1991, p 57.

bureaucracy, consultation and development. These sections display consistent evidence of a deep engagement with the arts sector, with recommendations that reflect the desires of that community.

The report's preface, authored by Wood, identified matters requiring urgent attention. The first of these, the immediate establishment of a cultural council 'to improve administration and planning and to provide a more powerful voice for the arts',[17] was made after the committee considered other models, including retaining the Arts Development Board (ADB). The second recommended the consolidation of all arts-related government agencies within one ministry. Both stemmed from the committee's belief that, having examined 'a great range of evidence that makes it feel very positive' it nevertheless had:

> some apprehension about the present administration of the arts in the ACT both in terms of funding and policy development. This apprehension in no way stems from the individuals involved with arts administration in Canberra. The committee's reservations emerge from the observation that the needs of arts development in the region have outstripped the original models set up to service the arts.[18]

Despite the recommendation from the Select Committee on the Establishment of a Casino, and the submissions supporting the construction of a new 2,000-seat lyric theatre, the Select Committee on Cultural Activities and Facilities determined that this expenditure was unwarranted, given the steady losses accumulated over a number of years by the CTC. Instead, in its third urgent recommendation, the committee advised that construction immediately begin on a community theatre in the Childers Street area. This 250-seat theatre, sited on the corner of Childers Street and University Avenue and renamed the Street Theatre, was completed in 1994. For over 20 years, the theatre has undergone several changes in management and style, but has remained a critical partner for Canberra's performing arts.

The urgent recommendation to set up a cultural council was enacted five months after the committee's final report was delivered to the Assembly. Like the Australia Council, the 15-member peak body was composed entirely of arts peers who aimed to 'promote the development and

---

17 Bill Wood, Preface, Select Committee on Cultural Activities and Facilities, 1991, p v.
18 Select Committee on Cultural Activities and Facilities, 1991, p 84.

continued growth of a creative, diverse and dynamic cultural sector in the ACT'.[19] The ADB was disbanded and replaced on 20 November 1991 with the ACT Cultural Council (1991–2013).[20] Williams, who was most recent head of the ADB, became the council's chair. The Cultural Council's formation was driven by Williams and Wood, and it answered the need, first voiced by the arts community in the mid-1980s, for long-term planning that was managed by community members. When announcing the council, Wood overtly recognised local artists and performers, thanking them 'for the essential spirit and vitality that they give to us all'. 'They should,' he said, 'take a bow.'[21]

Williams and Wood were powerful collaborators in the transformation of Canberra's arts culture from being a function of the national capital space to a vibrant expression of local community. Williams, who was previously director of the Australia Council's Crafts Board (1978–85), brought his considerable experience in infrastructure building to the table. Wood's impact on arts and culture development, from self-government until his retirement in 2004, cannot be overstated. In the second Follett Labor ministry he held the first designated arts and heritage portfolio, as well as the portfolio of planning. These concurrent portfolios enabled him to oversee the development of the Heritage Council and to identify and secure sites for arts facilities development. These included the Australian National Capital Artists (ANCA) artist studios in Mitchell in 1991 and ANCA artist studios and gallery in Dickson in November 1992. Canberra sculptor Jan Brown was a tireless advocate for the ANCA studios. In 1995, Wood was able to secure a permanent home for Canberra Contemporary Art Space (CCAS) Gallery 3 in the newly redeveloped commercial offices at Manuka, on the block that had housed Bitumen River Gallery (BRG).

The Cultural Council comprised two sets of committees: the Artform committees in visual arts, theatre, music, dance, literature, and – eventually – film, which considered all grant applications; and the Opportunities committee that considered entrepreneurial opportunities for the arts within the individual practices committees. The council strived for a holistic approach to overall arts and cultural development, with chairs of all committees involved in negotiating the best grant applications in terms of the overall development of the ACT arts and cultural landscape.

---

19   Bill Wood, quoted in Macklin, 1991, p 5.
20   The ADB presided over the $1.7 million in ACT government grants available from 1989.
21   Wood, quoted in Macklin, 1991, p 5.

The arts community was made aware of committee members, and members assessing grant applications were invited to see the work of companies/artists. This assisted with continued analysis of the sector and ensured feedback to applicants. Among the council's briefs was to seek multi-year funding for arts organisations through closer cooperation with the Australia Council. Analogous with bureaucratisation, this conversely assisted in reducing the administration associated with yearly grant applications and allowed planning beyond a 12-month period, thus answering a need that was first voiced in 1984.

Other initiatives

Important early initiatives from local government included a requirement that passed the Assembly in 1990 to include local art in all new buildings, and the establishment of a $15,000 ACT Literary Fellowship (1991–95), advocated by Canberra author Sara Dowse.

Community initiatives included the inauguration of the Canberra Critics Circle, convened in 1991 by Helen Musa. Critics across the art forms determined to vote every year, not for the 'best' in any category, but for those performances and exhibitions that stimulated the critic's imagination. In the same year, the Circle initiated the *Canberra Times* Artist of the Year award. In announcing the award, *Canberra Times* managing director Ian Meikle recognised the 'tremendous range and depth of artistic talent [that] contributes enormously to the quality of life in the national capital … a contribution which should be recognised and rewarded'.[22] The *Canberra Times* appointment of an arts editor and the paper's contribution to the arts in the ACT was recognised in the final report from the Select Committee on Cultural Activities and Facilities:

> The *Canberra Times* remains one of the most effective agents in the ACT for disseminating information about activities in the arts. Its regular and thorough coverage of the cultural life of the Territory is of enormous benefit to participants and audiences alike. The arts could not function effectively without this outstanding level of support.[23]

---

22   Ian Miekle, '*Times* backs artist award', *Canberra Times*, 17 August 1991, p 3.
23   Select Committee on Cultural Activities and Facilities, 1991, section 12.26, p 89. The *Canberra Times* was considered a great supporter of the arts well into the 2000s. More recent changes in ownership and staff brought a decrease in the coverage of local arts.

Canberra Arts Marketing (CAM) was another government-funded initiative that showed a commitment to modest developments benefiting the broad arts community. The small organisation was established in 1993 with Elizabeth Brown at its head. As local arts and cultural activity increased rapidly over the next decade, CAM kept its members apprised of each other's openings and events through an increasingly necessary arts calendar. From visual arts openings to orchestral presentations, CAM assisted, in its first decade, in cohering the sector by generating a powerful sense of local place.[24]

In the same year the term *cultural capital*, used to refer to Canberra as a city of culture and first coined in print by Williams, entered local language.[25] This highly significant adoption indicated that Canberrans had begun to see themselves as the drivers and providers of a vibrant local arts milieu. That the term was coined by the same lobbying body that was seeking validation and resources to grow local arts for the benefit of the local and regional communities is indicative of a vigorous surge towards a cultural future.

The Standing Committee on Planning, Development and Infrastructure

The second relevant committee, the Standing Committee on Planning, Development and Infrastructure was directed, in October 1992, to 'investigate and report on recommendations to the Assembly of the possible use of the $19 million casino premium, having regard to both the June 1991 report of the Select Committee on Cultural Activities and Facilities, and the government's stated objective to commit the funds to cultural facilities'.[26] The government reminded the committee that these objectives

---

24 By 2008, with the rapid uptake of social media communications across the arts in Canberra, government withdrew funding and the organisation folded.
25 David Williams in Robert Macklin, 'Cultural capital of Australia?', *Canberra Times*, 29 July 1990, p 17.
26 *Minutes of Proceedings*, 2nd Assembly, 22 October 1992 in *Report no. 9* of the Standing Committee on Planning Development and Infrastructure, Dec 1992, p iii. Established on 27 March 1992, this ACT-wide committee examined 'matters related to planning, land management, transport, economic development, commercial development, industrial and residential development, infrastructure and capital works, science and technology' (*Minutes of Proceedings*, 2nd Assembly, 27 March 1992 in *Report no. 9* of the Standing Committee on Planning Development and Infrastructure, Dec 1992, p iii). Committee members were David Lamont, Trevor Kaine, Tony De Domenico, Annette Ellis and Helen Szuty.

'have a long background and cover successive ACT Administrations'.[27] The committee was directed to report to the Legislative Assembly by 10 December 1992.[28] Public comment was sought, through local press advertisements, by 11 November. The committee heard 37 individuals and received 68 written submissions and 'numerous telephone calls'.[29] A public hearing on 13 November was attended by representatives of 20 arts organisations.

The impact of the report was stunning. The cost of all requests, excluding un-costed submissions, totalled $177,502,867. The many community submissions indicated peoples' ability to think large when given the opportunity to take part in generational planning. The committee's final recommendations reflected the breadth of community submissions over the two major enquiries. Their implementation over the next decade and beyond indicated the commitment of successive governments to supporting local arts and culture.

The recommendations were that:

- '$2.5 million … be allocated to assist in the provision of an Aboriginal Keeping Place/cultural centre … as proposed by the Ngunnawal aboriginal people and the Bogong Regional Council' (3.10, p 28)
- 'a trust arrangement along the lines discussed in this report be established to hold $2.75 million … pending the development of appropriate plans for regional facilities. These plans should result from extensive community consultation and negotiation, and take account of the diverse range of community and school-based needs that are demonstrated in the submissions to this inquiry' (3.22, p 31)
- 'the Government vary its land use policies in the Childers Street/Kingsley Street area to promote a mix of cultural and commercial activities' (3.33, p 34)
- '$250,000 … be allocated to equip the new community theatre on the corner of University Avenue and Childers Street, City' (3.37, p 35)

---

27   *Standing Committee on Planning Development and Infrastructure*, 1992, p 5.
28   *Standing Committee on Planning Development and Infrastructure*, 1992, p 3.
29   *Standing Committee on Planning Development and Infrastructure*, 1992, p 1.

- '$5 million ... be allocated to upgrading the Playhouse Theatre to a 600–650 seat theatre ... and $7 million be devoted to providing a cultural and heritage facility in the city centre ... either in the North Building of Civic Square or in the Childers Street/Kingsley Street area' (3.43, p 38)
- 'the Government facilitate the provision of space in the Kingston Foreshores area for visual and community performing artists, it being recognised that such space is provided on an interim basis pending the finalisation of plans for the whole Foreshores area' (3.48, p 39)
- '$1.5 million ... be devoted to the NATEX [National Exhibition Centre] site to provide for essential maintenance and a basic refurbishment program' (3.26, p 33).

Several recommendations of the report from the Select Committee on Cultural Activities and Facilities, delivered in June 1991, were enacted prior to the release of report no 9 of the Standing Committee on Planning Development and Infrastructure in December 1992. These included the establishment of the ACT Cultural Council, the beginnings of construction on what would become the Street Theatre in Childers Street (that street identified in June 1991 by the Select Committee on Cultural Activities and Facilities as a second area for cultural development), and the re-siting of the casino from its first proposed site in Civic Square to its present location at the eastern city edge.

Decisions flowing from the recommendations of both enquiries resulted in rapid growth across the sector. By 1994, two ACT Cultural Council project rounds each year were attracting 'up to 190 applications in an extremely competitive and vibrant arts scene'.[30] The perennial shortfall of available grant monies in this climate of rapidly increasing activity saw the arts community in turmoil once again following the council's announcement of funding for the 1995 year with a total of $1.8 million distributed. This was only $100,000 more than the $1.7 million distributed by the ADB in 1989. Council's then chairman, Richard Refshauge, reported that money:

---

30   Evol McLeod, chair, Practices Committee, 1994–97, interview with the author, 12 August 2015.

was extremely tight. In the past members were not fighting over particular projects. This time it would not be putting it too highly to say that they [members of council] were almost traumatised by the lack of available funds for good projects.[31]

In mid-1994, however, $108,000, 'designed to provide flexibility to arts clients',[32] was expended in 16 second-round grants for the period 1 August – 31 December. That these were, in the main, awarded to visual artists indicates a clear recognition of growth and response to the needs of this sector of the arts.

The realisation of successive local governments' visions for local arts and ambitious building programs manifested throughout the 1990s. In 1994, the Legislative Assembly moved to the South Building in Civic Square. *Ethos*, the Tom Bass sculpture erected in 1960 as a vision of a cultured national capital, then sat outside the front doors of the Assembly. In 1997, with the opening of Canberra Museum and Gallery (CMAG) approaching, a separate line in the ACT Government budget established the Cultural Facilities Corporation. This was given responsibility for the CTC, and for heritage cultural arts sites that included Lanyon Homestead, Calthorpes' House, and CMAG (then under construction). In 1998, CMAG was opened on the ground floor of the North Building in Civic Square, directly facing the Legislative Assembly, with the Craft Council and multicultural spaces housed above. The ACT Writers Centre, a principal recommendation from the Literature section of the 1991 Select Committee on Cultural Activities and Facilities final report, was located in the Gorman House Arts Centre. The need for a Territory-focused library was largely overtaken by emerging technology that allowed online catalogue research between specialist Canberra collections held by the ACT Heritage Library, the National Library of Australia, the National Gallery of Australia Research Library and the many university libraries across the city. The opening of the Civic branch of Libraries ACT in Civic Square in 2006 signalled the completion of the vision that emerged in the first months of self-government for a cultural precinct that included a theatre complex, a Territory museum and gallery, Craft ACT and a library housed together within Civic Square.

---

31 Robert Macklin, 'Turmoil in ACT Arts', *Canberra Times*, 19 November 1994, p 3.
32 Helen Musa, '$108 thousand in grants for arts: Wood', *Canberra Times*, 21 July 1994, p 6.

The $19 million casino premium, which had bipartisan support within successive ACT governments for the provision of arts and cultural infrastructure, funded the Aboriginal Cultural Centre in Yarramundi Reach on Canberra's southern edge ('Keeping Place/Cultural Centre' in the original recommendation), Street Theatre, Hawker College Theatre, the Canberra Institute of Technology (CIT) music campus in Woden, and the completion of the Tuggeranong Arts Centre. This latter, the first of Canberra's suburban community arts centres, was allocated funding of $4.183 million in 1987/88.[33] Over the next four years, a number of enquiries and steering committees were engaged in attempting to move the project through to architectural drawings. The centre finally opened in 1998.

The recommendations from both inquiries exemplify a quantum change in the government's perception of local arts and culture, indicating an increased level of respect for the wider arts community, as well as a clear understanding that the time had come to privilege local arts and culture. Over the decade, a rapid growth in arts activity resulted from the combination of successive willing governments and peer-supported, sector-directed planning, coupled with the growth of arts infrastructure. As the decade progressed, the visual arts – which from the 1960s to the end of the 1980s had struggled under the powerful federal rhetoric of national excellence in flagship performing arts companies – came to be perceived as equally important to the performing arts in the ACT.

The reports that anchored their respective decades of the 1980s and the 1990s – the Pascoe Report (1985), the Final Report of the Select Committee on Cultural Activities and Facilities (1991), and its follow-on report from the Standing Committee on Planning, Development and Infrastructure (1992) – paint a remarkably different picture of Canberra. The Pascoe Report was compiled by a consultant whose most recent position as head of the Australia Council meant he appeared to be the best prospect for the job – that is, to ascertain the way forward for arts and culture in the national capital. But Pascoe, in privileging national capital space over the local, misread both the nature of place and the powerful desire of local practitioners to drive their own future. In contrast, the findings and recommendations in the final report of the Select Committee on Cultural Activities and Facilities were made following an unprecedented

---

33   ACT Government, *ACT budget paper no 6, 1987/88*, Canberra, Government Printer, 1988, p 35.

level of community consultation. Many direct quotes from community members are scattered throughout the report, illustrating the committee's conclusions and indicating the depth of engagement undertaken by the committee and the seriousness with which the stated needs and indeed the cultural dreams of the community were taken. In them, civic pride was seen as stemming from local practice – in service to a city whose identity was culturally separate from the functions of national capital space, and where local arts practice was increasingly regarded as a dominant feature of Canberra life.

Additionally, many of the recommendations of the Standing Committee on Planning, Development and Infrastructure report, which clearly took into account the final report of the Select Committee on Cultural Activities and Facilities, continued to be activated over the next 25 years. This long-term fulfilment of the various recommendations stands as a testament to the original depth of arts community engagement over the first years of self-government, to the intelligent and far-sighted submissions by the broader arts community to these major committees of enquiry, and to the commitment of successive local governments to growing the sector.

4

BITUMEN RIVER GALLERY – EVOLUTION AND EARLY YEARS

Art is a Scheherazade job that goes night after night after night. The same anew. The main thing is … don't get involved with any of this if you can think of one other thing that, in your heart, you believe is a better thing to do with your life. If you can think of another life; a lawyer, nun, brain surgeon, jet pilot, do that thing and don't get involved. Don't do it, not just because the profession is over determined but because, if you go to it as a second choice, it is going to show in your work. Your work will be second rate and you will clutter up the place with overly managed bad art. Don't do it because you want 'to express yourself'. Don't do it because you want a career. Don't do it because you feel art needs you. Don't do it if you don't need art.[1]

This excerpt from Noel Sheridan's essay 'Yes Tasmania', in *Chameleon: a decade (1983–1993)* speaks of the compulsion that, from the beginning of the 1970s, drove small groups of artists and like-minded individuals to begin setting up alternative spaces. These spaces were for artists who, excluded by various art institutions because their youth and use of media such as prints, posters, photocopies and new media precluded serious collecting, were compelled to make and show work that was socially

---

1 Noel Sheridan, 'Yes Tasmania', in Hammond, 1993, p 14.

and politically relevant, on their own terms and of their own choosing. By 1980, this compulsive ethos had reached Australia's youngest city and national capital, Canberra.[2]

Canberra's alternative art space, Bitumen River Gallery (BRG), was not the first of Australia's alternative art spaces, nor was it modelled on those spaces that preceded it: Praxis in Perth, Australian Centre for Photography (ACP) in Sydney, Experimental Art Foundation (EAF) in Adelaide or Institute of Modern Art (IMA) in Brisbane. As national capital, Canberra differed significantly from other Australian cities and, as a result, critical differences are identifiable between the formation and early years of other art spaces and BRG.

BRG had its genesis in a small, fluid group of eight to 10 people, comprising printmakers, students from the Canberra School of Art (CSA) Printmaking Workshop, social activists, and beneficiaries of the late 1970s employment stimulus programs operating in Australia. That such a disparate group was responsible for the birth of alternative contemporary art practice can be traced to the first of these critical differences, which artist and filmmaker Tony Ayres identified as 'Canberra's subcultural homogeneity'.[3] The second critical difference was that the formation of BRG followed on swiftly from the beginnings of Megalo in 1980. In other words, the genesis of BRG was intrinsically connected to the formation of Canberra's first printmaking collective. Its alignment with Megalo ensured that, from the first exhibition opening on 4 April 1981, the gallery's focus, while predicated on the local, would never be parochial.

By 1980 Canberra, with a population of around 220,000, began to experience a cultural divide. On one side were public servants, who managed the day-to-day affairs of the federal government; an international conclave of ambassadors and staff from a number of embassies; military personnel attached to the Royal Military College, Duntroon; academic personnel attached to The Australian National University (ANU); along with professional advisers and private business owners constituting a large service sector. It could be argued that the occupants of this side

---

2   Noel Sheridan (1936–2006) was the inaugural paid secretary of the EAF. By the 1980s, titles such as 'secretary' and 'coordinator', which had previously been applied to those who led Australia's alternative art spaces, had evolved to the administrative term 'director'. This change in title, although not in job description, coincided with the change from alternative art spaces to contemporary art spaces, and was a harbinger of the creeping institutionalisation of art in Australia during the 1990s.
3   Tony Ayres, 'Space', *Art Network*, 11, 1983, p 4.

of the divide consumed imported culture. Broadly, the Canberra Theatre Centre (CTC) hosted interstate dance, opera and theatre companies and established artist societies held regular exhibitions at venues such as the Canberra Theatre Gallery, the Arts Council Gallery (ACG) and a number of commercial galleries around the city. Overwhelmingly, exhibitors for these events were drawn from visiting artists working in traditional areas, cultural exchange artists organised through the embassies or established artists recognised by the academy.

On the other side, although not completely in opposition, the city was experiencing growing unemployment and a steadily expanding community of students, including increasing numbers graduating from CSA.[4] From within these groups came the impetus and energy that created what Ayres has described as Canberra's 'cultural fringe'.[5] Smaller cultural groups active in 1980 that drew much of their audience and many of their members from these latter groups included theatre groups such as Fools Gallery Theatre Co, Canberra Youth Theatre (CYT) and Jigsaw Theatre Company,[6] dance companies and community arts groups such as Bluegum.

Ayres, an early BRG member, wrote that 1980 was:

> a prosperous time for the cultural fringe in Canberra. Given Canberra's size and subcultural homogeneity, it is not surprising that all of these organisations were linked by common threads – an inter-change of personnel whose consensus of opinion substituted for stated ideology. One could fairly describe most of these ventures as politically radical, in so far as their content tended towards leftist analyses of society.[7]

Julian Webb, who coordinated the work of Jobless Action (the employment-creation arm of the Community Youth Support Scheme (CYSS)), played a critical role in the unfolding story of contemporary art practice in Canberra. From a base in Ainslie,

---

[4] Indeed, many diplomatic representatives and some academics proved very sympathetic to 'fringe' art initiatives, indicating that the social divide was not entirely clear-cut.
[5] Ayres, 1983, p 11.
[6] Jigsaw's then artistic director, Joe Woodward, wrote, 'We tended to operate on a "Collective" basis with all cast, crew and director involved in decision making and artistic responsibility. It had a strong sense of "theatre for the community" and challenging privilege and establishment values. It tried to be a door to more cooperative and social values affirming people's culture and lives' (in 'Jigsaw Theatre Company history', www.jigsawtheatre.com.au/history, accessed 11 October 2012, site discontinued).
[7] Ayres, 1983, p 11.

Jobless Action provided moral and physical support for unemployed people, putting together income schemes and giving 'some focus to political activism'.[8]

Also central to the story were the political and arts practice choices made by a small number of CSA students. CSA opened its doors in its current location on the ANU campus in 1969. In 1980, a $3 million refurbishment program was completed. From 1978 onwards, the school had a strong printmaking focus under master printmaker Jorg Schmeisser and, critically, from the inaugural Print Workshop tutor, Mandy Martin. By 1980, Alison Alder was in her third year of a fine arts degree, majoring in printmaking. Part of an increasingly leftist, politicised youth arts scene, Alder was disenchanted with the technique-oriented master printmaker/apprentice paradigm championed by Schmeisser and she longed for a centralised collective that devolved control into the hands of makers. At that time, no such alternative existed. 'The Art School,' wrote Alder, 'was the pivot of art activity which was closed to artists outside of that system.'[9] She and her peers took matters into their own hands. They self-identified as having 'high energy and high levels of political and social commitment' and, in 1980, set about changing the face of art practice in Canberra.[10]

Megalo was the natural outcome of a poster-making culture that put itself in the service of minority social groups.[11] The poster's multiple production and wide dissemination was enabled in the 1960s through technological changes such as phototypesetting. Beginning as an underground political force in the 1960s connected with the 1968 Paris riots, poster making was legitimised through small poster collectives throughout Europe and the United States concerned predominantly with anti–Vietnam War protests,

---

8   Alison Alder, speech at the opening of Megalo Access Arts' new premises at the former Hackett Primary School, 1992, cited in *Printing history: 18 years of Megalo Access Arts*, Canberra Museum and Gallery, 1999.
9   Alder, 'Serving the needs of artists', 1983.
10 Alison Alder, interview with the author, 14 April 2010.
11 The history of poster making as art is lengthy and well documented, beginning with the work of the French poster designers Jules Chéret and Henri de Toulouse-Lautrec from the latter part of the 1800s; progressing to its use as a political propaganda tool through the twentieth century in both World War I and II and in countries including Spain, Russia and China; and produced as art objects in countries such as Japan. It is outside of the scope of this history. For the history of poster making in Australia see, for example, Roger Butler, *Poster art in Australia: the streets as art galleries – walls sometimes speak* (Canberra, National Gallery of Australia, 1993). Also see Therese Kenyon, *Under a hot tin roof: art, passion and politics at the Tin Sheds Art Workshop* (Sydney, State Library of New South Wales Press in association with Power Publications, 1995).

feminism and the women's movement, and the anti-nuclear movement. In the 1970s in Australia, a growing political activism and awareness of these social issues, coupled with the desire of art school graduates to develop an alternative creative environment, led to the formation of a loose association of print workshops. These workshops were:

> fundamentally committed to ensuring access to, and control of, information by those people whose interests and concerns are under-represented, or not represented at all, in the dominant media forms of radio, television and newspapers.[12]

Women's rights was the central issue for Canberra Women's Liberation (CWL), which set up a printmaking workshop in the garage of its home office at 12 Bremer Street in inner south Canberra in 1972. During 1972 and 1973, CWL members printed posters concerned with women's issues. Founding member Biff Ward remembered that member Eileen Haley 'knew a lot about' screen-printing and that CWL would have 'these big screen-printing working bees … working really hard, printing, printing, printing. We'd print posters for meetings and public meetings and maybe demonstrations'.[13]

The genesis of Megalo

By 1980, printmakers in Canberra were operating as a loose underground, 'screen-printing in garages around the place, mainly producing posters to advertise events and perhaps less often to express an ideological opinion'.[14] In May of that year, desire and momentum crystallised in the decision to set up a printmaking workshop. Jobless Action placed a tiny, unattributed advertisement in the *Canberra Times* requesting that people interested in a silk-screening collective enterprise telephone a business hours number.[15] The resulting well-attended inaugural meeting included 'many strangers'.[16]

---

12   Lee-Anne Hall, 'Who is Bill Posters? An examination of six Australian socially concerned alternative print media organisations', *Caper*, 27, special issue, 1988, p 3.
13   Biff Ward, interview with Sara Dowse, 26 September 1998, National Library of Australia oral history typescript, 30, quoted in Julia Ryan, email to the author, 20 June 2016.
14   Alder, cited in *Printing history*, 1992.
15   'Silk-screening. People interested in collective enterprise ph 811702 bh', advertisement, *Canberra Times*, 3 May 1980, p 21.
16   Alder, cited in *Printing history*, 1992.

Among those 'strangers' was Colin Little[17] – who established the Earthworks Poster Company[18] at the Tin Sheds, University of Sydney, in 1971 – and David Morrow, who produced work at Lucifoil in Sydney. These two brought collective experience to a group that also included Gaida Serilus, Paul Ford, Roland Manderson, Di Johnson and Webb's co-worker Annie Kavanagh. The meeting was an indication of Canberra's linked 'subcultural homogeneity'. Serilus, a 'hippie firebrand poster maker',[19] was Webb's partner and Ford was Alder's. These social interconnections were critical to the formation of both Megalo and, a year later, BRG.

When Megalo received its first funding through the Department of the Capital Territory (DCT) Arts Development Fund in 1981[20] it signalled the beginning of the Commonwealth's growing willingness to support emerging contemporary artists, albeit, at this time, as members of the unemployed. *Muse* magazine applauded the decision:

> The DCT is to be congratulated on its recent funding of Jobless Action's silk screening workshop at Ainslie Village. The workshop has received $5000 for equipment costs and is hoping to eventually employ a coordinator. Spokesperson Colin Little originally from the 'Tin Shed Collective' in Sydney told *Muse* that 'a major aim of the workshop was to improve the quality of poster graphics and street art in Canberra'. He saw the Village venture as a viable business capable of producing commercial posters as well as local social and non-profit prints. The collective hopes to involve the wider community by means of summer schools.[21]

---

17 Until his death on 4 October 1982, Little played an important role in the genesis and development of Megalo and BRG.
18 The Earthworks Poster Company (1971–79) became the Earthworks Poster Collective in 1972.
19 Alder, 2010.
20 ACT was funded through the Commonwealth Government's DCT until the Territory gained full self-government status in 1992. Chapters 1, 2 and 3 discuss local arts funding bodies.
21 'Museshorts', *Muse*, 5, p 37. This grant was the first awarded to a Canberra-based artist collective. While it was symptomatic of the increasing willingness of government funding bodies throughout Australia to support emerging artists, at this time in Canberra the focus was very much on support mechanisms for artists as members of the growing sector of unemployed, rather than as working artists.

The genesis of BRG

As the output of political posters from Megalo screen-printers continued to increase, it rapidly became apparent that a combined shop/exhibition space was needed. At the far edge of the former St Christopher's Catholic School grounds, on the corner of Furneaux and Bougainville streets, Manuka, was a derelict building that had consecutively operated as a milk shed, a shelter shed and, finally, a bus stop. In response to a resident's suggestion[22] to local Liberal member for Canberra, John Haslem,[23] that the building be used by the unemployed in some useful way, Robert Ellicott – minister for home affairs and the environment, and minister for the Capital Territory (1977–80) – handed the derelict structure over to Webb.

Alder, Ford, Webb and Serilus, together with CSA students Julia Church and Mark Denton, and Little and Morrow, had solidified their affiliations throughout the previous year with the establishment of Megalo. The shelter shed was an answer to the group's compelling need for an outlet for their screen prints. Jobless Action was closely aligned with the CYSS, and usage of the site was envisaged as a shopfront for Megalo posters and products from CYSS clients, with Jobless Action providing administrative assistance. The focus quickly turned to exhibition space, and a collective – comprising Megalo members, CSA students and Jobless Action members – was formed to transform the derelict building into a gallery. The DCT expedited an electricity pole to service the building and contributed $10,000 for urgent repairs. These included fitting a ceiling, mounting windows and doors, and replacing parts of the flooring.[24]

As with Megalo a year before, Jobless Action provided the official front for BRG. The focus was firmly on the unemployed and the public were advised that the gallery was run by a 'collective of unemployed people through Jobless Action, with the help of a number of committed employed people', and that it would 'sell art and some craft produced by unemployed people and other low income earners'.[25]

---

22   The resident's name was, unfortunately, not recorded.
23   John Haslem was the Liberal member for Canberra from 13 December 1975 to 8 October 1980.
24   'Future directions', a report of the Search Conference, 9 June 1985, BRG scrapbook, 1985, CCAS archives.
25   Julian Webb, 'Bill posters appreciated', *Hard Times*, 14, 1991.

It was a prosaic beginning with a modest vision. The name 'Bitumen River Gallery' encapsulates a particular spirit of the time: a do-it-yourself ethos, a close-to-the-ground approach to contemporary practice in the Canberra community, a sly take on social art within a city manufactured for twentieth-century urban and suburban living. The view from the proposed new gallery took in the vast bitumen car park that serviced the St Christopher's Church and the school. In retrospect, the name constitutes a parody. Bitumen, the symbol of the urban space, remade via a youthful collective into a gallery whose existence was charged with the compulsive spirit of renewal transforming international contemporary art.

Bill posters appreciated

BRG opened on 4 April 1981 with 60 posters in an exhibition titled *Bill posters appreciated*. Posters came from Sydney print collectives Jura Books, Earthworks, Lucifoil, Black Earth, Toby Zoates, Cockroach, Rouge, Wimmins Warehouse, Matilda Graphics, Movement Media, Pre-Natal Press, Resistance and Shopfront Theatre; and from Breadline (Melbourne); Redback Graphix (Wollongong); Without Authority (Lismore); Red Pepper (San Francisco); and Sisterwrite (London).

The exhibition's opening image, designed by Morrow and printed by him at Megalo, featured a wide-eyed, dark-haired toddler, with the words 'Well, I've never heard of YOU either' scrolling across the bottom of the image (see Figure 7).

The national and international prints on exhibition provided a window onto contemporary social concerns, with titles including *Share the shitwork* (see Figure 8), *Don't bomb the Pacific*, *El Salvador*, *Stop police harassment*, *Fight evictions*, and *For Aurukun and Mornington Island*.

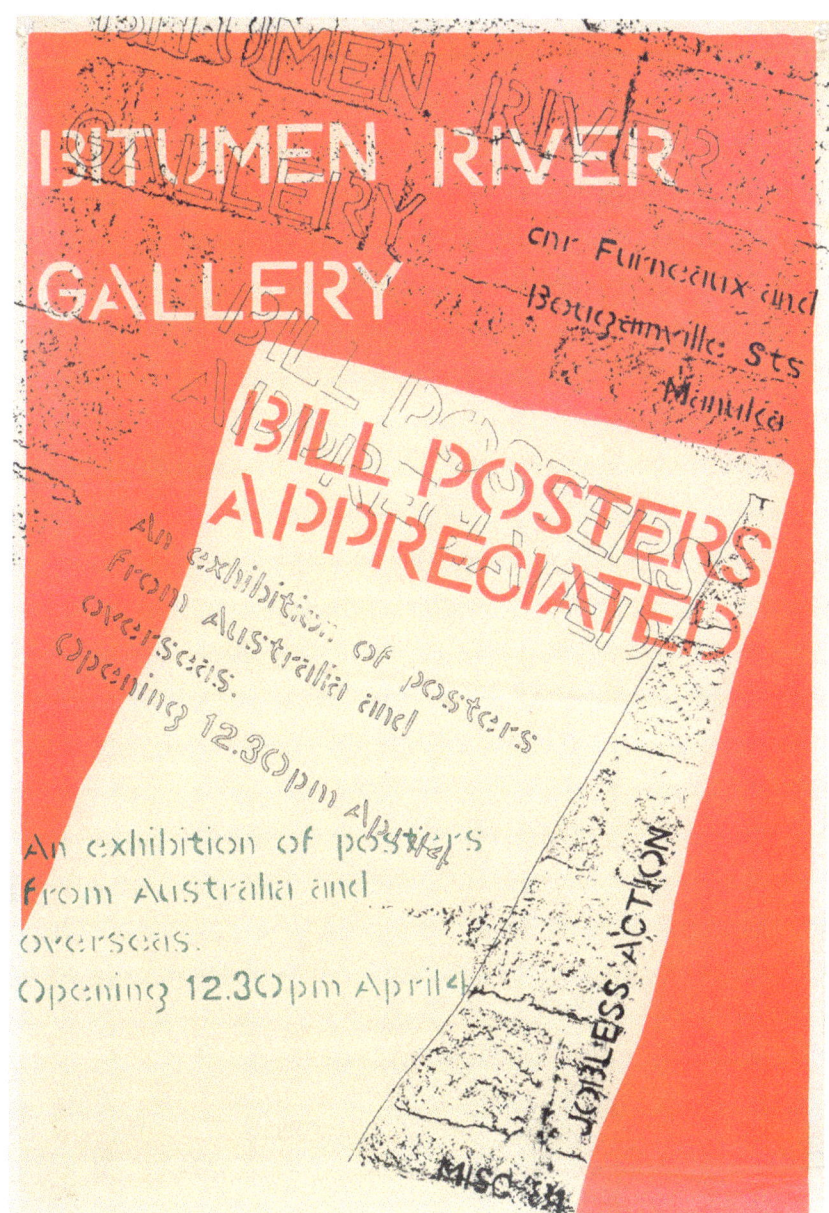

Figure 6. *Bill posters appreciated*, BRG opening exhibition poster, printed at Megalo, April 1981

Source. Photographer: Brenton McGeachie. CCAS image archive, reproduced with permission

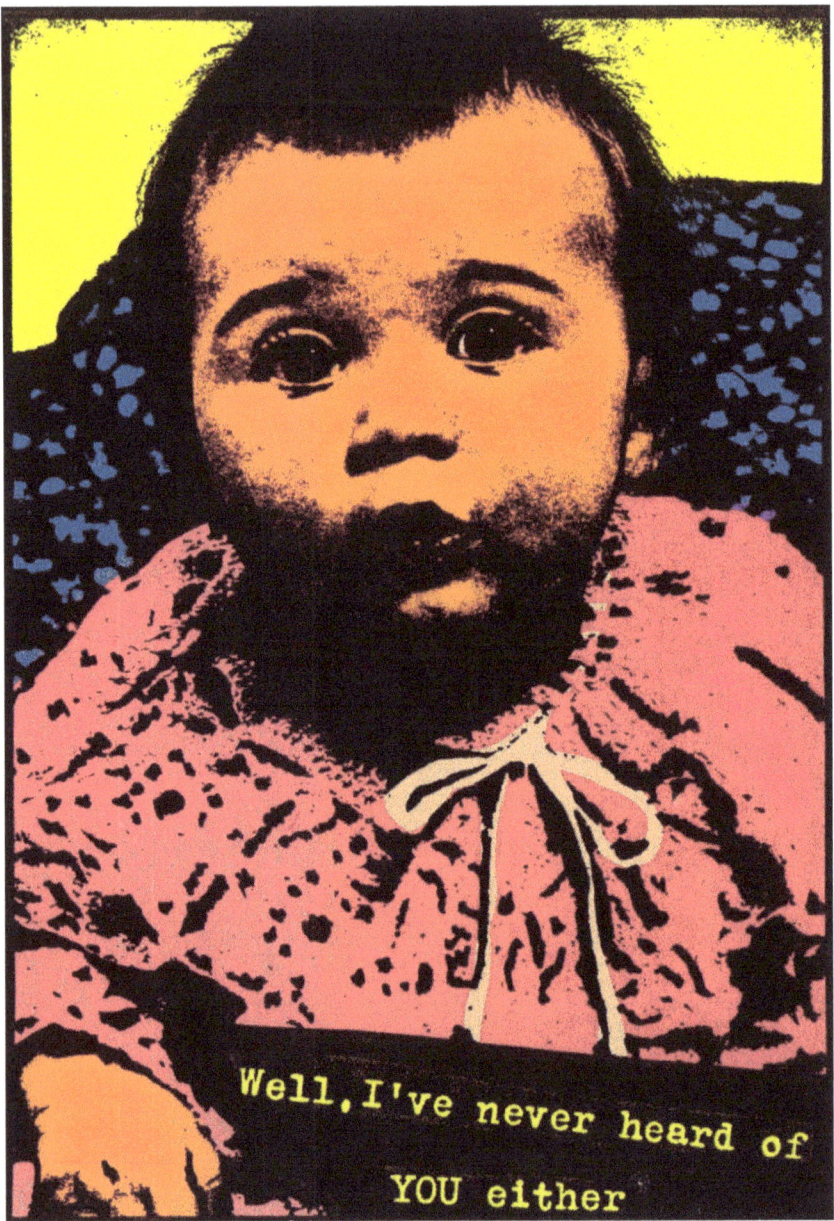

Figure 7. David Morrow, *Well I've never heard of YOU either*, screen print, postcard, BRG opening invitation for 4 April 1981
Source. CCAS image archive, reproduced with permission

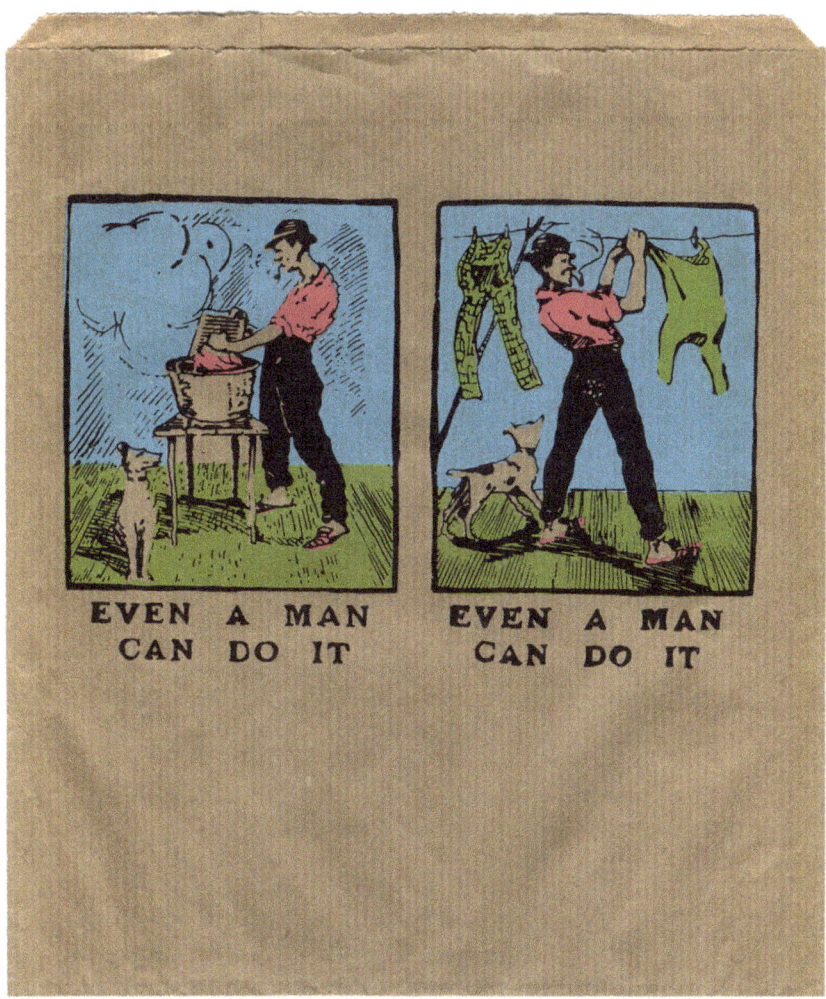

Figure 8. Alison Alder, *Share the shitwork: even a man can do it*, 1981, brown paper bag, screen print, 25 x 20 cm, Bill posters appreciated, BRG opening exhibition

Source. Photographer: Brenton McGeachie. CCAS image archive, reproduced with permission

Share the shitwork, designed by Alder and printed by her at Megalo, comprises two four-colour panels that reference early twentieth-century newspaper illustrations. The work features a lanky, hatted chap, with a pipe in his mouth and a dog at his feet. In the first panel, he is using a scrubbing board and tub and, in the second, a stick and wire clothesline. Subtitled *Even a man can do it*, the images use crafty humour to deliver a clear message: domestic equality in the late 1970s remained as elusive as it had been in the 1930s.

The opening exhibition was also an opportunity to make politicised statements in the press. These included an opinion piece by Webb in *Hard Times*, an occasional publication that was briefly produced by 'an independent autonomous collective', including Webb and 'various fringe dwellers'. Webb's review of the opening reflected the contemporary community backlash to the widening gap between the wealthy and the unemployed in Canberra. It incorporated a short thesis on the 'nature and value of work in terms other than the $' and urged readers to support the gallery:

> If the unemployed people running the place are to achieve their aim of satisfying employment, that is also paid, then your patronage is essential. If following exhibitions are of the calibre of this one then they will not be let down.[26]

Muse covered the opening with a statement from the exhibition's organisers that, in its impassioned political rhetoric, encapsulated a youthful, contemporary utopia:

> Co-operation is an essential part of this exhibition. The building was renovated through a group effort, the posters were made under a group system. The age of individual alienation is withering … we must oppose the terrorism of big business and its concomitant manipulative exploitation mentality; demand more humane and enduring social relationships; and develop community control of the streets and the country we/you share with all members of the world.[27]

The choice of *Bill posters appreciated* as an opening exhibition was important and prescient. It meant that, from its inception, BRG was contextualised within a national and international rubric. It heralded an intention to remain relevant within broad national and international social concerns, realising those through contemporary art practice. Posters were modestly priced at between $3 and $4 and embraced a wide spectrum of contemporary issues. They were overtly political, from poster number 1, titled *Dead men don't rape*, through to poster number 60, titled *Nuclear free Pacific*.[28]

---

26   Webb, 1991.
27   'Bill posters appreciated: a statement', *Muse*, April 1981.
28   List of works, *Bill posters appreciated*, 1981–83, CCAS archive.

4. BITUMEN RIVER GALLERY

From that first exhibition onwards, the gallery embraced and then transcended the local. The appellation 'parochial' would not then, or in the years to 1987, be applied to BRG, either by the public or by its members. Over the next six years, BRG members and early principal coordinators – Alder together with Ford, and Virgo together with Erica Green – would continue to impress the gallery's local relevance on artists, funding bodies and the public. Importantly, they also began to align its presence with the national agenda of emerging contemporary art spaces. They did this by attending seminal national arts conferences, beginning with the second ANZART conference in Hobart, 1983; instituting a series of travelling exhibitions between Canberra, Melbourne, Perth and Hobart; leading the push for the establishment of a local chapter of the Artworkers Union and for the national Campaign for Free Admission to the newly opened ANG; and bringing in national speakers on contemporary art, such as Terry Smith, to enliven local debate and arts practice.

In many ways, despite its strong opening exhibition, BRG's continuance seemed unlikely. On the general feeling that followed *Bill posters appreciated*, media commentator Marcus Breen noted in April 1982:

> When Humphrey McQueen[29] opened the Bitumen River Gallery in 1981 with the flourish of a glue brush and the flutter of a poster, few people expected to see the gallery thriving one year later.[30]

To begin with, the gallery was unfunded, relying on the young, inexperienced collective members to drive its future direction and undertake day-to-day management. It was a space run, according to one local wit, 'for all lost causes of humanity'.[31] In essence, it lurched through that first year, appearing to make it up as it went along, while managing to maintain a powerful, socially political focus. As Ayres would write from the perspective of 1985:

> The gallery came into being with each successive exhibition; the gallery became a 'political' one because the small circle of people involved, art school graduates and under-graduates, were at that time making overtly political imagery, not through a conscious collective decision to seek out that work.[32]

---

29 Humphrey McQueen was the teacher-in-charge of 'History and appreciation of art/architecture', a one- to two-hour course for Art Diploma 1 at CSA from 1978 to 1980.
30 Marcus Breen, 'Bitumen River Gallery – one year after', *Muse*, 2 April – 13 May 1982, p 15.
31 *Canberra and District Historical Society Newsletter*, June/July 1982, p 11.
32 Tony Ayres, '*Causes*: an exhibition of political posters and prints from Canberra, 1981 to 1983', *Imprint*, 1, 1985, np.

Recalling the climate that marked the collective's ability to move forward, Church married the high energy levels to the do-it-yourself ethos:

> We thought we had a licence to do whatever we wanted really and we kind of did. [We had] all the raw materials and that's partly what was such a charge-up about it – we could come up with the ideas, we could print the posters ourselves, we could take all the photos ourselves … and we could also build the workshops and build the galleries … [see Figures 9 and 10]. It was a very particular time in Australian history where people [working in the arts] did that all over the country and had done it for the generation before us too.[33]

The ANZART conference in Hobart in May 1983 was critical in establishing collaborative links between BRG and other artist-run spaces. Alder attended the conference, part of which included a breakaway three-day seminar, the *Open sandwich conference*, that brought together representatives from all Australia's existing contemporary art spaces for the first time. They came to share with, learn from and support each other.[34] The paper Alder gave at the conference provides a perspective on the volatile period immediately following the opening of BRG. She wrote:

> At this time there was no real conception of how the gallery was going to operate, to the point of not knowing what the next exhibition was going to be, and a number of problems began to surface.[35]

Among these problems was the question of how to select future exhibitors. BRG was an open-access gallery whose only exhibition policy was that the works shown would be non-racist and non-sexist. The group had neither the experience nor the desire to make value judgements on potential exhibitors. Ford explained:

> One woman said that she wanted to show – she was unemployed – so a number of us went along to look at her work and (sort of) pretend that we could decide whether she would show her work. So we all saw her work and thought, wow, what a responsibility, to say whether we like it or not and whether that person's work should be shown.[36]

---

33 Julia Church, interview with the author, 30 September 2012.
34 Pamela Zeplin, 'Crossing over: raising the ghosts of Tasman–Pacific art exchange: ANZART-in-Hobart, 1983', in '"Asian" media arts practice in/and Aotearoa New Zealand', *New Zealand Journal of Media Studies* 9, 1, 2005, nzetc.victoria.ac.nz/tm/scholarly/tei-Sch091JMS-t1-g1-t4.html, accessed 10 March 2015.
35 Alison Alder, 'Bitumen River', conference paper, *Open sandwich conference*, ANZART, Hobart, May 1983.
36 Breen, 1982, p 7.

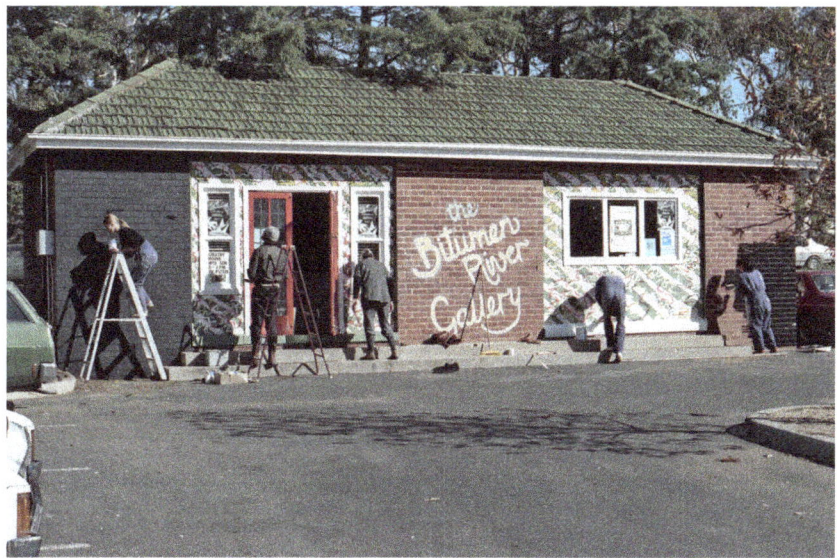

Figure 9. Collective members 'doing it for themselves', BRG Gallery
Source. CCAS image archive, reproduced with permission

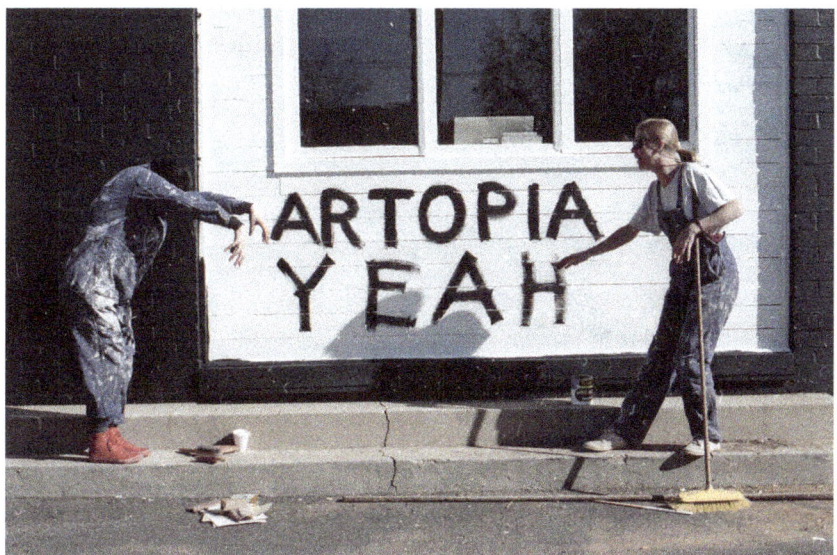

Figure 10. Collective members 'doing it for themselves', BRG Gallery
Source. CCAS image archive, reproduced with permission

Dreamtime machinetime

Given the lack of experience and skills in gallery management, it is extraordinary that the second exhibition at BRG, *Trevor Nickolls: from Dreamtime to machinetime* was, albeit for very different reasons, as remarkable as the first. This exhibition opened at BRG a full three years before *Koori art '84* introduced the work of contemporary city-based Aboriginal artists, previously known as 'Urban' artists, to Sydney. BRG's first exhibition centred it within national and international contemporary art discourses and its second exhibition anticipated a movement that has become one of the principal interests of art history since 1980: the transition of Indigenous art from ethnographica to contemporary visual art.

Nickolls, with dual Aboriginal/Irish heritage, graduated from the South Australian School of Art (SA SOA) (Dip Fine Art painting) in 1970.[37] The trajectory of his work, which as a student was wholly concerned with Western/European subject matter and styles, gradually turned towards the dichotomy of customary Aboriginal life versus alienated urban living. By the late 1970s, he had met central Australian Warlpiri/Anmatyerre painter and senior lawman Dinny Nolan Tjampitjinpa, and began to incorporate dots and traditional Aboriginal mark-making in his works, developing his Dreamtime/machinetime thesis.[38] In 1981 Nickolls arrived in Canberra as the HC Coombs Creative Arts Fellow at ANU.[39]

---

37 From the 1990s, Trevor Nickolls has been known as 'the father of urban Aboriginal art'.
38 Dinny Nolan Tjampitjinpa came from Yuendumu and moved to Papunya in 1972. He was one of the senior lawmen of the Warlpiri/Anmatyerre tribe who, with the support of teacher Geoffrey Bardon, began painting traditional designs on canvas, giving birth to the contemporary, grassroots (as opposed to the Urban Aboriginal art movement that would rise in the 1980s) Aboriginal art movement. Bardon characterised him as 'a wonderfully reliable man … a gentleman. He was a determined painter for Papunya Tula Artists Pty Ltd and was a fine ambassador for the company during his visits to Melbourne and Sydney' (Geoffrey Bardon and James Bardon, *Papunya: a place made after the story: the beginnings of the Western Desert Painting Movement*, Melbourne, The Miegunyah Press, 2004, p 87).
39 Nickolls was determined to access family history and resources at the Australian Institute of Aboriginal and Torres Strait Islander Affairs (AIATSIS) but, unable to prove his Indigeneity at that time, he was denied access to the archives.

4. BITUMEN RIVER GALLERY

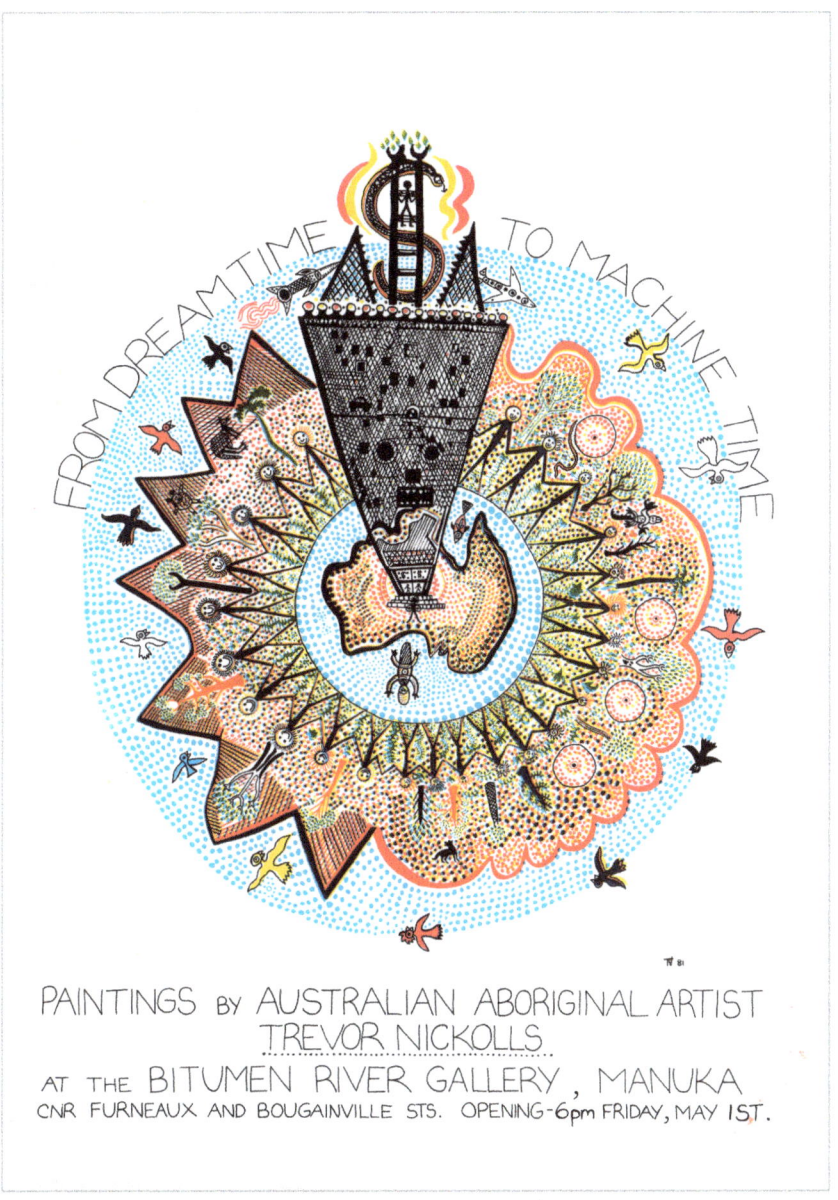

Figure 11. Alison Alder and Gaida Serilus, Trevor Nickolls, *From Dreamtime to machinetime*, exhibition poster, 1–17 May 1981
Source. Megalo archives, reproduced with permission

The physical proximity of Australia's national university and the art school fostered important collaborative links between radical students from both institutions. Ford, still a student at CSA, met Nickolls on campus and together with Little – who had met Nickolls during his time as arts adviser for Tiwi Designs from 1976 to 1980 – suggested that Nickolls hold an exhibition at the about-to-be-opened BRG.

Serilus and Alder printed exhibition posters and the invitation (see Figure 11) and, afterwards, Nickolls gave Alder a drawing. She remembers his work as 'luminous. It sang out from those red brick walls'.[40]

Nickolls exhibited 26 recent paintings at BRG. Comments in the visitors' book reflect an audience not yet literate in the language of contemporary Indigenous art, with responses ranging from 'Quite impressive (reminds me of Aboriginal work)' to 'Exciting, wonderful detail. Shows terrible dilemma of black culture – your women are so fierce!'[41] ANU head of Art History and *Canberra Times* reviewer Sasha Grishin applied his considerable scholarship in writing the first review of Nickolls' art practice by an art historian, noting that Nickolls was 'consciously creating his own personal expressive language freely using … a blend of forms drawn from traditionally Aboriginal arts and modern western conceptions of painting'.[42] While ultimately recognising Nickolls' work as 'coherent and potent', Grishin felt that 'in a number of his paintings, the imagery becomes too much an illustration of political ideas to work satisfactorily as a visual unity'.[43]

It was precisely the 'illustration of political ideas' that heralded the soon-to-explode phenomenon of contemporary Urban Aboriginal art. Grishin was not alone in failing to recognise Nickolls' exhibition as the beginning of what would become an internationally recognised art movement. Three years later, reviewers would misunderstand the work in the seminal Sydney exhibition *Koori art '84* as 'simulated and derived'[44] and dismiss

---

40 Alder, 2010.
41 Comments attributed respectively to Andrew Bray and Caroline Blesing, BRG visitors' book, 1981–83, CCAS archives.
42 Sasha Grishin, 'Aborigines in role of blood sacrifice', *Canberra Times*, 12 May 1981, p 15.
43 With reference to Adam Geczy's *Buried alive* (2007): 'Geczy is keenly aware of what he terms the "impossibility" of politically activist art, particularly in Australia' (Sasha Grishin, quoted in Jacqueline Millner, 'Elusive exigencies: art and social change', in *Conceptual beauty: perspectives on Australian contemporary art*, Sydney, Artspace, 2010, p 134).
44 Terence Maloon, 'Such sweet plunder', *Sydney Morning Herald*, 15 September 1984, p 49.

it as 'a passing fad'.[45] Yet, only six years after *Koori art '84*, Nickolls and Rover Thomas were the first Aboriginal artists to represent Australia at the Venice Biennale.[46] Nickolls was a heraldic messenger and his position as the second exhibitor at BRG presaged the gallery's position as a harbinger of contemporary trends.[47]

BRG quickly developed a following among Canberra's arts community. Alder recalls established artists such as Rosalie Gascoigne dropping in, as well as National Gallery director James Mollison, whose description of BRG as 'that little punk gallery' swiftly found its way into print[48] when, in his *Canberra Times* review of Nickolls' *From Dreamtime to machinetime*, Grishin wrote, '[Nickolls's works] are showing at the newly opened Bitumen River Gallery, a small punk gallery located at the Manuka car park'.[49]

It is possible that Mollison, who was a warmly supportive, frequent visitor to BRG, was misinterpreted. In comparison to the National Gallery, Bitumen River must have seemed like some 'punk' kid, flexing its puny muscles and cocking its nose at the establishment. In any case, the moniker stuck through the first year, although it seems probable that the original meaning, of what was most likely a throwaway line meant to highlight youth versus The Establishment, became confused with a contemporary social movement.[50] By 1983, Ayres took exception to the descriptive phrase, writing that BRG:

> is not a 'punk' gallery. It has none of the violent anarchy which typifies a punk visual style. None of the people who run it stick pins in themselves or make their hair stand up on end like used toothbrushes.[51]

---

45 Quoted in Brenda Croft, 'A change is gonna come', *Periphery*, 40–41, 1999–2000, p 52.
46 Ian McLean, *How Aborigines invented the idea of contemporary art: writings on Aboriginal contemporary art*, Brisbane, Institute of Modern Art and Sydney, Power Publications, 2011.
47 Nickolls' exhibition title shares a wonderful synergy with the name 'Bitumen River'.
48 Alder, 2010.
49 Grishin, 12 May 1981.
50 There was a vibrant punk scene in Canberra in the early 1980s.
51 Ayres, 1983, p 11.

Mollison continued to visit often. On 15 May 1982, artist Geoff Shera, who was sitting in the gallery, wrote in the visitors' book:

> visitors included students, diplomats, Welsh tourists and Canberran workers. The Director of the National Gallery came along to the Gallery. He remarked that the Gallery was 'a very lively one'. Mr Mollison said it was a 'crazy exhibition' with the pot-pourri of glass, leather shoe bespoking mixed media work & drawings. I asked him when the National Gallery was being opened and he said October 13 (or was 8th) [sic] this year. He asked me if I knew the 'Young Italians', 'who in particular' I asked. 'the young Italian painters', 'painting in Italy?' I asked. He said 'Yes, like Clemente' I said 'No, what do they paint like, what's their stuff like?' He laughed and said 'like this!'[52]

This anecdote illustrates the perceived gulf that existed at that time in the minds of collective members between national and local cultural spheres; between art in the institutions and art as practised by the members of BRG. On one hand, Mollison showed keen interest in the progress of this new wave of young artists; they were an accurate reflection of the thrust of broader contemporary art practice. Additionally, although the youth of these artists and the emergence of poster making and photocopy as mediums for artistic expression precluded serious collecting by other Australian art institutions, Roger Butler recognised the importance of the prints and posters being produced by both local and national collectives. With the support of Mollison and with funds supplied by then chairman of the National Gallery council, Gordon Darling, he immediately began acquiring posters and screen prints made by collective members for the national collection. Despite this quiet support, the about-to-be-opened National Gallery, with its prominent position in the national capital representing the apogee of the institutional model, epitomised a paradigm that these artists felt excluded them and that they rejected. Their focus lay in turning this paradigm on its head.

---

52   15 May 1982, BRG visitors' book, 1981–83. Shera's remarks are transcribed directly from the visitors' book.

CSA and BRG: the beginnings of a symbiotic relationship

CSA and BRG – and BRG's successor CCAS – have been engaged in a symbiotic and often complex relationship since 1980. The relationship between seminal staff and students at CSA from the latter years of the 1970s to the early 1980s reveals CSA's influence on BRG founding members. CSA, and in particular the Printmaking Workshop under senior lecturer Schmeisser and inaugural tutor Martin, provided a unique environment that directly contributed to the genesis of BRG. In this workshop a small group of politically inclined students were stimulated, particularly by Martin, who proved to be a politically and artistically literate tutor. While I acknowledge that other factors were important, the environment at CSA was critical to the growth of nascent contemporary arts exhibitions in Canberra, as evidenced through BRG's activities.

German-born Udo Sellbach, the school's inaugural director, took up his appointment in a period that Michael Agostino termed 'the financial halcyon days' of tertiary education in Australia.[53] Federal government support, which in the pre-self-government years liberally funded education in the Territory, enabled the implementation of Sellbach's Bauhaus-inspired vision. This involved setting up discrete workshops within CSA, one of which was printmaking, as well as the removal of previously accepted barriers between art and craft.[54] Importantly for the future of the Printmaking Workshop at CSA, Sellbach was a master printmaker trained in the European tradition who was active in furthering printmaking in Australia. In 1960, Sellbach and his printmaker wife Karin 'played a leading role in setting up the printmaking department at the SA SOA'.[55] In 1966, Sellbach, Ursula Hoff and Grahame King established the Print

---

53 Agostino, 2009, p 33.
54 The Bauhaus vision accepted other disciplines, such as craft, architecture and design, as art. Its architectural influence is seen in Canberra in several privately owned houses and in the 1962-built public housing of the Northbourne Housing Group – designed by Ancher, Mortlock and Murray for the National Capital Development Commission (NCDC) in 1959 – and the Bega and Allawah flats in Braddon designed by Richard Ure in 1954. The Northbourne Housing Group and Bega and Allawah flats were sold to developers from 2016 as part of the ACT government's public housing renewal program, with the money raised used to assist in funding the city's light rail network. These buildings, demolished during 2017, were 'Canberra's and probably Australia's first and only true example of the rationale of the Bauhaus principles used for public housing' (Martin Miles, 'Northbourne Housing Group', *Canberra house: mid-century modernist architecture*, www.canberrahouse.com.au/houses/northbourne-housing.html, accessed 23 March 2015).
55 Agostino, 2009, p 26.

Council of Australia in Melbourne.⁵⁶ In the 20 years before his arrival in Canberra, Sellbach lectured in printmaking in Adelaide, Melbourne, Brisbane and Hobart (where he was head of the Tasmanian School of Art). Agostino reveals that the Hobart appointment was rife with 'political infighting' and thus Sellbach, like many artists who migrated to Canberra from other Australian capitals, hoped that his appointment to CSA would provide 'a fresh start'.⁵⁷

Shortly after his arrival in Canberra he invited Schmeisser, who had trained in both Western and Eastern printmaking traditions in Germany and Kyoto, Japan, to set up a new printmaking workshop at CSA. At the same time, he approached Adelaide painter, printmaker and lecturer Robert Boynes to take up a position as head of the Painting Workshop. Boynes' partner, Martin, then a printmaker with an emerging national profile, had recently begun teaching at Salisbury TAFE.⁵⁸ Agreeing to come to Canberra if she could secure a tertiary position, she applied for and was accepted as the Printmaking Workshop tutor at CSA. Schmeisser, Boynes and Martin took up their positions together at the beginning of the 1978 academic year.⁵⁹

Mandy Martin: background and impacts

Martin had a profound influence from the late 1970s to the early 1980s on the students at CSA who founded and progressed Megalo and BRG, and on the development of contemporary political art in Canberra – particularly prints and posters. She was only 26 when she arrived at CSA, but she brought with her a sophisticated understanding of the nexus of art and politics. Her early political and artistic development was framed by South Australia's volatile political environment, and enacted through her involvement with the Progressive Art Movement (PAM) and women at the SA SOA, and the various left-wing political parties engaged in battles

---

56 'The Print Council of Australia (PCA) was established in 1966 to encourage the production and appreciation of hand-printed graphics. The intention of the PCA was to stimulate printmaking activities, to encourage understanding and appreciation of the original print and to define the various types of printmaking (wood-cut, etching, engraving, lithograph or serigraph)' (MS 49, Papers of the Print Council of Australia, Australian Prints and Printmaking Collection, NGA Research Library, nga.gov.au/Research/pdf/MS49_FindingAid.pdf, accessed 21 April 2012).
57 Agostino, 2009, p 27.
58 Martin's work was included in *Australian perspecta* in 1981 and again in 1983; she had the first of many solo shows at Roslyn Oxley 9 Gallery in 1983. Interest in her work grew nationally and internationally between 1977 and 1983.
59 Agostino (2009, p 29) incorrectly states Martin and Schmeisser as commencing at CSA in 1979.

in the SA car factories. Her political focus and her screen-printing skills, which she used on the ground in dangerous, real-life situations, directly influenced students who went on to establish Megalo and BRG, and therefore I make a close reading of her own influencing milieu.

At the beginning of 1972, Martin won one of five scholarships to the prestigious SA SOA. The early trajectory of Martin's career was set by three factors that, in turn, awakened her political conscience, gave her permission to make art outside of the academic paradigm, and furnished her with the skills to do so. The first, in the second semester of her first year, was the arrival from England of Clifford Frith as lecturer in Foundation Studies. Frith's novel approach to teaching – 'Why teach anything, why not do crochet classes?' – legitimised the making of art outside entrenched academic boundaries. Martin recalled, 'I headed to the Adelaide Hills and built a geodesic dome which was an "investigation of an interior space" … I never painted again at art school'.[60] The second, in 1973, was her decision to take Brian Medlin's course 'Politics and art' at Flinders University, which she found intellectually and politically stimulating as it explored the international intersections of art and politics. The third factor was her decision, in 1973, to seek out Boynes, who taught her to photo-screen print. This skill, which she passed on to her long-term collaborator Annie Newmarch, gave the two women an entrée into the highly politicised world of SA car manufacturing.

Under reforming Labor Premier Donald 'Don' Dunstan, South Australia styled itself as the 'State of the arts' and was arguably the most politically volatile of the Australian states and territories in the 1970s. Its industry was dominated by American car manufacturers Chrysler and General Motors Holden, which were the state's major employers and where the factory floors had, since the 1960s, become sites of escalating worker/management conflict. The complex industrial relations scenario was compounded by the number and diversity of small, left-wing political groups that were pitted against the companies, the state government, the industry's major union the Vehicle Builders Union (VBU) and, often, against themselves. Among the factions with a presence on the shop and

---

60 Mandy Martin, 'The South Australian School of Art at Stanley Street North Adelaide 1972–5', University of South Australia, School of Art, Architecture and Design, w3.unisa.edu.au/artarchitecturedesign/about/mandymartin.asp, accessed 17 April 2012, site discontinued.

factory floors were groups including the Communist Party of Australia Marxist Leninist (CPAML).[61] The CPAML played a pivotal role, firstly in Martin's political awakening and then in her disenchantment with the nexus of art and politics as evidenced in South Australia.

Martin became an early and active member of PAM. Centred around Flinders University, PAM was formed by a group of artists, performers, musicians, filmmakers and writers in 1974. This tendency towards cross–art form fertilisation was echoed in the Clifton Hill Community Music Centre in Melbourne and in Canberra's own fluid, homogenised subculture of artists, musicians and performers from the late 1970s. PAM comprised a like-minded group who had:

> turned their backs on conventional art modes and favoured mass-media forms of communication like video, photography and screenprinting rather than painting which we saw as an elitist and anachronistic activity.[62]

PAM quickly became a front organisation for WSA and for the secretive CPAML.

Martin's emerging political focus and photo-screen printing skills found their logical outlet in the Adelaide factories and workplaces of the American car manufacturers. The strategies employed by the CPAML on the factory floor followed the model of the Maoist two-stage revolution in working with the capitalists to expel the foreign imperialists – in this case, the American car manufacturer – and supporting the working-class struggle. The CPAML made effective use of cultural and arts workers, including Martin and Newmarch, to make rapid incursions onto the factory and shop floors with union-backed sloganeering that took the form of the immediately produced and disseminated screen-printed poster. In 1989 Martin recalled that:

---

61 Other groups included: the Communist Party of Australia (CPA); the Socialist Party of Australia; the Worker Student Alliance for Australian Independence (WSA); the Socialist Workers Party (SWP); the Socialist Labour League (SLL); the International Socialists (IS); and the Rank and File group (RAF), which was often accused of being a front for the WSA. List sourced from Garry Hill, 'Anatomy of an industrial struggle: Chrysler factory at Tonsley Park in Adelaide 1976–1978' (*Radical tradition: an Australian history page*, www.takver.com/history/chrysler.htm, accessed 18 April 2012).

62 Mandy Martin, 'Political posters in Adelaide', conference paper, *Australian Print symposium*, National Gallery of Australia, Canberra, 1989, www.printsandprintmaking.gov.au/references/409/, accessed 10 April 2012.

> Cultural workers had moved into the car factories and onto the rank and file of organisations in the car factories, and artists like Annie and I were right in behind, setting up exhibitions and demonstrations in the factories and workplaces. We screen-printed posters and stickers on the spot and images like *When workers unite, bosses tremble* and other plagiarised symbols from May 1968 in Paris, which enraged management as [posters and stickers] appeared minutes later on machinery and doors around the factories.[63]

Politics, both through the CPAML and via a growing interest in feminism, dominated this stage of Martin's life. She was printing political posters by day (at one stage she was banned from using SA SOA Printing Workshop inks and from using the workshop itself during school hours) and attending political meetings at night. As vice-president of the Student Representative Council (SRC), Martin 'donated the entire funds of the SRC, a whole $240, to the PLO'[64] and 'turned the office into a crèche for students with babies'.[65] Importantly, together with a group of women art school students, she founded what was arguably the first women's art group in an Australian art school. This energetic involvement with feminist politics, which Martin had viewed as contiguous to her leftist political endeavours, was in fact highly unwelcome within the CPAML cadre. Under the Maoist two-stage revolution concept, the women's revolution (along with gay rights) came in well behind the workers' revolution. Martin recalled: 'Even doing posters for things like the women's shelter was frowned on because the feminist, women's movement was considered a waste of energy'.[66]

This perceived incompatibility of her twin political interests was thrown into sharp focus by events that followed a visit by American feminist Lucy Lippard and Australian art critic Terry Smith. Lippard, visiting Adelaide as part of a lecture tour and to source images for the first issue of the American Feminist publication *Heresies*, stayed with Martin and Newmarch. In town at the same time was Smith, who had spent 1972–75 in New York, where he studied at The New York Institute of Fine Arts and Columbia University and joined the conceptual artists' group Art &

---

63 Martin, 1989.
64 Palestine Liberation Organization.
65 Mandy Martin, 'South Australian School of Art'.
66 Mandy Martin, interview with the author, 4 April 2012.

Language. The CPAML considered the two to be 'lackeys of American Imperialism'.[67] Lippard was a powerful advocate for feminist artists, and both she and Smith were working at the cutting edge of contemporary American arts criticism. Martin was 'pulled in for a whole day of disciplining by the cadre of the CPAML for fraternising with the enemy'.[68]

This experience led Martin to realise that membership of PAM, and by default the CPAML, curtailed her freedom of artistic thought and political will equally as restrictively as the academic art school paradigm. Allied to this sense of a loss of creative and political autonomy were her concerns over increasing violence at Chrysler's Tonsley Park factory in the lead-up to the riots and mass sackings of June/July 1977. Martin viewed the internecine factional wars as 'callous and interfering in working class peoples' lives. People [were] being beaten up by the police, going to jail, losing their jobs when they had families to support'.[69]

In the Australian car industry's history of significant unrest, the period of Martin's involvement as an active member of PAM is arguably the most bitter. Its intensity meant that Martin experienced an extreme introduction to the politics inherent in the trade union nexus of worker/unions/owners/political factions, and to art as a means of political activism at the coalface. The divisions and self-serving nature of much of the struggle, and the particularly bloody events leading up to and surrounding the July 1977 vote for increased workers' rights, signalled the end for Martin: 'I didn't want to hit people over the head any more, and I wanted to be able to critique both capitalism and socialism.'[70]

In other words, Martin required freedom to respond to the world as an artist, anticipating and reflecting change as her interests dictated, free of any imposed ideology. The time was ripe for the move to Canberra:

---

67 This phrase referred to anyone who sympathised with American concerns or worked within American cultural spheres.
68 Martin, 2012.
69 Martin, 2012.
70 Martin, 1989.

> By the time I left Adelaide I was pretty pissed off. I was looking for something that wasn't partisan, that was actually about fostering artistic practice and emerging artists, because I knew, as a fairly young artist myself, how difficult it was to bang your head against establishment walls. It still is, but it was particularly hard then.[71]

Martin and Boynes arrived in a Canberra that was 'a breath of fresh air', a sentiment that echoed Sellbach's feelings about his move to Canberra representing 'a fresh start'.[72] Martin's national reputation was on the rise and she was actively seeking a bipartisan and open forum within which to operate.[73] In 2012, she recalled that the move to Canberra signified:

> a clean slate because although people like Humphrey McQueen[74] for example had preconceptions about who Robert and I might be, in fact it was tremendously liberating to get over here and be able to paint without being criticised about not making political art. I'd come from a pretty tough ideological environment where every colour and every word and so on was analysed. If it wasn't approved by the rank and file of Chrysler and GMH [General Motors Holden] then you weren't allowed to do it. So yes it was really liberating coming to Canberra where you could reinvent the wheel a little bit.[75]

Martin's Adelaide experiences had a significant effect on the students under her tutelage in the Printmaking Workshop. When tasked with setting up the workshop, she first pasted the walls, floor to ceiling, with political posters, demonstrating her experience of photo-screen printing in a live political context. Additionally, her knowledge of and connection to the feminist and women's art movements and her relative youth provided a real alternative to Schmeisser's more traditional and technically rigorous approach to printmaking and teaching.

---

71 Martin, 2012. Although this intense period of art-making from within a political collective and for the collective cause was over, Martin has continued to paint works that reflect on the plight of the worker and the degradation of the environment by corporations.
72 Quotes respectively: Martin, 1989; and, Agostino, 2009, p 27.
73 Grishin reviewed Martin's drawings in the CSA staff exhibition of May 1979 as 'increasingly more powerful and intense' ('Diverse exhibition united by standard of excellence', *Canberra Times*, 15 May 1979, p 15).
74 McQueen resigned from CSA on 1 February 1979 to take up a two-year Australia Council Literature Board Fellowship. He returned to Canberra in time to open BRG in April 1981.
75 Martin, 2012.

Martin's appointment constituted the first full-time appointment of a female at the art school for six years.[76] She was at least a decade younger than any of her male colleagues and, therefore, closer in age to many of her students. Included in the first undergraduate intake of 1978 were Alder, Ford, Ayres, Morrow, Denton, Cassie Moulen, Nick Cosgrove and Di Wells. Church entered Photo Media in 1979 and, in the same year, Kath Walters enrolled in the Print Workshop.[77] Having completed a semester of Foundation Studies (later Core Studies), these radicalised, hippie-leaning, feminist, activist students, aged in their early 20s, were hungry and open to the idea of art as a socially useful vehicle. Martin was ideally suited to inspire and support their particular social agenda.[78]

With such vastly different backgrounds and trajectories of learning and teaching, it was inevitable that Schmeisser and Martin soon found themselves at odds, particularly with the concept of the value of the alternative within the student body and with the academic values placed on various students' work. As Martin noted: 'Jorg couldn't get it. He didn't understand my anti-establishmentness or that within rebellion and difference you could find immense creativity'.[79] Martin recognised the importance of the work being produced by students such as Denton, Moulen, Alder, Church, Ford and Ayres, and was determined to support and nurture their talents. 'I argued about the assessment of nearly every one of those students who was special to me'; it was 'a battle the whole time I was in printmaking … assessment was difficult; it needed a sympathetic outside examiner to understand the feminist, gay, Asian, student body'. In the end, Schmeisser and Martin 'came to a truce' and, with the support of students, essentially divided up the classes; the radicalised group of hippie firebrands came under the exclusive mentorship of Martin.[80]

---

76   Since Gillian Mann in 1972 (who, in addition to other contributions to the arts in Canberra, developed the printmaking curriculum for CSA) and Pat Harry, also in 1972, in painting.
77   Church remembers Walters as 'really the key person … [she] taught me screen-printing and she later became my partner in crime in Melbourne' (Church, 2012).
78   Martin's late-night experiences in the print room of the SA SOA were mirrored by the early 1980s cohort in Canberra. Printmakers whose work responded more to contemporary social concerns than to art orthodoxy were generally less inclined to play by the rules. Church recalled, 'I think the best times I had at the art school were when I used to break in at night and screen-print … doing experiments … printing on plastic and that was really lovely' (Church, 2012).
79   Martin, 2012.
80   Martin, 2012.

This informal arrangement didn't close the workshop to any student. There are many students from that time, including Canberra printmakers Julie Bradley, Dianne Fogwell and Ben Taylor, whose long careers benefited enormously from Schmeisser's rigorous training. Nor was Martin's tutelage any less rigorous. But it is arguably true that the energetic and understanding support extended by Martin impacted positively on the group of students who went on to form Megalo and BRG.[81]

This support was not limited to in-school experiences. Martin provided additional opportunities for her students to make art outside art school that encouraged the rise of the underground printmaking culture whose apogee was the establishment of Megalo by Alder and her fellow printmakers in 1980. Martin had shipped her Adelaide print studio to her new home in Queanbeyan and it became a focal point for that first group of students. She recalls that:

> In the second part of that first year when I went into printmaking [that group of students] all sort of became [friends]. They'd come out and do a bit of printing there because I had a full studio I'd brought over from Adelaide, racks and one arm bandit and dark room [which] I'd set up in Queanbeyan in the double garage.[82]

Later in that year, a pregnant Martin and Boynes moved their household from Queanbeyan to Canberra. Martin recalls the moving of her own print workshop to Gorman House:

> Alison and Paul and Mark and Julia and so on helped me move and [in 1982] we set up ACME Ink at Gorman House.[83] We rented those 4 little rooms there – one was the layout room, one was the office, one was the printing room and the other was the dark room. I'd pay the rent and, in exchange for helping print my work, they'd use the facilities. I didn't do a lot of printing at that stage – a couple of editions a year – and they'd print that work for me. So it was at that stage that we did things like *True Bird Grit*.[84]

---

81 By April 1981, Alder and her core group had set up BRG. Martin saw the gallery as 'an important way of developing the emerging artists – I did participate in a few shows there but it wasn't fundamental to my survival. I mean there was nothing here when we first came. Abraxas Gallery had just folded and the National Gallery wasn't open. There was just so little happening so it was great to have somewhere that became a focus' (Martin, 2012).
82 Martin, 2012.
83 For which Roger Butler did the plumbing!
84 Martin, 2012.

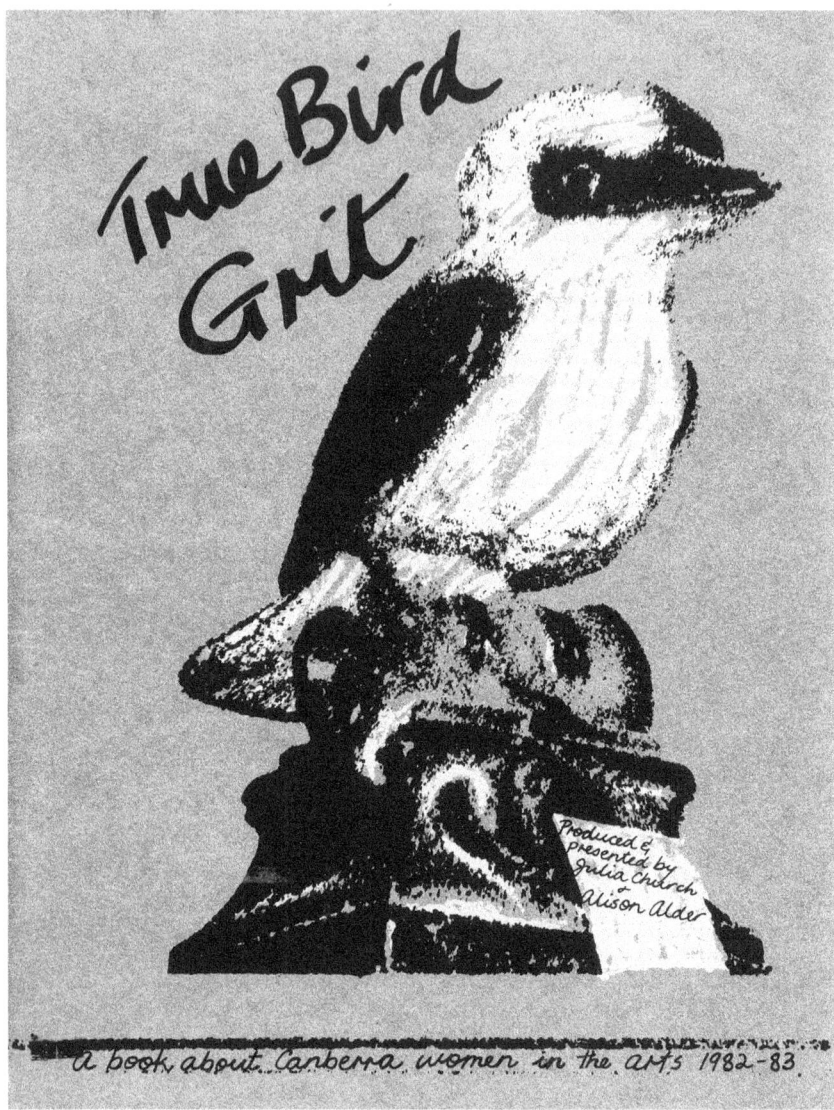

Figure 12. Alison Alder and Julia Church, *True bird grit*, book cover
Source. Photographer: Rob Little, reprinted with permission

Alder and Church printed *True bird grit* in 1982 at ACME Ink, and its production pulled together a diverse group of women working in multiple cross–art forms throughout Canberra. Martin remembers it as 'quite a funny document, really, and it was in response to looking at Canberra and thinking, "Well, where are the women artists?"'[85] Having already experienced the social and artistically nurturing value of a women's art group in Adelaide, Martin looked for evidence of a women's art movement when she first arrived in Canberra and established that there wasn't one:

> but there were a couple of women who were interested. There was Barbara Campbell the American feminist artist, who'd been friends with people like Nancy Spero and Lucy Lippard and she'd come straight from that [milieu] to Canberra. Also Karilyn Brown[86] came to Canberra around that time.[87]

Martin's contribution to the development of contemporary art in the region extended beyond the teaching experiences enjoyed by consecutive years of students during the period from 1978 until 2002, when, although she remained at CSA, she left the workshop.[88] Her sociopolitical conscience and knowledge and her involvement with current political thought were powerful motivating factors in the development of the political stance of that first group of students who went on to form Megalo and BRG. Her strong leadership likewise enabled enduring friendships between students, linked as they were by common ideas and burgeoning political awareness. Later, many of those who returned to or arrived in Canberra to teach at CSA, such as Toni Robertson and Nigel Lendon, applied for their roles with Martin's encouragement.

---

85 Martin, 2012.
86 Towards the end of 1982, Brown acted as temporary coordinator of BRG and was instrumental in mobilising the nationwide campaign for free admission to the National Gallery (see Chapter 2).
87 Martin, 2012.
88 Martin left the workshop in 2002 (although not the CSA) over increasing health and safety concerns regarding the effects of printing chemicals. The school later converted the workshop to use water-based inks (Agostino, 2009, p 26).

Ingo Kleinert and 3 Acts

It is timely at this point to highlight the tremendous contribution made by the CSA's Ingo Kleinert, who took early steps to illuminate the national contemporary scene for students, directing a series of three performance art festivals *ACT 1* (1978), *ACT 2* (1980), and *ACT 3* (1982).[89]

Kleinert (b 1941) migrated to Australia from Germany in 1949 and studied art at Caulfield Technical College and Melbourne Teachers' College. Dividing his time between Europe and Australia from the late 1960s to 1975, in June 1976 he was appointed to the Visual Communication Workshop in the newly independent CSA and he arrived in Canberra, from Adelaide, at the beginning of 1977.

The artists who coalesced around Adelaide's Experimental Art Foundation (EAF), which was established by Donald Brook in 1974, were working at the forefront of performance and experimental art in Australia in the last half of the 1970s. Kleinert's strong philosophical connections to Adelaide's experimental art scene were exemplified in *ACT 1: recent and experimental Australian art* in which half of the 22 artists were from the city, including Noel Sheridan, inaugural president of the EAF.[90]

A modest grant of $2,500 from the Australia Council and the ACT division of the Arts Council, plus a $1,000 in-kind administrative budget from the latter, supported the one-week festival. The majority of performances were held in the incomplete arts centre at ANU, 'a mass of brick spaces of varying sizes'.[91]

Joan Kerr, in one of the first Canberra art reviews in a national arts magazine, favourably reviewed *ACT 1* for *Art and Australia*, writing that 'national participation made [a] sense of common purpose comprehensible and gave greater strength to the individual works. For both participants and viewers it seemed an experience worth building on'.[92]

---

89   *ACT 1*: 4–17 November 1978, included 22 artists and a budget of $3,500; *ACT 2*: 18–20 April 1980, 41 artists, 60 performances, budget $8,000 ($4,000 from the Visual Arts Board (VAB), $2,000 from the Department of the Capital Territory (DCT), and $2,000 ($1,000 in kind) from the Arts Council (ACT division)); *ACT 3*, 8–10 October 1982, 10 invited artists, VAB funded. Kleinert's wife, Sylvia Kleinert, assisted him, as did workshop lecturer John Reid, from *ACT 2* on.
90   Artists included: Jim Cowley, John Davis, John Fisher, Marr Grounds, Ian Hamilton, Leigh Hobba, Liz Honybun, David Kerr, Richard and Pat Larter, Kevin Mortensen, John Nixon, Jillian Orr, Mike Parr, Bob Ramsay, Lesley Savage, Noel Sheridan, Terry Smith, Richard Tipping, Tony Twigg, Ken Unsworth, Donald Walters, Arthur Wicks.
91   Joan Kerr, '*Act 1*', *Art & Australia*, 16, 4, 1979, p 320.
92   Kerr, 1979, p 321.

The catalogue for *ACT 1* documents a pivotal moment in performance art in Australia. Internationally and at home, performance art had been circling the margins of contemporary art practice from the early 1970s. This was made explicit in the catalogue's title page, which defined works as 'innovative by operating on grounds not previously tested by time and general public acceptance'.[93] The catalogue documented the festival's performances and also included a trail of letters from artists, artist call-outs, support requests, responses from the Arts Council (ACT) and two essays on contemporary performance arts practice from Terry Smith and Paul McGillick.

The 1978 festival occurred two years before Canberra's poster and print makers came together under Megalo International Screenprint Collective and three years before the establishment of BRG. While it's difficult to quantify the effects that these three festivals had on emerging local contemporary arts practitioners, Kerr, alert to the creative power of visual memory, wrote of *ACT 1* that 'what stayed in the mind after the festival had ended was a series of images'.[94] Importantly, generous institutional support was on display; the support of the art school by ANU played out in the provision of spaces; the National Gallery's Daniel Thomas chaired an open panel, and Mollison extended moral and practical support; and the CSA, under Sellbach, gave unqualified support to Kleinert's endeavour. The exposure to national practitioners; the growing links between Adelaide and Canberra, which continued through the 1970s and 1980s with the arrival of Martin, Boynes, and other Adelaide artists; the fertile tensions emanating from national capital politics; and the exposure to incipient art forms, all contributed to a climate of possibility and open-ended practice.

This institutional support continued to play out through the late 1970s and early 1980s; however, other requirements for the flourishing of a contemporary arts practice were yet to evolve, and appropriate exhibition spaces and arts sector development funds were in short supply. In 1982, as *ACT 3* coincided with the opening of the National Gallery, Kleinert retired from festival production in order to concentrate on an increased teaching load and his own creative work. By then, performance

---

93 *Act 1: an exhibition of performance and participatory art*, exhibition catalogue, np.
94 Kerr, 1979, p 320.

art was being incorporated into the lexicon of contemporary practice internationally and nationally, and both Megalo and BRG had been established in the nation's capital.[95]

The BRG collective, through the making and exhibition of posters, was committed to local, national and international artistic political expression. Many of the issues expressed in the work of its members were indivisibly yoked to feminism. BRG artists were developing their local practice within the national capital at the heart of federal politics, but were mentored by older women artists with lived experiences of using art as a political tool, and were beneficiaries of the many advances for local women achieved since 1970 by CWL's second-wave feminist activism. It is fair to conclude that, by 1983, these young artists were exceptionally politically aware. How, then, to explain the rejection of a feminist poster titled *Slut*, made by Melbourne artist Catriona Holyoake in 1983 and heralding feminism's approaching third wave, that was offered to the BRG collective for sale? This fascinating and subtle conundrum, in which highly politically aware artists showed themselves to be out of touch with the earliest expressions of third-wave feminism that were burgeoning in Melbourne and other major centres, indicates that emerging changes in feminist theories and representations took hold differently in Canberra.[96]

---

95 As well as the aforementioned articles and catalogue, for more on these three festivals see: Anne Sanders, 'ACT 1, 2 & 3: Canberra's national performance art festivals' (*Art Monthly Australia*, 259, 2013, pp 51–54) and, Ingo Kleinert, '*Act 2*: for the record' (*Art Network*, 2, 1980, p 45).

96 First-wave feminism arose during the nineteenth century and continued into the early twentieth century. Its primary concerns – evidenced through the suffrage movements in the United States, the United Kingdom, Australia and New Zealand – centred around political equality for women, including the right to vote, the right to stand as candidates in elections, and rights around marriage and children. From 1949, a Marxist critique of capitalism as a root cause of women's inequality entered the discourse and remained a driving factor throughout second-wave feminism. Second-wave feminism arose in the United States from the early 1960s. It built on the political gains of first-wave feminism in that it sought to identify and remove cultural inequalities that the feminist movement recognised as barriers to full political equality. It was intrinsically linked with the women's liberation movement and it used cross-national consciousness-raising meetings to proselytise its aims. These disavowed all forms of patriarchy, including the uneven representation of women artists in museums and art galleries and issues around equality of career choice, remuneration and working conditions and physical and sexual safety for women and children. The concerns of third-wave feminism, made visible in posters from the early 1980s, arose as a sociopolitical movement during the early 1990s in the United States and co-exists to the present day with second-wave feminism. It is seen as a somewhat reactive movement to second-wave feminism's insistence on equalising sexual difference between men and women and it seeks to reclaim and celebrate women's differing sexuality. It includes a diversity of theories and a fluid approach to gender (see Cathia Jenainati and Judy Groves (eds), *Introducing feminism* (London, Icon Books, 2010); Rozsika Parker and Griselda Pollock, *Framing feminism: art and the women's movement, 1970–1985* (Kitchener, Canada, Pandora Press, 1987); Laura Meyer with Faith Wilding, 'Collaboration and conflict in the Fresno Feminist Art Program: an experiment in feminist pedagogy' (*N.paradoxa*, July 2010, vol 26)).

A close reading of the circumstances in Canberra and in Melbourne surrounding the rejection of *Slut* considers these emerging differences between second- and third-wave feminist representations of women. Further explaining why these young artists were so preoccupied with feminist concerns, are the following stories of the contrasting journeys to Canberra of Australia's foremost feminist artist Vivienne Binns and early BRG member Cherylynn Holmes. Their journeys and impacts, different again to that of Martin's, contextualise the various factors within the women's movement that marked this period of contemporary art development in Canberra.

Feminist politics and art: intersections

The young male and female students and activists who founded BRG were diverse but interconnected people engaged in various cultural and social justice organisations and collectives; as such, they could not help but be radically politicised. Activists were visible within a relatively small Canberra population that grew from around 140,000 in 1970 to around 235,000 by 1983. Additionally, they were agitating at the heart of political and judicial decision-making in Australia, which drew feminist activists from around the country at various times and increased both the sense of urgency and the perceived effectiveness of political actions.[97] BRG founders and early supporters, largely born around 1960, were beneficiaries of the gains won by second-wave feminists who had been active internationally, including in the United States from the late 1960s and in Australia since 1970. The ACT chapter of the Women's Liberation Movement, CWL, was formed in June 1970. Founding member Ward remembered that, in March/April 1970, she invited Sydney feminist Lyndall Ryan to Canberra:

---

97 For example, International Women's Day was revived on 8 March 1972. In 1973 women from around Australia set up a Tent Embassy outside Parliament House for three months in the lead up to and during the Lamb–McKenzie Private Members Anti-abortion Bill. In 1973, Ward, Haley, Daphne Gollan and Susan Magarey from CWL organised a national conference on feminist theory at Mt Beauty in Victoria (the 'Theory' very much tongue in cheek). International Women's Year in 1975 brought two conferences to Canberra: the *Women and politics national conference*, organised by Elizabeth Reid (who was appointed Whitlam's women's adviser in 1973), was held at ANU and the *Anarchist feminist conference* (again, organised by CWL). Some of the women who were instrumental in CWL and Women's Electoral Lobby (ACT) were Carol Ambrus, Sara Dowse, Gollan, Haley, Beryl Henderson, Magarey, Drusilla Modjeska, Gail Radford, Reid, Julia Ryan and Ward.

> She said 'Yes' and she and Coonie Sandford – an Australian woman who had been living in the US and later went back there – came here and spoke to us on a Saturday afternoon. The women there that day agreed to meet on Wednesday night and met every week for six years.[98]

Between 1970 and 1980, Australian women gained significant ground in the battle for equality on many fronts, with escalating gains made between 1972 and 1975 as a result of the swift implementation of useful legislation and funding by the Labor government under Gough Whitlam. In Canberra, the highly effective Women's Electoral Lobby (WEL) ACT (established 1972) made successful submissions to government that had far-reaching consequences. In the same year the Aboriginal Tent Embassy was founded and became a nationally recognised space for Indigenous political lobbying. WEL ACT and CWL supported Pat Eaton, the first Indigenous candidate, to stand (unsuccessfully) for federal parliament in 1972 as an independent candidate on women's and children's issues. In Canberra, women's services that received some level of government funding as a result of local lobbying included the Canberra Women's Refuge in 1975, followed in 1976 by the Rape Crisis Centre.[99] BRG opened in April 1981, in the same month in which women commemorating the rape of women in war first marched in Canberra's Anzac Day Parade and were arrested for doing so. Arguably, Canberra, from 1972, could be seen as operating at the cutting edge of political feminism in Australia.[100]

---

98 Biff Ward, email to the author, 11 July 2016.
99 Elsie House, Sydney's Women's Refuge, opened in Sydney in 1974. The Canberra Women's Refuge was opened on International Women's Day, 8 March 1975.
100 'Over its history as the national capital Canberra has witnessed a distinctive phenomenon: the capacity of activist women – many of them also public servants – to work within governmental structures to achieve broad-ranging improvements to the lives of women and families in Canberra and across Australia' (Roslyn Russell, 'Activists', *From Lady Denman to Katy Gallagher: a century of women's contributions to Canberra*, 21 February 2013, www.womenaustralia.info/exhib/ldkg/activists.html, accessed 15 August 2014).

4. BITUMEN RIVER GALLERY

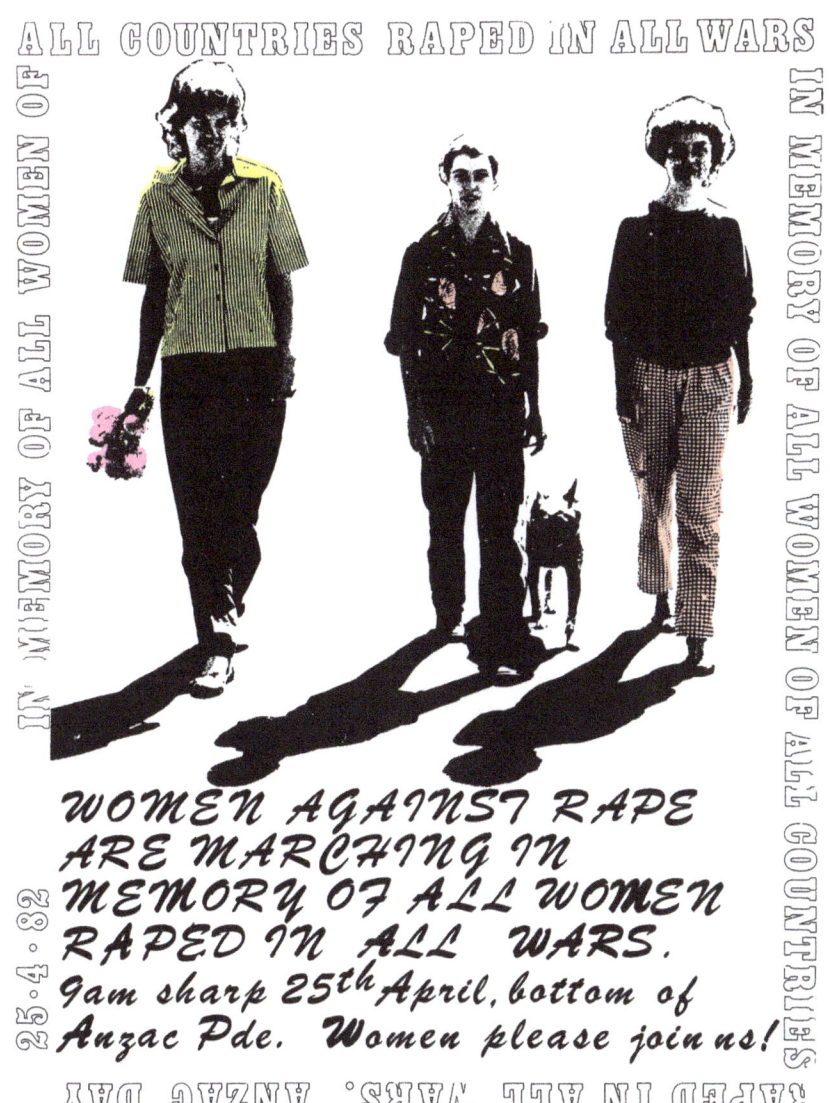

Figure 13. *Women against rape march*, poster, April 1982
Source. Printed by Megalo, Megalo poster archive, reprinted with permission

Cherylynn Holmes and the utopian ideal

In the late 1960s in Australia, the utopian ideal found political expression through the work of Jim Cairns, Labor Member for Yarra (1955–69) and Lalor (1969–77), and, briefly, deputy prime minister in the Whitlam government. He drove a relentless course for change, firstly as a spearhead of the anti-Vietnam protest movement and then as a leader of the countercultural movement. As the former, after several years of anti-war agitation, Cairns led an anti–Vietnam War street march in Melbourne in 1970 that attracted 100,000 peaceful protesters. Although he lost his position as deputy prime minister by early 1975, he continued to champion a countercultural philosophy for the rest of his life. In December 1976, prior to his resignation from politics, Cairns and his colleague Junie Morosi organised the first Down to Earth ConFest at the Cotter River Recreation Reserve,[101] just south of Canberra. It attracted 10,000 to 15,000 people. Holmes, a vigorous early BRG collective member and regular exhibitor who was then living in Kurrajong Heights in the Blue Mountains, came to Canberra for the first time in 1976 to attend the festival and recalls that 'everyone was very excited about it'.[102]

Canberra provided a haven and a home for Holmes, who came to CSA in 1979 aged 34. Her personal journey is different to those in the student cohort who were in their early twenties, and it stands in contrast to Martin's politicised, unionised background. Holmes exemplifies the generation of women for whom the women's liberation movement provided support and for whom art provided solace and inspiration. Because the story of her journey to CSA encapsulates the experience of a particular and large group of women of similar ages and from similar backgrounds, I quote her at length:

> I of course read *The female eunuch*. I was in a rather exploitative marriage in my twenties and left that in my thirties and went to live up in Northern NSW. I knew I was capable of a lot more than what I'd been indoctrinated as and I knew the pathway was through art. I had feminist friends in Sydney. [There was] a loose collection of women. We'd have dinner parties or go to restaurants. I read the *Sydney Morning Herald* advertisement for

---

101 ConFest was a manifestation of the Down to Earth Movement which Morosi and Cairns founded after Cairns lost his ministerial position in the Whitlam government and before his resignation from parliament. The movement folded in 1979.
102 Cherylynn Holmes, interview with the author, 30 August 2012.

> the art school and applied and got the train down to Canberra for the interview. On the way back out of town, I realised that one of my dearest friends from that first encounter [the Down to Earth ConFest in 1976] was working at the NGA and he said 'You're not getting on that train. Stay in Canberra overnight and I'll fly you back tomorrow'. He took me to dinner at Santa Lucia and we dined with Rosalie Gascoigne and her daughter. And then we went to a Vasarely exhibition in the Albert Hall. He was flying off next morning to collect some work from somewhere and a car picked us up in the morning and took us to the airport and we took separate planes. It was a magical journey to Canberra. [When I arrived to begin at CSA] I stayed with my sister for a week and somehow got into a group house briefly and then got a government house in O'Connor.[103]

This sympathetic environment was enhanced by the development of Ainslie Village. Opened as a military barracks during World War II, it provided accommodation for Canberra's migrant worker population after 1945 and, later, interim accommodation for migrants. From 1976 to 1980 the hostel, managed by private contractors and the DCT, provided short-term housing for migrants and those on low incomes. By 1980, years of neglect meant that buildings were in disrepair and the Village had gained a reputation for pervasive violence; those most in need were reluctant to accept emergency accommodation there. Jobless Action, whose initial support had enabled the creation of both Megalo and BRG, submitted to the DCT a joint proposal with the Salvation Army, St Vincent de Paul Society and Village residents to establish an incorporated body composed of residents and community organisations to manage the Village. The proposal was accepted and shortly thereafter, control of the Village passed to the new body. Jobless Action members comprised community workers, activists and artists, and an early decision was taken to set up Megalo in the Village.

When Megalo set up its rudimentary workshop at Ainslie Village, the anti-aesthetic ethos – which Hal Foster has defined as 'a will to grasp the present nexus of culture and politics and to affirm a practice resistant both to academic modernism and political reaction' – began to flower

---

103 Holmes, 2012. Holmes revealed that her friend and local wit Dennis Trigg, in the true spirit of the countercultural movement, named O'Connor as the Peoples Republic of O'Connor by which name it is still fondly known by many Canberrans.

collectively outside of CSA.[104] For a brief moment in the history of the village, the influence of European and Australian countercultural utopias manifested in a collective aesthetic. It was realised through the planting of common food gardens and particularly through the presence of a functioning creative workshop whose output was intrinsically tied to the concerns, both recreational and sociopolitical, of the Canberran subculture to which Megalo members belonged.

The cohort responsible for the birth of Megalo/BRG were themselves in an interstitial generational divide; the anti–Vietnam War protests, which attracted hundreds of thousands of protesters nationally and galvanised the previous generation, were replaced with a creeping disempowerment of a significant proportion of the Australian population. This was particularly obvious within the homogenised subcultural population in Canberra of which these young artist/activists were a part.

Coupled with their desire to make art that was recognised outside of the closed gallery system was this renewed ethos that borrowed from the 1968 European student uprisings and was influenced by the countercultural movement, the women's liberation movement, and locally rising levels of poverty and unemployment. This ethos stimulated their desire to make art that was 'useful, [art] that people needed. It was anti-individualist in that sense, anti-aesthetic in many ways and about empowering people'.[105]

In spite of the many serious concerns that were foregrounded through prints and posters, community action for these activist artists/printmakers was often actively based in light-hearted social engagement and, for Church and others, Megalo and BRG both provided 'another place to play':

> we had so much energy ... [S]ocially there was a lot of brainstorming. We were fortunate to be alive at a time when we really felt like we could do anything that we turned our hands to. And that, I suppose, was a little bit like what was happening in '68. It was an exciting time.[106]

Social play was boldly in evidence at the 1985 event *Off the beach*, for which the art deco environs of the Manuka Pool provided the frame for costumes constructed to theme by collective members (see Figures 14 and 15).

---

104 Hal Foster, 'Postmodernism: a preface', in *The anti-aesthetic: essays on postmodern culture*, Washington, Bay Press, 1983, p xv.
105 Church, 2012.
106 Church, 2012.

4. BITUMEN RIVER GALLERY

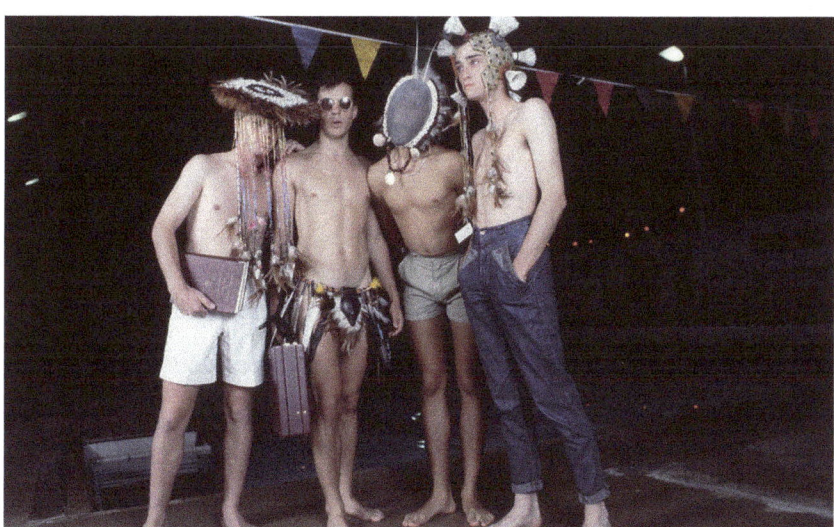

Figure 14. Collective members in costume for *Off the beach*, 27 February – 17 March 1985, 23 February 1985
Source. CCAS image archive, reproduced with permission

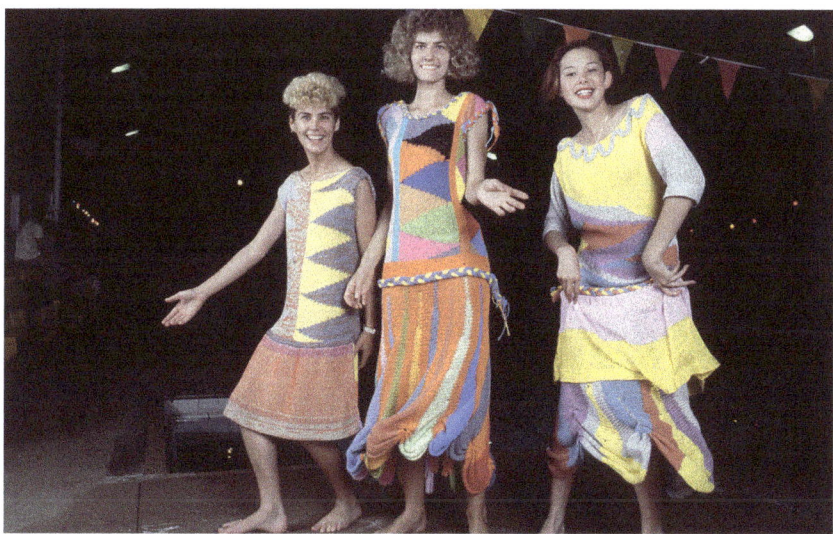

Figure 15. Collective members in costume for *Off the beach*, 27 February – 17 March 1985, 23 February 1985
Source. CCAS image archive, reproduced with permission

By the early 1980s, Australians were feeling the effects of the conservative Liberal government under Malcolm Fraser. Razor gangs slashed spending on women's health and social services and, consequently, on families and the unemployed; the changed policies bit deeply into previous gains. In 1981, the Single Women's Shelter Collective was established to push for single women's crisis accommodation and, after several years of intense negotiation and following high-profile community actions including squatting, the government provided some funding to establish the Toora Single Women's Shelter in 1983, followed by the Incest Centre in 1984.[107] The decrease in government support through the Fraser years led to an increase in radical expressions of the need for that support for women's services; in Canberra and elsewhere in Australia, poster makers played a pivotal role in getting these messages out into the public domain.[108]

Contributing to the charged political environment that came with living and working in the national capital, were older feminist women students and lecturers who arrived at CSA from other cities. They included Anne Morris who, like Binns, was an early contributor to community arts. Morris arrived at CSA in 1982 and positively influenced a number of students in the printmaking and photomedia workshops, including Church and Holmes. Holmes recalls travelling to Sydney with Morris to attend meetings for the Women's Art Register (the first of which Martin also attended), and the 1982 Women and Arts Festival: 'We thought, "Hey, there's nothing like this in Canberra", so we came back and organised an exhibition'.[109] The ACG, at that time in the Wales Centre on London Circuit, hosted this exhibition of work by 28 local women artists, titled *The first Super Doreen show*, which Holmes curated.

---

107 See, Elena Roseman, 'Talking like a Toora woman: the Herstory of Toora Women Inc', Toora Women Inc, Canberra, 2004, and 'From Lady Denman to Katy Gallagher: a century of woman's contribution to Canberra', www.womenaustralia.info/exhib/ldkg/. Conversations with Lee Collins, who was an active member of 2xx Community Radio and a member of the young 'punk' generation of lesbian feminists active in Canberra from the early 1980s, were revealing and useful.
108 Many of the posters in BRG's first exhibition carried messages of need for women's services. Additionally, in Canberra during 1972 and 1973, the posters printed by members of CWL were entirely concerned with women's issues (Ward, quoted in Julia Ryan, unpublished notes from 'Canberra Women's Liberation: main focus: 1970–75', talk, U3A Australian History, June 2012, email to the author, 20 June 2016).
109 Holmes, 2012.

4. BITUMEN RIVER GALLERY

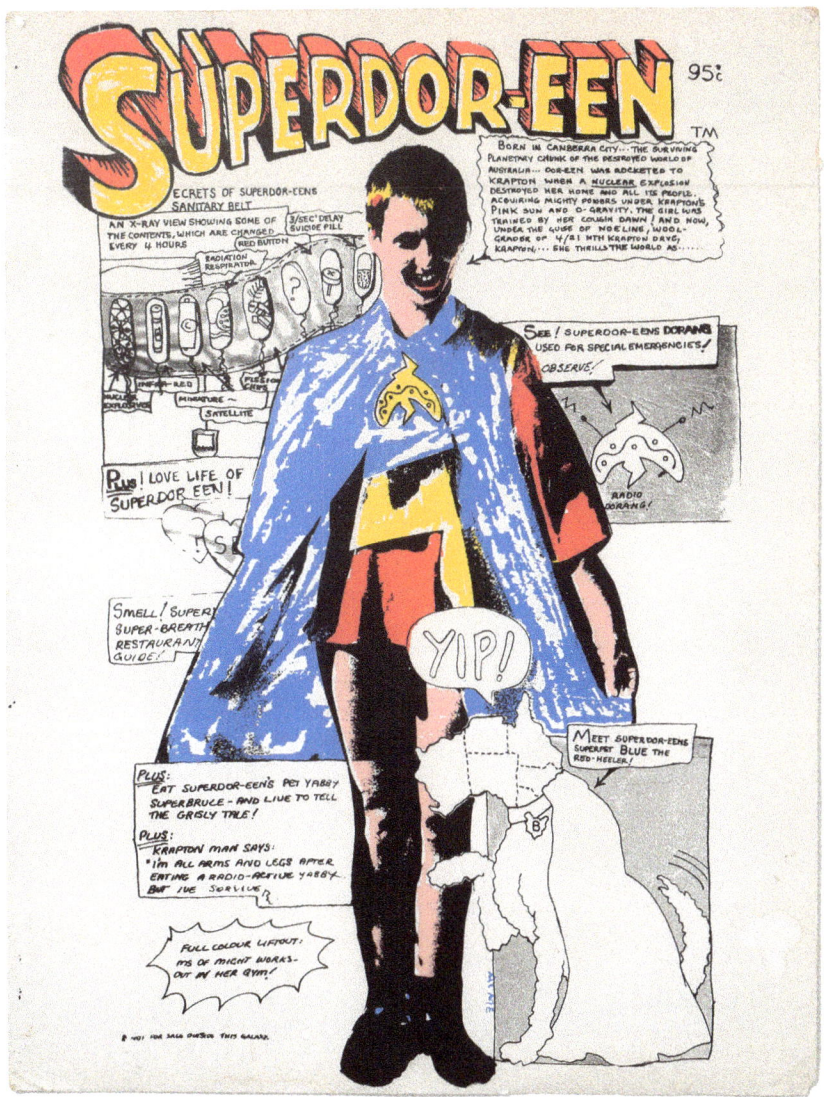

Figure 16. Julia Church, *Super Doreen*, 1982, poster, 102 x 76 cm
Source. Photographer: Brenton McGeachie. Private collection, reproduced with permission

Church, who created the cartoon character *Super Doreen* in early 1981 (see Figure 16), remembers Morris as:

> an inspiring figure. She had already been working in community arts before us and making a living out of it. She was incredibly well-organised but also an extraordinarily open and generous person with her knowledge and ideas, and very encouraging of everybody.[110]

Toni Robertson joined Martin in the Printmaking Workshop between 1982 and 1985. Robertson was an early member of the Earthworks Poster Collective at the Tin Sheds, and also a founder of the Sydney Women's Art Movement. Her presence in Canberra ensured that contemporary politics continued to be a focus at CSA and also encouraged more frequent visits from her colleague Binns.

Vivienne Binns

Binns' influence in the early 1980s on the burgeoning arts community in Canberra was subtle, but she was already disposed to view Canberra as a future home, eventually relocating in 1994 from the Blue Mountains to take up a position at CSA as lecturer in foundation studies, painting, sculpture and theory. She had in fact 'been up and down to Canberra'[111] since her 1975 and 1976 exhibitions at Fantasia and Abraxas Galleries respectively:

> Even with the women's art movement, back in the seventies when we formed groups in Sydney, we visited other states, searching out women artists. We'd made contact [in Canberra with] people like Rosalie Gascoigne and so on and I'd had fleeting visits with the place through the community arts, enough that I knew there was theatre and arts and the poster [movement]. There have always been lively activities and projects going on ... I always knew there was a community [of women artists].[112]

Canberra's strong community arts focus, recognised by Binns in the 1970s, was a clear reason for her growing interest in the city. By the time she settled permanently in Canberra, her experiences in this area assisted in maintaining the political focus of CSA students throughout the 1990s and 2000s.

---

110 Church, 2012.
111 Vivienne Binns, interview with the author, 26 February 2012.
112 Binns, 2012.

Binns' 'explosive' debut 1967 exhibition at Watters Gallery in Sydney is now generally seen as anticipating the rise of 1970s feminist art in Australia.[113] By the early 1970s, her fascination with craft and feminism was coalescing into what would become more than a decade of fertile engagement with community arts in both urban and rural women's communities, beginning with the travelling community arts project *Artsmobile* in 1972. Her best-known project from the period is *Mothers' memories others' memories* (*MMOM*) (1979–81), which focused on creative expression in the lives of women in Sydney's Blacktown area. The benefits experienced by a wide range of women as a result of their involvement in *MMOM* – and *Full flight* (1981–83), which was enacted in central and far-west New South Wales – was recognised with Binns award of an Order of Australia medal in 1983 for services to art and craft.[114] She is acknowledged as a founding member of the Women's Art Movement, a pioneer of community arts practice, and an enduring and effective advocate for women artists. Illustrating the latter is the following extract from Binns' 1977 letter to the Craft Council of NSW:

> The argument for excellence in arts is hard to dispute and because of this it is itself excellent as a subterfuge to disguise other motives. It is used for instance to disguise embedded sexual discrimination in job selection at some art colleges. It can be used to disguise a situation which by means of special selection criteria fosters and nurtures the needs of a few in the name of 'high standards'. It can be the death knell of creativity in the widest sense and blind people to a narrow view of what art is. Our view is already heavily blinkered.[115]

---

113 Deborah Clark's use of the word 'explosive' reflects the response of contemporary critics for whom the sexual imagery of the works, particularly coming from a young female artist, was entirely unexpected. Clark writes that 'this show marked a key moment in the nascent Women's Art Movement' (Deborah Clark, 'The painting of Vivienne Binns', in Craig Judd (ed), *Vivienne Binns*, exhibition catalogue, Hobart, Tasmanian Museum and Art Gallery, 2006, p 8).
114 Of *Full flight*, Binns wrote, 'As an Artist in Community in a large predominantly rural area of 60,000 square miles and a population of 200,000, I travel from town to town in a caravan which has living quarters and a small work space. I stay for 2–4 months in each place and visit small isolated towns as well as cities in the area. I see my role in *Full Flight* as that of an art worker travelling the country getting to know other art workers with whom I share, and who share with me experience, knowledge, ideas, skills, work projects and friendships' (Maria Kunda, 'The artist, the community, the land', in Judd, 2006, p 20).
115 Penny Peckham, 'Vivienne Binns biography', in Judd, 2012, pp 30–41.

Binns agreed with Martin's earlier assessment of Canberra as 'a breath of fresh air'. In 1993, at the tail end of a Keating Fellowship, Binns travelled again to Canberra to take up a residency in the Painting Workshop at CSA and later explained:

> I just found the CSA such a fabulous place by comparison to the politics and unpleasantness of the other major cities like Sydney and Melbourne where I might look for work [that] I sort of pestered them to give me a job. I knew there were people who were really happy to have me coming there.[116]

Canberra, therefore, was seen to be free of the pervasive art world politics – as identified by Sellbach, Martin and Binns – that characterised life in the southern Australian capitals from which these important practitioners came.[117]

Slut

In the middle of 1983, Alder, on behalf of the BRG collective, took receipt of a consignment of works on paper from the Jill Posters collective in Melbourne. Among them was *Slut*. Tellingly, it would prove to be the only poster ever rejected by the collective. *Slut*, now in the print collection at the National Gallery, differs markedly in two key respects from other posters in the gallery's collection from the period of 1983/84.[118] Firstly, it is printed on fine art paper in only two colours, blue and red. Secondly, and most significantly, the central figure, a woman, has long red hair and wears a red dress and red stiletto shoes. A thought bubble reads 'I won't see you in Paradise'. At the bottom right of the poster, a small clock shows five minutes to midnight; the text on the left of the clock face reads 'nuclear time'. Entering from the centre left, beginning outside the poster frame, is a quick rendering of a cruise missile, pointing at the figure and bearing the word 'slut'. Finally, the figure is fully outlined with a cut line in black from the knees up and the written exhortation to 'cut here' (see Figure 17).

---

116 Binns, 2012.
117 Canberra is still noted for its warm, inclusive and supportive arts community, particularly the local organisations CCAS, CMAG, M16, Megalo, Photo-Access and ANCA.
118 Roger Butler purchased the *Slut* poster to add to the National Gallery's collection of posters from BRG, Jill Posters and other Australian printmaking collectives, including, from 1973, 'almost a complete collection' of the Earthworks Poster Collective (Roger Butler, quoted in 'Posters for posterity', *Canberra Times*, 4 September 1986, p 1s).

4. BITUMEN RIVER GALLERY

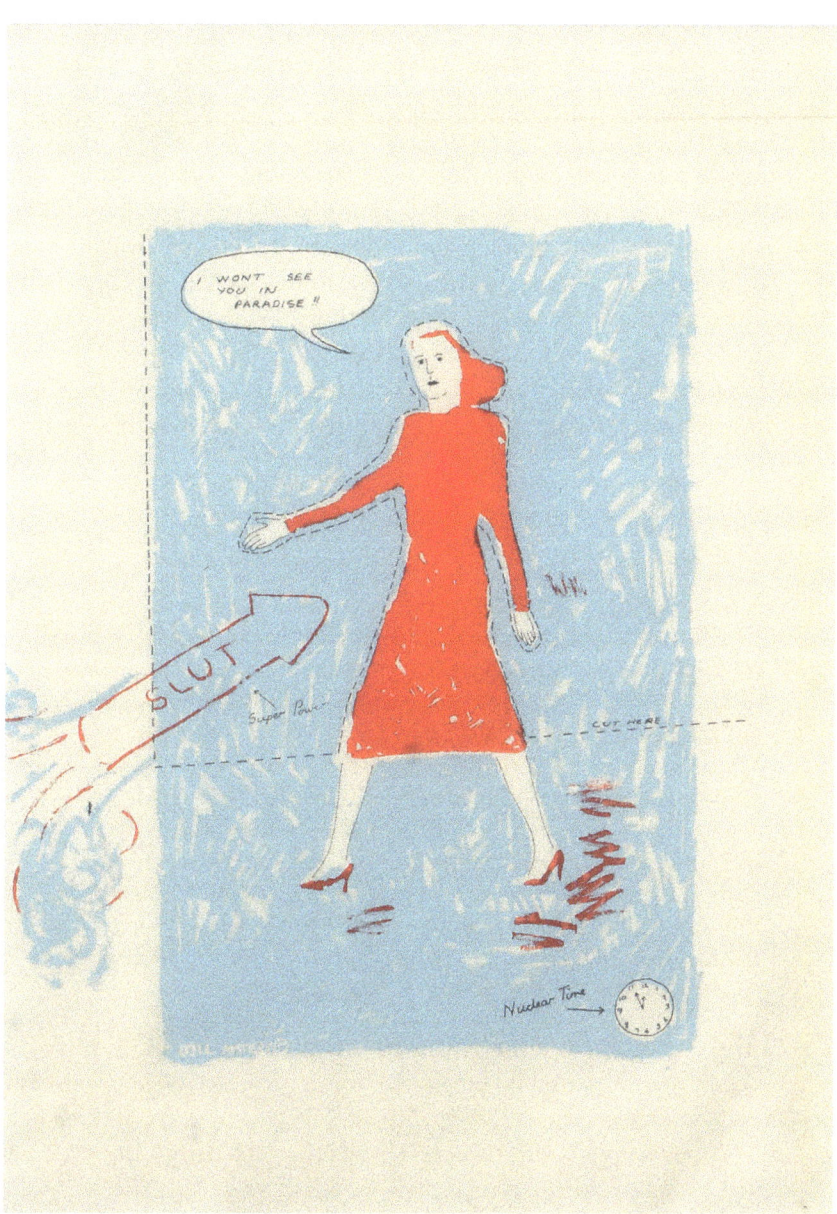

Figure 17. Catriona Holyoake, *I won't see you in paradise (slut)*, 1983, screen print, 100 x 80 cm
Source. Collection of the National Gallery of Australia. Photograph by Brenton McGeachie, CCAS image archive, reproduced with permission

Canberra's principal position as a fulcrum of political decision-making and social activism and as a nexus for the national expression of aspects of the women's liberation movement, among other social movements of the 1970s and 1980s, has been established. The strong feminist leanings of CSA student and graduate printmakers, Martin's role and the influences of community arts practitioners such as Binns and Morris, are clear. Given these facts, the 1983 rejection of *Slut* indicates that other factors were at play in Canberra's emerging contemporary arts scene. Among them was a continued emphasis on second-wave feminism, which Martin's Maoist political background may have subtly encouraged. Additionally, Canberra's status as a relatively isolated regional centre meant that collective members were less exposed to those early visual examples of third-wave feminism.

Alder's final day as coordinator of BRG was 11 August 1983. Her second-last letter, written on that day, was to the Jill Posters collective:

> Received your posters the other day and feel I must write to tell you that I don't feel the gallery can have the 'slut' poster in its racks. I realise that this poster has many intentions and that whoever did it hopefully meant to put across a message of 'super powers = penis [leads to] oppression of women'. However, visually that message is not clear and the poster puts across an extremely negative image. My main argument is that the woman is portrayed as a totally passive helpless victim. Personally I find this very offensive. Women must be made aware of the negative aspects of our society but at the same time as commenting on this oppression women must give other women positive models to act upon. I find that this is not the case in this instance. Please let me know what you think, and I look forward to hearing from you. Yours sincerely, Alison Alder for Bitumen River.[119]

On 24 November 1983, Colin Russell wrote to Jill Posters in his capacity as temporary coordinator. Having carried out a BRG stocktake of posters, postcards and books, Russell acknowledged receipt of three lots of five posters, and sought clarification as to whether the BRG commission should be added on to the poster price of $3.75 or deducted from it.[120] The letter also enclosed copies of *Slut* that Alder and Russell agreed could not be carried by BRG due to its 'ambiguity and its negative projection':

---

119 Alison Alder, letter to Jill Posters, 11 August 1983.
120 The reply from Jill Posters indicates that galleries in Melbourne added 25 per cent to take the retail price to $5.00. BRG had been adding 20 per cent on for a price of $4.50.

Also enclosed are posters that had been sent to us about three or four months ago. At that time Alison, who was the co-ordinator, sent a letter expressing her misgivings towards that poster and if it would be suitable for the gallery to have placed it in our racks, mainly for reasons of ambiguity and its negative projection. She had written with the intention of finding out how you felt and personally as a postermaker myself, I supported her on this point. Since we received no reply and a stocktake was under way, the collective, at a general meeting, decided that the 'slut' poster not be exhibited, and be returned to the Jillposters collective. I hope that you don't view this as a harsh action or that any prejudices against the <u>intended meaning</u> of the work are being enforced.[121]

A very informal note came back from Carole Wilson, a founding member of Jill Posters:

> Colin darling you are oh so formal, yes we are horrendously offended by the fact that you didn't display the 'slut' poster and we are planning to execute a subversive, terrorist action on Bitumen River Gallery and especially you.

The letter, succinctly displaying the ad hoc nature of the small Australian print collective, continued:

> Thank you for being so terribly tactful & polite – I'm usually the only one who reads Jill Posters mail anyway ... Jillposters couldn't possibly get itself together enough to write a reply to Alison's letter. Very strange collective we have lots of money & no one prints posters; we are given a free workshop & we give it back; etc, etc.[122]

Russell appended a note to the Jill Posters letter before filing: 'Ha Ha – personal friend not to be taken as a need for military armament! Colin'.

As already noted, the BRG collective determined at the outset that the only requirement for work to be accepted for exhibition was that it be non-sexist and non-racist. *Slut* was clearly non-racist and therefore Alder's reasons for rejecting the poster centred on constructions of female sexuality. Her objections to the poster – that it put across 'an extremely negative image'; that the woman 'was portrayed as a totally passive victim'; that she, Alder, personally found it 'very offensive'; and that 'women

---

121 Colin Russell, letter to Jill Posters, 24 November 1983. Original emphasis.
122 Carole [now known to be Carole Wilson], letter to Colin Russell, Tuesday (undated), 1983, CCAS archives.

[in this case, poster makers] must give other women positive models to act upon', which she felt this poster did not do – speak to the image of woman in second-wave feminism as constructed by issues of equality.

This construction eschewed references to femininity; beauty, inextricably linked to objectification, was to be avoided. The 1984 *Post-atomic card*, produced for the Campaign for International Co-operation and Disarmament, illustrates this type of representation of women in anti-nuclear posters. Printed in four colours, including a radioactive green/yellow, its two female workers are dressed in overalls and boots and wielding shovels, with a banner that reads 'Bury it Mac' (see Figure 18).[123]

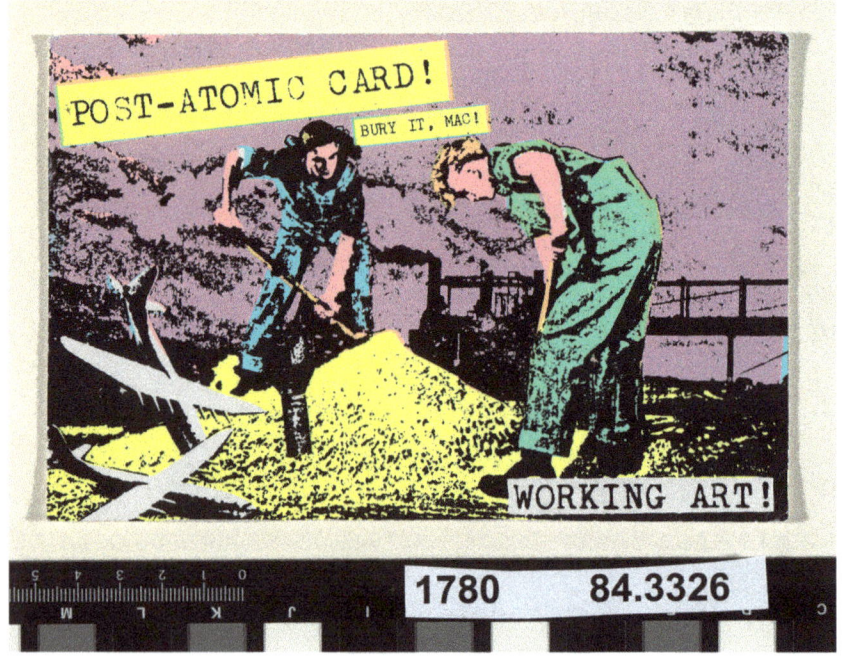

Figure 18. *Post-atomic card!: Working art!*, **colour postcard**
Source. Designed and printed by the Fallout Committee for the Post-atomic postcard show, 1984. Collection of the National Gallery of Australia, reproduced with permission

---

123 Anti-nuclear posters were produced at all poster-making collectives in the early 1980s, encouraging and encouraged by the Women's Peace Camp and protests at Pine Gap in the Northern Territory in 1983. 'Feminists in Australia pioneered new forms of activity in opposition to USA bases, uranium mining and the threat of nuclear war' (Joyce Stevens, 'The nineteen seventies and eighties continued', *A history of International Women's Day in words and images*, www.isis.aust.com/iwd/stevens/70s80s_3.htm, accessed 14 May 2012).

The blatant femininity of the *Slut* poster's protagonist – her long red hair, red dress and red stiletto shoes – was in stark opposition to these representations. Red was a colour still associated with female sexual promiscuity, with the term 'scarlet woman', and a general sense of moral laxity inherent in the potent combination of colour and stilettos. If Holyoake's woman had been wearing boots and overalls, the poster may have passed. But Alder was herself a second-wave feminist and the collective, inclined by virtue of political and social choices to walk the feminist talk, were unable to accept this construction of the feminine as anything other than a weak or 'passive' sexual stereotype.

The collective may also have been influenced by what Laura Meyer has identified as the 'heavy fire' that key feminist art strategies came under in the 1980s. The feminist art movement began with the Fresno Feminist Art Program at Fresno State College (now University) in California's San Joaquin Valley in 1970 under visiting artist Judy Chicago. Meyer identifies two of its main 'pedagogical artmaking strategies' as 'the quest for new kinds of female body imagery, or so-called cunt art' and the use of 'female media', which – under the rubric of 'women's work' – included performance art, photography, filmmaking, needlework, and the use of costume and make-up. Meyer posits that, by the 1980s, these formerly key strategies were seen to be negatively 'reinforc[ing] an essentialist [or in other words a collection of fixed traits] view of women'.[124] Despite the fact that words such as 'slut' and 'cunt' had gained widespread currency through the female art movement and the women's liberation movement of the 1970s, they nonetheless retained a seedy pejorative quality; the collective would have been hard-pressed not to identify the use of 'slut' in this instance as essentialising.

It was not until the early 1990s and the rise of 'lipstick feminism' that feminism and femininity were seen to cohabit, evidenced publicly through the use of make-up and the wearing of dresses and high heels. Additionally, the use of female-centric language such as 'slut' and 'cunt' was widely reclaimed by women in the 1990s as potent symbols of personal power.

---

124 Meyer with Wilding, 2010.

In Australia, the cyberfeminist[125] collective VNS Matrix (1991–97) is credited with launching the cyberfeminist movement – which is charged with examining the multiple intersections between women and computer technologies – that made this reclamation of language visible, referring to themselves in their 1991 manifesto as 'the modern cunt' pitted against the referent of 'big daddy mainframe' in the continuing war against patriarchy.[126] Despite the coming changes, language, as it applied to gender and sexuality in the early 1980s, was essentially neutralising: Alder's reading of the poster, as 'super powers = penis [leads to] oppression of women', is a response that is indivisibly tied to the constructions of second-wave feminism.

Arguably, the BRG collective's response says more about the nature of the engagement with feminism in Canberra and the heightened politicisation inherent in the national capital than it does about the wider national and international feminist movement. In other words, Alder's and the collective's response may have been more politically charged, by virtue of being located at the centre of Australia's political decision-making, than Holyoake anticipated. This would therefore reflect a disconnect between the Melbourne-based artist and the Canberra collective and thus between the politically heightened but, at the same time, relatively more insular art world of Canberra and that of the more established scene in Melbourne. Additionally, during the early 1980s, the BRG collective largely comprised

---

125 Cyberfeminism arose in 1991 with artist collective VNS Matrix in Australia and in 1992 with philosopher Sadie Plant in the United Kingdom. Both built on the initial work of US scholar Donna Haraway in her 1985 article, 'The cyborg manifesto: science, technology and socialist feminism in the late twentieth century' (in David Bell and Barbara M Kennedy (eds), *The cybercultures reader*, London, New York, Routledge, 2000, pp 291–324). In 'Cyberfeminism(s): origins, definitions and overview', Vesna Dragojlov gives a comprehensive examination of cyberfeminism's history and argues that, broadly speaking, cyberfeminism's main goal 'has been to analyze issues of gender, new technologies and, especially, the internet' (25) that 'sit at the crossroads of art, theory and activism' (23) (University of Advancing Technology, www.uat.edu/webmedia/pdf/Cyberfem_14066.pdf, accessed 24 June 2012, site discontinued).

126 VNS Matrix's manifesto reads as follows:
CYBERFEMINIST MANIFESTO FOR THE 21ST CENTURY
We are the modern cunt / positive anti reason / unbounded unleashed unforgiving / we see art with our cunt we make art with our cunt / we believe in jouissance madness holiness and poetry / we are the virus of the new world disorder / rupturing the symbolic from within / saboteurs of big daddy mainframe / the clitoris is a direct line to the matrix / VNS MATRIX / terminators of the moral codes / mercenaries of slime / go down on the altar of abjection / probing the visceral temple we speak in tongues / infiltrating disrupting disseminating / corrupting the discourse / we are the future cunt.

Manifesto first declared by VNS Matrix1991, Adelaide & Sydney, Australia (www.sterneck.net/cyber/vns-matrix/index.php, accessed 24 June 2012).

present and past students from CSA who were influenced by the emphasis on emancipation inherent in Martin's Marxist/Maoist Adelaide background. It can therefore be argued that the politics of second-wave feminism was a driving force in the context of the collective's view of *Slut* rather than the changing constructions of feminism emerging in southern capitals. Melbourne artists on the other hand were arguably more exposed, through the rapidly increasing movement of artists and ideas in and out of the country, to European and North American trends, which included the theories and practices of third-wave feminism.[127]

Holyoake was a member of the Jill Posters collective that, for a time, included former BRG members Church, Walters and Deej Fabyc, all of whom moved to Melbourne in 1983. Like Martin and Binns, Church regarded Canberra as a centre where political orthodoxy held less sway. As an activist printmaker who was heavily involved in CSA's scene from 1979 to 1982, a member of the loose network of underground printers in Canberra, a founding member of Megalo and BRG, and then as a founding member, along with Kath Walters, of several print workshops in Melbourne from 1983 onwards,[128] Church later reflected:

> I think in Canberra there was more flexibility, there was less political orthodoxy. In Melbourne and Sydney I think there was a lot more orthodoxy and you could get into some really terrible stoushes. I'm just thinking about Jill Posters for example which had all sorts of political problems because people held very strong political positions; they were polar opposites sometimes or imagined that they were. I think Canberra was quite liberating in that way.[129]

---

127 This may seem unlikely today when images and movements are instantaneously transferred across borders. Movements grew more slowly in the early 1980s in the absence of email and internet.
128 Julia Church and Kath Walters arrived in Melbourne from Canberra at the beginning of 1983. Church immediately set up Bloody Good Graffix at University of Melbourne where the duo printed and taught printmaking skills to community members. Church recalled that 'Bloody Good Graphics became one of the base camps for Jill Posters. Contemporaneously we applied for a grant to set up Another Planet and for a Victorian Department of the Arts Community Arts Grant and got both. So [with the latter] we worked with the Hospital Employees Federation creating banners for them and going out as roaming artists-in-residence creating visual [material] with their membership. That was a really interesting period of time. Then we employed people to set up Another Planet and some of those people came from [Canberra including] Diana Wells and Julie Shiels who'd been involved in Jill Posters' (Church, 2012).
129 Church, 2012.

Many Jill Posters members were lesbian separatists, although Holyoake 'was heterosexual, liked men, liked having sex with men'.[130] Holyoake was the same age as her Megalo/BRG contemporaries but was both subject to and took advantage of a more diverse social and artistic milieu. While others 'tended to work in their groups', Holyoake 'mix[ed] about with a lot of different groups', including Melbourne's Clifton Hill art community and other groups making films and music. Friends and 'artist feminists' returning to Melbourne from visits to the United Kingdom and New York were inspired by emerging pop-cultural feminist icons in fashion – such as Vivienne Westwood – and music, such as Madonna. 'Red lipstick was "in" – sluttish-ness was out there, female sexuality was definitely being pushed into the mix in the early 80s.'[131] Also emerging in Europe at the time was New Romanticism and Holyoake recalled wanting to 'dress up in 50s–60s retro feminine'.

Holyoake embraced these many and diverse influences and crafted a poster that proved unacceptable to the BRG collective and difficult to accept, even for her more internationally influenced Melbourne contemporaries. Despite the fact that Holyoake characterises early 1980s Melbourne as 'a post-feminist/post-punk era' during which she and other women peers 'reacted to and questioned the exclusivity' of hard-core feminist ideas – including the benefit of following masculine forms of dress – it is clear that the central female figure in *Slut* presents a construction of 'woman' that was unusually feminine within the context of imagery favoured by a second-wave feminist collective such as Jill Posters.[132]

Jill Posters collective members were primarily printing posters to be pasted up in the street, occasionally working in two colours, which allowed the poster makers to maximise limited printing time and funds and suited the postmodern use of photographic images. Artist and founding Jill Posters member Wilson secured access to the print room at University of Melbourne, where *Slut* was printed out of hours.[133] It was here also that

---

130 Catriona Holyoake, email to the author, 24 December 2011. Jill Posters members included Lesley Baxter, Ally Black, Linda Brassel, Church, Zana Dare, Fabyc, Maggie Fooke, Julie Higginbotham, Holyoake, Barbara Miles, Kate Reeves, Linda Rhodes, Julie Shiels, Lin Tobias, Julia Tobin, Walters, Wilson.
131 Holyoake, 2011.
132 Holyoake, 2011.
133 I am grateful to Carole Wilson, formerly of Jill Posters, who remembered Holyoake as the *Slut* poster maker and set me on the path to finding her. I was then able to attribute the poster in the NGA collection. Holyoake has taught digital media at RMIT for 15 years and is currently the senior digital strategist for Red Cross Blood Service in Melbourne.

the Jill Posters' printmakers made small editions on quality paper for their portfolios. Holyoake writes that 'A lot of the work I did at this time was based on a simple illustrative style – juxtaposing images to create a story or project an idea'.[134]

Holyoake's central female figure was a photographic image of a woman striding across a street, taken from *Vogue* magazine. The image appealed to her as it was:

> a positive active image for a fashion magazine, which usually shows women as the object. [The model] was one of my favourites and I really liked the dress; it was very simple and elegant. I was a bit of a chameleon—overalls one day and skirts and heels the next ... you had to blend in when required.[135]

Slut, with its appropriation of this photographic image and its gathering of messages and images from the immediate contemporary milieu, can be seen as a deployment of Julia Kristeva's 'fragmentation of the imaginary', which Kristeva identified as a marker of postmodernist art strategies.[136] Holyoake was, therefore, exquisitely of her time, elaborating in *Slut* the 'real mix of feminist and postmodern theory' to which she was exposed.[137]

Alder's initial reading of the poster's message – that is, that 'super powers = penis [leads to] oppression of women' – was at odds with the artist's intentions. As Holyoake remembered it:

> I was trying to subvert the penis by making it look like a toy rocket (silly boy missile) in relation to the woman in red who is striding out confidently – separate and oblivious of the rocket ... it's half rocket half penis. I was trying to make fun of it (Germaine Greer style). It's just a penis! – Boys and their toys, men and their rockets. The cut out is to add to the idea that this is a game and yes we can change the play.[138]

And, indeed, if the cut line were to be employed and the figure pulled forward out of the poster frame, then the rocket/penis, on a trajectory towards the model's midriff, would simply pass by into open space.

---

134 Holyoake, 2011.
135 Holyoake, 2011.
136 Julia Kristeva, in 'Interview with Catherine Francklin', part VIIIA, 'The critique of originality', in Charles Harrison and Paul Wood (eds), *Art in theory: 1900–2000: an anthology of changing ideas*, Blackwell Publishing, 2003, p 1055.
137 Holyoake, 2011.
138 Holyoake, 2011.

In the 30 years since the poster was made, the word 'Paradise', when combined with the sexualised image of woman, calls up fallout from nuclear activity in the Pacific Islands or Islamic extremist definitions of Paradise. In fact, Holyoake's use of 'Paradise' in the thought bubble was designed to be ambiguous: constructed as a series of comments on perceptions of female sexuality and the threat of nuclear holocaust. The artist's intended readings included firstly, 'I've sinned, I'm a slut (in the conservative male sense of the word), I won't get to heaven [as in the Judeo-Christian construction of paradise] and I don't care I'm having a great time'. And, secondly, 'Paradise; I won't see you there because we will be dead and the world/nature/ beauty will be destroyed'.[139]

Even in her hometown of Melbourne, a city subject to the ebb and flow of artists and ideas moving rapidly between Australia, America and Europe, Holyoake's collective struggled with the blatant femininity of the poster's protagonist. Reflecting in 2011 on the reception of the poster from other Jill Posters members, Holyoake – describing herself as 'deliberately trying to take a more Warholian/post-modernist tack' – wrote:

> I think the reading of the poster was that it was offensive to women as in sexist. Carole Wilson was at least prepared to listen and out of friendship agreed we should still post it up in the street ... I did remember being disappointed that the poster didn't fit with what was PC [politically correct]. Failure more on my part I thought to not meet the criteria. But I have to say I do remember thinking that a lot of the PC art was really dull and that some PC people were already being a bit colloquial. So the *Vogue* magazine image was, I thought, going to have more impact; [in that the woman at the centre of the poster was] a civilian rather than a feminist. [I thought] no-one is going to care about a feminist in boots and overalls, people hated them.[140]

The rejection of *Slut* in Canberra, in an environment that was noted more for flexibility than for political orthodoxy, illustrates the critical importance of artists' access to diverse influences and opinions. While the proposed public display of the poster created disquiet among some members of Jill Posters, Melbourne afforded greater access to rapidly changing international constructions of, in this case, feminism and allowed for an acceptance, albeit somewhat grudging, of *Slut*'s message.

---

139 Holyoake, 2011.
140 Holyoake, 2011.

Canberra's contemporary artists, particularly as evidenced through BRG, were distinctly less impacted by the flood of disparate internationalist ideas that were making their way through southern capitals.

The decision to reject *Slut* occurred in what is now categorised as a postmodernist, post-feminist era. Arguably this brief period in the early 1980s could be understood *not* as post-feminist but as an interstitial moment; between second- and third-wave feminism and, importantly, as the 1980s unfolded, between the death of the artist-run space and the birth of more highly administered art centres, in Canberra, nationally and internationally.

5
TRANSITION: BRG TO CCAS

In July 1987, Bitumen River Gallery (BRG) was amalgamated with the Arts Council Gallery (ACG) to create Canberra Contemporary Art Space (CCAS). Anne Virgo played a seminal role in the amalgamation; she began as BRG's second coordinator during 1984/85, became ACG director in 1986, and was appointed as inaugural director of CCAS in 1987. Her 10 years in Canberra coincided with the transformation of local contemporary art practice from a youthful collective operating at the margins – as reflected at BRG – into an expression of contemporary art operating in a national mainstream context – as demonstrated through CCAS.

The notion and reality of collective practice at BRG, and the consequences of the loss of the collective model speaks to the important philosophical schism that characterised the wider national development of contemporary art: whether arts practitioners were better served by spaces run by artists, for artists; or whether contemporary art should take its place within the network of funded art galleries and museums.

Anne Virgo

Virgo arrived in Canberra at the beginning of 1984 as one of two part-time coordinators at BRG. After her appointment as inaugural director of CCAS in 1987, she remained in that position until 1993 when she left for Melbourne to become director of the Australian Print Workshop (APW).

Virgo completed a fine arts degree at the South Australian School of Art (SA SOA), majoring in printmaking and photography. For a year or so after graduation, she shared studio space in Adelaide, making prints and photographs and working part-time to pay the rent. Along with many of her early 1980s cohort from the SA SOA – and like Mandy Martin in the decade before her – she left art school with an expanded social and political consciousness:

> I had focused specifically on what, at that time, was called community arts practice. When I went through art school and did a fine art degree my mentors at the time were very much the socialist drivers, part of the socialist party agitators in Adelaide, and so I grew up in a very political environment.[1]

Passing through Canberra in December 1983 and knowing only one person in the city, the 22-year-old Virgo read the *Canberra Times* advertisement for a shared coordinator's position at BRG. She submitted an application and returned to Adelaide. Within weeks she was back in Canberra for an interview in the gallery, with a panel comprising Sasha Grishin and artists Kay Ransome, Tony Ayres and Stephanie Radok. 'We were sitting around on chairs, someone was sitting on a metal garbage tin – it was pretty rudimentary.'[2] Virgo was offered the job and started at the beginning of 1984 in a job-share position with BRG stalwart Mark Denton:

> Mark was a local Canberra person and I was the person completely left of centre because I'd come from outside of Canberra. I hadn't made a conscious decision to move to Canberra – it was just one of those things that happened. I didn't know anyone in the art world [in Canberra]. [I was] totally disconnected.[3]

Despite this self-identified outsider status, Virgo was well-suited for the shared coordinator's position in the young collective. At SA SOA, she had had it 'drummed into [her] psyche' that 'to be an individual artist was almost self-indulgent, that it wasn't about the individual it was about working collectively, working in a different way'.[4] Arriving in Canberra, she moved into a share house in Yarralumla. The salary for the two-and-a-half-day a week position was $7,500, at that time 'not much more' than the dole:

---

1 Anne Virgo, interview with the author, 17 September 2013.
2 Virgo, 2013.
3 Virgo, 2013.
4 Virgo, 2013.

> [T]o supplement our income from the Gallery we both took on other jobs; Mark worked on the merry-go-round in Civic and I cleaned the offices of an architect. Both Mark and I intended to continue with our practice as the role of coordinator was a shared position, but it wasn't long before we realised that this was almost impossible. It seemed that we were both working full-time on a part-time wage – not unusual for an arts-related job.[5]

When Denton left BRG to work with Julia Church and Kath Walters at their Redletter imprint in Melbourne in the middle of 1984, Virgo took on the coordinator's role full-time. She was drawn to arts administration and, with Denton's departure, decided to pack away her 'paints and palettes' and pursue a career supporting artists.[6] 'I realised,' she wrote in 1986, 'that arts administration was my first love and that my practice was secondary. For the next year and a half Bitumen River was my life.'[7] Virgo's introduction to the 1984 BRG scrapbook serves to underline the fledgling collective's ability to survive, despite tenuous circumstances, to the point where it could attract the beginnings of a useful funding base. Its survival to that point is testament to the continuing support of the local community. She named the year as 'a "turning point"' for the gallery:

> After two years [and ten months] of surviving on volunteer labour, on an inadequate budget, often witnessing 'burn-out' by key members due to the enormous task of running an organisation with no or very little financial reward for their work, BRG was able to employ a full-time co-ordinator. This position enabled such basic administrative functions as a book-keeping system, a filing system and a more efficient program of activities to operate.[8]

Importantly, it also allowed the new coordinator to travel. It is clear that, from her arrival, Virgo was interested in the wider arts community, both in Canberra and nationally. Throughout Australia, collectives and artist-run spaces that were opened and staffed by young artists, as well as funded contemporary art spaces, were proliferating. By 1984, only the Northern Territory and the Australian Capital Territory (ACT) were without a federally funded contemporary art space. The contemporary arts sector was on the cusp of enormous change and Virgo, who proved to be both ambitious and strategic, arrived in Canberra at a pivotal moment in the development of contemporary art in the city.

---

5   BRG, '5th birthday show', CCAS archives.
6   Virgo, 2013.
7   Virgo, 2013.
8   Anne Virgo, 'Introduction', BRG scrapbook, 1984, CCAS archives.

Virgo's two years with BRG were characterised by tremendous energy and curiosity. She travelled widely and frequently with the aim of progressing national relationships and building the Territory's capacity in contemporary arts practice. In 1984, she attended four state conferences: 'Artists' week' at the *Adelaide festival of the arts* from 9–19 March; the *Regional development and touring exhibition* conference in Melbourne on 27 April; the *Art of survival* conference in Melbourne on 29 April; and, on 2 June, the Contemporary Art Spaces Association conference in Sydney.[9] There she met with 'representatives from each state to discuss common issues and develop a stronger network'.[10] Continuing the gallery's relationship with Canberra School of Art (CSA), Virgo gave a lecture there midway through 1984 as part of the *Art forum* public lectures program.[11]

Virgo's first working contact with the ACG at Gorman House, then directed by Ben Grady, also occurred in 1984 when a year of planning resulted in the BRG collective coordinating, with ACG, the local tour of the travelling political poster exhibition *Truth rules OK?* This exhibition, arising at the Experimental Art Foundation (EAF) in Adelaide, toured to the Woden and Belconnen shopping centres.[12] At BRG, an arts fashion parade heralded the exhibition *This year's model*, a china-painting workshop presaged *A new spirit in china painting*, and women's films were shown at the opening of the *Women's archives exhibition*. In addition, BRG hosted lectures by Terry Smith (on Frida Kahlo), Gary Sangster from Sydney's Artspace, Robert McDonald and Juilee Pryor from Sydney's Art Unit, and Juan Davila (whom Ayres had met and invited to Canberra).

Modelling a collective ethos, Virgo, Ayres, Denton and BRG member Robert Saxton all engaged in correspondence on behalf of the gallery through the first half of 1984. By March, approximately 100 people and organisations were on BRG's mailing list.[13] Potential exhibitors were given the aims and objectives of BRG, the current gallery roster, a membership form and an exhibition agreement. In an ad hoc manner, CSA often

---

9   The Contemporary Art Spaces Association was the first iteration of the peak organisation Contemporary Art Organisations Australia (CAOA).
10 BRG scrapbook, 1984.
11 This initial contact progressed to a four-year teaching stint in professional practice at CSA from 1988 to 1991. CSA amalgamated with the Canberra School of Music to form the Canberra Institute of the Arts in 1988. *Art forum* was initiated by Sellbach in 1983 as the *Living arts program*.
12 *Truth rules OK?* was co-curated by Ken Bolton and Christine Goodwin and opened at the EAF in Adelaide in September 1983.
13 Anne Virgo, letter to Marcus [unattributed, but most likely Marcus Breen], 7 March 1984, 'Correspondence', 1984/2, CCAS archives.

loaned frames for works in exhibitions, and members of the collective were prepared to frame and hang works for visiting artists, to sit the gallery for a shows' duration and to provide a bed for visiting artists. Artists were asked to print invitations and posters if possible, and posters continued to be sold from the BRG poster racks during and after exhibition. Members collectively mailed exhibition invitations out and postered details of up-coming events widely around the city.

By mid-1984, a core group of those BRG members who guided the gallery through its considerable early difficulties had left Canberra for capitals interstate. Denton was in Melbourne, as was Ayres who enrolled to study film at Swinburne and was writing for *Art Network*; Karilyn Brown, stepping in as BRG coordinator for three months after Alison Alder's departure for Melbourne in early 1983, was working with the Visual Arts Board (VAB) of the Australia Council in Sydney. After a year in Melbourne, Alder was on the move to Redback Graphix, which was founded by Michael Callaghan and Gregor Cullen in Brisbane in 1979 (one year before Megalo), before moving to Wollongong in 1980 and then to Sydney in 1985. Collective members were buoyed by the backing of their peers who had left Canberra for positions interstate and who continued to support the gallery in various ways, including being present at openings. These former colleagues continued their support through the next few years, visiting when in town, exchanging contacts, showing in exhibitions at BRG and, importantly, facilitating national touring shows between artist-run spaces.

Reflecting the growing profile of contemporary art in Canberra and the increased national visibility of BRG and its activities, the gallery's 1985 Community Development Fund (CDF) grant, which was announced in November 1984, was increased to $27,000 and BRG also received $8,750, its first grant, from the VAB of the Australia Council.

The ongoing difficulties of operating effectively in a collective environment were reflected at the end of Virgo's first year. The November BRG meeting unanimously agreed that Virgo should continue in the coordinator's position if she wished to. Virgo *was* willing to continue if members made themselves more available for consultation and support.[14]

---

14   BRG, minutes from meeting, 13 November 1984, 'Meeting minutes, 1984', CCAS archives.

One of the defining characteristics of the BRG journey during the period from 1981 to 1985 was the number of reactive meetings called. This was a result of the gallery's ad hoc genesis and the ongoing problems caused by inadequate funding and staffing, pitted against the strong desire for the gallery to succeed.

Having run BRG almost singlehandedly through to the beginning of 1983, Alder's 'burnout' precipitated an emergency meeting of members in late 1982 to assess future directions.[15] On that occasion a decision was taken to institute a formal collective membership base in an effort to streamline procedures and to spread the administrative load across members. In August 1983, BRG's *Future directions forum*, which included Grishin among its attendees, determined that the collective should commence proceedings to become either an incorporated association or a registered business, and on 6 September 1984 – in an act that conferred a public legitimacy on the collective – BRG was incorporated as an association in the ACT.[16] This was a fundamentally important step that, in its formality, signalled maturity and a desire among members to secure the collective's future.

The 1983 conference elicited a letter from artist, teacher and BRG member Neil Roberts (1954–2002) who, unable to attend, wrote that 'the survival of the gallery or something similar' was 'vital' to the development of the visual arts in Canberra.[17] Roberts accepted that 'a collective-run gallery is a desirable ideal' but believed that innovations such as 'performances, installations and various one night wonders … could be more difficult to undertake given the trials and tribulations of a truly collective model'. Roberts was an active collective member from 1982 with strong ties to CSA, particularly the Glass Workshop that, with Klaus Moje, he was instrumental in setting up in 1983. He was acutely aware of the inherent difficulties in maintaining a long-term collective consensus, given the members' relative youth, poverty and lack of experience. He personally believed that in the interests of:

---

15 Alison Alder, letter to Geoff Shera, Brisbane, undated, 'Correspondence, 1984', CCAS archives.
16 Another compelling reason for this decision was so that the telephone number could be listed as 'Bitumen River Gallery', rather than 'A Alder'.
17 Roberts was also instrumental in developing the Ingo Kleinart-led *ACT 1* (1978), *ACT 2* (1980), and *ACT 3* (1982).

maximising … influence both here and interstate … especially at this point of time in Canberra, the appointment of a decisive and forward-looking director with the power to respond quickly to opportunity and change would be an exciting step in the right direction.[18]

A series of forums and meetings held from 1981 to the end of 1983 resulted in actions that enabled the gallery to stay open in the lead-up to Virgo's appointment. Virgo recalled that during her two-year period from the beginning of 1984 to early 1986:

> there were many times along the way – 'crisis meetings' they were called – where you'd pull the group together and 'There's no energy, what are we doing, who's involved, who's doing this, what's going to happen' – so many moments where it just could have fallen over.[19]

On 2 May 1984, during Virgo's first year at BRG, around 30 people attended the gallery to reflect on the present and discuss future directions. A year later, in the wake of the 1985 Pascoe Report,[20] 17 members attended a BRG 'search conference', again titled 'Future directions', at the premises of the community theatre company Through Art Unity (TAU).[21] That only half the number of members who attended the previous year's forum were present in 1985 indicates that the collective membership continued to be unstable, a consequence of the still peripatetic nature of the lives of the city's visual artists.

There were limited opportunities for visual artists to progress their career while remaining in Canberra. In response to a question posed about changes in Canberra and what opportunities and constraints such changes might represent for BRG, members' responses included that, while acknowledging 'an increased interest in galleries and art in general', Canberra:

> Offer[ed] limited opportunities as a place for artists to live and work, especially after the publication of the Pascoe Report; rather Canberra was perceived as a stepping-stone en route to Sydney or Melbourne.[22]

---

18   Neil Roberts, letter to Alison Alder, 3 August 1983. CCAS archives.
19   Virgo, 2013.
20   See Chapter 2, 'The Pascoe Report', for an examination of the report's wider effects on the ACT arts community.
21   Geoffrey Milne named TAU as the 'only orthodox community theatre company in Canberra' (*Theatre Australia (un)limited: Australian theatre since the 1950s*, Australian Playwrights, no 10, Rodopi, Amsterdam, New York, 2004, p 45).
22   'Future directions', a report of the search conference, compiled by Greg Sugden, TAU, 9 June 1985, 'Future directions', envelope, CCAS archives.

The Pascoe Report cast a long shadow on BRG members. Emerging into a more receptive milieu, Pascoe's recommendations gave little hope of future federal government–assisted growth. With the beginnings of the handover to self-government only four years away, concern was also voiced about self-government's economic effects on the local visual arts sector and the proposed concomitant federal government cutbacks to the Community Employment Programs (CEPs), which continued to provide start-up funds for community cultural projects.

Possible futures that privileged growth in both space and programming were envisioned when members were asked to consider what BRG would 'ideally' look like in five years. A key concern was to seek out a larger space, 'more space and more staff', based in the old GPO or in a 'large warehouse or building that the collective had "seized"'.[23] This larger space would allow the 'staging [of] dual shows (thematic and experimental) at the same time' with performance art, sculpture, large installations and 'risky and innovative' art.[24] A focus on artists and the community also prevailed, indicating the deep connections between artists and community that informed the collective's decisions, with responses such as 'working artists should dominate gallery directions', that BRG be 'a base/umbrella for other activities and a resource centre for artists', that it 'remain accessible to community exhibitions e.g. mural artists', and that it 'connects with community events'.[25]

While most responses envisioned a larger space within Canberra that continued to focus on emerging artists and the community, a few suggestions concerned BRG's place in the wider visual arts community – that BRG be 'part of an integrated network with *all* the visual arts groups in Canberra and interstate', or in a more defined way, that it be 'part of the contemporary art network undergoing radical growth'.[26] The response that BRG could be 'either emerging artist based, community based or part of a major contemporary art network but not both' is evidence of the respondent's broad understanding of national funding trends.[27]

---

23 'Future directions', 1985.
24 'Future directions', 1985.
25 'Future directions', 1985.
26 'Future directions', 1985, original emphasis on all.
27 'Future directions', 1985.

Virgo was arguably the first person able to progress the idea of a fully funded contemporary art space in Canberra. While it is unlikely that she arrived in the city with that in mind, it is feasible that, by the end of 1984, supported by her many national professional encounters, the imminent possibility of creating such a space had taken hold. The list of 17 members who attended the 1985 forum included six current CSA students, nine working artists, a community artist/administrator who was also a member of the Arts Development Board and Virgo. Five were new members and six had been members for a year. Only four, including Cherylynn Holmes, had exhibited and become members within the first year. Virgo was the least Canberra-centric of the attendees and arguably the most aware, given her exposure through national travel, of the rapid changes occurring in the visual arts sector. It is likely that responses pointing towards BRG's inclusion in a national contemporary art network came from Virgo and, therefore, it can be assumed this meeting in mid-1985 saw a firming of her intention to further such an agenda. A number of factors, however, were yet to align.

The question of appropriate space would have been uppermost in Virgo's mind. BRG was clearly too small to accommodate any possible contemporary art space and the city, planned and constructed largely to purpose, did not provide access to suitable 'spare' real estate – unlike the warehouses of Melbourne or Sydney or the bond stores of Adelaide and Hobart – that could be re-visioned and re-purposed as centres for art. Additionally, BRG was deeply imbued with the ethos of a collectively run space. The make-up of the small group who continued to lend day-to-day assistance in the running of BRG remained somewhat unstable, but the gallery's slowly increasing annual funding, growing membership and the fact of its presence demonstrated its relevance to the sector through its five years of continuous operation.

By the end of 1985, Virgo was having trouble seeing a future for herself at BRG. When Grady resigned from his position as director of ACG – leaving the community sector in the wake of the Pascoe Report to open his eponymously titled commercial gallery in Canberra's southern suburb of Kingston – Virgo applied for and was given the ACG director's job, commencing in March 1986.[28] She resigned from BRG on 14 February 1986 and eX de Medici and Greg Sugden stepped temporarily into the coordinator's position. Virgo recalled the reasons for her resignation:

---

28   Grady was one of a number of arts workers in the ACT who resigned at the end of 1985, following widespread dissatisfaction with the ADB's handling of arts funding in the ACT; see Chapter 3.

> I guess I'd done what I needed to do, it wasn't progressing anywhere, it was a bit cyclic, you know it was a limited life there and in a sense it was time for Bitumen River to die. And the energy and the enthusiasm had gone ... [I]t was time to move on.[29]

Virgo's position as director of ACG attracted more gravitas and greater visibility than the BRG coordinator's role. Coupled with the excellent gallery facilities, it placed Virgo in a stronger position to begin progressing plans for a local contemporary art space. It was not within ACG's purview to show emerging artists and thus Virgo planned to continue its emphasis 'on local professional artists: people who have perhaps exhibited before or have been painting for a number of years'.[30] She stated that she was 'keen to provide gallery space for major exhibitions from contemporary art spaces and regional and State galleries'.[31] This would indicate that she imagined the ACG as a de facto regional gallery. It would be another 12 years before CMAG, Canberra's purpose-built regional gallery, joined the city's growing collection of cultural institutions.

Erica Green, who worked under Virgo at BRG and was appointed BRG's coordinator on 1 April 1986, described 1986 as 'a year that embraced divisiveness, dialogue, rationalisation and review ... culminat[ing] in many new and exciting initiatives'.[32] The gallery hosted nine solo exhibitions from local artists, the majority of whom were early career artists, rather than the current or recently graduated students from CSA whose emerging careers had been incubated at BRG.[33] Three interstate exhibitions – including the touring exhibition *Truth rules II*, the second iteration of this concept from the EAF – and three theme shows – comprising an exhibition of printed works using multiple techniques, a members' Christmas show of edible art and BRG's *5th birthday show* – completed the calendar. It was clear that the local visual arts sector was strengthening as applications from potential exhibitors continued to increase throughout the year, and Green and collective members worked to build the profile of BRG and to emphasise both growing achievements and growing need within the visual arts sector.

---

29 Virgo, 2013.
30 Virginia Cook, 'Director drafts policy: gallery emphasis on ACT artists', 20 March 1986, p 5.
31 *Canberra Times*, 20 March 1986.
32 BRG scrapbook, 1986.
33 The nine artists were eX de Medici (*Work saints*), Michael Cartwright (*Recent works*), Stephanie Radok (*The garden of earthly delights*), Wendy Ann Rose (*Up the garden path*), CSA graduate student Julianna Balla (*Layers within*), Jackie Gorring (*These things of mine*), Sylvia Convey (*A coloured life*), Gaynor Cardew (*The great graffiti show*), and Monica Luff (*Luminus*).

Amalgamation: from collective to contemporary art space

By the time of BRG's fifth birthday celebrations, the vote that legitimised the merger of BRG/ACG into a single contemporary art space was less than a year away. The agreement necessary to proceed with the merger was based on consultation with many parties, including BRG members, ACT Arts Development Board (ADB), the Arts Council (ACT) board and its CEO, the Australia Council's VAB, the wider ACT arts community and Canberra's art-consuming public. Virgo had strong support from Ross Wolfe, who was director of the VAB from 1983 to 1988 and who, among other 'policy initiatives of consequence', was concerned that each capital city would have a funded contemporary art space.[34] She could also arguably be certain of support from Green, who was her co-worker at BRG and remained her friend and confidante after Virgo's move to the ACG precipitated Green's step to the coordinator's position at BRG.

Unhappy with the proposed move were the Arts Council (ACT) – which had only recently acquired its excellently appointed new exhibition space at Gorman House, 'a space to work with that would turn many gallery directors' eyes green'[35] – and those members of BRG who believed that Canberra needed an artist-run space that catered for newly emerged artists and for works that would not find a home in either the commercial or funded spaces. This last, above all, was intrinsic to the ongoing ethos of BRG.

Virgo's note, in materials pertaining to the fifth birthday celebrations, gave no clue of any future plans. She wrote:

> Most of my memories of Bitumen River are people, not only the visitors to the gallery but those that were involved and dedicated to the concept of an artist run space. The energies of these members built Bitumen River into a viable and valuable visual arts space, a space unique to Canberra and perhaps to Australia because we are now celebrating our fifth birthday proving that the ideals of an artists-run space can be sustained. Although I have now left Bitumen River in my capacity as Co-ordinator, I still feel

---

34   Ross Wolfe's policy initiatives included agreements for a permanent Australian Pavilion at the *Venice biennale* and establishment of the National Exhibitions Touring Support Program (now known as National Exhibitions Touring Support (NETS) Australia).
35   Cook, 20 March 1986.

very attached to that small building in the car park that was often mistaken for a toilet block and hope that in a few years' time we will be celebrating our tenth birthday.[36]

The first public outing of the proposed idea of a merger between BRG and the ACG occurred on 21 October 1986 at a meeting at BRG convened by the Contemporary Art Space Working Group. The group included Gaynor Cardew, Sylvia Convey, Paul Costigan, de Medici, Elizabeth Frewin, Radok, Roberts, Veet Sandeha, and Virgo and was responsible for lobbying, advertising and organising the public meeting.

Arguably neither BRG members, who made up the bulk of the working group, nor the ADB, were fully aware that a contemporary art space for Canberra would mean an end to BRG. The ADB intended to fund both BRG and the ACG going forward and, on 4 December 1986, the board announced that, from a total ACT pool of $1,105,063 in operational grants for 1987, BRG would receive $33,000, an increase of $5,000 on the previous year. ACG was awarded $45,000.[37]

Just six months after that first public meeting, the members of BRG voted in April 1987 to hand their constitution over to Virgo and the ACG, and the new organisation, CCAS, was incorporated with Virgo as its director. On the surface, the transition to a contemporary art space appeared to be both welcome and logical, reflecting what English artist, curator and writer Richard Grayson – who first came to EAF in Adelaide in 1982 – called the 'victory of contemporary art'.[38] There was, however, opposition from those who believed that Canberra's arts community needed an independent artist-run space. These individuals believed that the local arts community needed a messy, open, emerging arts incubator – that is, the community needed BRG. Vocal opposition came from de Medici, Roberts and Huw Davies, who photographed the crowd as the vote was taken. A hard and successful drive for membership was instituted some weeks before the vote and many of those voting in favour were new recruits. Among the naysayers, folded arms eloquently but ineffectually signified opposition to the merger.

---

36   BRG, '5th birthday show'.
37   Megalo was awarded $29,000, Photo Access $21,340 and Studio One $25,000. Gorman House Community Arts Centre was awarded $22,640. In all, 26 ACT arts organisations were awarded a total of $1,105,063. The largest grant by far, $200,000, was given to the newly formed Fortune Theatre.
38   Richard Grayson, interview with the author, 14 September 2011, Istanbul.

The opening of CCAS marked the beginning of fully funded contemporary art exhibition practice, bringing the ACT into line with each of the Australian states and their respective contemporary art spaces.[39]

On 4 July 1987, CCAS held an opening party prior to the official opening on 10 July by Daniel Thomas, director of the Art Gallery of South Australia. In interview with the *Canberra Times*, Virgo stated that CCAS's aim was to 'facilitate and encourage a program of activities that address the concerns and issues associated with innovative and experimental contemporary visual arts practice'.[40] It planned to do so by supporting emerging and established artists, responding to the needs of its arts community, initiating activities and providing a forum for special events, lectures and discussions.[41]

BRG's and the ACG's existing funding became seed funding for the new organisation and the ADB announced that, from the total pool of $1 million for the ACT for the year 1988, the operational grant extended to CCAS would be $83,000, an increase of $5,000 on the previous year's combined BRG and ACG grants.

The opening of CCAS thus marked the end to an ACT-based, independent, artist-run space with all of its attendant possibilities and frustrations. Six years after it opened its doors in April 1981, BRG – subsumed and renamed – entered the mainstream.

Australian writer/curator Julie Ewington,[42] reflecting on the merger in *Art Monthly*, wrote at the end of 1987 that it provided 'one of the few admirable examples of "rationalization" here or anywhere else. The Canberra art community and its audiences have come out the richer'.

> This is despite regrets I share about the immolation of the old Bitumen River and its Collective ... [T]he exhibition program has always been wonderful and wacky, a combination of work from local artists and small touring shows, a haven for group shows by recent graduates and students from the Canberra School of Art, and a focus for art community energies. Quite simply Bitumen

---

39   The Northern Territory established a contemporary art space, 24HR Art (now Northern Centre for Contemporary Art), in 1989.
40   *Canberra Times*, 'Contemporary art space', 9 July 1987, p 6s.
41   *Canberra Times*, 1987.
42   Ewington was head of the Art Theory Workshop at CSA from 1986 to 1989 when she resigned to become curator of CSA's SofA Gallery. She moved to a position at the Museum of Contemporary Art in Sydney in 1994, later becoming head of Australian Art at Queensland Art Gallery.

River sheltered some of the liveliest art in Canberra, and just about the only scurrilous art, thereby standing as a beacon of resistance in this sanitized city.[43]

The crossover exhibitions at BRG and CCAS – that is, the last to be held at BRG and the first at CCAS – were *Salon coda: the making of history* (10 June – 5 July, BRG) and *Site specific city* (10 July – 2 August, CCAS). Ewington described the former as 'typical of the Bitumen River's style' given its 'less-cash-more-dash verve'.[44] *Salon coda* comprised 99 works from over 50 artists hung in the nineteenth-century salon manner. The exhibition's title was timely: salon, from the method that 'provided an unparalleled opportunity for seeing what was being done by nearly every artist of consequence and seeing it at the same time and place',[45] and Coda, to mark the end of an extraordinary period in Canberra's contemporary art history. The exhibition's tagline referenced the preceding six years of works from BRG artists, as the artists in the exhibition were drawn from the ranks of previous exhibitors and included student artists, emerging artists, and early and mid-career artists. Arguably, outside of CSA and discounting community art exhibitions, *Salon coda* (see Figure 19) constituted the largest number of local contemporary artists yet hung in the city. 'Unhappily, perhaps,' wrote Ewington, 'modern exhibition strategies ensure this is a rare opportunity.'[46]

On the other side of the lake at CCAS, Gorman House, *Site specific city* exhibited the works of five BRG stalwarts: Ayres, de Medici, Radok, Roberts and Arthur Wicks (see Figure 21), represented with works on paper, installations, constructions and video. De Medici and Ayres, both emerging artists at this point, had previously specifically activated the gallery with works that provided a 'beacon of resistance' to Canberra audiences. Here, de Medici and Roberts contributed installations inside and across the outside wall of the gallery (See Figure 22). Wicks, an early BRG exhibitor, was an established artist who had worked in Berlin, New York and Paris, with works held in the national and many regional galleries.[47]

---

43   Julie Ewington, 'Canberra commentary', *Art Monthly*, November 1987, p 16.
44   Ewington, November 1987.
45   Erica Green, '*Salon coda: the making of history*', fragment, 'Salon Coda', CCAS archives.
46   Ewington, 1987.
47   In 2017, CCAS curator Alexander Boynes exhibited Wick's work in *Ex machina*.

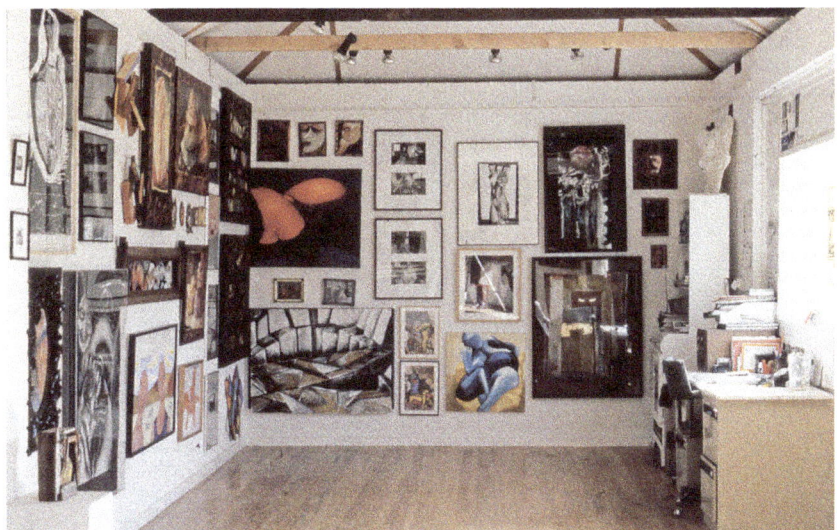

Figure 19. BRG group exhibition, *Salon coda: the making of history*, 10 June – 5 July 1987, installation photograph, detail
Source. CCAS image archive, reproduced with permission

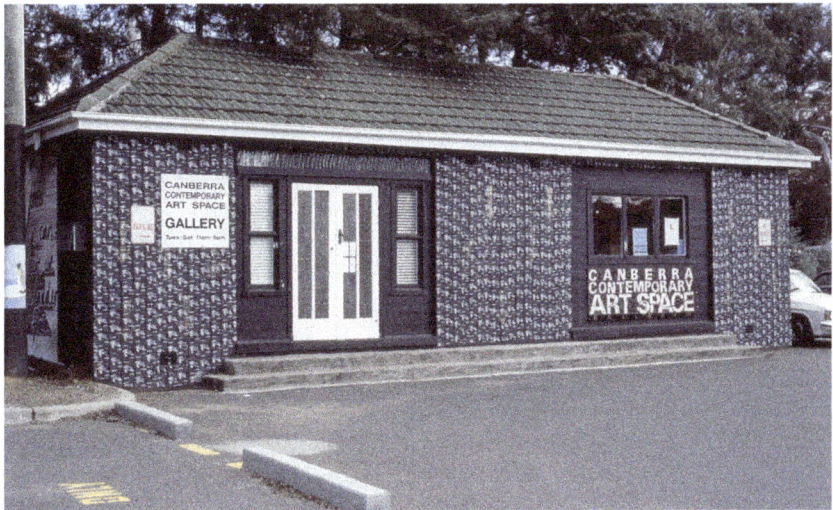

Figure 20. Exterior, BRG renamed CCAS Gallery 3
Source. CCAS image archive, reproduced with permission

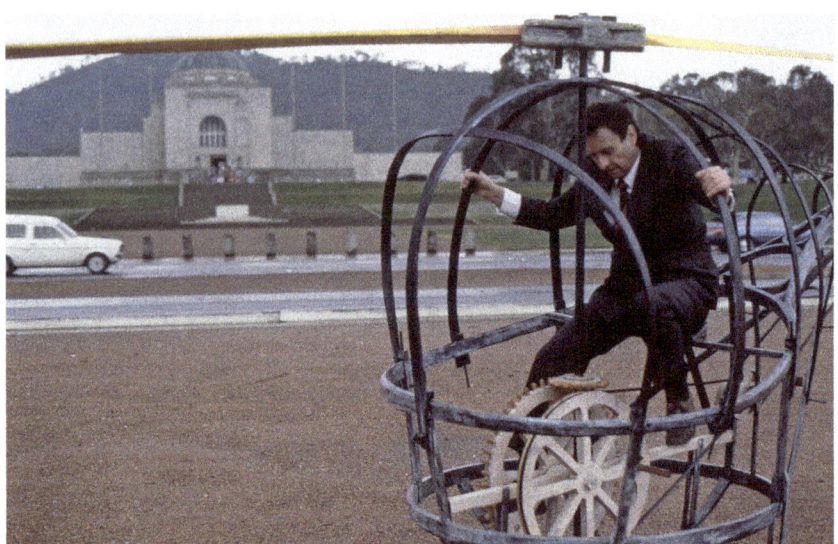

Figure 21. Arthur Wicks, *Mobile observatory*, wooden machine (working), main blades 4 m, total length 2 x 1.3 m, installed in gallery in *Site specific city*, CCAS group exhibition, 10 July – 2 August 1987
Source. CCAS image archive, reproduced with permission

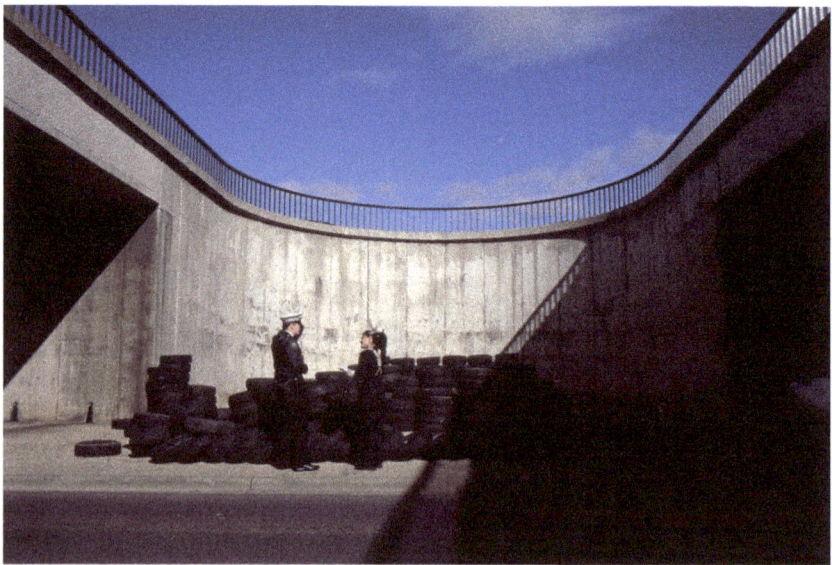

Figure 22. Artist and policeman, preparing tyre tower; tyre tower detritus installed in gallery in *Site specific city*, CCAS group exhibition, 10 July – 2 August 1987
Source. CCAS image archive, reproduced with permission

During the rest of 1987, Virgo and Green began to build a combined profile as CCAS. *Site specific city* and *Salon coda* were followed by the national travelling exhibition *Domestic contradictions: perceptions of the domestic sphere* and the local *At home with Megalo maniacs*. The former was a national look at contemporary feminism curated by Ewington, organised by the Power Gallery of Contemporary Art, and funded by the Australia Council's VAB. It comprised nine artists from four states – including Annie Newmarch, who had been Martin's Adelaide compatriot – with works spanning 1974 to 1987. It opened at the Power Gallery of Contemporary Art before travelling to Canberra, Shepparton and Adelaide. Works in the exhibition vigorously interrogated contemporary pressures on women's domestic life and the uncomfortable and growing intersections with public life.[48] Importantly, it showed an early commitment at CCAS to accepting national touring exhibitions.

At home with Megalo maniacs at the newly named CCAS Gallery 3 – which would be referred to as 'BRG' by Canberra's art community for some time to come, and would continue to stubbornly resist efforts to sanitise its exhibition program – exhibited six artists who worked together during the previous year at Megalo. Printmakers Costigan[49] and Cardew, together with Annie Trevillian and Angelic Oltolgyi working in textiles and Lynn Dickens and Annie Franklin in photomedia, presented a different take on the domestic. Reviewing both exhibitions, Sonia Barron was able to find common ground, conflating their disparate domestic views with a Lippard quote:

> What seems to be most important in this whole matter is that we focus our eyes and our feelings upon the flashes of insight which our feminine sensitivity affords us.[50]

The exhibition that followed *Domestic contradictions* constituted the only public display of a selection of works from the Parliament House collection prior to their in situ installation. Given that CCAS was relatively small and very much less physically secure than any of the national institutions, hosting *Art in architecture: selections from the new Parliament House Collection*, was a coup for the gallery. Virgo publicly

---

48   Artists included Elizabeth Gower, Helen Grace, Wendy Kelly, Jan Mackay, Leah MacKinnon, Margaret Morgan, Ann Newmarch, Stephen Robinson and Lynn Smith.
49   Costigan was director of Megalo during the later 1980s and visual arts representative on the ACT Cultural Council during the early 1990s.
50   Sonia Barron, 'Perceptions of domesticity', *Canberra Times*, 19 August 1987, p 29.

declared her desire to host exhibitions from other state galleries when she was appointed to ACG, but it was not until late 1987 that she achieved this. The exhibition was presented by the Parliament House Construction Authority in association with the Rotary Club of Canberra and it was opened by the Hon Stewart West, Minister for Administrative Services, on 3 September. Artists included Martin, Arthur Boyd, Robert Klippel, Grant Mudford, Sidney Nolan, Gareth Sansom, Imants Tillers, Vicki Varvaressos and Fred Williams. It provided one of the few examples of exhibitions at BRG/CCAS throughout the period covered in this history in which male artists outnumbered female artists, although it could hardly be considered as representative of local or national contemporary practice.

CCAS's next two exhibitions enlarged its horizons, cemented its links with CSA, and privileged women artists. When the gallery showed *Janenne Eaton: recent paintings* from 1–25 October, Grishin wrote that in:

> presenting the first Canberra exhibition of Janenne Eaton's work, the Canberra Contemporary Art Space has staged its first significant solo exhibition in its three months of operation.[51]

Eaton taught de Medici drawing at CSA, won the 1987 *Canberra Times* National Art Award, and was represented at that time by Grady. According to Grishin, Eaton 'presented the work of a mature, questioning artist … of remarkable pictorial powers and considerable spiritual insight'.[52] Following Eaton's exhibition was *The crossing*, from two Sydney artists: Adrienne Gaha, who was artist in residence in the Painting Workshop at CSA, and Narelle Jubelin, the co-founder/co-coordinator of First Draft, an artist-run gallery in Chippendale, Sydney, with which BRG had previously exchanged exhibitions.

The decision to show senior BRG artists in the first CCAS show was inspired, and from these examples of the first exhibitions under the CCAS banner in galleries 1 and 2 at Gorman House, it is clear that Virgo successfully transitioned the Gorman House location from ACG to CCAS. Illustrating that Gallery 3 in this early period continued to function in much the same way as BRG had previously done, the *Canberra Times* 'Exhibitions list' for 29 October 1987 informed readers that 'in Gallery 3 (formerly Bitumen River Gallery) … is a group exhibition by members of the BRG collective, titled *Nowhere Utopia*'. A photocopy exhibition investigating

---

51 Sasha Grishin, 'Cosmic forces that control our lives', *Canberra Times*, 15 October 1987, p 19.
52 Grishin, 1987.

Canberra's peculiarities, *Nowhere utopia* is revisited in Chapter 6 as an example of touring shows from the 1980s. The title – while reflecting Canberra's history as a largely unsuccessful utopian social experiment – acts, inchoately, as a paean to loss, a true reflection of the displacement felt by the BRG collective at the 'immolation' of their collective's home.

Notions of the collective: defining BRG

In conclusion, it is important to reflect on the notion of the collective as evidenced at BRG. This history contends that BRG is most usefully defined, considered and remembered as a collective. Virgo, in interview in 2012, objected to the definition, saying:

> When I started there the organisation was already funded. To me it was always an artist-run initiative that did receive a government grant. People didn't pay to have an exhibition – it was all supported and it had a committee, like a committee of management or an honorary board of management … so it wasn't really a collective in the true sense of collective.[53]

Disallowing the use of the term 'collective' once funding has been received, however, has little to do with the notion of the collective as evidenced at BRG. BRG's principal raison d'être was to provide exhibition space for those locked out of other spaces, whose work evinced the 'lost causes of humanity'.[54] In setting up BRG (and Megalo before it) as collectives, members were following the historical precedents of oppressed peoples who have always formed groups of various kinds to gain combined strength to face their struggles. Artists with views that ran counter to established positions or to regain visibility within their society formed collectives to conduct their mission with the relative support and protection of the group.

Although by the beginning of 1984 the collective attracted local funding of $21,000, the grant was only enough to support a small salary for a coordinator and minimal running costs. This therefore meant that the day-to-day running of the space continued to fall to the collective. Thus, CCAS operated from 1984 as a minimally funded collective, with jobs

---

53 Anne Virgo, interview, 17 September 2013.
54 *Canberra and District Historical Society Newsletter*, June/July 1982, p 11.

continuing to be allocated across a broad member base in spite of the small but growing amounts of funding extended to it after its first two years of operation.

Members were publicly referred to and self-identified as being the BRG collective even after BRG had been subsumed into CCAS. Virgo freely deployed the term during 1984/85 while working with the collective and then directly after amalgamation in the press release that announced *Nowhere utopia* as 'a group exhibition by members of the BRG collective'.[55]

The BRG community's self-identification as a collective is referred to in numerous general meeting notes over the period. Point one of the minutes from the general meeting of 19 members on 20 October 1982 states: 'That even though a co-ordinator is to be appointed, the collective is still valid for all major decision making, and through working in all the various sub-committees.'[56] A year later, minutes from the general meeting of Sunday 7 August 1983, under 'Any other business', state that a 'Process of "intuitive consensus" be upheld'.[57] Among the possible futures envisaged during the 1984 *Future directions forum* were that 'an active collective would be reflected in BRG'.[58] De Medici, co-opted by Ayres onto the management committee of BRG after returning to Canberra from Brisbane in early 1984, remembers that BRG was 'called a collective', even though by September that year it was an incorporated association: 'The membership was functioning as a collective where everything's shared. You just did it as a group because it had to be done.'[59] Printmaker and BRG member Deej Fabyc, commenting during BRG's fifth birthday on the collective mindset, wrote: 'I believe in working against the dominant ideology whenever I can … I was involved in BRG because … artist run galleries are important.'[60] Finally – as previously noted – Ewington, in reviewing the crossover exhibitions after amalgamation, lamented the 'immolation' of the 'BRG collective'.[61]

---

55 *Nowhere utopia*, media release, March 1987, CCAS scrapbook, 1987, CCAS archives.
56 BRG meeting minutes, 20 October 1982, 'Meeting minutes, 1982', CCAS archives.
57 BRG meeting minutes, 7 August 1983, 'Meeting minutes, 1983', CCAS archives.
58 BRG 'Future directions forum' minutes, May 1984, 'Future directions, 1984', CCAS archives.
59 eX de Medici, interview with the author, 9 April 2012.
60 BRG, '5th birthday show'.
61 Ewington, 1987.

The contention that BRG was not a collective in the true sense disavows both the collective ethos that drove its founding and BRG's continued focus on work that manifested the concerns of marginalised groups. Artist and art critic Mark Alice Durant writes that a community-based art collective 'gives voice to the voiceless'.[62] BRG showed the work of minorities who would otherwise have remained invisible within Canberra's available exhibition spaces, including Indigenous artists, intellectually and physically disabled children, and other socially and economically marginalised groups. That ethos remained alive throughout 1984 and 1985 during Virgo's role as coordinator, and up to and for a brief time after the merger. Indeed, pockets of resistance continued to surface right through to 1994.

Ultimately, it is BRG's locus as a continued point of resistance throughout the period from foundation to after amalgamation, together with an unbroken line of collective decision-making and job-sharing processes, that defines BRG as a collective. In interview, Virgo warned generally against romanticising the gallery's memory, but it is equally impossible to overstate the importance of BRG in the development of contemporary art in Canberra.[63] Its mission was to show art of the moment, made by those at the forefront of, and agitating for, social and economic change. Many of those who first exhibited with BRG would go on to become senior figures in the local, national and international art communities. Throughout the period from the late 1970s up to the early 2000s, their work bore witness to the movement of contemporary alternative art from the margins to the mainstream.

---

62 Mark Alice Durant, 'Activist art in the shadow of rebellion', *Art in America*, 80, July 1992, pp 31–35.
63 Virgo, 2013.

6

TRANSFORMATION: TRANSCENDING THE LOCAL

Trevor Smith's appointment as director of Canberra Contemporary Art Space (CCAS) in 1994, and his curatorial decisions during his first year, reflected international paradigmatic changes around the definition and role of the curator. These changes began to manifest from the 1970s, in exhibitions developed by Swiss curator Harald Szeemann from 1969 and Australian curator Daniel Thomas from 1972. By the late 1980s, as 'curators began more and more to be creatively and conceptually involved in the making of exhibitions' and professional roles changed accordingly, the professionalisation of curatorial practice was reflected in new academic courses.[1] JJ Charlesworth has written that 'the term "curator" has been around for as long as there were bodies of objects and bodies of knowledge to preserve and perpetuate'.[2] By the mid-1990s, however, curators had

---

1   'The formalized study of curating first properly emerged at the École du Magasin in Grenoble, France, in 1987 with a 10-month course dedicated to curatorship. This was followed by a permanent two-year Master's degree course at the Royal College of Art in London in 1992. These programs recognized the importance of curatorship and heralded a new place for the curator – emphasizing the position's essential responsibility in the creation of an exhibition or display' (Alice Pfeiffer, 'Delving into the art of curating: as job enjoys a star turn, several new degrees offer "a passport for life"', *International Herald Tribune* (Paris), 11 October 2012, p 202). Jens Hoffman, 'The next *Documenta* should be curated by an artist', 2002, quoted in Nicola Trezzi, 'The art of curating', *Flash Art International*, 45, March/April 2010, pp 62–66.
2   JJ Charlesworth, 'Curating doubt', *Art Monthly*, 294, March 2006, p 1.

transitioned from their supportive role in developing collections and exhibitions to acting as, and importantly being perceived as, cultural protagonists in their creative exhibition-making.[3]

Among others who have written on these decades of transition is American arts writer Nicola Trezzi, who identified the curatorial shift as a move to 'the practice of curating as an art in its own right, with its own structure and language'.[4] Trezzi writes of the 'passage from a historical, "temporal" perception … to a "spatial" understanding of art'.[5] In other words, a move away from curating as being solely aligned to the academic discipline of art history towards an approach dominated by artists and other multidisciplinary practitioners. This change was apparent internationally as the 1990s progressed through the rapid growth of biennales of contemporary art with governing bodies that extended curatorial invitations to artists and when artists began curating satellite exhibitions during biennales.[6] In Australia in 2002, Richard Grayson was invited to curate Sydney's biennale, (*The world may be) fantastic*.[7] As well, in the mid-2000s, the Australia Council instituted a funded program that invited international curators to tour Australian art spaces in order to assist in expanding the local understanding of the role of the curator and positively impact international perceptions of Australian artists.

---

3   In 1990 artist and founding director Jeffrey Moore of Blue Star Contemporary Art Museum (established 1986) in San Antonio, Texas, convened a workshop to answer questions about the notion of the curator within the contemporary art space and the curator's relationship to artists and exhibitions. The questions were reflective of a growing liminality around the role and included: 'What is a curator? What does he or she do? What is the role of the curator in the art community? Why does someone have the right to call himself or herself a curator? Why is this or that curator's taste better than mine? Is it who you know? In other words, does a buddy system between curators and favorite artists exist? Do curators have a responsibility to exhibit artists from their own communities? How do the duties, goals, etc. of a museum curator differ from those of a director/curator at an alternative space? How do the local arts community, the size of the exhibition space, etc. influence curatorial decisions?' This chapter illustrates how the spirit of these questions manifested at CCAS.
4   Trezzi, 2015.
5   Trezzi, 2015.
6   This relatively new field of scholarly enquiry into the artist as curator is examined by Costa Rican curator Jens Hoffman in 'The art of curating and the curating of art' (*The utopian display platform*, Milan, Nuova Accademia di Belle Arti Milano). See also, Elena Filipovic, 'When exhibitions become form: on the history of the artist as curator, *Mousse*, 41, moussemagazine.it/taac0/, accessed 4 August 2016.
7   Grayson was one of a handful of artist/curators at the forefront of the discipline's rapidly changing construct in contemporary art in the 1990s. (*The world may be) fantastic* included 'quirky and unpredictable' artists from 21 countries. Grayson stated that his artistic intention was to 'look at "approaches that are fantastic, partial, various, suggestive, ambitious, subjective, wobbly and eccentric to normal orbits"' (Michael Duncan, 'Report from Sydney: self-created worlds', *Art in America*, 90, 10, 2002, pp 60–65).

At CCAS, this change was manifested through the appointment of Jane Barney as curator in 1995, whose own curatorial trajectory emanated from her arts practice.

Along with these paradigmatic changes in curatorial process, Smith's appointment occurred during the decade in which contemporary art spaces in Australia were seeking to establish identities that distinguished them from the collective artist-run spaces of the 1970s and 1980s. By the beginning of the 1990s, having successfully transitioned to funded organisations, the inexorable tendency towards expansion foregrounded the desire for further legitimisation for contemporary art spaces. This tendency became intrinsically connected to the requirement to show funding bodies, tangible need for increased support.

Having completed the first step in this larger acceptance of contemporary art, contemporary art spaces looked forward. The art museum, exclusion from which had provided the impetus for establishing the collective artist-run spaces that gave rise to contemporary art spaces, continued to provide an aspirational model. This desire for legitimacy by alternative artists was present from the 1970s, a period that Grayson recalled as one where alternative artists, relegated to basements and clubs, would walk past the art museums dreaming of a day when their art would be hung on art museum walls.[8]

As a result of this relentless drive towards ever larger models of institutionalisation, tensions arose between contemporary art space directors and the boards who supported continued growth, and local emerging and established contemporary artists who needed contemporary art spaces to enable the development and showing of new works that fell outside the exhibition parameters of the commercial galleries and art museums. A particular example of this is Sydney artist Dale Frank's exhibition *Satellite of love*, co-curated by Smith and the artist, and shown at CCAS in association with the National Gallery of Australia's exhibition *Virtual reality* over the summer of 1994/95.

The structure of the contemporary art space during the 1980s allowed for an intense, personal, start-to-finish engagement with exhibiting artists. This 'grassroots' curatorial input had a decisive impact on the growth of contemporary art practice and its increased visibility within the community.

---

8   Grayson, 2011.

The position of the director/curator provided an opportunity to broadly affect the contemporary arts milieu. During the 1990s, this position became increasingly critical to the success or otherwise of contemporary art spaces in general. One of the changes in curatorial practice during the 1990s was that, while contemporary art spaces continued to exhibit artists excluded from the mainstream, by the mid-1990s the focus was moving to artists who were very much included. The mark of an effective curator became about the quality of artists that could be attracted to the contemporary art space.

Previous chapters explored the roles of coordinators and the collective in two quite different iterations of the space: the collective, and the funded organisation. These chapters consider the institutionalisation of the space and what effects this had on the exhibition of contemporary art in the capital, as the culture of the collective, artist-run space transformed to a fully funded and administered contemporary art space. One consequence of this more highly administered structure was that successive boards came to play an increasingly important role in decision-making, particularly in setting different curatorial agendas through the hiring of directors. At the end of 1993, the CCAS board sought to bring the organisation into line with changing national and international curatorial parameters by hiring a director whose focus would transform the organisation.

A new direction: Trevor Smith

After almost 10 years in arts management in Canberra, inaugural CCAS director Anne Virgo began transitioning to a new life in Melbourne. The experienced administrator and artist Brenda Runnegar stepped into the role of acting director, supported by CCAS members. In October 1993, the CCAS board – which then included Christopher Chapman (chair); Deborah Clark (secretary); and, from the Canberra School of Art (CSA), artist/lecturers David Watt, Ruth Waller, Pam Debenham, Martyn Jolly and Anna Eggert – accepted Virgo's resignation and advertised the director's position.

The board's membership reflected the paradigmatic changes occurring throughout the 1980s as collective artist-run spaces transitioned to funded contemporary art spaces. Board members were educated and progressive arts professionals who supported the contemporary art space model. Six years and three months had passed since amalgamation and, with CCAS now established as the principal conduit for the exhibition of contemporary art in Canberra, the board sought a new type of director/curator who would bring national experience and international perspectives to the organisation and therefore to the capital's contemporary arts community.[9]

A nationally placed advertisement, 'seeking a Director with substantial curatorial, managerial and administrative abilities', required that, along with 'relevant tertiary qualifications in Contemporary Art History, Practice or Administration', the applicant should have 'a demonstrated ability to effectively liaise with government funding agencies, corporate and community organisations, all levels of the art museum and gallery profession, and especially artists'.[10] The position attracted a salary of $36,638–$40,946 per annum, more than twice the annual salary of $15,000 offered 10 years previously for the coordinator's position at BRG.[11]

The interviews took place over a day at CSA, in a room whose long windows revealed the length of Childers Street. As Jolly recalled it, towards day's end, he looked up and out through the windows to see a tall, dark-haired man, 'striding with great energy and purpose' towards the school's entrance.[12] This, it transpired, was Smith. Successful in interview, he was appointed as CCAS director at the end of 1993. He commenced a three-year term on 9 March 1994,[13] by which time Runnegar – CCAS's highly experienced administrator of eight years – had been acting director for the five months since Virgo's move to the Australian Print Workshop (APW) in Melbourne.

---

9   Deborah Clark, at that time chair of CCAS, conversation with the author, March 2013.
10 'Gallery co-ordinator', advertisement, *Canberra Times*, 25 September 1993, p 10s.
11 'Gallery co-ordinator', advertisement, *Canberra Times*, 5 November 1983, p 28.
12 Martyn Jolly, conversation with the author, October 2014.
13 The *Canberra Times* welcomed Smith in print a full month before he arrived (Robert Macklin, 'A capital life', *Canberra Times*, 5 February 1994, p 49), attributing Mark Dubner's exhibition, *The querulous quest of quiff*, to Smith. Perhaps the title and the subject matter – 'humour, pathos and sexuality are used within a narrative structure to illustrate the protagonist's travails' – sounded like something a young Canadian contemporary art space director would come up with? In fact, this exhibition was organised some months before Virgo's resignation. Smith's appointment was ultimately announced under the headline 'New director for Contemporary Art Space', giving his starting date as 9 March 1994 (*Canberra Times*, 28 February 1994, p 11). On Thursday 17 March, the Board of Management held meet-and-greet drinks in the gallery for Smith, prior to the opening of the touring exhibition *Queerography*.

Following Smith's appointment, arts journalist Helen Musa identified an initial feeling of surprise among the local arts community, reporting in *Muse* in March 1994 that 'As a Canadian trained overseas [Smith's] appointment may at first appear surprising'.[14] Smith was 29 years old when he arrived in Canberra, having graduated with a BA in art history from the University of British Columbia in 1986, and then working as a curatorial assistant at the Mackenzie Art Gallery, established in 1953 in Regina, the capital of Canadian province Saskatchewan. After moving to Sydney with his Australian wife, he spent 18 months as site manager at the Art Gallery of New South Wales (AGNSW) for Sydney's ninth biennale (1992/93). This engagement, *Muse* reported, 'obviously gave him a valuable insight into the contemporary art scene here in Australia'.[15]

The use of the word 'obviously' may have been somewhat tongue-in-cheek; Smith's brief exposure to Australian art since his arrival in the country was largely Sydney-centric. Both his Canadian training and employment and his biennale engagement, however, were important factors in the board's decision to hire him and greatly influenced his curatorial decisions over his three years at CCAS. He had, firstly, a demonstrated commitment to the exhibition of Indigenous art. The Mackenzie Art Gallery had a proud record of achievement as a leader in First Nation exhibitions. Smith's time there, the recent foregrounding of Australian Indigenous art through Australia's 1988 bicentenary, as well as his Sydney gallery connections, contributed to his curatorial commitment to Indigenous art. Secondly, Smith worked with and must have been influenced by Anthony Bond, artistic director of the 1992/93 *Biennale of Sydney*, who sought to 'expand the understanding of Internationalism' in his selection of 'mainstream artists' and 'emerging artists from beyond the traditional centres'.[16] Thirdly, Chapman's position as CCAS chair and connection to Frank and the Sydney gallery scene meant that the two shared similar concerns and interests and were able to collaborate on *Satellite of love* over the 1995/96 summer. Smith's high energy and internationalist viewpoint were exactly the qualities the board sought, qualities that outweighed his lack of local knowledge, restricted Australian art knowledge and inexperience as a director.[17]

---

14 *Muse*, March 1994.
15 *Muse*, March 1994.
16 Anthony Bond, 'The boundary rider', foreword, catalogue, *9th Biennale of Sydney* (1992/93).
17 Smith derived, in a sense, his regional service from his tenure at CCAS, enabling him to apply for and accept a position three years later as curator of contemporary art at the Art Gallery of Western Australia.

By the time Smith arrived, the bulk of the 1994 exhibition program was in place at both Gorman House and at the Manuka space. The program included receiving (as opposed to sending out) international and national touring exhibitions; exhibitions from queer and outsider artists; sculpture and performance exhibitions; and continued forums on arts connectedness and the state of the arts in the Australian Capital Territory (ACT). A period in July was set aside for the new director's first exhibition.

Romantisystem

Smith's Sydney connections were a strong contributing factor to his curatorial decisions at CCAS. His first exhibition, three-and-a-half months after arrival, was the group show *Romantisystem*, which hung in the Gorman House gallery from 1–31 July. According to its press release, the exhibition explored 'the intermingling of subjective and systematic approaches to artmaking'[18] and featured 14 artists from Canberra and 'around Australia'. Of the artists in the exhibition, Rosalie Gascoigne and Neil Roberts were from Canberra, and Robert MacPherson was from Brisbane. The balance included Sydney artists Paul Saint, Ian Burn, Maria Cruz, Bronwyn Clark-Coolee, Matthys Gerber, Lindy Lee, Ruark Lewis, Euan McDonald, Susan Norrie, Jacqueline Rose and sculptor Kathy Temin. Smith's selection of artists, who were mainly luminaries of the Sydney gallery scene, speaks to the change occurring in curatorial practice by which a curator's worth was judged by the quality of artists he or she could attract to an exhibition.

During the 1990s the exhibition catalogue also assumed a heightened importance within exhibitions. The press release for *Romantisystem* promised 'A post-event catalogue of the exhibition … including essays and installation photographs'.[19] Although in this instance the catalogue failed to materialise, it nonetheless retained a sort of ghost-life throughout the exhibition, featuring, in its non-presence, in the many reviews that *Romantisystem* generated.[20] Faced with a somewhat curly curatorial

---

18 *Romantisystem*, media release, 21 June 1994, '*Romantisystem*', CCAS archives.
19 *Romantisystem*, 1994.
20 Sasha Grishin, reviewing Ruth Waller and Tess Horwitz's October 1995 exhibition at CCAS for the *Canberra Times*, acerbically wrote at the end of that review, 'I still have not seen the catalogue for the *Romantisystem* which the curator Trevor Smith promised to issue to explain his thinking behind the exhibition. A year has passed so I have stopped holding my breath' ('Conventional departures', *Canberra Times*, 24 October 1995, p 18).

premise and with this 'catalogue to come' promise central to the press release and exhibition, and additionally without wall text or other textual markers, local reviewers Peter Haynes, Sasha Grishin and Kerry-Anne Cousins rose to the exhibition's challenge with mixed responses.

Haynes' review in *Art and Australia* comprised one of a slowly increasing number of texts in national art magazines about Canberra's local art scene, reflecting the growth of the visual arts sector and its increasing national penetration. Haynes began and ended his review with comments relating to the absence of a catalogue and he elliptically wrote that, because of this absence, 'the works in the exhibition therefore operated as illustrations for an unarticulated text which paradoxically opened them to a wider dialogue about the nature of (some) contemporary art practice'. What are we to make of Haynes' comments that 'the clues though, are those plastic expressions deployed around the gallery space and it is precisely these which Smith used as the unarticulated text'? Does Haynes mean that the works speak for themselves? Concluding, 'we must engage directly with the works if we are to begin to understand the impulse for Smith's curatorial premise', Haynes seemed relieved that there was no catalogue, as 'too often the text becomes the exhibition'.

Discussing a work by Roberts, Haynes wrote that 'Within a minimal, formal vocabulary he creates a highly expressive amalgam theoretically contradictory to its imposed limitations'. 'Other artists [in the exhibition],' he continued, 'adopt an assertively interrogative approach to the art history of which they are a part', citing Norrie, Lee and Rose (three of the six woman artists in the exhibition) as 'clear though complex examples of this'. Haynes concluded that the exhibition's 'challenge' was 'the directness of the confrontation offered by the works chosen by the curator. Its meaning lay in this challenge and *not* in the unseen/unread verbal defence'.[21] This review, while it indicated a willingness to engage with Smith's curatorial premise, was ambivalent.

Grishin, a regular visitor to national and international galleries, wrote for the *Canberra Times* that '"Romantisystem" is a curious word invented to describe a curious exhibition representing the work of 15 artists, most of whom are from Sydney'. He reminded readers that most artists were well known to Canberra audiences, thus underscoring the art literacy of the 1994 population, but was largely unmoved by the curatorial premise:

---

21 Peter Haynes, 'Antisystem', *Art and Australia*, 32, 3, 1995, p 444. Emphasis in original.

While it is difficult not to be impressed by this selection of some very fine work in a wide range of mediums, even if much of it is predictable in its unconventional properties, the lack of surprises or startling discoveries makes this for me a somewhat directionless exhibition, a show case rather than an argument.

Grishin illuminated Smith's curatorial premise for *Canberra Times* readers in writing that the exhibition:

> is built around the notion of a dialectic between what could be termed a subjective approach to art making and a systematic approach … The two are generally viewed as antithetic to one another, and the curator … has attempted to set up unexpected contrasts and oppositions to form new relationships between the works … Without the assistance of a wall text or catalogue (although one is promised for September), the beholder is thrown in to the exhibition to form his or her own associations and interpretations of the curatorial intent. This is only a partly satisfactory approach.[22]

What is interesting about these critical reviews is their charting of the mixed community reception surrounding this change in the presentation of contemporary art in Canberra. The lack of a catalogue and wall texts as a point of contention in Haynes', Grishin's, and in Kerry-Anne Cousins' review (a discussion of which follows) masks what was really happening. The change in emphasis from local to national during Smith's directorship occurred a short time after Canberra artists had succeeded in carving out their local identity from within the cultural and funding imperatives of a national capital space. Some members of Canberra's arts community were understandably reluctant to relinquish this local focus in favour of national representations. Smith had, however, been hired to bring art within the local space into line with national curatorial and exhibition agendas. His perceived radical approach, which was brought to the fore with this exhibition, was not well understood within the local context in this first showing of his curatorial intent. As a sign of Canberra's growing maturity, however, his effort was appreciated. Cousins' review sums up this dichotomy of confusion and support.

---

22 Sasha Grishin, 'No discoveries in a "showcase" display', *Canberra Times*, 26 July 1994, p 16.

Reviewing for the August edition of *Muse*, Cousins felt the lack of supporting documentation made the exhibition unnecessarily opaque to viewers:

> Smith suggests that two traditionally opposing artistic approaches can be present together in the same artist's work ... Unfortunately this is not communicated to the viewer who is required to accept these theories without being given the necessary background knowledge to take part in the debate.

Cousins believed that the terminology lacked 'any clear definition'. With the title eliding 'Romanticism' and 'systemic', she wondered if the Romanti[cism] of the title was 'used in an art historical sense' or if it was 'equated, as it appears to be in this context, with expressionism'? Cousins pointed out that, while systemic related to 1950s/60s American colour field painting, Smith equated the term with a 'cool and impersonal' artistic choice. Cousins claimed that without any explanation of the terms:

> the point of the exhibition's unifying theme becomes lost and meaningless. Paradoxically, the catalogue in which all these ideas may have been able to be discussed at greater length and presumably be made clear, will not be appearing until later.

Despite these reservations, Cousins concluded that the exhibition was:

> one of the best surveys we have had in Canberra recently of contemporary art trends ... It is to be welcomed that [Smith] is looking towards creating an exciting, interesting and thought provoking forum for contemporary art in Canberra.[23]

Romantisystem highlighted emerging problems that were connected to the appointment of an inexperienced director. These included a lack of record-keeping and a perceived disconnect between the CCAS charter and its implementation, which in itself was a clear marker of the tensions surrounding the changing identity of contemporary art spaces nationally. The former manifested early in the media release with errors relating to artists' names and the total number of exhibiting artists, the decision to do away with a visitors' book – which precludes an examination of public response to this and other exhibitions in Smith's first year, the lack of wall texts and the non-appearance of the catalogue. Although these could be explained by a postmodern anti-systems bent, they are more likely due to

---

23 Kerry-Anne Cousins, 'Art', *Muse*, August 1994.

the new director's administrative inexperience, the lack of staff at the time within CCAS and of funding alternatives to pay for an accompanying catalogue.[24] It is likely that Smith – having come from a commercial, highly resourced, Sydney contemporary arts scene – would have believed that the national capital would deliver a similarly resourced contemporary arts milieu.

Cousins' comments welcomed *Romantisystem* as heralding a wider contemporary arts dialogue, thus underscoring one of the board's primary reasons for hiring Smith. However, the privileging of Sydney's commercially successful artists sat uncomfortably with some CCAS members and pointed to a lack of understanding concerning the previously accepted CCAS core policy of supporting local emerging artists. eX de Medici believed that the contemporary art space charter was to:

> promote the work of emerging artists, not promote the work of commercially successful artists from very successful hard-core commercial galleries. It's sort of like a cultural cringe inside another cultural cringe inside another one whereas I believe the Bitumen River Gallery didn't really care about those debates at all.[25]

De Medici's multiple iterations of 'cultural cringe' identified national and local tendencies to validate, as culture, that which came from outside. In the first instance (as examined in Chapter 2 in the context of national arts funding), the cringe as an Australian phenomenon speaks to the national tendency that – until the rise of a Labor government under Gough Whitlam in the early 1970s – classed culture as that which came specifically from England.[26] Locally, the cringe referenced the trend that saw successive intakes of graduating students from CSA leave Canberra after graduation to make their careers in southern capitals, particularly Melbourne; many of the founding members of the Bitumen River Gallery (BRG) collective had left the Territory by mid-1984 to further their careers. De Medici's third iteration of the cringe draws attention to the culture she saw developing within CCAS; this was reflected more widely in the national contemporary art spaces that eschewed exhibiting work by local contemporary artists in favour of those from other Australian

---

24 Smith is now a highly respected and experienced curator of contemporary art with more than 25 years' experience. He is currently curator of the *Present tense* initiative at the Peabody Essex Museum in Salem, Massachusetts.
25 De Medici, 2012.
26 AA Phillips, 'The cultural cringe', *Meanjin*, 9, 4, 1950, pp 299–302.

capitals, especially Sydney. This speaks again to the growing tendency of the curator as star and the quality of that curator being verified in the quality of artists they attracted.

There is no doubting Smith's energy and optimism, nor the local arts community's efforts to make him welcome. Interviewed by Musa at the end of July and asked how he was settling in, he replied 'Obviously, it has been a huge learning curve, but people have been generous … [T]hey mightn't agree, but there is a willingness to be open to possibilities'.[27] During his first active year in the local arts community he was interviewed regularly on local radio 2xx; opened the mid-year graduate diploma exhibition at the ANU Drill Hall Gallery in August, the ANCA tenants' exhibition in September, and an exhibition at Jardine Gallery in October; chaired panels; spoke at conferences; and instituted a program of studio visits to local artists in an effort to get an overview of current arts practice in the ACT.

Satellite of love

A powerful example of Smith's curatorial intent occurred at the end of 1994, when Canberra's contemporary arts consumers were invited to take a bold leap into the conceptual contemporary. Frank's solo exhibition *Satellite of love* (see Figure 23) garnered reviews that indicated some critical resistance to continued theoretically conceptual work from interstate artists. The exhibition was installed at CCAS from 11 December 1994 to 29 January 1995. At the same time, from 10 December 1994 to 5 February 1995, Frank was included in the group exhibition *Virtual reality* at the National Gallery of Australia (NGA). *Satellite of love* and Frank's works in *Virtual reality* provide a comprehensive example of the differences in curatorial possibilities between CCAS and NGA during this period; while Frank's works at NGA could have migrated across to CCAS, *Satellite of love* could not have been shown at NGA. This is mainly because exhibits in *Satellite of love* were designed to cause perceptible and, at times, negative physical impacts on viewers. Equally, these concurrent exhibitions illustrate the particularity of Canberra's small and interconnected arts community, which made curatorial collaboration possible – in this instance, between those working within the institutional museum model on one hand and within the contemporary art space model on the other.

---

27   Helen Musa, 'Drawing an artists' map for Canberra', *Canberra Times*, 31 July, 1994, p 24.

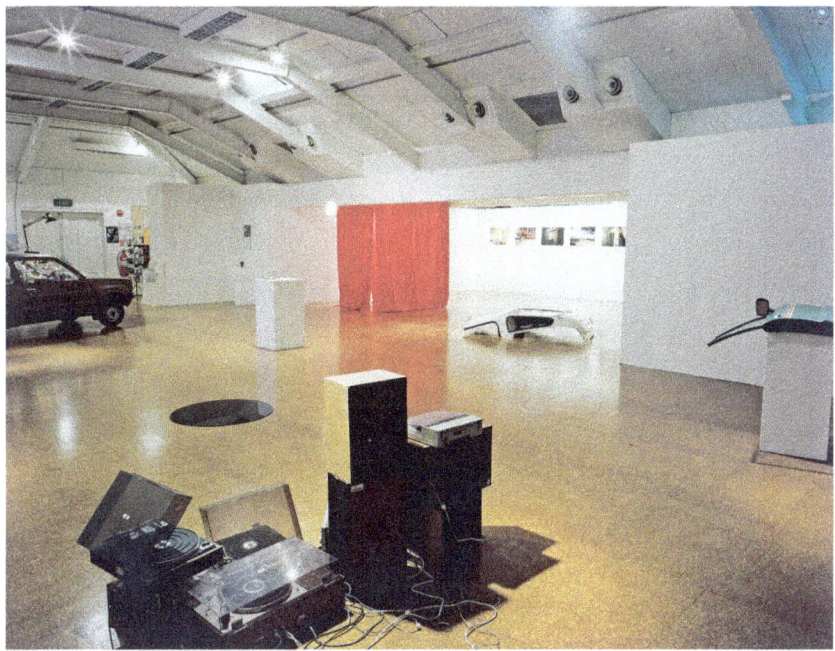

Figure 23. Dale Frank, *Satellite of love*, CCAS, 11 December 1994 – 29 January 1995, installation photograph
Source. Photographer: Brenton McGeachie. CCAS image archive, reproduced with permission

Chapman, then an assistant curator in Australian art at the NGA, provided the critical collaborative link in assisting Mary Eagle, the curator of *Virtual reality*. Chapman was chairman of the CCAS board when Smith was hired and the two shared an interest in contemporary theories and conceptual art, and they were both passionate supporters of Frank's work.[28] Frank's Sydney gallerist, Roslyn Oxley, supplied a number of the artists for Smith's *Romantisystem* exhibition earlier that year. Smith, wrote an essay for the *Virtual reality* catalogue,[29] and Chapman wrote the catalogue essay for *Satellite of love*[30] and the Frank essay in the *Virtual reality* catalogue. The exhibitions were billed as being 'in association with' each other.

---

28   Christopher Chapman, 'Dale Frank and the Diamond Dogs', in *Virtual reality*, exhibition catalogue, Canberra, National Gallery of Australia, 1994.
29   Trevor Smith, 'Ronald Jones: contagion cultures', in *Virtual reality*, 1994.
30   Christopher Chapman, 'Reality used to be a friend of mine', *Satellite of love*, exhibition catalogue, Canberra, CCAS, 1994, np.

The exhibition signalled CCAS's emergence as a relevant national contemporary arts space. By 1994, Frank was widely known for his conceptual, performative, mercurial and challenging art practice. *Satellite of love* approached the apogee of conceptual art practice in Australia at the time, with a mix of objects with conceptual links that proved challenging to reviewers, audiences and gallery staff (see below). A wish list from the artist to Smith, written some weeks before installation, exemplifies Frank's free-ranging, fearless, associative approach. Despite these inherent challenges, Smith and Chapman were able to mediate the installation process to successful conclusion.

Once again, the local critical reception to Smith's curatorial intent indicated a residual intolerance to theoretically challenging contemporary art from a non-Canberra-based artist. The November media release informed readers that 'automobiles, family snapshots [and] bodies' would be 'touchstones' in the body of work and that a 32-page colour catalogue would be available at the opening. Chapman's catalogue essay was contentious for Sonia Barron, who reviewed the exhibition for the *Canberra Times* in January 1995. Barron wrote that Chapman had gone to 'extraordinary lengths to justify, in terms of current and not-so-current art practices and theoretical writings, what I can only describe as a deliberate assault on the senses'. Thinking at first that she had walked into a 'post Christmas disaster site', Barron concluded:

> After reading the catalogue and looking again, it all became a bit nasty and a deadly serious mind-bending exercise. The artist as victim, or a proxy for perceived social ills, is a fashionable posture. The twist with this installation is that the viewer is being deliberately victimised by the artist.[31]

Barron picked up on the artist's use of the word 'victimisation', as quoted in Chapman's catalogue essay;[32] arguably, in this instance, the word victim has been hijacked in service to the reviewer's negative response. Rather than viewers being 'deliberately victimised'; however, the artist was hoping to engage the audience in a duologue. In a fax to Chapman, Frank wrote, 'All participants in this work including the audience could be seen as part of the terrorism/victimisation here. The roles are not clear'.[33] The review indicates that Frank, whose work is essentially 'concerned with

---

31 Sonia Barron, 'Viewers are deliberately victimised', *Canberra Times*, 13 January 1995, p 12.
32 Chapman, *Satellite of love*, 1994.
33 Chapman, *Satellite of love*, 1994.

notions of the physical, the physiological and psychological',[34] succeeded, as Chapman writes, in his aim of '[creating] a shift in perception which is actualised and apprehended directly by the viewer … [An intense experience] we are unfamiliar with and deeply unsure of'.[35] Chapman believed that, in reference to the viewer, 'What is at stake is the possibility of complete surrender'.[36] Frank's purpose was, therefore, not to victimise the audience but to continue to explore the very concept of reality and to push the boundaries of conceptual art practice in the interests of this exploration. In fact, his aim was to invite the audience, in the most visceral way, to act as a participant in this questioning of reality.

An unexpected consequence of the exhibition was that it led to a formalising of management's responsibilities to gallery visitors. The 17 works on the final exhibition list for *Satellite of love* are essentially not very different from the wish list Frank faxed to Smith in November 1994. Components of works included 'a small colony of red-back spiders' and 'chemically active paint'.[37] At the last minute,[38] exhibit no 17, *For John (no, not John N.) this is not a disco, I'm only dancing* (disc-jockey, living sculpture, music, lights, atmospheric fog), was dropped, as the requirement to have a live DJ and a 'living sculpture' in residence throughout the life of the exhibition proved impossible to accommodate.[39] Elements of the exhibition *were* contentious, including no 7, *Tolerance + acceptance – Fatima's global cannon with the allure and acid of the fat cow's afterbirth*, which constituted a hip-high swimming pool with a slick of varnish covering the water's surface. The ACT Department of Health directed the work be removed shortly into the exhibition's run after the water began to evaporate, the varnish fumes permeated the gallery and several staff members experienced headaches and nausea.

---

34 Chapman, *Satellite of love*, 1994.
35 Chapman, *Satellite of love*, 1994.
36 Chapman, *Satellite of love*, 1994.
37 'List of works', *Satellite of love*, CCAS.
38 Room sheets have exhibits no 7 and no 17 ruled through with black lines.
39 Exhibit no 15, *Untitled (for Christopher) – after Joseph Beuys* (television monitor, VCR, selection of four videos – *The abyss, Point break, Starman, The last American hero*), is a homage to Chapman who has written extensively on Frank's oeuvre.

CCAS chairperson (1994–95) Deborah Clark understatedly writes in her 1995 report that '*Satellite of love* proved to be something of a learning experience for all concerned'.[40] The Department of Health's intervention led to CCAS developing a draft health and safety policy at the beginning of 1995:

> Recognising the hazards occurring in the arts industry, the CCAS will take every practicable step to provide and maintain a safe and healthy work environment for all employees. Although the CCAS exists to promote and support experimental art practices, when proposed work includes potentially noxious substances or other elements which may have a deleterious effect upon the workplace environment, this must be taken into consideration in the assessment of exhibition proposals.[41]

Despite the exhibition's critical reception, and irrespective of the scandal associated with the Department of Health's removal of exhibit no 7 and the artist's unhappiness with that intervention, *Satellite of love* was a memorable harbinger of change in the history of contemporary art exhibition in Canberra.

Smith came to Canberra with some international experience, a sound knowledge of contemporary theories and a brief but intense exposure to Sydney's contemporary arts milieu. His first solo year could not have been an easy transition for him and was obviously not for some others, including incumbent CCAS staff and those members who were committed to the local model. It can be argued, however, that this same lack of experience allowed him to move beyond the status quo of the nationally accepted, bureaucratised, contemporary art space model that was in place by 1994. By not understanding that status quo and by virtue of having only had 18 months of experience in Australia, Smith was less likely to be burdened by the accepted/expected paradigm.

At the heart of Smith's lukewarm reception from some quarters was an unshakeable belief that the contemporary art space model's primary agency was in its privileging of local emerging and mid-career contemporary artists. In hiring Smith, however, the CCAS board flagged a desire for a more internationalist curatorial approach to inject a contemporary theoretical component into the CCAS exhibition calendar.

---

40   Deborah Clark, 'CCAS Chairperson's report 1995', 1995 scrapbook, CCAS archives.
41   'Draft Health and Safety Policy', 7 February, 1995 scrapbook.

Ultimately, *Romantisystem* and *Satellite of love* were a distinct alternative to all that had gone before. They provided a permissive model for the flowering of performative and travelling exhibitions that Barney, as assistant curator and then as director, instituted from 1995 to 2002. Barney defined Smith as 'hard-core, deeply passionate about contemporary art. He swept away any cobwebs or conservatism that may have crept into the program'.[42] This 'passionate' commitment to difficult contemporary art set the tone for the next period at CCAS.

With Smith's appointment, the CCAS board fulfilled their criteria of positioning CCAS as nationally relevant within a rapidly changing sector. They were so successful in this endeavour that, 12 months after Smith's appointment, they were forced to make another appointment. The following section investigates Barney's appointment and her local focus, which acted as a balance to Smith's internationalism.

Jane Barney

By November 1994, the CCAS board was grappling with a breakdown in the relationship between Runnegar and Smith.[43] Ill-suited professionally, their relationship deteriorated over the months leading up to November. Vivienne Binns, living in Canberra and teaching at CSA, joined the board in 1994 and remembers that Runnegar and Smith were 'like chalk and cheese, really different, really didn't understand one another'.[44] Smith's postmodern, internationalised, urban conceptualism and Runnegar's local community orientation were deeply at odds: 'she didn't like or understand what he wanted to do and he didn't like her style and what she was doing and there just developed a standoff'.[45] With a great deal of experience leading community organisations through successful creative endeavours, Binns and Clark took on the responsibility of negotiating a détente. The board verbally supported both Runnegar and Smith for their different but equally valuable approaches and required that Smith take separate management/coaching classes. Binns arranged mediation sessions for the

---

42   Jane Barney, interview with the author, 19 September 2012.
43   Runnegar was CCAS administrator for eight years and acting director on a number of occasions, including during the eight months prior to Smith's appointment. At the end of 1993, Runnegar endured the disappointment of being overlooked for the director's position in favour of Smith.
44   Binns, 2012.
45   Binns, 2012.

two and 'smoothed things over'.⁴⁶ She believes that by the time Runnegar resigned at the end of January 1995, 'it felt OK … whereas the other way [without mediation] everyone would have been hurt and damaged'.⁴⁷

The loss of long-term workers reduced the previously deep connection between the gallery and the local contemporary art community. In December 1994 administrative assistant Lois Selby also resigned, after four years of service. This meant that, by February 1995, CCAS staff comprised Smith, who had been in Canberra for 10 months, and newly appointed gallery assistant Megan Elliot. Reflecting on the period directly preceding her appointment as assistant curator, Barney believed that the board had realised there was 'potentially a risk of disenfranchising'⁴⁸ local artists by hiring someone who was more connected to art and artists outside of Canberra. In April 1995, Barney began her new role as assistant curator.

The appointment had far-reaching consequences in positioning CCAS nationally as a dynamic contemporary institution and presenting Canberra artists to national and international audiences. It made the best of Smith, allowing him time, within a more structured workspace, to continue to move the organisation forward. Barney and Smith worked closely together over the next two years. They were a well-matched team, personally compatible and professionally complementary. Barney was and remains a supporter of Smith's achievements and of their time together, crediting the success of their professional partnership with a division of duties that allowed her to 'focus on the Canberra connections [while] he was more focused on the bigger connections'.⁴⁹

In contrast to Smith's academic path to CCAS, Barney's trajectory, both in her photographic practice and her career as a curator and director, was elliptical. She came to Canberra as a three-year-old in 1963 and, like many Canberrans, moved away from and back to the city at various times. She was awarded degrees in political science and history from The Australian National University (ANU) and then worked under a Community Development Program (CDP) trainee scheme at 2xx. This community radio station was a conduit for multi–art form practitioners, interviewing local and visiting artists and employing, in various

---

46   Binns, 2012.
47   Binns, 2012.
48   Jane Barney, interview with the author, 19 September 2012.
49   Barney, 2012.

capacities, numerous arts practitioners. Barney had been taking her own photographs, mostly still lifes, for some time and, through 2xx, was exposed to a variety of artists and creatives. She approached Photo Access with a request to do a Cibachrome colour course and 'had this fantastic experience … I hadn't done the basic introduction to black and white. They said "don't worry we're doing this intensive weekend course"'.[50] This led to two years as Photo Access project officer. After this she moved to CSA where, from 1990, she was employed as an assistant at the CSA Gallery and, from 1992 to 1994, as professional practice coordinator. In 1993, while the SofA Gallery curator Julie Ewington took up an Australia Council Visual Arts Board (VAB) Writer's Fellowship, Barney stepped in as acting curator, assuming the role in her own right in 1994. During this time, she curated, among others, two graduate exhibitions and a staff exhibition. By the time she arrived at CCAS in April 1995, she had amassed a depth of local arts knowledge, and developed an energetic curatorial vision and a commitment to expanding national and international exhibition opportunities for local artists.

Smith's inexperience was confirmed when Barney, a week into her appointment in April 1995, asked where the exhibition program was so she could begin planning. She later recounted:

> [H]e said 'Well I haven't really got it written down anywhere.' He was actually running three spaces in his head. I would be getting calls from artists and they would be saying 'I think I have a show on then' and I would ask Trevor and he would say 'No, so-and-so has a show on then and this one is on the following month'.[51]

She immediately set to work getting relevant systems into place, the first of which was a spreadsheet that timetabled upcoming exhibitions in the Main Space and the Cube at Gorman House and at the Manuka gallery.[52] Barney then launched into exhibition planning and she recalls making a conscious curatorial decision from the beginning:

---

50   Barney, 2012.
51   Barney, 2012.
52   Making it even more extraordinary that Smith was keeping the exhibitions list in his head was the fact that the CCAS Manuka gallery moved to fortnightly exhibitions at the beginning of 1995. CCAS's press release from 1 February 1995 states that this doubling of the number of exhibitions hosted annually '[reflects] the diversity and excitement in the Canberra arts scene [providing] even more opportunity for local artists and audiences to participate in the excitement of contemporary art'. Curiously, however, the opening exhibition at Manuka for 1995 was a show of 'exciting works by young Melbourne artists', graduates of the Victorian College of the Arts, titled *Displacement on a summer holiday*. Smith, as reflected in the article in 'Art' in *Chronicle*, 20 February 1995, was by then marketing the Manuka gallery as 'recognised in Sydney and Melbourne as being on the cutting edge of Australian art'.

> I took it into my head as a bit of my mantra [to] actively embrace messy stuff when it came along because I think you can't be in a contemporary art space and be hanging things on the wall all the time – you've got to have some mess.[53]

Among Barney's many achievements at CCAS was her implementation, with Smith's support, of a national touring program and her forays into international touring, and international/local artist exchange. She was deeply committed to the Canberra community and to revealing local artists to local audiences and then moving the works of Canberra artists out into the wider national and international arts communities. It was Barney who provided the impetus and energy for the international tours that marked the organisation's growing confidence and maturity in contemporary art practice. By the end of her time with CCAS in 2002, the BRG collective, which began as a local response to a lack of space and exhibition opportunities for emerging artists, had completed its transformation to an internationally confident and relevant contemporary art space.

Barney staged important exhibitions of local Indigenous art, works in the intersections between new media and art, and performance art exhibitions and programs. The latter, particularly if it involved 'a bit of fun', was a strength throughout her seven years at CCAS. Of the period from 1995 onwards, she recalls that performance art 'was quite mature for a town of this age'.[54] Performance art was one strand of the multi-arts practice in the young arts community where multiple art forms were blended in backyard gatherings, garages and at early openings at Megalo, BRG and CCAS Gorman House. Barney's aim was to have 'at least some [and] sometimes whole programs of performance art where the gallery space would be taken up for four weeks with a series of performances'.[55] This was possible because of the number of performance artists living in the city, the majority of whom were students in CSA's Sculpture Department under then head of sculpture and CCAS board member David Watt. Barney's time at CSA meant she was intimately aware of the trend towards performance in the Sculpture Workshop. Her desire to open the gallery to performance art and to offer performance opportunities to the artists helped it to flourish in Canberra and at CCAS during the period from 1995 to 2002. (See Figures 24, 25 and 26)

---

53 Barney, 2012.
54 Barney, 2012.
55 Barney, 2012.

6. TRANSFORMATION

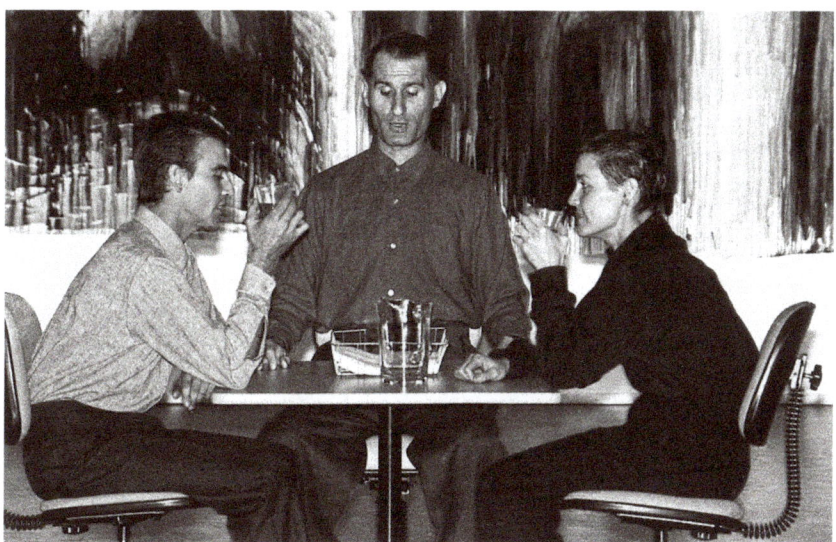

Figure 24. Left to right: Hawk McLean, Renald Navilly (formerly Navarro) and eX de Medici, 'Inside out', performance art season, 26 September – 24 October 1998, CCAS Gorman House
Source. CCAS image archive, reproduced with permission

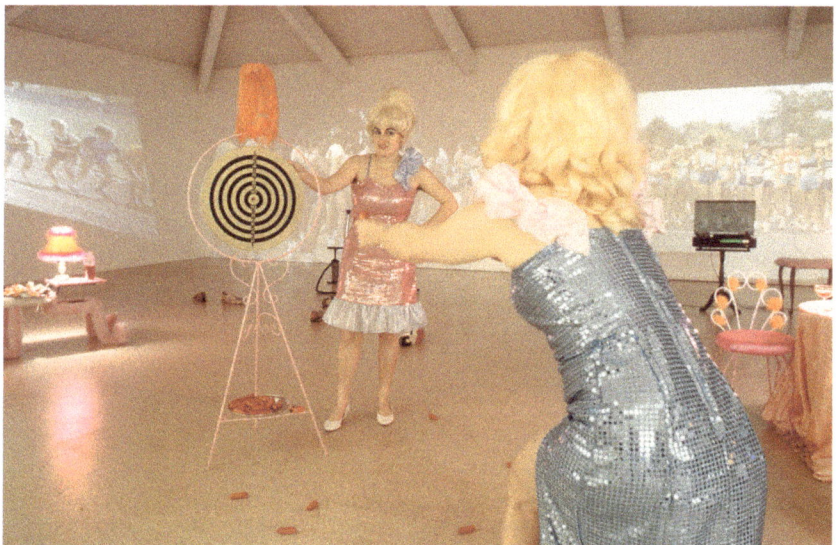

Figure 25. Cristy Gilbert and Anna Simic, *Edible art*, 'Inside out', performance art season, 26 September – 24 October 1998, CCAS Gorman House
Source. CCAS image archive, reproduced with permission

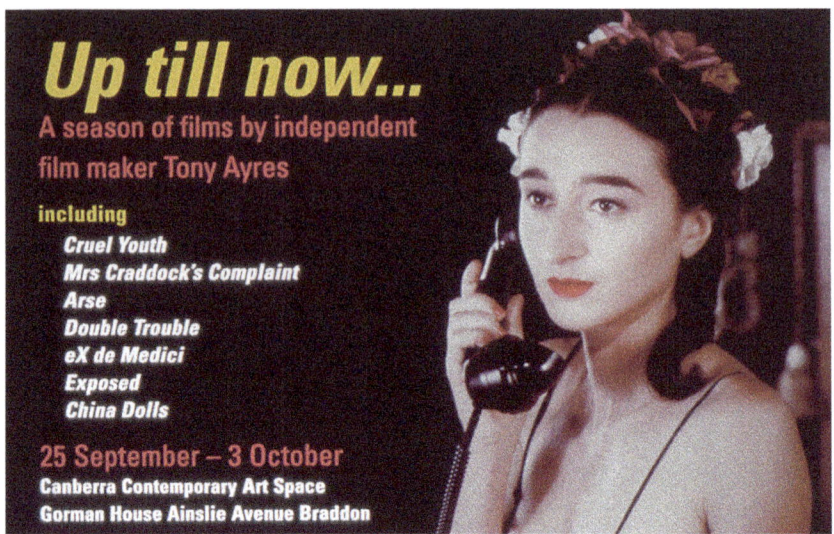

Figure 26. Poster advertising 'Up till now … a season of films by independent filmmaker Tony Ayres', 'Inside out', curated by Jane Barney, 25 September – 3 October 1998, CCAS Gorman House
Source. CCAS image archive, reproduced with permission

Beautiful home

Beautiful home: just what is it that makes today's homes so different, so appealing? remains a singular example of an artist-occupied gallery exhibition in Canberra.[56] This local affair inhabited the gallery over five weeks, from 11 July to 8 August 1998. Canberra artists and CSA students Bronwen Sandland and Paull McKee brought the concept of a transformed, occupied main gallery space to Barney. It would be messy, which Barney liked, and, even better, had the potential to be transgressive. Artist-driven, with an over-arching performative ethos and ripe with multiple transformative possibilities, the proposal fulfilled many of Barney's objectives and fitted closely with her personal CCAS mantra. The exhibition manifestly occupied the gallery space by importing the artists, the objects and the 1970s time period into the space in such a way that space, artists and audiences were transformed. Essentially, for five weeks, the gallery became home for a 1970s couple (see Figure 27), 'the perfect couple, liv[ing] the dream politics of domesticity under the microscope'.[57]

---

56 For international precedents, see Chris Burden and *White light white heat*, Robert Feldman Gallery, New York, 1974; and *Doomed*, Museum of Contemporary Art Chicago, 1975.
57 Naomi Horridge, 'Spending time at home', *Beautiful home*, exhibition catalogue, CCAS, 1998.

6. TRANSFORMATION

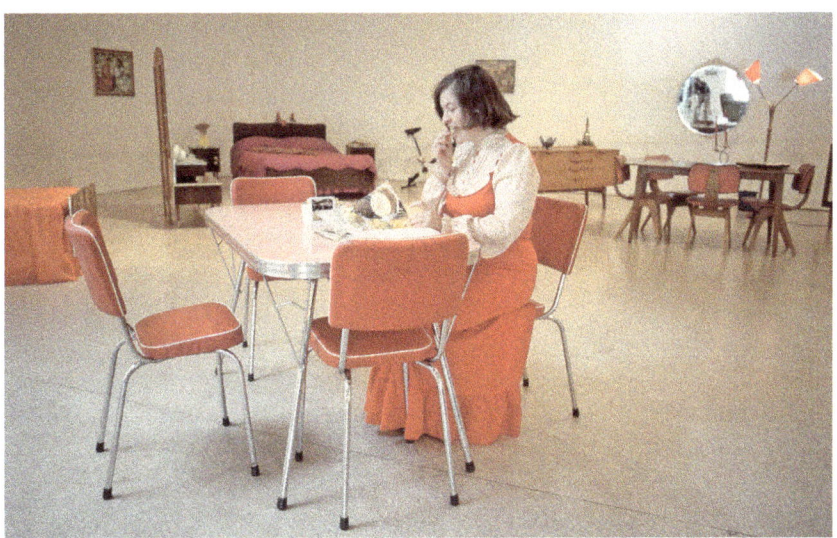

Figure 27. Bronwyn Sandland and Paull McKee, *Beautiful home: just what is it that makes today's home so different, so appealing?*, CCAS, 11 July – 8 August 1998, installation photograph
Source. CCAS image archive, reproduced with permission

The original first phrase of the exhibition title was *Home beautiful*, a deliberate borrowing from the eponymous magazine that had for some time been an arbiter of domestic Australian taste and homemaking. Barney was still amused 15 years later retelling the story of the unexpected and unsuccessful negotiations that ensued between CCAS and *Home beautiful*:

> One of the people on our team said, 'I know someone on the magazine and I'll write to her and see if they want to put in some sponsorship or have their editor come down and talk about the history of the magazine or have some other involvement.' Anyway, she wrote and we got a letter back from their lawyer saying, 'Desist from using our name *Home beautiful* or we will sue you.' So I thought, 'OK there's no spirit of fun there.' So we wrote back and said 'OK we won't use *Home beautiful*. Are you comfortable with us using *Beautiful home*?' and they said 'Yes that would be fine.' The invitations had been sent [under the name *Home beautiful*] and there was a bit of pre-publicity in *Art almanac*. I had to name all the places where the name *Home beautiful* would appear and make a disclaimer in the back of the catalogue.[58]

---

58 Barney, 2012. The catalogue for *Beautiful home* bears the following disclaimer: 'Re: *Beautiful home* – the exhibition formerly known as *Home beautiful*. The exhibition *Beautiful home*, formerly known as *Home beautiful*, has no connection with the magazine 'Australian Home Beautiful' published by Pacific Publications Pty. Ltd. Canberra Contemporary Art Space apologises unreservedly to Pacific Publications Pty. Ltd. for the use of the name 'Home Beautiful'.'

The exhibition's tag line, 'just what is it that makes today's homes so different, so appealing?', is taken from the title of Richard Hamilton's 1956 iconic pop art mixed-media collage, created for the group exhibition *This is tomorrow* at London's Whitechapel Art Gallery. A staple study image for art school students, *Just what is it that makes today's homes so different, so appealing?*, was remade by Hamilton in 1992 as *Just what is it that makes today's homes so different?* for the BBC series *QED*. This second incarnation, which Hamilton created on new media software, reworked original elements to reflect changes between 1956 and 1992, both in the international political arena and within the domestic realm. Sandland could not recall whether she and McKee were aware of this second incarnation, but it is possible that it was referred to during art theory lessons.[59] In any case, it seems clear that in *Beautiful home*, the tagline operated to signify that the exhibition occupied a time frame outside of the contemporary, that the installation constituted domesticity as art and that its intended import was rather more humorous than serious.

Sandland and McKee were little more than acquaintances when they conceived the idea for an exhibition that required them to act as husband and wife for the duration. In presenting the idea to Barney they indicated that they wanted to begin as if at the start of the marriage, enjoy the loveliness of that early relationship, and then proceed through turmoil to the eventual dissolution of the relationship. Barney remembers that she warned them:

> Be careful. You'll be in a public space performing this and you don't want to get to the breakup too early because we don't want a whole month of you in the gallery fighting. And neither do you.[60]

Initially the artists planned to leave the gallery and go to their respective homes on Mondays and Tuesdays when the gallery was closed to the public. On the first of these Mondays both left the gallery but before the end of the day 'they came rushing back and said, "Actually, we've decided not to go home because it's too hard to extract. We want to just stay here and live here".'[61] Their self-imposed exile from their everyday lives constituted a gallery-based immersion that has remained unparalleled

---

59 Bronwyn Sandland, conversation with the author, 16 February 2013.
60 Barney, 2012.
61 Barney, 2012.

in Canberra.⁶² The artists filled their co-opted space with furniture and objects that referenced home decor of the 1950s, 1960s and 1970s. These were not beautiful objects but rather mismatched signifiers of an 'everyperson's' home, chosen for their power to elicit layers of memories. McKee, sporting mutton-chop sideburns, shoulder length hair and a beard, had a wardrobe of vintage outfits, and Sandland chose her many outfit changes from a rack of vintage op-shop clothes. Curiously, as Naomi Horridge writes in the catalogue essay that followed the exhibition: 'In the melange of styles time slipped and it became apparent that neither artists nor audience were sure what actually happened in which decade'.⁶³ Nor did they appear to mind.

For *Beautiful home*, the gallery was set up as a notional house, albeit one without physical walls. Spaces quickly assumed gendered identities; McKee commandeered his 'den', Sandland personalised the 'bedroom'. The exhibition also became, as Barney remembers 'very much about their relationship', and an example of the power of space to transform those who inhabit it versus those who visit it, in unexpected ways:

> It was a very brave thing to do and it did at times become almost them versus the intruders, the visitors; there were moments when it would become stressful for them and then they remembered that they wanted people to come and visit.⁶⁴

The enormous public response to *Beautiful home* surprised artists and gallery staff. A much larger than expected number of visitors attended the exhibition and took part in various events. Of the opening day McKee wrote:

> [W]e had three hundred people. We were overawed. We put Skippy on the tele, wrapped a rug around us and said 'Hey'. Everyone sat down in the lounge. A German woman said, 'this is the first bit of Australia I saw' … At the housewarming [that night] two hundred people partied, it was a hoot. We had a guy playing the Hammond

---

62   In 1978, the artist Micky Allen staged *Photography, drawing and poetry: a live-in show* at Ewing and George Paton galleries, University of Melbourne. In 2008, she remembered the experience: 'The live-in show was my first solo exhibition. In it I wanted to change the experience of the gallery goer from one of white walls, hush, hush, don't speak, say what you really think when you get out of here – to one of sit down, relax, absorb the work at varying rates, discussing as you go, integrating the experience of being in a gallery with other life activities' ('*Photography, drawing and poetry: a live-in show*, 1978', *Mickey Allen*, www.mickyallan.com/Bodies/Live-inShow.html, accessed 10 July 2016).
63   Horridge, 1998.
64   Barney, 2012.

Organ and a cover band playing Burt Bacharach. A dapper silver moustachioed man in his sixties came in, to tell the staff that his wife had asked for something really unusual to do on Friday night. They came for the pyjama party ... in red dressing gowns and pyjamas.[65]

Beautiful home's extensive public program encompassed the opening night housewarming, a pyjama party, a fondue evening hosted by the artists, video nights and a bridge afternoon. Of the latter, Barney recalls:

> [I] got my old mum who played bridge to come and do a bridge day and we got the *Canberra Times* bridge writer to come down and he did a real analysis of one of the hands in his bridge column. [*Beautiful home*] went to all of these illogical extremes.[66]

There were unexpected audience interactions. While nostalgia was deliberately privileged in the exhibition plan, objects familiar to viewers from their youth or childhood elicited life stories that were at times exhaustingly personal for the artists to hear; neither artist was expecting the level of intimacy that evolved between themselves and audiences. Following the exhibition Sandland wrote, 'We didn't prepare ourselves for how much energy it takes to listen to everyone'.[67] Barney, who was a keen observer and a willing participant in the unfolding process, retains clear memories:

> The punters would come in on the weekend and they'd be rifling through ... as Bronwyn said '... our undies'. Things were left open and a bit spilly and a bit messy. Bronwyn was a big knitter and she would create giant pompoms, often in colours to match her clothes.[68]

The immersive nature of the exhibition affected the relationship between artists and gallery staff as much as between artists and audiences. In reminiscing about the exhibition, which she remembers as 'an amazing

---

65 Paull McKee, in Horridge, 1998.
66 Barney, 2012.
67 Bronwyn Sandland, in Horridge, 1998, p 7.
68 Barney, 2012. Sandland has continued to knit. Her large knitted interventions into the Canberra landscape have included covering 'a two-storey modernist maisonette'. See Merryn Gates, 'Bronwen Sandland: *Housecosy*', *Artlink*, 23, 1, March 2003, www.artlink.com.au/articles/2438/bronwen-sandland-housecosy/, accessed 3 August 2016.

experience', and which required gallery staff to negotiate their working space differently, Barney reflected more widely on this concept of navigated, negotiated space:

> As people working there you had to navigate your way around. Our office at that time was right next to their home. You were conscious that you couldn't just walk through the gallery to the storeroom, for example, as there were people living there. So the gallery became our negotiated space [in this exhibition and others]. We used to comment sometimes that you would quite enjoy the reclamation that used to go on for four days between exhibitions. It was our space in that time; it was as though you would wipe the space clean and start again.[69]

Some gallery staff had more difficulty than others negotiating this separation between exhibition and working spaces. While Sandland didn't have a 'day job' and was therefore in the exhibition space full-time, McKee, as did most 'husbands' during the period represented in exhibition, went out to work every day. Barney was made aware after the exhibition came down that:

> one of the staff working with me, who was this little skinny person that was always hungry, would suddenly materialise in the gallery every time they would organise lunch or dinner. 'Oh we were feeding three people,' Bronwyn said. 'You know, it was our home and we were getting a little bit sick of it because she would turn up for lunch every day.'[70]

The variables inherent in the exhibition concept and design for *Beautiful home* included this always-present, transgressive potential between artists and staff associated with negotiating the transformed gallery space. Additionally, they included the unpredictable nature of artist/audience interaction. With the latter, any perceived control that the artists may have thought they had rapidly slipped away. The combinations of objects, artists/performers and an audience for whom the usual boundaries were removed created a volatile, liminal environment. While other artists were making performative interventions into historic homes in this period, the particular 24-hour-a-day immersion practised by Sandland and McKee was unique in Canberra. The Western gallery construct is essentially designed to house static exhibitions with which viewers do not

---

69 Barney, 2012.
70 Barney, 2012.

interact. In any single exhibition period, each viewer, although his or her individual responses will vary, can generally expect to encounter the same exhibition. Performance art at CCAS, and in particular in *Beautiful home*, became a product of many interactions that were unknown before they occurred. The usual boundaries were absent, the number of visitors was high and the results were, therefore, unpredictable.

Exhibiting minorities and touring exhibitions at BRG/CCAS: a comparison

The presentations of minorities in exhibition at BRG/CCAS were largely successful and often groundbreaking incursions that provided a foil to the growing number of official cultural spaces and institutional exhibitions that marked Canberra as a national capital space. BRG and CCAS were contiguous iterations of the same physical and conceptual space, although their governance and funding parameters were different. Both iterations showed a commitment to exhibiting the works of artists who were members of minority groups or who worked in mediums that fell well outside established parameters. During BRG's existence, when the local community was vigorously agitating for recognition within the national capital space, 'minority exhibitions' served to clearly differentiate between local emerging art and the institutional/commercial national capital space reality. Minority exhibitions at CCAS gradually moved away from this focus on creating a clearly differentiated local community to display a growing maturity and confidence within national and, from the mid-1990s, international markets.

BRG was in essence anti-establishment, acting in opposition to both the institutional and the commercial gallery models in the city from foundation in 1981 through to merger in 1987. Both the first and second exhibitions at BRG, *Bill posters appreciated* and *Dreamtime machinetime*, heralded profound changes in the reception of contemporary poster making and urban Indigenous art respectively. Toward the end of the 1980s, escalating changes saw both art forms move from the margins into the mainstream.

The position of the poster in Australian art history in the 1980s made visible the end of modernism and the rise of popular culture. Posters and prints in *Bill posters appreciated* were sourced from local, national and international printmakers and cooperatives making works at the margins of art practice, championing causes whose protagonists came from minority social groups. Roger Butler recalls this period as a time when the National Gallery was 'putting in place strategies for acquisitions on a number of fronts Australia wide'.[71] These included the acquisition for the national collection of more than 30 posters in the period from 1981 to 1983, from members of Megalo who were exhibiting at BRG and the artists from Australian and international collectives who were represented in *Bill posters appreciated*. Butler's reaction to the exhibition caused him to think of:

> the whole movement and all those that were producing posters in the ACT and elsewhere. Colin Little was a focus; the example of Earthworks and then his work at Megalo highlighted the diverse strength of the movement.[72]

Little died in October 1982 at the age of 30, a decade after he had established the Earthworks Poster Collective (1972–79, Tin Sheds, Sydney). Butler contextualised Little's oeuvre within a short history of poster making, in his essay for the *Colin Little retrospective* exhibition at BRG (10–23 August 1983). The exhibition underlined the primary link between the genesis of BRG and its roots as an outlet for the poster-making culture that Megalo demonstrated in Canberra. Throwing light on the wider national context, Butler concluded that, 'A fitting response to [Little's] career is that the poster, traditionally regarded by Australian art museums as ephemeral and unimportant, has had to be reassessed'.[73] BRG continued to engage with printmaking throughout the period leading to amalgamation in 1987.

BRG's engagement with Indigenous Australia was uneven during the period to amalgamation. It was not until 1995, when Smith conceived the exhibition *Naii Ngarrambai Wanggirali Burrangiri Nangi Dyannai Ngurui* (*the lay of the land is how you know your country; when you look behind you, you can always see your tracks*), which was subsequently developed by Elliot, that Indigenous exhibitions were scheduled on the annual CCAS calendar.

---

71 Roger Butler, email to the author, 3 August 2011.
72 Butler, 2011.
73 Roger Butler, 'Colin Little: poster maker', *Colin Little retrospective*, exhibition catalogue, Canberra, BRG, 1983, pp 3–4.

Trevor Nickolls' *Dreamtime machinetime* was the first of the Indigenous exhibitions at BRG. Nickolls was already in a minority as an Indigenous Australian and, as a manifestation of urban Indigenous art in 1981, *Dreamtime machinetime* positioned him further as a minority of one. Nickolls, who in 1976 was a prize winner in Canberra's Civic Permanent Art Award (established 1971), first exhibited works in Canberra with the Arts Council of Australia (ACT) in May 1977 at its CTC Gallery location. This brief showing at CTC Gallery, from 11 am to 10 pm over four days, passed largely unnoticed, although WL Hoffman mentioned it in his May 26 'The world of music' column in the *Canberra Times*, writing that the exhibition showed 'how people of a different culture and a different frame of reference see modern society'.[74] Nickolls himself, who in that year was studying at the Canberra College of Advanced Education (CCAE),[75] hoped the works would 'show people how to appreciate the search by black people for identity and dignity in our modern technological society'.[76] Nickolls' return to Canberra in 1981 to take up the HC Coombs Creative Arts Fellowship at the ANU led to a meeting on campus with Little that resulted in the decision to stage *Dreamtime machinetime* at BRG.

Nickolls' exhibition was seminally important. Much more than just another step in the paradigmatic shift of Indigenous art from ethnographic display in museums to fine art exhibition in institutional and commercial galleries, it constituted the first cohesive manifestation of urban Indigenous art in exhibition in Australia. The following discussion outlines the trajectory of Indigenous art in exhibition in Australia preceding *Dreamtime machinetime* and looks briefly at the reception and flowering of Urban Indigenous art post–*Dreamtime machinetime* to further illuminate this shifting paradigm.

---

74   WL Hoffman, 'The world of music', *Canberra Times*, 26 May 1977, p 25.
75   CCAE (which became the University of Canberra in 1990) was established in 1967. Prime Minister John Gorton's speech at the unveiling of its foundation stone in October 1968 reminds us how geographically small Canberra was: 'One more thing, Sir, I would say. This college is being built in open country, but within measurable time, within a short time, there will be around it the new town of Belconnen' ('Speech at unveiling of foundation stone, Canberra College of Advanced Education', 28 October 1968, pmtranscripts.pmc.gov.au/sites/default/files/original/00001945.pdf, accessed 3 September 2012).
76   Hoffman, 1977.

In 1959, Tony Tuckson, at the time the deputy director of AGNSW, made the pioneering taxonomic leap to exhibit Indigenous art in a gallery context for the first time. The National Gallery of Victoria (NGV) was the only Australian institution in the 1970s to purchase contemporary Aboriginal art for its permanent collection. The NGV opened its gallery of Oceanic art 'whose prime purpose [was] the exhibition of Aboriginal art' in 1984.[77] In the 1980s, the NGA and the Art Gallery of Western Australia included the acquisition of Indigenous art in their collection policies, but it was not until the 1990s that Australia's other state galleries began to purchase contemporary Indigenous art. Commercial galleries also began to curate exhibitions of Western Desert and Arnhem Land art during the 1980s. A handful of government-funded exhibitions toured internationally towards the end of the 1980s, reflecting the federal government's interest in promoting the iconography of North Australian Aboriginal art as the international cultural face of Australia's bicentennial celebrations. The highest profile was *Dreamings: the art of Aboriginal Australia*, organised by the Asia Society with professional input from the collections and anthropology staff of the South Australian Museum.[78] In its contemporary form and reclassified as fine art, the exhibition of an efflorescence of Indigenous art practice – including, since the 1990s, urban Indigenous art – has become increasingly intense.

Nickolls' relationship with BRG forged an early link between BRG and the NGA. Three years after *Dreamtime machinetime*, *Koori art '84* introduced Sydney audiences to contemporary urban Indigenous artists. Curator Wally Caruana characterised the exhibition, which was held at Artspace in Sydney, as 'a watershed … for urban Aboriginal art and artists'.[79] AGNSW's purchase from this exhibition of Jeffrey Samuels' *This changing continent of Australia* has previously been recognised as the first acquisition of urban Indigenous art by a national or state gallery.[80] The National Gallery, however, acquired Nickolls' eponymous painting *Dreamtime machinetime* in 1982 as a result of seeing it in exhibition at BRG in 1981, thus making it the first institution to purchase an urban Indigenous work.

---

77 'Aboriginal art and the National Gallery of Victoria', *National Gallery of Victoria: annual report 1984–85*.
78 *Dreamings: the art of Aboriginal Australia* opened in New York in October 1988, then toured to Chicago, Melbourne and, finally, in 1990, to the South Australian Museum.
79 Wally Caruana, *Aboriginal art*, London, Thames and Hudson, 2003, p 201.
80 Caruana, 2003.

Many of the 30 Indigenous artists involved in *Koori art '84* worked in isolation. With the aim of increasing exhibition, curatorship and professional development opportunities, a number of these artists founded Boomalli Artist's Co-operative in 1987. 'Boomalli' means 'to strike or make a mark' and, from the end of the 1980s and into the 1990s, Boomalli acted to significantly increase the profile of a number of city-based Indigenous artists. By the early 1990s, Bronwyn Bancroft, Brenda L Croft, Fiona Foley, Djon Mundine, Hetti Perkins and Daphne Wallace had emerged as the first generation of Indigenous individuals working in the combined roles of artists-curators in Australia.

Nickolls' seminal importance to urban Indigenous art cannot be overstated. On hearing of his death in October 2012, Vernon Ah Kee, a founding member of proppaNow, Brisbane's urban Indigenous artists' collective wrote:

> In 2012 we are still grappling with identity and art. It is a healthy dialogue I think. And Nickolls is as much a part of that discourse as he ever was. I think back to when I first moved to Brisbane in the early 1990s and people began talking more and more about this thing called 'Urban' Aboriginal art. Trevor Nickolls was before all that.[81]

The exhibition of non-Indigenous Judo (now Juno) Gemes' photographic portraits of Indigenous Australians, *We wait no more: a selection of photographs and textures*, was also held in BRG's first year and illustrates the gallery's engagement with Indigenous Australia. Photography was familiar to gallery visitors and presented a generally more accessible view of Aboriginal people than had Nickolls' *Dreamtime machinetime* thesis. Responses in the visitors' book included: 'Impressed with stillness and respect for the people. Can feel the hope and strength'; 'Very impressed with poetry, stillness & feeling in images'. The colonial concept of the noble savage, however, was also alive and well. This was evidenced by the response 'Thanks for the faces – noble. I was impressed by how well the people looked', and a comment that, in its admittance of 'a lack of knowledge', echoed the wider non-Indigenous understanding of 1980s Aboriginal Australia:

---

81   Vernon Ah Kee, 'Trevor Nickolls 1949–2012', 30 October 2012, vernonahkee.blogspot.com/2012/10/trevor-nickolls-1949-2012.html, accessed 15 August 2016.

> Impressed by openness honesty of the faces. Felt in harmony with their strong identification with the land. Felt backward about my lack of knowledge about Aboriginal achievement. Renewed my belief in equality, identity and people. Tremendous eye-opener. I hope this exhibition travels across the country.[82]

It was 13 years before BRG's successor, CCAS, hosted another exhibition of Indigenous art in what was, by then, a very different national environment, both politically and for contemporary art. Contemporary Indigenous art in the 1990s, including urban art, had gained national and international currency.

Two other exhibitions during BRG's first year, *Our place* and *The Foundry – on the road*, continued the collective's sociopolitical engagement, giving visibility to disenfranchised Canberrans.

The Foundry, like Jobless Action, was a Community Youth Support Scheme (CYSS)–funded employment-creation enterprise managed by one part-time and two full-time co-coordinators, whose programs were designed to equip unemployed young people with new skills. Charles Livingstone, chair of The Foundry Association (which managed The Foundry) described the organisation's house in Braddon, which attracted around 50 people a day, as 'an important clearing house for people's problems – a place where there is always someone to talk to'.[83] Funding enabled The Foundry to provide opportunities for clients to work with craftspeople at Ainslie Village. Previously, artworks made by Foundry clients would not have progressed to exhibition; BRG's open-access policies, however, were expressly designed to accommodate such a group. While the works displayed by the 18 artists did not act as 'a personal expression of frustration or a political bludgeon',[84] the exhibition politicised the proposed cuts to CYSS programs that would directly affect The Foundry. Importantly, through coverage on ABC TV's *Nationwide* program, BRG was contextualised nationally, for the first time, as socially relevant.

---

82 BRG visitors' book, 1981–83.
83 Charles Livingstone, quoted in Sonja Kaleski, 'Art "on the road"', *Canberra Times*, 27 September 1981, p 10.
84 Kaleski, 1981.

Figure 28. Poster, The Foundry, printed at Megalo, artists unknown
Source. Photographer: Dean Butters. Megalo poster archives, reproduced with permission

The second exhibition, *Our place*, initiated by Julia Church, showed work by children with disabilities from Chapman Hostel, and included wall hangings, pastel drawings, paintings, T-shirts and bags. In 1976, the UN General Assembly declared 1981 as the International Year of Disabled Persons. *Our place* constituted Church and BRG's response to this international initiative and provided a locus for Church's community-focused practice. The Chapman Hostel children went on to stage performances with the money raised from artwork sales. The exhibition was linked to the idea, strong in the 1960s, that art was a useful tool for social change and it provided an example of art practice with the intent to improve the quality of life for minorities at the margins of Canberra society.[85] Church recalls that she and Mark Denton were then among a handful of artists working in the community in this way:

> When I was still at art school Mark and I used to go out to various care centres and work with people and do occupational art – in some way helping people to deal with the frustration of being institutionalised. I used to work with intellectually disabled

---

85 Community practice is still in evidence at Megalo today, and remains a central tenet of the community art centres that were established in Canberra's Belconnen and Tuggeranong town centres in the 1990s.

kids; they were really frustrated with their situation, they were in a hostel and a lot of them were quite capable of living in the community [and] wanted their independence. I'd taken them to Bitumen River before so we decided to make an exhibition together. I taught them how to screenprint … that was a lot of fun and [later] we did performance stuff as well, but not at BRG.[86]

Reviewing for the *Canberra Times*, Grishin noted that 'it was yet another important undertaking by the Bitumen River Gallery'. That Church was well suited to supporting community art projects is made obvious by Grishin, whose descriptions of the works foregrounded their 'vigour … stunning boldness and a strong expressive use of colour' and 'immediate unimpeded vision':

> *Our Place* is not an exhibition that you need to approach with charitable intention; as an exhibition of art it is a bold, brilliant and rewarding experience. There is a richness and vitality in the range of the imagination in the work on display … What emerges from this exhibition is a range of strong artistic personalities with real emotive, expressive and imaginary powers that speak of an unusual sense of creativity.[87]

Tony Ayres

Tony Ayres and de Medici joined the BRG collective in 1983. Both were destined for international careers and they made significant contributions to the collective's continuing commitment to exhibit work from members of minority groups and artists working in non-traditional mediums.

Ayres came to Australia from Macau with his mother and sister in 1964, towards the end of the White Australia policy and before the first wave of Asian immigration that brought Vietnamese students and the first 'boat people' to Australia. 'We were,' remembers Ayres, 'pretty much in white Australia.'[88] After two years at ANU, in 1983 he transferred to CSA where he majored in photography but found himself drawn to printmaking. Ayres was among the student artists particularly supported by Mandy Martin. He began working with the members of BRG in 1983, and in that year 'co-opted' de Medici – who had returned to Canberra to take

---

86 Church, 2012.
87 Sasha Grishin, 'Bold and brilliant and rewarding', *Canberra Times*, 20 November 1981, p 10.
88 'Tony Ayres' new film echoes stories from his own life', ABC *Conversations with Richard Fidler*, 10 August 2007, www.abc.net.au/local/stories/2007/08/10/2001814.htm, accessed 15 August 2016.

up painting at CSA – to the collective.[89] Ayres was a polymath whose developing interests, after art school, included filmmaking. De Medici remembers him as 'a good member … a brilliant guy [with] an amazing work ethic'.[90]

Ayres' presence as an openly gay, Asian man opened up an aesthetic not otherwise easily accessed by collective members or the wider Canberra public. A number of his prints referenced issues faced by gay men in Australia in the first half of the 1980s and were purchased from the artist for the NGA collection in 1993.[91] They included *Vogue man* (1982), *Skeleton* (1982), *I am the Nazi I am the Jew* (1984), *Glamour men and S-P* (1984) and *Behind the wall* (c 1984).[92]

In 1984, Ayres brought Chilean-born artist Juan Davila to Canberra. A proponent of art in service to social and political change, Davila was 28 when he immigrated to Melbourne in 1976. Ayres had met and spoken 'briefly' to Davila during Artist Week in Adelaide in March 1984, having attended with Virgo, then in her first year as BRG co-coordinator. He wrote to Davila on 1 April about the possibility of Davila speaking during the *Art forum* program at CSA, 'through the auspices of Bitumen River'. Asking for 'some kind of continuation of your artist week talk', Ayres requested 'a subject such as the direction that socially progressive artists should/could be taking, the limitations of the current state of painting in terms of the politically radical etc'. Davila was paid a fee of $60 plus accommodation, meals 'or anything like that'.[93]

Ayres continued to explore gay themes in an exhibition of manipulated screenprints titled *The image of desire*, which was shown at BRG from 10–28 April 1985. These works had, in the main, been produced during the artist's final year at CSA in 1984, and included the prints purchased by NGA in 1993. CCAS gifted the screenprinted poster advertising the exhibition to the NGA in 1993. Darkly homoerotic and intimating violence, the exhibition provided previously unseen content for audiences, many of whom appreciated the essay that made them feel 'ok about

---

89   De Medici, 2012.
90   De Medici, 2012.
91   See list of Ayres' posters held by the NGA, www.printsandprintmaking.gov.au/artists/10662/works/, accessed 29 August 2016.
92   Ayres' poster advertising the 1984 BRG exhibition *A new spirit in china painting* – to which Grishin acerbically responded in the visitor's book 'Where's the new spirit?' – was gifted to the NGA by CCAS in 1993.
93   Tony Ayres, letter to Juan Davila, 1 April 1984, CCAS archives.

not understanding the visual leads!' Included among these was Roland Manderson who wrote, 'Thanks very much for the essay. I'm sick of art speaking for itself … I am thankful for the view of the person responsible for making it'.[94] Ayres' catalogue introduction provides a superb example of how important and effective written mediation from the artist can be for viewers; the essay was perfectly attuned to an audience unfamiliar with the intense visual language of gay culture, the words gently leading viewers to a contextual understanding:

> Initially the prints operate to a highly specific sense of audience. They are meant to be viewed by gay men. The images, words and situations they describe are drawn from contemporary urban homosexual terminology – s/m, gloryholes, pornography. The content acts as a critique of the way in which desire is represented within this context. Understanding of this critique is most available to gay men who are familiar with the imagery.[95]

Grishin believed that the images provided 'a brilliant and provocative critique of the modern western society's homosexual subculture'. He wrote that the work was 'sophisticated … technically and in its thinking … going considerably beyond making a simple social statement or seeking to be attractive aesthetic objects'. Grishin also noted that BRG was about to mark its fourth year in operation, 'continuing to provide an outlet for important art otherwise not seen in Canberra'.[96]

eX de Medici and CCAS: minorities and touring exhibitions

eX de Medici, who grew up in Canberra in a politically active family, explored minority forms of art practice and championed disenfranchised minorities from the beginning of her career. She attended art schools at Riverina CAE and Darling Downs Institute and completed her undergraduate degree in visual arts at CSA in the mid-1980s, majoring in painting and photo media. She also studied multi-track recording and sound sampling at Canberra School of Music.

---

94 BRG visitors' book, 1985, CCAS archives.
95 Tony Ayres, 'Introduction', *The image of desire*, exhibition catalogue, Canberra, BRG, 1985.
96 Sasha Grishin, '*Images of desire*', *Canberra Times*, 23 April 1985, p 28.

Her early works included a two-hour performance on the Cahill Expressway – 'a really good place to place flesh ... it is completely artificial'[97] – in which she crossed the road 27 times, making a chalk line as she reached each verge, before she was removed by officers of the Department of Main Roads; and a performance at the Canberra rubbish tip where she hung her unsuccessful works among the city's messy detritus. She described this latter performance to reviewer Virginia Cook as being 'about success ... how to have a successful exhibition at the dump is really quite difficult'.[98] During the BRG exhibition titled *Work saints*, de Medici created a large charcoal drawing each day, working for five consecutive days from 9 am to 5 pm, reflecting Canberra's bureaucratic working hours. The message behind the performance and exhibition was the concept of the artist as a worker like any other:

> [O]ne of the reasons I am doing 'Work saints' is that artists are not seen as workers ... [T]hree per cent is magic, ninety-seven per cent is work ... [Y]ou get dirty, you get tired, you want to have a break.[99]

The touring BRG members' show *Nowhere utopia* (3–14 March 1987) spanned the crossover period that took BRG through to CCAS. The exhibition of photocopy works evidenced minority arts practices, as well as commenting, through its title, on the dissolution of the utopian ideals of the collective/artist-run space. Ironically, it provided an example of how a medium that was first shown in a collective, then rejected as 'not art' by an established art space, could be subsequently invited, three years later, into the space that had previously rejected it. De Medici recalls that:

> Andy [Hurrell], Elena [Gallegos] and I approached the ACP for a show of [these photocopied works] and we got back a letter (and they were the cutting edge of photography in Australia at that time) and they wrote back and said, 'We're sorry, this isn't photography, goodbye'. And then about three years later we were invited to show and we told them to fuck off. Because by then we'd finished with it and they were just finding it.[100]

---

97 Virginia Cook, "'Artist shown as worker'", *Canberra Times*, 20 February 1986, p 5.
98 Cook, 1986.
99 Cook, 1986.
100 De Medici, 2012.

6. TRANSFORMATION

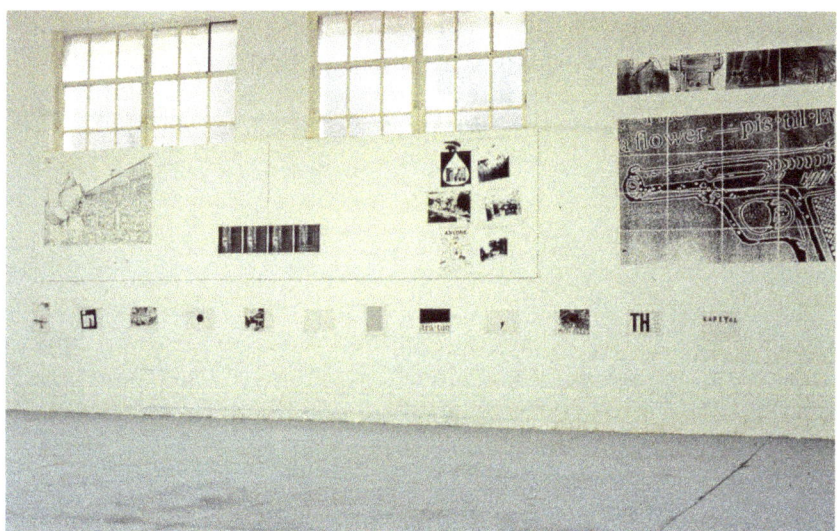

Figure 29. *Nowhere utopia*. BRG touring group exhibition at THAT Space, Brisbane, 3–14 March 1987, installation photograph. Far right: eX de Medici's *Pistol*, 1985, gridded black-and-white laser-copied image, 1200 x 1600 cm, printed on Canon's first prototype laser photocopier as a 16-piece gridded image
Source. CCAS image archive, reproduced with permission

In this way, the medium of photocopy traversed a path from marginality to mainstream acceptance. This path to acceptance was likewise enacted in: print/poster making, on which Megalo and BRG were founded; urban Indigenous art, with Nickolls' *Dreamtime machinetime*; and exhibitions by people with disabilities, as in *Our place*. A difference with the photocopy medium in *Nowhere utopia* is that its use was a knowing exercise; for the artists, the worthlessness of the materials provided their political raison d'être; an opportunity to say something worthwhile through a medium rejected by the established art world.

Nowhere utopia included the first of de Medici's geo-political gun imagery.[101] *Pistol* (1985, gridded black-and-white laser-copied image, 1200 x 1600 cm), 'a revolver from a very old dictionary',[102] was printed on Canon's first prototype laser photocopier as a 16-piece gridded image (see Figure 29). This and two other works were the early results of the artist's residencies around Australia, working with Canon multifunction

---

101 *Pistol* and *knife* were exhibited 25 years later in the CCAS Canberra centenary show *Bad girls* (8 February – 16 March 2013), curated by the author.
102 De Medici, 2012.

laser printers/photocopiers that allowed her to increase the size of images until they were 'building size ... whacked up with wallpaper paste'.[103] De Medici remembered that 'It was very tedious because you'd have to get them all cut properly and the machine didn't quite grid them all up correctly'.[104] At the time, clean finishes were secondary to the primary aim of the work; de Medici recalls that 'It wasn't a big issue about making perfect things because no-one was going to buy them; you were just going to throw them away anyway'.[105] Images were sourced from 'everywhere'.[106] The second work in the series, *knife* (1985, gridded black-and-white laser-copied image, 15 panels, 2000 x 1500 cm), blown out and mysterious, was from 'a very strange small photograph of my deceased grandmother's wedding cake with a hand with a big knife coming into the picture'. The third work, damaged in transit on return from Brisbane, was a colour photocopy of a scene from *South Pacific* privileging the homoerotic in the poses of the male protagonists.[107]

De Medici has been 'fascinated with signifiers of power for as long as [she] can remember. It's the one thing that just never goes away; [power] and the paradoxes within [its signifiers]'.[108] This fascination with power and its effect on the powerless drove de Medici's attempts to subvert what she regarded as Virgo's increasingly mainstream curatorial aesthetic. De Medici advocated for the continuance of BRG as an artist-run collective space, believing that the mandate of such a space should be the support and guidance of emerging artists. She voted against the handover of the BRG constitution that allowed the formation of CCAS and, throughout the period of Virgo's directorship of CCAS, took every opportunity to subvert what she saw as creeping institutionalisation.

Over the five years following the handover of BRG's constitution to CCAS (1987–92), de Medici and Runnegar sought to inject alternative notes of performance and messiness back into the exhibition calendar – tropes that

---

103 De Medici worked again with Canon in producing her billboard for *I am you: artists against violence, artists for tolerance*, the Goethe Institut travelling exhibition at CCAS in 1994.
104 De Medici, 2012.
105 By 2012, when I sat with de Medici choosing works for *Bad girls*, *Pistol* and *knife* had attained an iconic status and I was excited but nervous about putting these fragile pieces on the wall in case they were damaged. eX remarked 'If they get damaged don't worry. Do remember it's just a miracle that these have survived. They're photocopies. It's raw and base and it's not a problem for me if they get damaged' (eX de Medici, interview with the author, 1 February 2013).
106 De Medici, 2013.
107 The blacks retain their crisp outlines even today, belying the passage of years.
108 De Medici, 2012.

had defined the early days of BRG. De Medici believed then, as she does today, that 'a contemporary arts space should be a place where emerging artists should be given the correct respect … and assistance'.[109] As time went on, the relationship between Virgo and de Medici soured:

> Issues arose between me and Anne and older members who slipped away … [G]radually through Anne's [time] it became much more conservative, although at the same time we would do things, Brenda and I; Anne would go [out of Canberra] and Brenda and I would be scrabbling through the proposals and [would then] notify people and say 'you've got a show' without [Anne's] permission – subversive incursions while she was away.[110]

De Medici's early explorations into art forms that the establishment considered worthless, such as performance and photocopy, reached the apex of alternative, minority art practice with tattooing. In 1989, an Australia Council grant afforded her the opportunity to spend a year studying the medium in California. Tattooing provided a medium in which her primary interests coalesced: minorities; minority practice; power and its signifiers; and gay culture, which was flourishing in the tattoo world between the 1950s and the 1980s. Importantly, it also fundamentally changed her manner of working and set her up for the later execution of the powerful, intricate, large-scale works on paper that would make her international reputation:

> I'm very ordered when I work. Tattooing made me that way because you're dealing with blood and diseases – I started tattooing at the height of HIV/AIDS so everything had to become absolutely ordered. I believe tattooing absolutely changed every aspect of how I worked.[111]

By the beginning of 1994, de Medici had fully incorporated tattooing into her art practice. During the next 18 months, exhibitions at CCAS and australian Girls Own Gallery (aGOG) – respectively titled *Inside out: out of the mainstream: a group exhibition* and *Scratching* – illustrated her seminal engagement with this minority form and cemented her position as the only contemporary artist in Australia working with this medium as an alternative contemporary art practice.

---

109 De Medici, 2012.
110 De Medici, 2012.
111 De Medici, 2012.

These two concurrent exhibitions highlighted the *process* of tattooing. Runnegar and de Medici curated *Inside out*, which ran from 3–26 June 1994, immediately preceding Smith's *Romantisystem*. This marked the last of their many ventures together for BRG/CCAS. In title and in content, the exhibition privileged those on the fringe. Included were the detritus of de Medici's tattooing practice in the form of 100 bloody napkins. De Medici is explicitly not named as an artist in the exhibition; her choice was to acknowledge the contribution of the blood patches as artworks provided by the 100 tattooed people from whom they came. Deborah Clark, reviewing de Medici's concurrent solo exhibition *Scratching* at aGOG, brought the focus back to the artist, writing of de Medici's work in *Inside out* that:

> [The napkins] were displayed in plastic bags, like a body of specimens, and their nauseating quality was somehow cumulative. The work was called *The blood of others* and its reference to scientific samples was underscored by the idea of guilt and bad conscience, making mileage out of the blood of others. Implicit here is the complicity of the artist, like the imperialist, exploiting and souveniring the bodies of her subjects.[112]

Inside out also included a number of air-brushed motorcycle bike tanks that, as with de Medici's bloody napkins, were unattributed. Ruth Ellis, in the brief catalogue essay, writes that 'The act of customising the motorcycle to an internal and personal agenda flows clearly to the act of tattooing and customising the flesh machine through pigment and blood'.[113] Other works in *Inside out* were: a tipi erected in the gallery from the nomadic and mutable outsider collective Electric Tipi; a selection of woodworks from NSW prison inmate and former Canberran Bob Cummins; embroidered skulls from Vicki Bell; and an installation from two ex-Brickworks artists and Canberra performance group Splinters members Stuart Vaskess and Adam Herbst. The installation's notes instructed the:

> guest [to] enter through The Bower, make obeisance at the Dragon Flower Shrine, cook the sacred sausage on the Barbecue of Desire (dedicated to an armless yet devastating deity, devoted to the cooking of meat) light the sacred candles (3) and eat the sandwich provided by the fruits of heaven.[114]

---

112 Deborah Clark, 'Scratching the surface', *Art Monthly Australia*, July 1994, p 30.
113 Ruth Ellis, *Inside out – out of the main stream: a group exhibition*, exhibition catalogue, Canberra, CCAS, 1994.
114 Stuart Vaskess and Adam Herbst, in Ellis, 1994.

The next showing of de Medici's tattoo practice took place outdoors. Smith's Sydney connections facilitated the Goethe-Institut's international travelling exhibition *I am you: artists against violence, art for tolerance* from 12 October to 6 November 1994. The works, by 20 artists from Europe and the United States (including Marina Abramovic), were joined by de Medici's CCAS-commissioned work (see Figure 30) and erected on large billboards erected on the median strip in front of Gorman House. The location was one of 200 around the world exhibiting the billboards throughout 1994. *I am you* aimed to bring world attention to growing aggression in Europe against refugees and political minorities. The press release stated, 'Racism, intolerance and xenophobia are unfortunately global phenomena and their effects are also felt here in Australia'.[115] De Medici's billboard presented a group of tattooed people, an outsider minority in the mid-1990s, in various linked poses.

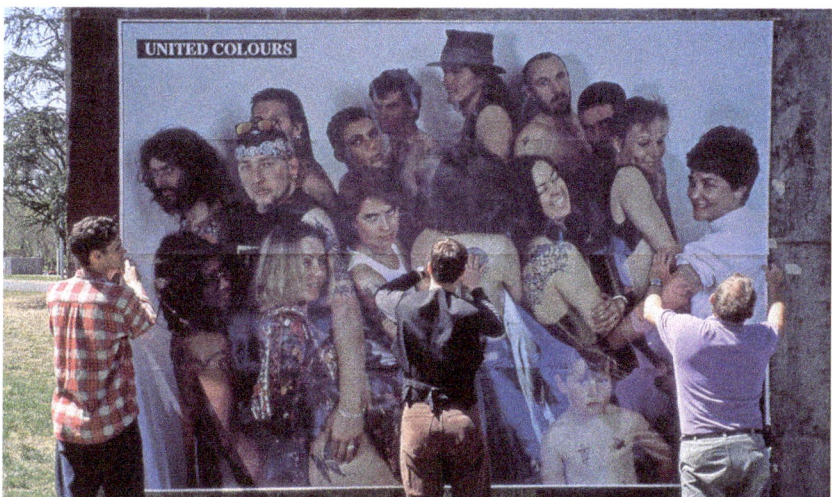

Figure 30. eX de Medici, *United colours*, gridded colour laser-copied image, in Goethe-Institut's international travelling exhibition, *I am you: artists against violence, art for tolerance*, CCAS, 12 October – 6 November 1994, installation photograph
Source. CCAS image archive, reproduced with permission

---

115 Media release, *I am you: artists against violence, art for tolerance*, October 1994, CCAS archives.

Staging the exhibition on Ainslie Avenue was a bold intervention into public space, years before the ACT's Labor government under Jon Stanhope enacted a public arts policy (2001–11) that made public art commonplace. The exhibition's reception was not entirely positive. Canberra was then and is now a billboard-free city; for local residents living at Reid's outer edge, the global implications of tolerance paled beside their sympathy for those who they thought were being hectored. In a letter to the *Canberra Times*, titled 'Billboard horror', (Ms) P Sanders of Reid complained:

> I am writing in protest at the erection of certain hideous billboards, which have appeared recently in the centre of Ainslie Avenue. These billboards carry messages such as 'Clean your house' and 'I am you' (referring to the human brain.) One could only conclude from these that the government tenants, who are obliged to gaze on them every day of their lives, instead of enjoying the previously aesthetically beautiful Ainslie Avenue, are perhaps not quite normal and need to be given a visual moral lesson. Perhaps those who have provided this lesson in morality could arrange to put their own houses in order first.[116]

The last of de Medici's exhibitions foregrounding tattooing opened at CCAS in March 1996. In *60 heads*, the tattoo was overtly presented as contemporary art, in a whole-of-gallery exhibition that provided another example of CCAS's attention to minority groups and art forms. One result was that an entirely new demographic entered the gallery, setting a new benchmark for visitor numbers. Barney, then CCAS assistant curator, remembers the exhibition as 'a real pleasure to work on. It was a beautiful moment where the tattoo levelled the playing field'.[117] In assessing the diversity among exhibition visitors, Barney concluded that:

> eX was ahead of her time. Every tattooed person in Canberra and the surrounding region visited that show. We had truckies, bus drivers, bikers … not our normal clientele, but our normal clientele were there too because some of our regular clientele were in the photos.[118]

---

116 Ms P Sanders, letter to the editor, *Canberra Times*, 21 October 1994, p 10.
117 Barney, 2012.
118 Barney, 2012.

A full-colour catalogue, supported by the ACT Cultural Council, accompanied the exhibition. It included essays by Gordon Bull, then head of the Art Theory Workshop at ANU School of Art; and Jenny McFarlane, then assistant curator at City Gallery, Canberra, who previously wrote about the artist's work, and who – along with Barney – was instrumental in bringing the concept of *60 heads* to exhibition.[119] Encapsulated in the essays was the idea – new for Western society in the mid-1990s – that the tattoo and contemporary art are joined at an interface. Long the terrain of bikers, jail inmates and sailors – and devoid of the cultural signifiers that marked the place of the tattoo in non-Anglo societies – the tattooed in Western society were, at the end of the last century, perceived as outsiders and not as the representatives of a contemporary arts practice.

Seventy-four candid snapshots, without artifice, many taken just after the tattoo had been placed on the skin, were chosen (see Figure 31) from around 400 of the photographs in the rapidly growing photographic database that de Medici collected from 1989 to 1995 in studios in Europe, North America and Australia. Tattoos ranged from the wonky, homemade *Dad* and *Mom*, to exquisite miniatures, and complex sleeves and body suits, while the portrait subjects ranged from young boys to hard men to girls next door. Not all of the tattoos were de Medici's work. She recalled the 'groups within the groups':

> Some of them were the ultra-young, 14 or so, with home tattoos. They would come into the tattoo shop and [I'd say] 'get out, you're a baby – you're not even allowed to be in here.' [But I'd ask] can I take a photograph of that and they'd go 'Yeah whatever.' Then there are [those people] directly after the tattoo process, they're dishevelled, they're bursting with endorphins, they're kind of not there – I find they're post-coital or something – you know, post-pain. Maybe 10 per cent of the *60 heads* photographs are tattoos I've done and 90 per cent are just post-tattoo people. I'd be in studios anywhere in the world and I'd [ask] 'Oh can I take a photo?'[120]

---

119 McFarlane continues to write about de Medici's work to the present day.
120 De Medici, 2012.

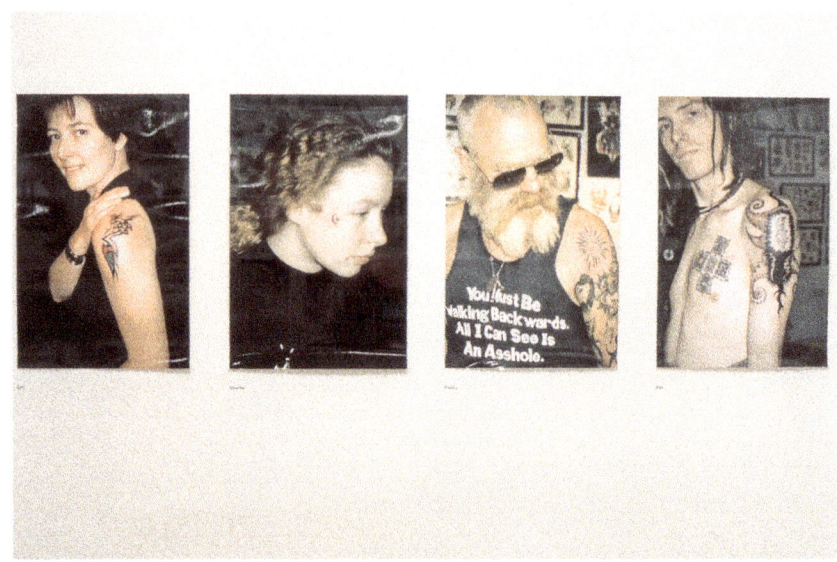

Figure 31. eX de Medici, *60 heads*, exhibition detail, laminated inkjet prints, 59.4 x 84.1 cm, CCAS travelling exhibition, ACCA, Melbourne, 24 January – 2 March 1997, installation photograph
Source. Photographer: K Pleban. CCAS image archive, reproduced with permission

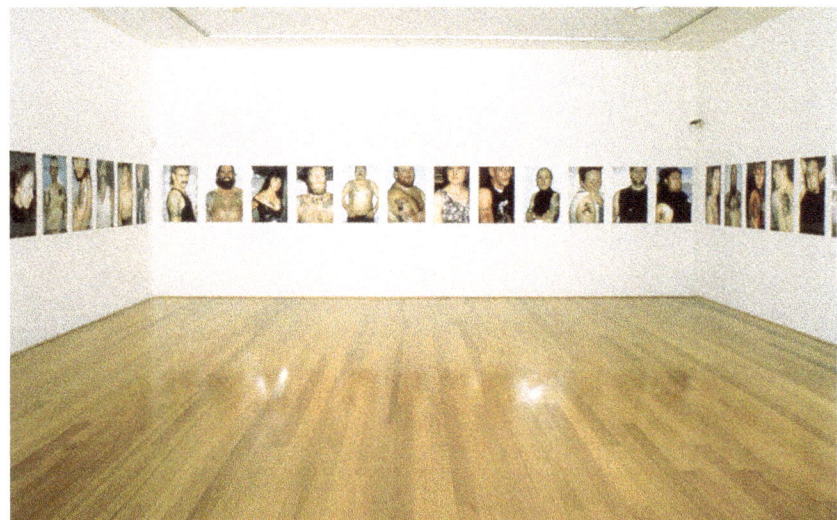

Figure 32. eX de Medici, *60 heads*, laminated inkjet prints, 59.4 x 84.1 cm, CCAS travelling exhibition, ACCA, Melbourne, 24 January – 2 March 1997, installation photograph
Source. Photographer: K Pleban. CCAS image archive, reproduced with permission

The exhibition design was intentionally egalitarian and, as a touring exhibition, was beautifully conceived. It was cheap and practical to travel and uncomplicated to install. All 74 portraits were hung in a straight line at eye height, so that no single subject took precedence over any other (see Figure 32). The snapshots were prepared for exhibition as laminated A1 inkjet prints, again courtesy of de Medici's collaboration with Canon Australia, combining her then dual interests of photocopy and tattoo. These could be sponged clean and packed into one A4-size wooden crate. The number of works could be expanded or contracted depending on the size of the receiving venue. Barney remembers calls from venue curators who, with a show called *60 heads*, were surprised to find 74 portraits inside the travelling case. Smith had chosen the exhibition's name; confusing perhaps in its non-matching numbers, but it rolled off the tongue and had a clean graphic presence in publicity. It was 'hugely popular'[121] with venues, touring from its opening at CCAS in March 1996, to Performance Space in Sydney (May 1996), Australian Centre for Contemporary Art (ACCA) in Melbourne (March 1997), Institute of Modern Art (IMA) in Brisbane (June/July 1997), 24HR Art in Darwin (August 1997), through to its final Australian destination at the Goldfields Art Centre, Kalgoorlie in January 1998,[122] where de Medici recalled that it was 'the first time miners had stepped into their regional gallery'.[123] The exhibition concluded touring, three years later, with an international showing at the *1998 fotofeis: survey of international photography* in Glasgow, Scotland. 'Eventually,' recalled Barney, 'we had to say enough.'[124]

The exhibition also marked the end of de Medici's long and fruitful alliance with BRG/CCAS. 'I felt that *60 heads* was a big effort and [that] afterwards it was time to step away and let other people in.'[125]

The success of *60 heads* was assisted by its egalitarian structure, ease of touring and installation, and the curatorial ethos that was inherent to CCAS and driven largely by Barney during the period from 1995 to 2002. This ethos privileged the artist-generated exhibition, which was then supported and facilitated by intelligent curatorial guidance and often grounded with a sophisticated catalogue. De Medici was ahead of

---

121 Barney, 2012.
122 Touring of the exhibition to ACCA, IMA and 24HR Art was announced in a National Exhibitions Touring Support (NETS) media release, 19 October 1995, 1995 scrapbook, CCAS archives.
123 De Medici, 2012.
124 Barney, 2012.
125 De Medici, 2012.

her time, as was Barney for recognising the potential of the exhibition to transcend simple portraits. De Medici – who brought the concept to a receptive Barney as assistant curator – harbours a belief that then director Smith was less than enthusiastic about the exhibition concept, initially feeling that it was 'too rough, it wasn't glam, it wasn't associated with a commercial gallery'.[126] The exhibition's long touring life and high visitor numbers, however, bear out Barney's judgement to proceed and, importantly, Smith's support for her decision.

A second wave

60 heads marked the beginning of a second wave of touring exhibitions from CCAS from 1996 to 2002. Smith's director's report at the end of 1995 commented that, 'To my knowledge before 1994, the CCAS had never organised an exhibition tour',[127] but this claim is erroneous and reflects not only the lack of corporate memory available within CCAS by 1995, but also points to a reading of CCAS that disavows its historical links to BRG.

Arrangements made between Virgo, Ross Wolfe of the Australia Council's VAB, and Arts ACT, included provision for CCAS to assume the funding previously given to BRG. This, with the approval of BRG members to hand over the BRG constitution to the newly incorporated CCAS, shows that, although BRG and CCAS embodied different constitutional frameworks, they were indivisibly linked as a contiguous organisation. A comparison of touring shows between BRG and CCAS reveals that the collective's touring exhibitions were predicated on taking the local to a national audience in a necessarily modest way; by the mid-1990s, however, CCAS was confidently operating in the international market and asserting its right to international recognition.

BRG's scrapbooks reveal three significant examples of interstate touring shows: an exchange with Iceberg Gallery in Melbourne in 1983; the tour of *Causes* to Hobart, Launceston, Perth and Adelaide in 1984; and the touring of *Nowhere utopia* to Brisbane in 1986. The impetus for the Iceberg show came from ex-BRG member Karilyn Brown, who was working at the Melbourne gallery in early 1983. Soon after her arrival in Melbourne, she wrote to Alder: 'I was pondering the idea of a group show

---

126 De Medici, 2012.
127 Trevor Smith, 'Director's report', 1995 Scrapbook, CCAS archives.

at Iceberg, representing the Bitumen River Gallery artists, what do you think?'[128] This first BRG travelling exhibition showed works by 14 artists using a variety of mediums including sculpture, lithographs, silk-screened posters, oil paintings, and crayon and pencil drawings.[129] Marcus Breen reviewed the show for the *Melbourne Times*, highlighting Tony Ayres' silk-screens, Andrew Powell's sculptures, and works by Stephanie Radok and Colin Russell. Alluding to Canberra's dual national capital/local dichotomy, Breen wrote: 'Stephanie Radok's work exemplifies something of the restraint of the Canberra mentality, with some of the edge still intact.'[130] The exhibition provided the first non-institutional opportunity for Melbourne audiences to witness expressions of local emerging art from Canberra.

One memory collected from early BRG members on the occasion of BRG's fifth birthday was from Powell, who submitted a pencil drawing of his Canberra lounge room that showed posters from early Canberra printmakers, along with a story of getting the work to Iceberg Gallery:

> I remember some good things that happened in the early days of BRG – like our trip to Iceberg Gallery in Melbourne. 12 members submitted about 4 or 5 works each, [then] Dave Turnbull, myself and Nick Cosgrove drove my Kombi and Dave's FC packed with all this art to Rankin Lane and the next day we hung the show. We stayed for a few days, across the lane in Julie Higginbotham's studio, felt a bit funny hanging around all the rad femmes – but they were good to us, Julie and her friends drove us around and we pasted up posters (on a couple of the posh gallery art marts as well) bit like a cloak and dagger scene – anyway we drank lots of wine and coffee and the local Iceberg crowd seemed happy with the work, we even had some air time on [community radio station] 3cr … [I]t was an interesting time – I remember the effort by people like Alison Alder and Paul Ford and others that made B>R>G> [sic] progress when the gallery was young – [N]o wage, living [sic] on the dole, making good out of not much – so good on them.[131]

---

128 Karilyn Brown, letter to Dianne, BRG, undated [c February/March 1983].
129 It was the second time that the work of young Canberra artists had been exhibited interstate; first showings from CSA student printmakers took place at the George Paton Gallery at the University of Melbourne in the early 1980s, organised by head of the Printmaking Workshop, Jorg Schmeisser.
130 Marcus Breen, 'Life after Canberra', *Melbourne Times*, June 1983.
131 BRG, '5th birthday show', CCAS archives.

Less than three years after BRG opened, its tenacity and relevance were recognised when its second touring show gained modest local and Commonwealth funding. In early 1984, BRG for the first time secured funding from the Department of Territories and Local Government and the ACT Community Development Fund to tour the exhibition *Causes* to Praxis Gallery in Perth for an arrival date of 27 April. Ayres, who was travelling to Perth for Easter, offered to print the invitations at the Praxis workshop. March dates were added for Cockatoo Workshop in Launceston and Chameleon Gallery in Hobart, with the tour ending at the Experimental Art Foundation in Adelaide in May. Denton wrote to Chameleon in March to thank the gallery for 'the enthusiasm shown towards the "Causes" show.'[132]

The last of the BRG travelling shows prior to amalgamation was *Nowhere utopia*. Norman Ainsworth and de Medici took two briefcases containing the photocopied works of 27 members to THAT Gallery, Brisbane, by train in June 1987, because, as de Medici recalled, 'We couldn't afford to freight the show'.[133] The show's poster was printed at Megalo.

There are significant differences in funding and organisation between BRG's exhibition tours of the 1980s and the CCAS touring programs of the mid-90s to early 2000s. The BRG collective tours exemplify the necessarily ad hoc approach of the time in which the elements to tour an exhibition were cobbled together; there were no precedents for touring prior to *Causes* and, in spite of the small one-off grant that facilitated its travel to Praxis, there was no ongoing funding to support a touring program and little experience to draw upon within the collective.

The touring programs from 1995 to 1997, with Barney and Smith working together, and from 1997 to 2002 with Barney as director, were markedly different. Barney's funded, full-time position encouraged long-term program planning and she was committed to touring CCAS-generated exhibitions nationally on a regular basis and internationally where possible. Planning and commitment, however, required funding. During the period from 1994 to 2002, which included the appointments of both Smith and Barney, there was no CPI increase in the annual Australia Council or Arts ACT grant to CCAS. As the Canberra-based exhibition program became increasingly ambitious, Barney needed to raise

---

132 Mark Denton, letter to Chameleon, 7 March 1984, CCAS archives.
133 De Medici, 2012.

additional funding for touring opportunities. Her solution was to raise money for one major touring show a year. Securing funding for an annual touring exhibition had positive ongoing repercussions throughout the program. It meant that Smith was able to announce in the 1995 director's report that, between the end of 1995 and 1997, 'there [will be] at least three exhibitions touring with a total of thirteen dates between them'.[134] These exhibitions would be developed by and open at CCAS and 'could be paid for with the touring funding and that would free us up a bit more money to spend on the rest of the year'.[135]

CCAS sent a strong message of continuing support for Indigenous artists when Barney and Smith decided that the first exhibition to tour internationally would be the Indigenous exhibition *Black books*. The show had its genesis in 1994 when Barney, in her final year at the CSA Gallery, curated an exhibition of the same name of journals made by Aboriginal and Maori women. Including local Ngunnawal Aboriginal elder Matilda House and Canberra-based Maori musician Mereana Otene Waaka, the women were given loose-leaf journals in which they wrote every day for a month. The resulting works were exhibited on black plinths and patrons were given black gloves to wear while turning the pages.

Another manifestation of local/national collaboration through CCAS occurred when Smith offered Aboriginal urban artist Gordon Hookey, whom he met in Sydney, an artist-in-residence placement at Gorman House for early 1995. During the residency, Hookey developed a body of work for a solo show, *Interface inyaface*, that opened at CCAS Manuka gallery in April 1995. At the same time, Smith envisaged that Hookey would work with local Indigenous artists from the Ngunnawal, Wiradguri and other nations, on a collaborative exhibition as part of the Inaugural National Sculpture Forum. The resulting exhibition, *Naii Ngarrambai Wanggirali Burrangiri Nangi Dyannai Ngurui* (*the lay of the land is how you know your country; when you look behind you, you can always see your tracks*) (see Figure 33), was developed by gallery assistant Megan Elliot and opened at CCAS on 8 April.

---

134 Trevor Smith, 1995.
135 Barney, 2012.

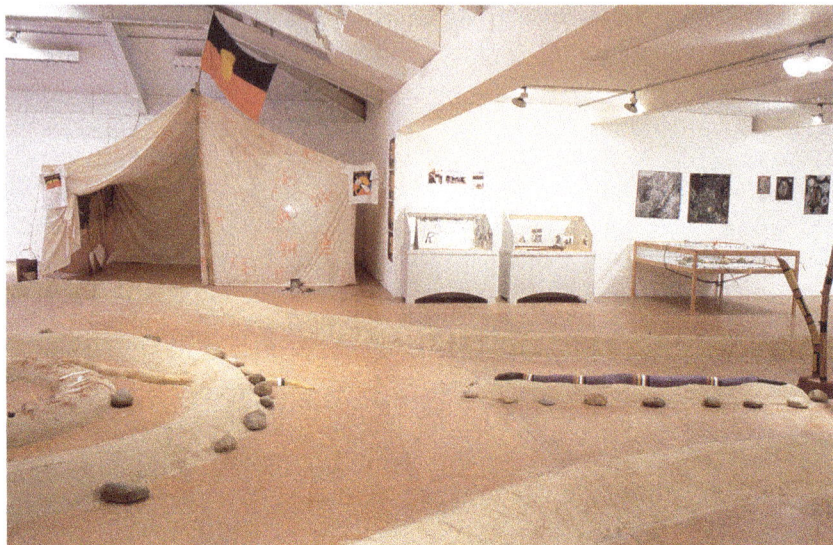

Figure 33. *Naii Ngarrambai Wanggirali Burrangiri Nangi Dyannai Ngurui (the lay of the land is how you know your country; when you look behind you, can always see your tracks)*, **installation photograph, detail**
Source. CCAS image archive, reproduced with permission

The media release stated that the exhibition comprised 'Work by artists from the Ngunnawal community and Aboriginal artists living and working in Canberra focus[ing] on the region's past, present and future'.[136] The exhibition garnered wide local press with reviews from Barron (*Canberra Times*) and Cousins (*Muse*), a story in *Canberra City News*, and two articles in the *Chronicle* – one on *Naii Ngarrambai Wanggirali Burrangiri Nangi Dyannai Ngurui* and one on Hookey.[137] The latter article described the exhibition as providing a 'commentary on issues which arise from western cultural encroachment and impositions'.[138] *Work in progress*, the briefly-produced member's newsletter of Gorman House Arts Centre, also featured Hookey's story on its front page.[139]

---

136 *What's On?*, Gorman House Arts Centre newsletter, April 1995.
137 *Naii Ngarrambai Wanggirali Burrangiri Nangi Dyannai Ngurui*, 1995, CCAS archives.
138 *Chronicle*, 'Encroachment and impositions', 17 April 1995.
139 *Work in progress*, 4, 1, April 1995, Gorman House Arts Centre.

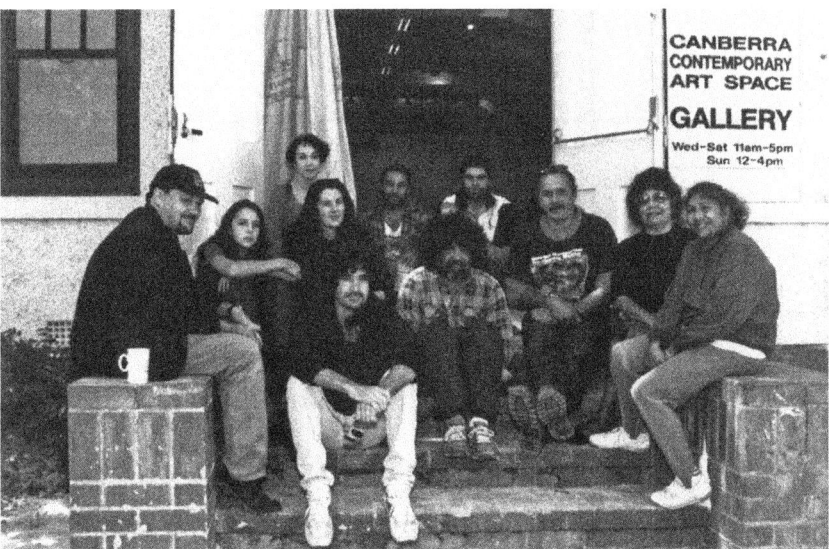

Figure 34. *Naii Ngarrambai Wanggirali Burrangiri Nangi Dyannai Ngurui (the lay of the land is how you know your country; when you look behind you, you can always see your tracks)*, **artists: Neville O'Neill, Kalara Gilbert, Megan Elliot, Gail Harradine, Michael Kennedy, Gordon Hookey, Arnold Williams, Jim 'Boza' Williams, Johnno Johnson, Aunty Matilda House, Joan Wingfield; exterior CCAS, Gorman House, April 1995**
Source. Photographer: Eleanor Williams, reproduced with permission

Works from Barney's CSA Gallery exhibition *Black books*, and Smith and Elliot's CCAS exhibition *Naii Ngarrambai Wanggirali Burrangiri Nangi Dyannai Ngurui*, were also selected for an international showing. At the end of 1996, CCAS, in association with local Aboriginal elders Iris Clayton and House, toured *Black books* to the Australian Embassy in Manila via Barney's relationship with April Pressler, who was at that time Australia's cultural attaché to the Philippines. In this instance Barney maximised exhibition opportunities with work already at hand, a strategy she would continue to employ over the next five years at CCAS.[140]

---

140 Another example of the CCAS commitment to Indigenous artists was the exhibition *Black humour*, which opened at CCAS on 12 July 1997. This exhibition subsequently toured to IMA, 24HR Art, Boomalli Gallery, Koorie Heritage Trust in Melbourne and Tandanya in Adelaide.

Canberra/Brasilia

Twenty years after the unfunded BRG collective opened the doors of its tiny reclaimed gallery space in the old shelter shed of St Christopher's School in Manuka, CCAS embarked on an international artist exchange. Smith conceived the ambitious idea to link the world's two 20th-century, planned national capitals, Canberra, Australia, and Brasilia, Brazil. He left CCAS in 1997 before the concept could be realised but, in 2001, with the Centenary of Federation providing additional funding for the contemporary art sector, Barney realised the concept with Smith's unqualified support. Through the process of developing the exchange, the parameters that previously governed CCAS touring exhibitions were extended to include the movement of and collaboration between artists from both countries. *Canberra/Brasilia* provides an outstanding example of a successful inter-country artist exchange using the relatively small resources of a regional contemporary art space. The project highlighted how effectively CCAS could perform when acting as host to a visiting international artist and, importantly, how far the organisation had come from its early preoccupation with supporting the development of local visual arts practice, to a mutually supported international undertaking.

This project would not have been undertaken by the NGA, nor would it, with its negligible potential for profit, have found a place within the commercial milieu. Moreover, the exchange could only have happened between Canberra and Brasilia. It was a site-specific collaboration on an international scale and yet the resulting exhibitions were inherently and intrinsically communal and personal; using a combination of old technology, Indigenous materials, and expressions of nature, the artists' works were enacted within and against outstanding planned-city designs. In thinking about *Canberra/Brasilia*, Barney's only givens were the major similarity between the two cities as planned capitals and the decision to use Shane Breynard as the Canberra artist. It was an open-ended, curatorially fertile space.

Breynard had lived in Canberra for 27 years and graduated from ANU SOA with first-class honours, the University medal and a Master of arts degree by research. His photographic art was concerned with the interaction of cultural values, specific architectures of the built environment, and its surrounding landscape. When Barney approached him to ask if he was interested in the concept that Smith had broached five years previously, he was coming to the end of four years in London and returning to Canberra as managing editor of *Art Monthly Australia*. The timing was good. Barney additionally liked his 'odd, esoteric take on things'.[141] With Breynard locked in, Barney travelled to Brasilia to find a local artist, who 'knew Brasilia in the same way that Shane was really embedded in Canberra'.[142]

The most interesting contemporary art is often generated by artists working at the margins and, for this reason, international visiting curators reliant on in-country dealers for introductions can find it difficult to access the artists they are hoping to find. This was the problem that Barney faced:

> We got introduced to painter after painter after painter after painter – we were getting a really hard sell from dealers – we went to Sao Paolo but I was pretty clear in my mind that it wasn't going to be a Sao Paolo or a Rio artist.[143]

Back in Brasilia and at the end of another long day of consecutive meetings where the art on show included 'painting, more painting; kind of irrelevant subject matter that had nothing to do with the city', Barney was beginning to feel 'hysterical'.[144] She arrived for the day's last meeting – at a classic Oscar Niemeyer–designed apartment block in the heart of the original 1960s-built accommodation precinct – to meet with artist Marta Penner:

> [T]here were kids everywhere and mess everywhere and she's pulling out these pinhole photographs of the Brasilia interstices, all the crummy places between the shiny designed Oscar Niemeyer bits that only someone who lives there could possibly know. I knew the moment I saw those things that this was it. I got back to her and I said 'I want you to do the show' and she said 'I'm amazed that you picked me because I'm not really in the crowd and my partner said to me "Why are you even bothering to meet with those people? They never pick us"' and I said 'No you're definitely it. You're it. I have no doubt'.[145]

---

141 Barney, 2012.
142 Barney, 2012.
143 Barney, 2012.
144 Barney, 2012.
145 Barney, 2012.

Barney determined that Breynard and Penner would travel to each other's cities to make individual and collaborative works: Breynard to Brasilia in June and Penner to Canberra in late August – early September, with the results being exhibited at CCAS and in Brasilia and Rio. The catalogue essay reveals that the exhibition incorporated:

> a collection of the documents, objects and photographs from [the artists'] urban work. It is a coalescence of visual art, urban planning, public art, text and architecture; and a contemporary reflection on life in two of the world's most unusual cities.[146]

The artists' experiences whilst in each other's countries were markedly different. While Penner had all the advantages of the CCAS networks to support the development of her work in Canberra, Breynard's experience was somewhat negatively coloured by not having a host gallery in Brasilia. Based at the university, he was more reliant on Penner as a facilitator and a working partner. Barney believes this meant it took longer for Breynard's concept to emerge. 'His experience wasn't as streamlined as hers [but] in the end it all came together'.[147]

Breynard pursued two ideas in Brasilia. The first was working with Brazil's ubiquitous, Indigenous bed, the hammock, designed to be cool and transportable. The second comprised laser-cut timber names – painted in eucalypt colours – of the eucalypt trees native to the Canberra region. These were installed in the Roberto Burle Marx–designed landscape around Niemeyer's superquadra apartment blocks, and then displayed on the walls at CCAS (see Figure 35).

Breynard's laser-cut works, and the catalogue essays, are indicative of a major problem with international touring shows with a text component that are enacted between countries without a common language. The tree names and the catalogue essays were both being shown/read in Canberra and Brasilia and so needed to be translated into Portuguese. Barney recalls the process:

> The first translator we had was a bit of a clunker and the second had a nice turn of phrase so some of those essays in the catalogue are a pleasure to read and some are not so pleasurable.[148]

---

146 Jane Barney (ed), *Canberra/Brasilia*, exhibition catalogue, Canberra Contemporary Art Space, 2001, p 10.
147 Barney, 2012.
148 Barney, 2012.

6. TRANSFORMATION

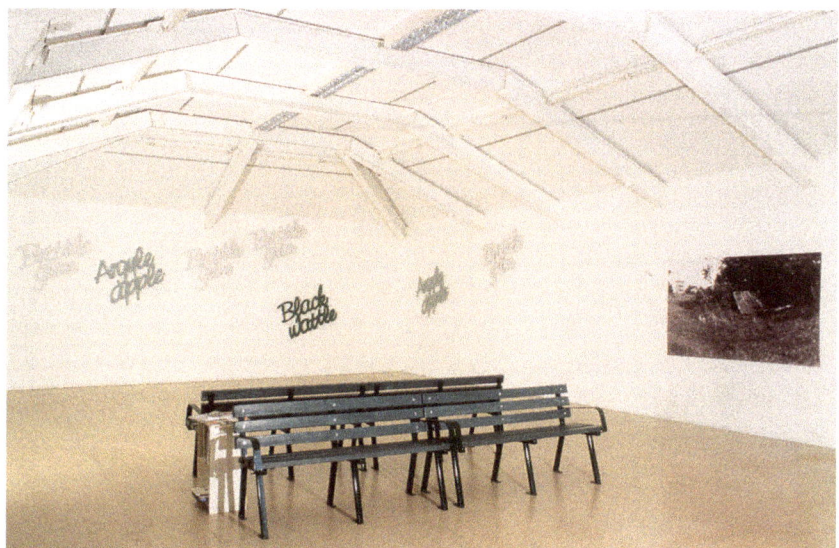

Figure 35. Shane Breynard and Marta Penner, *Canberra Brasilia,* **CCAS artist exchange and travelling exhibition at CCAS, 8 September – 20 October 2001, installation photograph**
Source. CCAS image archive, reproduced with permission

Penner shared that characteristic of Breynard's that Barney had so liked: 'an odd esoteric take on things'. She had lived in Brasilia for 15 years and began photographing around the city during her master's degree, three years before Barney met her. The pinhole camera images – realised using a coffee can with a hole punched in its base – that excited Barney ostensibly had little to do with the modernist Niemeyer-designed city. Penner photographed the city from an entirely unexpected and quirky perspective that could only have been obvious to someone whose knowledge of the shining planned spaces extended to the interstitial; those unseen or otherwise forgotten places inhabited and traversed by the marginalised and dispossessed; spaces that neither Brasilia nor Canberra allowed for in the city planning process.[149]

When Penner arrived in Canberra, she went straight to CCAS and immediately set off on foot with her pinhole camera towards the Commonwealth Science and Industrial Research Organisation (CSIRO)

---

149 The question of whether cultural precincts can be effectively imposed on spaces in a city or should be allowed to arise naturally is one that comes up in forums in Canberra. It is currently particularly relevant to the developing Kingston Foreshore precinct, as first mooted in the *Final report* of the Select Committee on Cultural Activities and Facilities, ACT Legislative Assembly (June 1991).

building. From that first walk she began taking 'these amazing pictures … She kept coming across homeless people'.¹⁵⁰ As with her work in Brasilia, however, Penner was not interested in photographing the people but in exploring the in-between spaces, situated around the designed spaces, that these people inhabited. The resulting body of work from Canberra bears many similarities to those photographs made by her in Brasilia.

In Canberra and Brasilia, Breynard and Penner worked with hammocks. In Brasilia, in a collaborative work titled *entre-redes*, reflecting Breynard's interest in the intersections between the built environment and nature, the artists suspended hammocks between the uppermost branches of the large trees that ringed the superquadra apartment blocks, connecting individual apartments to the natural environment. In Canberra, Penner's installation of hammocks, which were hung through the stairwells of the inner-city Currong Apartments, fulfilled the artist's interest in spaces that existed within and yet outside planned affluence (see Figure 36). Additionally, this installation reflected the gulf between contemporary art practice and civic rules, recalling the tone of some of the public response to the 1994 Ainslie Avenue billboards exhibition *I am you*. Barney related the brush with officialdom:

> [Penner] strung up hammocks between the stairwells and all the tenants were coming up and saying it looks great and taking pictures and within an hour and a half the housing people had turned up and said 'Get those hammocks down from there someone might jump'!¹⁵¹

Breynard's Brasilia experience and the touring component of the exhibition to Brasilia would have been more effective with a host gallery in place in Brasilia that was able to facilitate Breynard's work as CCAS facilitated Penner's visit and exhibition. As it was, Barney arrived at the Brasilia exhibition to find herself in the kind of Niemeyer-designed gallery space that, in Brasilia, are 'a dime a dozen'.¹⁵² The thrill of attending opening night within the iconic architecture was tempered by the realisation that the exhibition was being held in an 'under-funded, government-owned Niemeyer space that [was] falling apart [with] three people and a dog coming through for an exhibition opening'.¹⁵³

---

150   Barney, 2012.
151   Barney, 2012.
152   Barney, 2012.
153   Barney, 2012.

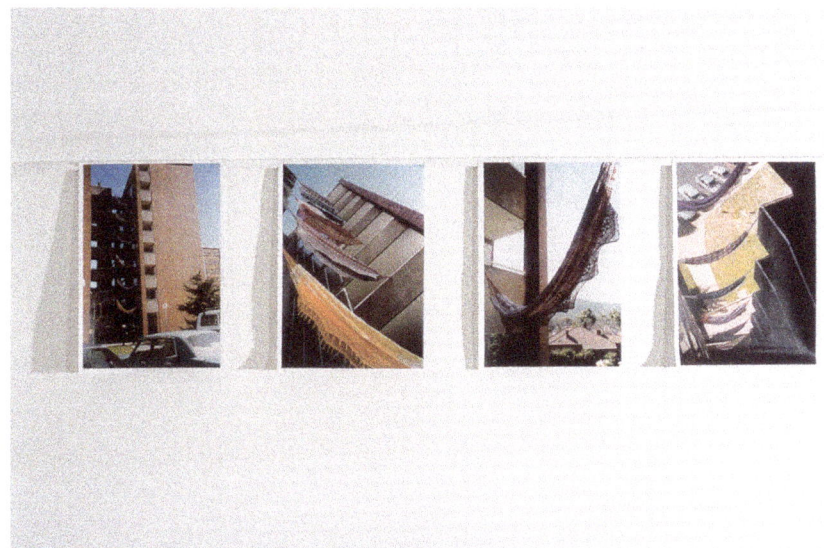

Figure 36. Shane Breynard and Marta Penner, *Canberra Brasilia*, CCAS artist exchange and travelling exhibition at CCAS, 8 September – 20 October 2001, installation photograph of hammocks strung between apartments in the Currong apartments, Canberra
Source. CCAS image archive, reproduced with permission

The value of the project lay in more than the sum of its parts. Its successful conclusion signalled the maturing of an arts space that began as a contested, local, unfunded collective space arising in response to local social and political imperatives at the beginning of the 1980s. The BRG collective displayed an early commitment to increasing the national profile of local artists with several modest tours of BRG exhibitions and through its initial coordinators, Alder and Virgo, attending national forums. When the CCAS board hired Smith as director at the end of 1993, it did so in order to bring CCAS into line with national and international paradigmatic changes in curatorial and exhibition practice. Although the decision was not without detractors, the appointments of Smith, and then Barney, transformed CCAS. During their collaboration as director/curator in the mid-1990s and subsequently though Barney's time as director, national and international touring programs reflected the growing maturity of the Canberra visual arts community. *Canberra/Brasilia*, Barney's last major project for CCAS before she left the organisation in 2002, positioned CCAS as a nationally relevant, fully funded, confident contemporary art space, executing curatorial decisions that defined local practice as internationally relevant and mutually supported.

CONCLUSION

Late autumn in the Australian Capital Territory is all limpid sky and crisp outline. In 2013, as Canberra turned 100 years old, a remarkable work of art rose through the crystalline air: an otherworldly creature, exuding symbolic references to the ancient natural environment below and to the planned, twentieth-century capital nestled within. *Skywhale*, the hot air balloon designed by Australian artist Patricia Piccinini, was aloft (see Figure 37). Piccinini's breathtakingly strange creature, whose evolutions and adaptations are connected to ideas of human intervention into the natural world, reflects the Canberra in which she grew up. In its colours of sky, limestone plains, treed ridges and escarpments, in its imaginative physical characteristics that combine allusions to the natural and the man-made, and in the passionate conversations that surrounded its commissioning and delivery, *Skywhale*'s artistic complexity echoes Canberra's own.

This national capital is enlivened and humanised by its warm and inclusive arts community. Outsiders might perceive that the currently well-resourced local arts sector is a direct outcome of Commonwealth-supported national capital life. This is simply wrong. It is instead, and overwhelmingly, the product of passionate, consistent, local community engagement and activism over more than 40 years. Today, the city benefits from the inspired, local political and arts leadership of the past and the continuing spirit of mentorship, collaboration and friendship that pervades the broad arts community. The deep regard for excellence in visual arts education through the ANU School of Art and Design (SofA) has continued to grow throughout this new century. A broad, tightly knit spread of student, emerging, mid-career and senior artists make their homes and their works in the ACT.

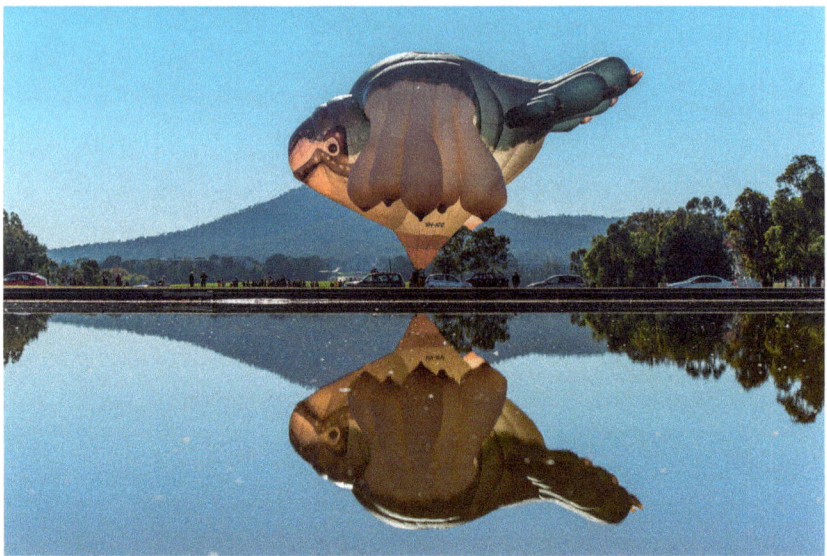

Figure 37. Patricia Piccinini, *Skywhale*, 2013
Source. Photographer: Martin Ollman, reproduced with permission

Echoes of the burgeoning arts community of the early 1980s resonate strongly in Canberra today. Artists, arts workers and institutions that emerged at that time are now nationally and internationally effective and highly visible protagonists and crucibles of Australian art development and practice. Among them is nationally acclaimed artist Alison Alder, who returned to Canberra in 2010 to head Megalo Print Studios, the organisation whose birth she assisted 30 years before. Alder transferred to the ANU SofA in 2012 as head of the Printmaking Workshop; the same workshop where she trained from 1978 to 1981. Only a brave person would have predicted that the small group of impoverished students, emerging artists and activists who established Megalo in the tumbledown shed in Ainslie Village, and then Bitumen River Gallery (BRG) in the abandoned bus shelter at St Christopher's Church, would go on to have national and international careers. The organisations they founded in activism and hope have retained their individuality and are vital threads in the contemporary cultural fabric of both the ACT and Australia.

Statistics reveal that the ACT has the highest per-capita involvement in arts and culture in the country. Within a population of just over 400,000, this reflects the community's continued arts and cultural literacy and its hunger for the social enhancements that cultural engagement offers. Statistics likewise support the tremendous economic contribution that the arts bring to the national capital.

There remains, however, an inherent fragility in the ACT's arts and cultural fabric. Without a local council and, therefore, no access to council arts funding, continued sustainable funding is dependent on the vagaries of elected local governments, ministerial appointments and bureaucratic support; the quality of incumbent ministerial engagement and bureaucratic follow-through. Historically, those periods when the sector has flourished in Canberra have occurred when the needs of the vibrant arts and cultural communities are met by an engaged government that courageously implements responsive arts policy. Until sustainable local arts funding is mandated as bipartisan, each generation will be called to activism for survival.

A confluence of events in 2016–17 exquisitely illustrated this recurrent fragility. In 2011, senior arts figures, concerned with a steady decline in local arts funding from a high of $1.1 million in 2005, established an independent forum, The Childers Group. The group aimed to advocate for arts workers and practitioners and, through public forums and the compilation of statistics, provide timely, ongoing information to assist government in decision-making. In early 2016, the Australia Council (which makes the second-lowest per-capita contribution to the ACT)[1] announced catastrophic de-funding of the national visual arts sector. These cuts were met with an entirely unexpected decrease in local project funding, 'the largest decrease in living memory'.[2] Despite the flurry of broad arts activity in the lead-up to the national capital's centenary in 2013, in late December 2016, when the ACT's principal funding body, Arts ACT, finally released its 2017 project funding commitment, the local arts community were blindsided. At just $300,000, it reflected a significant and unaccountable loss in funding from the 2005 high of $1.1 million.

---

1   In 2014/15 the ACT received $1.5 million from the Australia Council, the least of all jurisdictions and equivalent to the second-least per capita at around $3.84 each – just slightly better than Queensland which received $17.6 million, around $3.68 each. See 'Facts', *The Childers Group*, childersgroup.com.au.
2   The Childers Group archive, February 2017, www.childersgroup.com.au/2017/02/.

Once more, as it had throughout the 1970s, 1980s and 1990s, the community rose as one, wasting no time in alerting the new Arts Minister, Gordon Ramsay, who was confirmed by the Labor government under Chief Minister Andrew Barr in the portfolios of Attorney General, and Arts, Community and Veteran Affairs in September 2016, to the parlous state of project funding and ministerial and bureaucratic support for sustainable practice. Activism arose on several united fronts – from the general community, from practitioners and workers, and through the Childers Group. It included activist events, public rallies, panels and forums, submissions to the minister and presentations to the Legislative Assembly.

The new minister's extensive background in community consultation was immediately apparent. An additional $230,000 in project funding was released in early 2017, with recipients to come from those who had applied for the 2017 round. Reflecting Ramsay's serious intent, Arts ACT was incorporated into the department of the Chief Minister and Ramsay and his staff embarked on a period of broad community consultation. Speaking at the *Arts value forum* in August 2017, his commitment to arts and culture as a prerequisite for a healthy polis was clear:

> If the ability to access the arts and the capability to make art are inherently important to human wellbeing and community, we must ensure we are fostering cultural democracy – providing the places, spaces, empowerment, and resources – the capability – for everyone to engage with the creative process in whatever way brings added fulfilment their lives.

The results of broad arts community consultation are reflected in the June 2018/19 ACT budget, which delivered highly significant growth in funding for local arts, including: a $750,000 annual commitment for project funding, $230,000 for arts events, and a commitment to return any underspends in the arts budget directly back to arts endeavours. In 2018, this has yielded an additional one-off $325,000 for community outreach art projects. In all, the government commitment to local grant funding has exceeded $1 million for the 2018 year. Additionally, application processes for project funding have been streamlined with application dates consistent across years.

The minister and the government's commitment to the sector as a whole is borne out by increased and new funding for: a dedicated Aboriginal and Torres Strait Islander arts officer; funds for sector capacity building; an asset replacement scheme; funds to support innovative programming at community centres; training in the stage and theatre industry; artist exchanges, upgrades to CMAG and the CTC and conservation works and improvements to the ACT's Historic Places, Lanyon Homestead, Calthorpes' House and Mugga Mugga; as well as a one-off, $5 million grant to establish a screen industry development fund. Funding continues for arts organisations, the Cultural Facilities Corporation, the ACT Book of the Year award and community outreach programs. In all, the government's budgetary commitment to arts and culture in the 2018/19 year exceeds $26 million. This time around, great need has been met by a courageous ministerial response.

In charting the development of arts practice in the city between the 1920s and 2001, and within BRG and Canberra Contemporary Art Space (CCAS) between 1978 and 2001, this history has exposed the rapid evolution of Australia's modern national capital. Created principally as the federal capital, the city has been transformed into a national capital space that is a complex, dynamic centre for contemporary arts practice and exhibition.

There are fertile opportunities for further research in this area. The loss of Australia Council funding to the contemporary arts sector in May 2016 indicates a clear and pressing need to assist arts funding bodies and arts ministers' understanding of the critical importance of not only restoring but increasing funding to contemporary visual art organisations in every state and territory. These spaces are vital to Australian artists' continued development and to international perceptions of Australia as contemporarily culturally relevant. This could be done through an analysis of the history and importance of the sector's national body, Contemporary Art Organisations Australia. Comparative studies of regional and city-based contemporary art spaces would also assist relevant bodies in understanding their importance. A comparative study of contemporary art spaces in the modern planned federal capitals of Canberra and Brasilia would be fascinating and timely. These two cities, which Trevor Smith and, later, Jane Barney so creatively conceived as ripe for artists' exchanges and exhibitions in the 1990s, would today present opportunities for assessing the impacts of local and federal funding on the development of contemporary art and the effects of that funding and development on international perceptions of two modern, national federal capitals.[3]

---

3   Over summer 2018/19 the author and her Brasilian collaborator conceived a long-form, collaborative curatorial/multiple-artist exhibition and exchange project, titled '*Curating Canberra Brasilia*', between these two planned capitals, with exhibitions to be staged in both cities in autumn 2021.

One of Australia's most pressing issues concerns reconciliation between, and rehabilitation of, Indigenous/non-Indigenous relations. Locally, the BRG/CCAS archives provide considerable material for research into its engagement with local and national Indigenous artists in exhibition, building on the work done in this research. While the parameters of this history do not allow for an in-depth study in this area, further research would contribute to positive public perceptions of contemporary Indigeneity in Australia. A deeper analysis of CCAS's engagement with performance art during the 1990s is also rich in research possibilities. Analysing the connections between the Sculpture Workshop at Canberra School of Art (CSA) and performance art emanating from CCAS would further unique aspects of art practice in the national capital and assist today's artists, arts workers, art consumers and local and national funding bodies in continuing to build a picture of Canberra's contemporary arts development.

One of the aims of this history has been to make a thorough analytical response to Timothy Pascoe's misconception of the importance of visual arts development in Canberra. He characterised this, in the mid-1980s, as 'not particularly strong' and as lacking the 'opportunity for uniqueness'.[4] While those with a vested interest in local contemporary arts initiatives would intuitively oppose such claims, recent federal government funding policy has revealed a return to views that devalue the importance of local contemporary arts spaces in our communities. CCAS, along with Australia's network of contemporary art spaces, arose as an unfunded collective in response to local needs. Federal and local arts funding from the mid-1980s through to the present day has assisted the ongoing development of these grassroots organisations. Today they are profoundly effective conduits for artists in their journey from art schools through to their representation in commercial, regional, state and national galleries; in international art museums; and in Australian and international biennales. Donal Fitzpatrick, head of the School of Design and Art at Curtin University of Technology, characterises the contemporary art space as providing: 'The heavy lifting of a vibrant visual culture,' allowing for 'the unsteady and the tumultuous, in spaces electric with the risk of failure and prickling with unease.'[5]

---

4 Pascoe, 1985, p 57.
5 Donal Fitzpatrick, *21st century CAOs: a forward plan for contemporary art*, Sydney, Contemporary Art Organisations Australia, 2010, p 19.

CONCLUSION

CCAS developed a solution-focused response to the 2016 decrease in Australia Council funding. In the week prior to the announcement, director David Broker successfully interpreted the political mood and, in preparing CCAS curator Alexander Boynes and then gallery manager Sabrina Baker for funding cuts, called a meeting to consider the gallery's guiding principles of innovation and resilience: innovation in maintaining a vital and relevant exhibition program with reduced resources, and resilience in the face of necessary changes, the most confronting of which was the need to temporarily abort the long-established residency program, which had provided year-long residencies to emerging artists. In the immediate short-term, and reflective of the unique local solutions to funding crises enacted in the 1980s, CCAS announced a fundraising auction for which the $250 tickets sold out on release.[6] Fifty-two local artists, from emerging to those with international reputations, who had exhibited at CCAS over the preceding three years, donated works that were then awarded, in blind pairings, to 52 ticketed patrons. The success of the auction showed the Canberra community's deep affection for, engagement with and understanding of CCAS's critical importance to Canberra's continued contemporary arts development.

In 2017, the organisation decreased staffing to two – Broker and curator Alexander Boynes – and staged another successful fundraiser. After a one-year hiatus during 2017, CCAS has extended three residencies to emerging artists in 2018. While this vitally important contemporary arts organisation has displayed great resilience since Australia Council funding cuts in 2016, it is imperative that funding be restored.

For over 30 years, the CCAS gallery has occupied exhibition space at Gorman House within the recently rebadged Ainslie and Gorman Art Centres. Now, with significant expenditure required to bring the current gallery up to standard, it is undeniably past time for the organisation to relocate to more appropriate premises.

The arrangement between the Drill Hall Gallery and the Australian National Gallery in the 1980s allowed the best of contemporary Australian and international art exhibitions to be staged outside the confines of the National Gallery. The arrangement came to an end, under director Betty Churcher in 1991, in the face of staffing and budget cuts. NGA Contemporary was revived by director Ron Radford in 2014, with

---

6   Conceived and managed by then CCAS Gallery Manager, Sabrina Baker.

exhibitions staged in the architecturally significant lakeside building, East Space, owned by the National Capital Authority, adjacent to the NGA and the National Portrait Gallery (NPG). The final of three exhibitions in that space, *The last temptation: the art of Ken and Julia Yonetani*, provided a provocative, visually stunning conclusion to this second iteration of an NGA-run contemporary art annexe. Under the yoke of continued efficiency dividends applied to the federally funded national institutions, director Gerard Vaughan closed NGA Contemporary in 2016.

This now empty gallery space, situated within the national capital cultural triangle, in close proximity to the nation's major cultural institutions, provides a logical and ideal location for the next chapter in the CCAS journey, allowing for increased public accessibility and profile for the national capital's critically important contemporary art space and its exhibiting artists.[7]

The second decade of the twenty-first century in Canberra has witnessed increasing activity in contemporary art, dance, music, performance, design and literature from young practitioners with an emphasis on cross–art form collaboration. What distinguishes this surge from that occurring in the late 1970s and 1980s is that today's artists stand on the shoulders of giants; of those whose early and, ultimately, successful battles for recognition, for spaces and for funding, amongst the clamorous rhetoric of the national capital space's cultural pre-eminence, laid the fertile ground for subsequent generations of arts practitioners. This study, and the continued writing of our local art history, means that their early achievements, critical to the success of today's visual arts community, will not remain unsung.

---

7   In January 2020, Canberra Contemporary Art Space relocated to East Space after 32 years at Gorman House. It will remain in this location until it moves with other arts organisations, including ArtSound, Canberra Glassworks, CraftACT, M16, Megalo Access Arts and Photo Access, to the Kingston Arts Precinct in 2023–24. In February 2017 the ACT government announced developer Geocon, with partners Fender Katsalidis architects and Oculus, as successful tenderers for construction of the Kingston Arts Precinct. Contracts were exchanged in July 2019. The development will comprise offices, gallery spaces and workshops for Canberra arts organisations, accommodation for visiting artists, outdoor arts and recreation areas, carparking and mixed residential. Construction for all stages is to be completed by mid-2026. The development completes the plan first outlined 28 years ago in the final report of the Bill Wood–chaired Select Committee on Cultural Activities and Facilities, in consultation with the Canberra arts and culture community.

REFERENCES

21 years of hybrid arts practice, Sydney, Performance Space, 2004.

ACT Arts Development Board, *Arts development in the Australian Capital Territory: a discussion paper*, Canberra, 1984.

ACT Government, *ACT budget paper no 6, 1987/88*, Canberra, Government Printer, 1988.

ACT Government Genealogy Project, *Our kin our country*, Canberra, ACT Government, August 2012, www.communityservices.act.gov.au/__data/assets/pdf_file/0005/394385/CSD_GSR_web.pdf, accessed 7 November 2015.

Age, 'Australia shuns its artists: inquiry', 1 February 1984, p 3.

Agnello, Chiara and Roberta Tenconi, 'Taking the initiative: DIY in Australia's cultural capital', Julia Helm (trans), *Modern painters*, October 2006, pp 94–95.

Agostino, Michael, *The Australian National University School of Art: a history of the first 65 years*, Canberra, ANU School of Art, 2009.

Ah Kee, Vernon, 'Trevor Nickolls 1949–2012', 30 October 2012, vernonahkee.blogspot.com/2012/10/trevor-nickolls-1949-2012.html.

Alder, Alison, 'Bitumen River', conference paper, *Open sandwich conference*, ANZART, Hobart, May 1983.

——, 'Serving the needs of artists', conference paper, *Open sandwich conference*, ANZART, Hobart, May 1983.

Allen, Micky, '*Photography, drawing and poetry: a live-in show*, 1978', *Mickey Allen*, www.mickyallan.com/Bodies/Live-inShow.html, accessed 10 July 2016.

Andrews, Ross, 'From pasture to gala dinner', *Canberra Times*, 23 October 1983, p 11.

Australian Bureau of Statistics, Australia Historical Population Statistics (cat no 3105.0.65.001), 2014.

Australian Government, 'National Gallery regulations 1982', Federal Register of Legislation, www.legislation.gov.au/Details/C2004H02339, accessed 2 May 2014.

Ayres, Tony, 'Space', *Art Network*, 11, 1983, p 42.

——, '*Causes*: an exhibition of political posters and prints from Canberra, 1981 to 1983', *Imprint*, 1, 1985, np.

——, 'Introduction', *The image of desire*, exhibition catalogue, Canberra, BRG, 1985.

Bardon, Geoffrey and James Bardon, *Papunya: a place made after the story: the beginnings of the Western Desert Painting Movement*, Melbourne, The Miegunyah Press, 2004.

Barker, Heather and Charles Green, 'The provincialism problem: Terry Smith and centre–periphery art history', *Journal of Art Historiography*, 3, 2010, pp 54–59.

Barney, Jane (ed), *60 heads*, exhibition catalogue, Canberra Contemporary Art Space, 1996.

—— (ed), *Breath of life: moments in transit towards Aboriginal sovereignty*, Canberra Contemporary Art Space, 1996, exhibition catalogue.

—— (ed), *Performance season*, exhibition catalogue, Canberra Contemporary Art Space, 2000.

——, *Canberra/Brasilia*, exhibition catalogue, Canberra Contemporary Art Space, 2001.

——, *Sex and the settee*, exhibition catalogue, Canberra Contemporary Art Space, 2002.

Barron, Sonia, 'Light as the medium', *Canberra Times*, 1 February 1986, p 6.

——, 'Perceptions of domesticity', *Canberra Times*, 19 August 1987, p 29.

——, 'Viewers are deliberately victimised', *Canberra Times*, 13 January 1995.

Battersby, Jean, *Cultural policy in Australia*, Paris, UNESCO, 2000.

Beer, Chris, 'The production of Canberra and its national cultural institutions: imagination and practice of national capital space, national leadership and transnational and national museum practice, and Commonwealth managerial space', conference paper, Australasian Political Studies Association, Newcastle, New South Wales, 25–27 September 2006.

Bell, Alison, *Intensity of purpose: 21 years of ANCA*, exhibition catalogue, Canberra, Australian National Capital Artists, 2013.

Bereson, Ruth, 'Advance Australia – fair or foul? Observing Australian arts policies', *Journal of Arts Management, Law, and Society*, 35, 1, 2005, pp 49–59.

Bitumen River Gallery, 'Braidwood seminar of Canberra's arts organisations', *BRG Newsletter*, 6(b), November 1983, p 2.

Black, Lawrence, 'Not only a source of expenditure but a source of income', in Christiane Eisenberg, Rita Gerlach and Christian Handke (eds), *Cultural industries: the British experience in international perspective*, Berlin, Humboldt University, 2006, p 120, edoc.hu-berlin.de/conferences/culturalindustries/proc/culturalindustries.pdf, accessed 22 May 2013.

Boling, Edna, 'Auctioneer has sociable way to raise money', *Canberra Times*, 10 November 1983, p 8.

Bond, Anthony, 'The boundary rider', Foreword, *9th Biennale of Sydney* (1992/93), www.biennaleofsydney.com.au/20bos/about-us/history/1992-93/, accessed 15 August 2016.

Breen, Marcus, 'Bitumen River Gallery – one year after', *Muse*, 2 April – 13 May 1982, p 15.

——, 'Life after Canberra', *Melbourne Times*, June 1983.

Britton, Stephanie, (ed), *A decade at the EAF: a history of the Experimental Art Foundation 1974–1984*, Adelaide, Australian Experimental Art Foundation, 1984.

Broker, David, 'Quo vadis: 1994 to 2004: the Snelling years', Brisbane, Institute of Modern Art, 2005, web.archive.org/web/20140306081944/http://www.ima.org.au/pages/history/1994E280932004-the-snelling-years.php, last captured 6 March 2014, accessed 2 August 2012.

Brook, Donald, *The awful truth about what art is*, Adelaide, Artlink Australia, 2008.

——, 'The art school way back when', *Artlink*, 31, 3, 2011, pp 80–82.

Brough, Jodie, 'Gallery goes out in spectacular style – the Tully style', *Canberra Times*, 7 July 1991, p 1.

Brown, Nicholas, *A history of Canberra*, Cambridge University Press, 2014.

——, 'Never lost for words: Canberra's archives', *Public History Review*, 21, 2014, pp 81–101, epress.lib.uts.edu.au/journals/index.php/phrj/article/download/3928/4411, accessed 15 January 2015.

Bruton, Dean (ed), *The contemporary art society of South Australia 1942–86: recollections*, Adelaide, The Contemporary Art Society of South Australia, 1986.

Bull, Gordon, 'A front', *Site specific city*, exhibition catalogue, Canberra Contemporary Art Space, 1987.

Butler, Roger, 'Colin Little: poster maker', *Colin Little retrospective*, exhibition catalogue, Canberra, BRG, 1983, pp 3–4.

——, *Poster art in Australia: the streets as art galleries – walls sometimes speak*, Canberra, National Gallery of Australia, 1993.

Cameron, Debbie, 'Kingston space launched for art', *Canberra Times*, 31 March 1984, p 9.

'Campaign for free admission to the Australian National Gallery', press release, 22 September 1982.

Canberra and District Historical Society Newsletter, June/July 1982.

Canberra Times, 'Canberra's population', 19 July 1927, p 4.

——, 'Petitions to parliament: voice in local affairs: seat in parliament', 1 November 1927, p 4.

——, 'Canberra division of Arts Council: new name for CEMA', 26 May 1948, p 2.

——, 'Art and craft prizes at Hall', 16 February 1952, p 2.

——, 'Artist finishes school murals', 13 September 1960, p 7.

——, 'Council grants to arts', 12 December 1968, p 33.

——, 'Arts grants criticised', 13 December 1968, p 19.

——, 'Diary dates', 14 May 1971, p 9.

——, 'Theatre's runs could be longer', 28 November 1972, p 3.

——, 'Major grants for the arts announced', 12 December 1972, p 3.

——, 'Tour of craft studios', 8 August 1974, p 14.

——, '"Sunday in the Park" praised', 26 October 1977, p 9.

——, 'Gallery fee discussed', 24 September 1982, p 7.

——, 'Auction to benefit arts organisations', 30 November 1983, p 9.

——, 'Chairman appointed for arts review', 30 November 1984, p 13.

——, 'Bid for your own star', 26 April 1985, p 7.

——, 'Timing of arts funding decision', 25 May 1985, p 7.

——, 'Call for change for arts sake', 5 December 1985, p 8.

——, 'Posters for posterity', 4 September 1986, p 1s.

——, 'Contemporary art space', 9 July 1987, p 6s.

Caruana, Wally, *Aboriginal art*, London, Thames and Hudson, 2003.

Chapman, Christopher, 'Dale Frank and the Diamond Dogs', *Virtual reality*, exhibition catalogue, Canberra, National Gallery of Australia, 1994.

——, *Satellite of love*, exhibition catalogue, Canberra, CCAS, 1994.

Charlesworth, JJ, 'Curating doubt', *Art Monthly*, 294, March 2006, p 1.

Charlton, Ken, *Federal capital architecture: Canberra, 1911–1939*, Canberra, National Trust of Australia, 1984.

Charlton, Ken, Paola Favaro and Bronwen Jones, *The contribution of Enrico Taglietti to Canberra's architecture*, Canberra, Royal Australian Institute of Architects, ACT Chapter, 2007.

Choudhury, Farzana (ed), *Opening a new door: the herstory of Beryl Women Inc (1975–2015)*, Canberra, Beryl Women Inc, 2015.

Chronicle, 'Encroachment and impositions', 17 April 1995.

——, 'Art' 20 February 1995.

Church, Julia and Alison Alder, *True bird grit: a book about Canberra women in the arts*, Canberra, Acme Ink, 1982.

Churcher, Betty and Lucy Quinn, *Treasures of Canberra*, Canberra, Halstead Press, 2013.

Clark, Deborah, 'Scratching the surface', *Art Monthly Australia*, July 1994, p 30.

——, 'The painting of Vivienne Binns', in Craig Judd (ed), Vivienne Binns, exhibition catalogue, Hobart, Tasmanian Museum and Art Gallery, 2006.

—— (ed), *Imitation of life: memory and mimicry in Canberra region art*, exhibition catalogue, Canberra, CMAG, 2011.

Clark, Deborah and Mark Van Veen, *Something in the air: collage and assemblage in Canberra region art*, exhibition catalogue, Canberra, CMAG, 2010.

Coltheart, Lenore, *Albert Hall: the heart of Canberra*, Sydney, UNSW Press/ NewSouth Publishing, 2014.

Cook, Virginia, '"Artist shown as worker"', *Canberra Times*, 20 February 1986, p 5.

——, 'Director drafts policy: gallery emphasis on ACT artists', 20 March 1986, p 5.

Cousins, Kerry-Anne, 'Art', *Muse*, August 1994.

Crass art II, exhibition catalogue, Sydney, The Art Unit with Redfern Black Rose Anarchist Bookshop, 1984.

Croft, Brenda, 'A change is gonna come', *Periphery*, 40–41, 1999–2000, p 52.

Daley, Paul, *Canberra*, City Series, Sydney, NewSouth Publishing, 2012.

Davies, Fiona, *That's such a pretty dress dear*, exhibition catalogue, Canberra Contemporary Art Space, 1994.

Day, Charlotte (ed), *A short ride in a fast machine: Gertrude Contemporary Art Spaces 1985–2005*, Melbourne, Gertrude Contemporary, 2006.

Duncan, Michael, 'Report from Sydney: self-created worlds', *Art in America*, 90, 10, 2002, pp 60–65.

Durant, Mark Alice, 'Activist art in the shadow of rebellion', *Art in America*, 80, July 1992, pp 31–35.

Eagle, Mary, 'Archives', conference paper, *ARLIS/ANZ conference 2004, ARLIS/ ANZ Journal*, 58, 2004, pp 28–34.

Elliot, Megan (ed), *Naii Ngarrambai Wanggirali Burrangiri Nangi Dyannai Ngurui (The lay of the land is how you know your country; when you look behind you, you can always see your tracks)*, exhibition catalogue, Canberra Contemporary Art Space, 1995.

Ellis, Ruth, *Inside out – out of the main stream: a group exhibition*, exhibition catalogue, Canberra, CCAS, 1994.

Ernst & Young, *Casino Canberra: Casino Canberra's contribution to the ACT economy*, March 2006.

Ewington, Julie, 'Canberra commentary', *Art Monthly*, November 1987, p 16.

——, *Domestic contradictions: an exhibition of contemporary Australian art*, exhibition catalogue, Sydney, Power Gallery of Contemporary Art, 1987.

Farquharson, John, 'Warren, Robert George (Bob) (1920–2002)', *Obituaries Australia*, oa.anu.edu.au/obituary/warren-robert–george-bob-1002, accessed 2 April 2012.

Filipovic, Elena, 'When exhibitions become form: on the history of the artist as curator', *Mousse*, 41, moussemagazine.it/taac0/, accessed 4 August 2016.

Findlay, Gavin and Robertson, Jose, *Splinters Theatre of Spectacle: massive love of risk*, exhibition catalogue, Canberra Museum and Gallery, 2013.

Fitzpatrick, Donal, *21st century CAOs: a forward plan for contemporary art*, Sydney, Contemporary Art Organisations Australia, 2010.

Foster, Hal, 'Postmodernism: a preface', in *The anti-aesthetic: essays on postmodern culture*, Washington, Bay Press, 1983, p xv.

Foster, Michael, 'Jobless paint a plea for artists' space', *Canberra Times*, 8 July 1983, p 1.

Freeman, Peter, 'Building Canberra to 1958', National Capital Authority fact sheets, www.nca.gov.au/factsheet/building-canberra-1958-0.

Gardiner-Garden, John, *Commonwealth arts policy and administration*, Social Policy Section, Parliament of Australia, Canberra, Department of Parliamentary Services, 7 May 2009.

Gates, Merryn, 'Bronwen Sandland: *Housecosy*', *Artlink*, 23, 1, March 2003, www.artlink.com.au/articles/2438/bronwen-sandland-housecosy/, accessed 3 August 2016.

—— (ed), *Shit*, exhibition catalogue, Canberra Contemporary Art Space, 2003.

George, Peter, 'For art's sake', *Canberra Times*, 29 April 1976, p 3.

Gorton, John, 'Speech at unveiling of foundation stone, Canberra College of Advanced Education', 28 October 1968, pmtranscripts.pmc.gov.au/sites/default/files/original/00001945.pdf, accessed 3 September 2012.

——, 'Recommendations of the Australian Council for the Arts for 1969/1970', news release, PM No 85/1969, 3 December 1969, pmtranscripts.dpmc.gov.au/release/transcript-2145, accessed 11 February 2015.

Green, Erica, *Salon coda: the making of history*, exhibition catalogue, Canberra, Bitumen River Gallery, 1987.

Grishin, Sasha, 'A festival-like atmosphere', *Canberra Times*, 8 October 1977, p 18.

——, 'Diverse exhibition united by standard of excellence', *Canberra Times*, 15 May 1979, p 15.

——, 'Aborigines in role of blood sacrifice', *Canberra Times*, 12 May 1981, p 15.

——, 'Bold and brilliant and rewarding', *Canberra Times*, 20 November 1981, p 10.

——, 'Visiting the National Gallery: should owners pay twice?', *Canberra Times*, 19 September 1982, p 7.

——, '*Images of desire*', *Canberra Times*, 23 April 1985, p 28.

——, '*First look* of high quality', *Canberra Times*, 14 October 1986, p 14.

——, 'Cosmic forces that control our lives', *Canberra Times*, 15 October 1987, p 19.

——, 'No discoveries in a "showcase" display', *Canberra Times*, 26 July 1994, p 16.

——, 'Conventional departures', *Canberra Times*, 24 October 1995, p 18.

——, 'Canberra's visual arts landscape: an art critic's view', *Art Monthly Australia*, 259, May 2013, p 28.

——, 'A gift our city can savour', *Sydney Morning Herald*, 13 March 2012, www.smh.com.au/entertainment/a-gift-our-city-can-savour-20120312-1uubu.html, accessed 11 November 2015.

Guldberg, Hans, *The arts economy: 1968–1998. Three decades of growth in Australia*, Sydney, Australia Council for the Arts, 2000.

Hall, Lee-Anne, 'Who is Bill Posters? An examination of six Australian socially concerned alternative print media organisations', *Caper* 27, special issue, 1988, p 3.

Hammond, Victoria (ed), *Chameleon: a decade*, Hobart, Contemporary Art Services Tasmania, 1993.

Haraway, Donna, 'The cyborg manifesto: science, technology and socialist feminism in the late twentieth century', in David Bell and Barbara M Kennedy (eds), *The cybercultures reader*, London; New York, Routledge, 2000, pp 291–324.

Harrison, Charles and Wood, Paul (eds), *Art in theory – 1900–2000: an anthology of changing ideas*, Malden, MA, Blackwell Publishing, 2003.

Hayden, Bill, 'Aboriginals', House of Representatives, 26th Parliament, 2 November 1967, p 2629, *Historic Hansard*, built by Tim Sherratt, historichansard.net/hofreps/1967/19671102_reps_26_hor57/#debate-22, accessed 11 February 2015.

Haynes, Peter, 'Antisystem', *Art and Australia*, 32, 3, 1995, p 444.

Headon, David, *Beyond the boundaries*, Canberra, Chief Minister's Department, 2009.

———, *Crystal palace to golden trowels*, Canberra, Chief Minister's Department, 2009.

———, *Those other Americans*, Canberra, Chief Minister's Department, 2009.

Healey, Ken, 'Practical Pascoe sheds light on art wars', *Canberra Times*, 12 May 1985, p 12.

———, 'Disheartened arts workers leave their jobs: 1986 grants meet silence of the defeated', *Canberra Times*, 30 November 1985, p 18.

———, 'FOI adds material to arts funding debate', *Canberra Times*, 13 December 1985, p 21.

Henningham, Nikki, 'From Lady Denman to Katy Gallagher: a century of women's contributions to Canberra', *The Australian Womens' Register Blog*, 21 February 2013, www.womenaustralia.info/blog/2013/02/21/from-lady-denman-to-katy-gallagher-a-century-of-womens-contributions-to-canberra/, accessed 15 August 2014.

Hill, Garry, 'Anatomy of an industrial struggle: Chrysler factory at Tonsley Park in Adelaide 1976–1978', *Radical tradition: an Australian history page*, www.takver.com/history/chrysler.htm, accessed 18 April 2012.

Hinchliffe, Meredith, 'Fragile tenancy but exceptional art', *Canberra Times*, 18 October 1986, p 7s.

Hoffman, Jens, 'The art of curating and the curating of art', *The utopian display platform*, Milan, Nuova Accademia di Belle Arti Milano.

Hoffman, WL, 'The world of music', *Canberra Times*, 26 May 1977, p 25.

Holt, Harold, 'Australian cultural activities', Ministerial statement, House of Representatives, 1 November 1967, parlinfo.aph.gov.au/parlInfo/genpdf/hansard80/hansardr80/1967-11-01/0077/hansard_frag.pdf;fileType=application%2Fpdf, accessed 22 May 2013.

Horridge, Naomi, 'Spending time at home', *Beautiful home*, exhibition catalogue, CCAS, 1998.

Jackson-Nakano, Ann, *The Kamberri: a history from the records of Aboriginal families in the Canberra–Queanbeyan district and surrounds 1820–1927 and historical overview 1928–2001*, Weerawa History Series, Canberra, 2001.

Jenainati, Cathia and Judy Groves (eds), *Introducing feminism*, London, Icon Books, 2010.

Judd, Craig (ed), *Vivienne Binns*, exhibition catalogue, Hobart, Tasmanian Museum and Art Gallery, 2006.

Kaleski, Sonja, 'Art "on the road"', *Canberra Times*, 27 September 1981, p 10.

——, 'City's private galleries versus keeping art for the people', *Canberra Times*, 3 December 1981, p 29.

——, 'Strong criticisms of society', *Canberra Times*, 17 November 1982.

Kelly, Francis, 'A national gallery but when?', *Canberra Times*, 15 February 1969, p 11.

——, 'ALP man says gallery delay "an insult"', *Canberra Times*, 13 May 1970.

Kenyon, Therese, *Under a hot tin roof: art, passion and politics at the Tin Sheds Art Workshop*, Sydney, State Library of New South Wales Press in association with Power Publications, 1995.

Kerr, Joan, '*Act 1*', *Art & Australia*, 16, 4, 1979, p 320.

——, 'Colonial quotations', *Art and Australia* 33, 3, 1996, pp 376–87.

Kleinert, Ingo, '*Act 2*: for the record', *Art Network*, 2, 1980, p 45.

Kristeva Julia, 'Interview with Catherine Francklin', in Charles Harrison and Paul Wood (eds), *Art in theory: 1900–2000: an anthology of changing ideas*, Blackwell Publishing, 2003, pp 1054–56.

Kunda, Maria, 'The artist, the community, the land', in Craig Judd (ed), *Vivienne Binns*, exhibition catalogue, Hobart, Tasmanian Museum and Art Gallery, 2006.

Lee, Jennie, *A policy for the arts – the first steps*, London, HMSO, 15 February 1965, p 6, action.labour.org.uk/page/-/blog%20images/policy_for_the_arts.pdf, accessed 26 May 2013.

Ling, Ted, *Government records about the Australian Capital Territory*, Canberra, National Archives of Australia, 2013, www.archives.act.gov.au/__data/assets/pdf_file/0008/562544/Canberra_Research_Guide.pdf, accessed 3 April 2015.

Lingard, Bob and Sue Cramer (eds), *Institute of Modern Art: a documentary history 1975–1989*, Brisbane, Institute of Modern Art, 1989.

Macklin, Robert, 'Cultural capital of Australia?', *Canberra Times*, 29 July 1990, p 17.

——, 'Cultural scene transformed under council', *Canberra Times*, 21 November 1991, p 5.

——, 'A capital life', *Canberra Times*, 5 February 1994, p 49.

——, 'Turmoil in ACT Arts', *Canberra Times*, 19 November 1994, p 3.

Maloon, Terence, 'Such sweet plunder', *Sydney Morning Herald*, 15 September 1984, p 49.

Martin, Mandy, 'Political posters in Adelaide', conference paper, *Australian Print symposium*, National Gallery of Australia, Canberra, 1989, www.printsandprintmaking.gov.au/references/409/, accessed 10 April 2012.

Mayhew, Louise, 'Jill Posters will be prosecuted: Australia's women-only print collectives from the 1970s and 1980s', conference paper, *Impact7: intersections and counterpoints*, Monash University, Melbourne, September 2011.

McKinnon, Malcolm, *The hottest gallery in the world: 10 years at 24HR Art – Northern Territory Centre for Contemporary Art (1990–2000)*, Darwin, 24HR Art, 2001.

McLean, Ian, *How Aborigines invented the idea of contemporary art: writings on Aboriginal contemporary art*, Brisbane, Institute of Modern Art and Sydney, Power Publications, 2011.

McLeod, Pamela and Lisa Anderson, *Preliminary audit of support infrastructures for creative professionals in the ACT: a pilot study of design, crafts, visual arts, dance and theatre for the Cultural Asset Mapping in Regional Australia (CAMRA) research project*, Sydney, University of Technology, November 2008.

Merewether, Charles and Julie Ewington, *Working with the enemy*, exhibition catalogue, Bitumen River Gallery with Canberra Contemporary Art Space; Sydney, First Draft.

Metcalfe, Andrew, *Canberra architecture*, Watermark Architectural Guides, Boorowa, NSW, Watermark, 2006.

Meyer, Laura with Faith Wilding, 'Collaboration and conflict in the Fresno Feminist Art Program: an experiment in feminist pedagogy', *N.paradoxa*, July 2010, vol 26.

Miekle, Ian, '*Times* backs artist award', *Canberra Times*, 17 August 1991, p 3.

Miles, Martin, 'Northbourne Housing Group', *Canberra house: mid-century modernist architecture*, www.canberrahouse.com.au/houses/northbourne-housing.html, accessed 23 March 2015.

Millner, Jacqueline, *Conceptual beauty: perspectives on Australian contemporary art*, Sydney, Artspace, 2010.

Milne, Geoffrey, *Theatre Australia (un)limited: Australian theatre since the 1950s*, Australian Playwrights, no 10, Rodopi, Amsterdam, New York, 2004, doi.org/10.1017/s0307883305301416.

Moore Milroy, Beth, 'Commentary: what is a capital?', in John Taylor, Jean G Lengellé and Caroline Andrew (eds), *Capital cities/les capitales: international perspectives/perspectives internationales*, Montreal, McGill-Queens University Press, 1993, p 86, doi.org/10.7202/1016599ar.

Musa, Helen, '$108 thousand in grants for arts: Wood', *Canberra Times*, 21 July 1994, p 6.

——, 'Drawing an artists' map for Canberra', *Canberra Times*, 31 July, 1994, p 24.

——, 'Michael le Grand: sculptor or "boy racer"?' *World of Antiques and Art*, 81, August 2011 – February 2012, p 78.

Muse, 'Bill posters appreciated: a statement', *Muse*, April 1981.

National Capital Development Commission, *Sixth annual report*, Canberra, 1962/63.

——, 'Draft land use policy concerning art galleries on residential leases', *Canberra Times*, 6 August 1983, public notice.

National Council on the Arts, *The first annual report on the National Council on the Arts*, 1964–65, Washington DC, 1965, www.arts.gov/sites/default/files/NEA-Annual-Report-1964-1965.pdf, accessed 23 May 2013.

National Gallery of Australia, *Living in the seventies: works of art made in Canberra and region in the Nineteen Seventies – selected from the collection of the National Gallery of Australia*, exhibition catalogue, Canberra Museum and Gallery, 1999.

O'Neill, Neville and Jane Barney, *Black humour*, Canberra Contemporary Art Space, 1997.

Parker, Rozsika and Griselda Pollock, *Framing feminism: art and the women's movement, 1970–1985*, Pandora Press, Kitchener, Canada, 1987.

Pascoe, Timothy, *Arts in the ACT: funding priorities and grant administration*, Canberra, ACT Arts Development Board, Commonwealth of Australia, 1985.

Payne, Stephen, 'Sir Richard named arts chairman', *Canberra Times*, 11 December 1981, p 7.

Peckham, Penny, 'Vivienne Binns biography', in Craig Judd (ed), *Vivienne Binns*, exhibition catalogue, Hobart, Tasmanian Museum and Art Gallery, 2006.

Pfeiffer, Alice, 'Delving into the art of curating: as job enjoys a star turn, several new degrees offer "a passport for life"', *International Herald Tribune* (Paris), 11 October 2012, p 202.

Phillips, AA, 'The cultural cringe', *Meanjin*, 9, 4, 1950, pp 299–302.

Printing history: 18 years of Megalo Access Arts, Canberra Museum and Gallery, 1999.

Pryor, Sally, '40 years since the day art came to town', *Canberra Times*, 29 June 2013, www.canberratimes.com.au/act-news/40-years-since-the-day-art-came-to-town-20130628-2p33h.html, accessed 2 July 2014.

——, 'Canberra farewells Joy Warren, doyenne of the local art scene', *Canberra Times*, 5 January 2015, www.canberratimes.com.au/act-news/canberra-life/canberra-farewells-joy-warren-doyenne-of-the-local-art-scene-20150105-12i598.html, accessed 8 November 2015.

Radok, Stephanie, 'Future directions forum', *Bitumen River Gallery Newletter*, 5 ½, September 1983, p 2.

——, '*Black humour*', *Artlink*, 18, 3, 1998, www.artlink.com.au/articles/205/black-humour/, accessed 12 January 2016.

Reeves, Tim and Alan Roberts, *100 Canberra houses: a century of capital architecture*, Canberra, Halstead Press, 2013.

Richardson, Elvis, *CoUNTess: women count in the artworld*, blog, countesses.blogspot.com.au.

Rood, Sarah and Belinda Ensor, *Olims Hotel Canberra: through the ages*, Sydney, CL Creations, 2007.

Roseman, Elena, *Talking like a Toora woman*, Canberra, Toora Women Inc, 2004.

Russell, Roslyn, 'Activists', *From Lady Denman to Katy Gallagher: a century of women's contributions to Canberra*, 21 February 2013, www.womenaustralia.info/exhib/ldkg/activists.html, accessed 15 August 2014.

——, 'Helen Maxwell', *The Australian Women's Register*, www.womenaustralia.info/biogs/AWE2104b.htm, accessed 17 July 2014.

Ryan, Julia, 'Canberra Women's Liberation – mainfocus: 1970–1975', lecture notes, Australian History, U3A, University of Canberra, June 2012.

Sanders, Anne, '*ACT 1, 2 & 3*: Canberra's national performance art festivals', *Art Monthly Australia*, 259, 2013, pp 51–54.

Seares, Margaret, with John Gardiner-Garden, *Cultural policies in Australia*, Sydney, Australia Council, June 2011.

Select Committee on Cultural Activities and Facilities, *Final report*, Legislative Assembly for the ACT, June 1991.

Select Committee on the Establishment of a Casino, *Report*, Canberra, Legislative Assembly for the ACT, July 1989.

Skeat, Helen (ed), *Majura Women's Group celebrating 25 years: a selection of recollections, reflections, images and quotations*, Canberra, Majura Women's Group, 2006.

Slack, Enid and Rupak Chattopadhyay (eds), *Finance and governance of capital cities in federal systems*, vol 1, *Thematic issues in federalism*, Montreal, McGill-Queen's University Press, 2009.

Smith, Brian, and Heide Smith, *A portrait of Canberra and of Canberrans 1979–2012*, Narooma, NSW, Hobbs Point Publishing, 2012.

Smith, Terry, 'The provincialism problem', *Artforum*, 13, 1, 1974, pp 54–59.

——, 'Writing the history of Australian art: its past, present and possible future', *Australian Journal of Art*, 3, 1983, pp 10–29.

——, 'The state of art history: contemporary art', *The Art Bulletin*, December 2010, p 380.

Smith, Trevor, 'Ronald Jones: contagion cultures', in Mary Eagle (ed), *Virtual reality*, exhibition catalogue, Canberra, National Gallery of Australia, 1994.

Standing Committee on Planning Development and Infrastructure, *Inquiry into the possible use of the $19 million casino premium, report no 9*, Legislative Assembly for the ACT, December 1992.

Stevens, Joyce, 'The nineteen seventies and eighties continued', *A history of International Women's Day in words and images*, accessed 14 May 2012.

Sydney Morning Herald, 'Canberra Mothercraft Society', 26 July 1929.

'Tony Ayres' new film echoes stories from his own life', ABC *Conversations with Richard Fidler*, 10 August 2007, www.abc.net.au/local/stories/2007/08/10/2001814.htm, accessed 15 August 2016.

Trezzi, Nicola, 'The art of curating', *Flash Art International*, 45, March/April 2010, pp 62–66.

Virgo, Anne (ed), *Conversions 1–8*, exhibition catalogue, Canberra Contemporary Art Space, 1992.

VNS Matrix, 'Cyberfeministmanifesto for the 21st Century', www.sterneck.net/cyber/vns-matrix/index.php, accessed 24 June 2012.

Wallace, Chris, with Robyn Archer, Kathryn Ross, and Emily Sykes, *Megalomania: 33 years of posters made at Megalo Print Studio 1980–2013*, Canberra, Megalo Print Studio + Gallery, 2013.

Warden, Ian, 'Getting our $2 worth', *Canberra Times*, 22 September 1982, p 21.

Warden, Ian, *Think of it! Dream of it! In six snapshots*, Canberra, Chief Minister's Department, 2009.

Webb, Julian, 'Bill posters appreciated', *Hard Times*, 14, 1991.

Weereewa Ngunnawal, exhibition catalogue, Canberra Contemporary Art Space, 1999.

What's On?, Gorman House Arts Centre newsletter, April 1995.

Whitlam, Gough, 'It's time', Labor Party election policy speech, Blacktown Civic Centre, Sydney, 13 November 1972, whitlamdismissal.com/1972/11/13/whitlam-1972-election-policy-speech.html, accessed 24 May 2013.

——, 'Major grants for the arts', media release, 11 December 1972, pmtranscripts.dpmc.gov.au/release/transcript-2740, accessed 14 February 2015.

Winning, Fiona (ed), *21st century CAOs: a forward plan for contemporary art*, Sydney, Contemporary Art Organisations Australia, 2010.

——, Hansard, Parliamentary Debates, Legislative Assembly, Australian Capital Territory, 22 October 1992, p 2874.

——, Hansard, Parliamentary Debates, Legislative Assembly, Australian Capital Territory, 26 August 2004, p 4323.

Wood, Greg, *Maps and makers*, Canberra, Chief Minister's Department, 2009.

——, *The community that was*, Canberra, Chief Minister's Department, 2009.

Work in progress, 4, 1, April 1995, Gorman House Arts Centre.

Woroni, 'The story of Reid House', 4 March 1974, p 5.

——, 'Reid House: innovative theatre', 18 September 1980, pp 26–27.

Zeplin, Pamela, 'Crossing over: raising the ghosts of Tasman–Pacific art exchange: ANZART-in-Hobart, 1983', in '"Asian" media arts practice in/and Aotearoa New Zealand', *New Zealand Journal of Media Studies*, 9, 1, 2005, nzetc.victoria.ac.nz/tm/scholarly/tei-Sch091JMS-t1-g1-t4.html, accessed 10 March 2015, doi.org/10.11157/medianz-vol9iss1id84.

INDEX

Page numbers in *italic* indicate illustrations. Page numbers containing 'n' indicate footnotes; for example, '7n21' is note 21 on page 7.

2CA Theatrette, 32
2xx (radio station), 50, 146n107, 196, 202–203
24HR Art, 10, 12, 15, 175n39, 231, 237n140 *see also* Northern Centre for Contemporary Art, Darwin
60 heads exhibition, 1997, 228–232, *230*

Aboriginal art *see* Indigenous art
Aboriginal Cultural Centre, 102
Aboriginal Tent Embassy, 140
Abraxas Gallery, 30, 148
ACA *see* Arts Council of Australia
ACME Ink, 133, 135
ACME Silkscreen Workshop, 59
ACT (territory) *see* Australian Capital Territory
ACT 1 (1978), *ACT* 2 (1980) and *ACT* 3 (1982) performance art festivals, 136–137
ACT Advisory Committee on the Arts, 49, 51
ACT Arts Development Board (ADB), 48, 49, 51
 community organisation recommendations to, 55–56, 59–60
 difficulty of reaching consensus, 58
 disbanded, 96
 discussion paper (1984), 55, 56, 58–60
 funding distribution, 68–70, 72–73, 174, 175
 funding mechanisms, 61
 members, 58
 review of funding priorities *see* Pascoe, Timothy, 1985 report on arts funding
 under-resourced, 72
ACT Committee on Cultural Development, 49
ACT Community Development Fund (CDF), 49, 52, 55, 57, 60, 92, 167, 234
ACT Cultural Council, 71, 95–97, 100, 179n49, 229 *see also* Cultural Facilities Corporation, ACT
ACT Literary Fellowship, 97
ACT Pastoral and Agricultural Association annual show, 26–27
ACT Writers Centre, 94n15, 101
activism *see* arts community: activism; social activism
ADB *see* ACT Arts Development Board (ADB)
advocacy for the arts, 57–58, 60–61, 247–248 *see also* arts community: activism

AETT *see* Australian Elizabethan
    Theatre Trust (AETT)
aGOG *see* australian Girls Own
    Gallery (aGOG)
Agostino, Michael, 5, 125, 126
Ah Kee, Vernon, 216
Ainslie, ACT, 22, 45
Ainslie Village, 80, 110, 143–144,
    217 *see also* Megalo
Ainsworth, Norman, 234
Albert Hall, 32, 33, 38n78, 41
Alder, Alison
    art student, 108, 132
    on BRG, 11, 118, 123
    BRG coordinator, 15n39, 17, 51,
        117, 152, 168, 233
    career, 167, 246
    Megalo and, 110, 111, 133, 246
    prints by, 13n32, 115, *115, 121,*
        122, *134,* 135
    and *Slut* poster, 152–155
Alewood, Robyn, 49–50
Allawah flats, 125n54
Alliance Française, 55
alternative art spaces, 105–106 *see also*
    Bitumen River Gallery (BRG);
    contemporary art spaces
Ambrus, Carol, 139n97
Amesbury, Avi, 27n34
ANCA *see* Australian National
    Capital Artists (ANCA)
Ancher, Mortlock and Murray,
    125n54
Anderson, Sir Colin, 34
ANG/NGA *see* National Gallery
    of Australia (NGA)
Anna Simons Gallery, 31
anti-aesthetic ethos, 143–144
anti-nuclear posters, 13, 154
ANU *see* Australian National
    University, The (ANU)
ANZART conference, Hobart, 1983,
    117, 118

Apex Club of Ginninderra, 41
architecture
    Bauhaus influence, 125n54
    Canberra histories, 4
    see also Canberra Brasilia
        exhibition, 2001
Arnold, Raymond, 82 *see also*
    Coward, Dan
Art Forum program, 166, 220
art galleries, 28–33, 58
    commercial, 28–32, 54, 60, 81,
        215
    home-based, 28, 31–32, 53–54
    see also art museums; exhibition
        venues
Art Gallery of New South Wales, 190,
    215
Art Gallery of South Australia, 85
Art Gallery of Western Australia, 215
*Art in architecture: selections from the
    new Parliament House Collection*
    exhibition, 1987, 179–180
art institutions, studies of, 5–6
art museums, 33, 59, 94, 187, 213
    admission fees, 81–86
    curatorial practices, 185–187, 196
    and ephemera, 124, 213
    Indigenous art acquisitions,
        215–216
    see also Canberra Museum and
        Gallery (CMAG); National
        Gallery of Australia (NGA)
Art Museums Association
    of Australia, 84
art patrons
    CAPO, 53, 71, 72, 73–77, 78
    CCAS fundraising auction, 251
art schools, 5, 11, 26
    accommodation, 6–7
    graduate opportunities, 11–12,
        77–80, 109
    hobbyist classes, 7
    Pascoe on arts education, 67
    student gender, 14

see also The Australian National University: School of Art; Canberra School of Art (CSA); Canberra Technical College art school
art societies, 2, 3–4, 26–29, 107
art spaces *see* contemporary art spaces; studio spaces
Arthouse, Launceston, 10
Arthur, Jay, 78
Artillion, 79n84
Artist of the Year award, 97
artist-run spaces *see* collectives
artists *see* arts community; arts workers; women artists
Artists' Society of Canberra, 26
Arts ACT, 232, 234, 247, 248
arts administration in the ACT, 49, 71
    gender representation, 15
    Pascoe recommendations, 67
    Virgo and, 165–172
    see also arts funding bodies; Australian Capital Territory Legislative Assembly; federal government
arts community
    activism, 2, 47–48, 57–58, 59, 81–86, 106–109, 117, 126–130
    flexibility versus political orthodoxy, 131, 132, 150, 157, 160
    nature of, 1–2, 150n117, 245–249, 252
    networks, 50–51, 118, 133, 150, 157, 165–167, 170
    response to Pascoe report, 68–71
    see also arts workers; Bitumen River Gallery (BRG); community arts organisations; Megalo
Arts Council Australia, ACT Division, 39–40 *see also* Arts Council of Australia ACT (ACA ACT)
Arts Council Gallery (ACG), 50, 51, 55, 57, 107, 174
    exhibitions, 78–79, 107, 146, 166–167, 172
    merged with BRG to form CCAS, 9, 163, 173–176, 180, 232 *see also* Canberra Contemporary Art Space (CCAS)
    Virgo and, 163, 166, 171, 172, 173–174, 180
Arts Council of Australia (ACA), 28, 38–39, 42
Arts Council of Australia ACT (ACA ACT), 39–40, 53, 56n22, 70, 214
    and BRG/ACG merger, 173
    funding, 60–61, 70, 75
    and Kingston Art Centre, 60
    Muse magazine, 72–73
    Pascoe recommendation on, 67
    representation on ADB, 55
Arts development in the Australian Capital Territory: a discussion paper (1984), 58–60
Arts Development program, General Grants Scheme, 59
    review of, 61–62
arts funding, 9, 17
    1960s and 1970s, 36–43
    1980s, 49–62 *see also* Pascoe, Timothy, 1985 report on arts funding
    after ACT self-government, 76, 92–103, 247–249 *see also* Australian Capital Territory: self-government
    casino premium, 49, 71, 89, 92, 93, 98–99, 102
    community arts, 49–50, 52–53
    decline in, 247–248, 249
    focus on 'flagship' performing arts companies, 2–3, 17, 36–39, 41, 47–48, 63, 66–67, 69, 71–72

government payment practices, 61, 97
models, 2–3
non-government, 72, 73–78
arts funding bodies *see* ACT Advisory Committee on the Arts; ACT Arts Development Board (ADB); Arts Council of Australia (ACA); Arts Council of Australia ACT (ACA ACT); Australia Council for the Arts (from 1973); Australian Council for the Arts (1967–73); Australian Elizabethan Theatre Trust (AETT)
arts infrastructure *see* arts precincts; contemporary art spaces; cultural infrastructure; exhibition venues; studio spaces
arts lobby *see* advocacy for the arts; arts community: activism
arts organisations *see* community arts organisations; contemporary art spaces
arts precincts
   Belconnen, 50, 218n85
   Canberra Brickworks, 78–79
   Civic Square, 33n60, 34, 93, 94, 100, 101
   Kingston, 57, 58, 60, 78, 79, 100, 241n149, 252n7
   planned versus natural growth, 57, 241n149
   Tuggeranong, 50, 102, 218n85
   see also contemporary art spaces; cultural infrastructure
Arts Value Forum, 2017, 248
arts workers
   advocacy for, 247–248
   artist as worker, 222
   campaign against NGA admission fee, 81–86
   and CPAML, 128–130
   remuneration/unremunerated working hours, 56n27, 70
   responses to Pascoe report, 68–70, 169–170
   union, 59, 84, 117
   see also arts community
ArtSound FM, 75
Artspace Visual Arts Centre, Sydney, 10, 166, 215
Artworkers Union, 59, 84, 117
Arunta Galleries, 32
Asker, Don, 65n51
At home with Megalo maniacs exhibition, 1987, 179
Australia Council for the Arts (from 1973), 249–250
   ACT representation, 56
   Community Arts Board, 51
   Crafts Board, 96
   curator program, 186–187
   elitism allegations, 63
   establishment, 36–37, 43, 64
   funding cuts, 247, 249, 251
   funding distribution, 9, 40, 49, 63, 136, 167, 225, 234, 247n1
   funding focus and practice, 36–37, 58–59, 61, 63
   international curator program, 186
   Pascoe's role, 62, 63–64, 102
   role of, 43
   Visual Arts Board, 9, 43, 167, 173, 179, 232
   see also Australian Council for the Arts (1967–73)
Australia Drama Company, 38n78
Australian Ballet, 39n81, 63
Australian Capital Territory
   administration, 17, 47–48, 61
   arts funding *see* arts funding
   representation on Australia Council, 56
   self-government, 2, 3, 17–18, 89–92

INDEX

see also Canberra; National Capital Development Commission (NCDC); *and names beginning with* 'ACT'
Australian Capital Territory
   Legislative Assembly, 17–18, 91
   arts and cultural agenda, 2, 3, 90, 91, 92–103, 247–249
   first elections, 91
   responsibility for public artworks, 36, 228
   Select Committee on Cultural Activities and Facilities, 89, 91, 93–97, 98, 100, 101, 102–103, 252n7
   Select Committee on the Establishment of a Casino, 91, 92–93, 95
   Standing Committee on Planning, Development and Infrastructure, 89, 91, 98–100, 102, 103
Australian Centre for Contemporary Art, 231
Australian Centre for Photography, Sydney, 10, 106, 222
Australian Choreographic Centre, 65n51
Australian Council for the Arts (1967–73), 7n21, 41–43
   chairmen, 38
   elitism allegations, 63
   establishment, 36
   funding distribution, 39, 40, 41–42
   overhaul of, 43
   see also Australia Council for the Arts (from 1973)
Australian Elizabethan Theatre Trust (AETT), 36–39, 42n94
australian Girls Own Gallery (aGOG), 15, 79, 80–81, 225–226
Australian National Capital Artists (ANCA), 5, 96, 150n117

Australian National Eisteddfod Society, 53
Australian National Gallery (ANG) *see* National Gallery of Australia (NGA)
Australian National University (ANU), The
   art collection, 87n110
   Department of Fine Art, 30
   Drill Hall Gallery, 86–87, 251
   establishment, 20
   exhibition spaces/arts venues, 32, 55, 86–87, 251
   HC Coombs Creative Arts Fellowship, 120, 214
   public artworks, 34
   School of Art, 5, 20, 245, 246
   see also Canberra School of Art (CSA)
Australian Opera Company, 39n81, 63
Australian perspecta, 87, 126n58
Australian Print Workshop, 163
Australian Sculpture Centre, 32
Australian War Memorial (AWM), 6, 20, 21, 55, 84
Australian Women's archive project, 5
awards, 33
AWM *see* Australian War Memorial (AWM)
Ayres, Tony, 219–221
   art practice, 206, 220–221
   art student, 132, 167
   BRG and, 106, 107, 117, 123, 164, 166, 182, 219–221, 234
   exhibitions, 176, 220–221, 233

Bad girls: twenty witness 1000 exhibition, 2013, 13, *14*, 223n101, 224n105
Bailey, John, 85
Baker, Sabrina, 251
Bancroft, Bronwyn, 216
Bardon, Geoffrey, 120n38

273

Barney, Jane, 13n32, 15, 17, 187, 201–212, 228–243, 249
Barr government (ACT), 248–249
Barron, Sonia, 73, 179, 198, 236
Bass, Tom, *Ethos,* 1961, 34, 101
Batt, Beverley, 7
Bauhaus tradition, 7, 48, 125
Baxter, Lesley, 158n130
Bean, Charles, 6, 26
Beauchamp House, Acton, ACT, 57
Beautiful home: just what is it that makes today's home so different, so appealing? exhibition, 1998, 206–212, *207*
Beaver Galleries, 30
Bega flats, 125n54
Behan, Judith, 31
Belconnen, ACT, 50, 56, 214, 218n85
Bell, Vicki, 226
Beryl (women's refuge), 2, 5, 24, 25
biennales of contemporary art, 15–16, 123, 173n34, 186, 190
Bill posters appreciated exhibition, 1981, 112, *113–115,* 115–116, 212–213
Binns, Vivienne, 13n32, 32, 51, 139, 148–150, 152, 201–202
Bischoff, Theo, 28
Bitumen River Gallery (BRG), 4, 10–12, 44, 56n22, 59, 60n39, *177,* 213, 217
  administration, 163–172
  Ayres and, 219–221
  'collective' notion, 181–183
  coordinators, 15, 17, 117, 163, 171, 172
  CSA and, 106, 107, 108, 125, 166–167, 175
  de Medici and, 219, 221–222, 224
  establishment, 1, 9, 58, 106–107, 133
  exhibitions *see* Bitumen River Gallery (BRG) exhibitions
  feminist concerns, 138–139
  funding, 174, 181, 234
  'future directions' forums, 54–55, 168, 169–171
  gender representation in exhibitions, 13–15
  incorporation, 168
  initiatives, 117, 118
  lectures, 16, 166
  Megalo and, 106, 108, 111–112, 212–213
  merged with ACG to form CCAS, 9, 163, 173–176, 180, 232 *see also* Canberra Contemporary Art Space (CCAS)
  merger opposition, 173, 174, 224
  NGA free admission campaign, 81–86
  opening, 112–116, 117
  precarious nature of, 117–118, 165, 167–168
  premises and name, 12, 111–112, *119, 177*
  purpose, 10–11, 181, 183, 217
  significance of, 183, 213, 243, 246
  Slut poster rejection, 138–139, 150–161
  social relevance, 217–218
  Virgo and, 163, 164–167, 169–172, 181, 183, 224
Bitumen River Gallery (BRG) exhibitions, 166–167, 175–176, *177,* 180–181
  Foundry clients' work, 217–218
  Indigenous art, 120–124, 212, 213–214, 215, 217
  performance art, 222
  photography, 216–217
  posters and prints, 112–116, 166, 212–213
  travelling exhibitions, 166, 172, 222–223, 232–234, 243
  work by children with disabilities, 218–219
  see also minority exhibitions at BRG/CCAS

Black, Ally, 158n130
Black books exhibition, 1996, 235, 237
Blacktown City Council, 84–85
Blue Folk Community Arts Association, 50, 53, 56n22, 60n39
Blunden, Camilla, 49–50
Bond, Anthony, 190
Boomalli Artist's Co-operative, 216
Bowak, Rachel, 13n32
Boynes, Alexander, 176n47, 251
Boynes, Robert, 126, 127, 131, 133, 137
Braddon, ACT, 45
Bradley, Jacqueline, 13n32
Bradley, Julie, 13n32, 133
Brasilia, Brazil *see Canberra Brasilia* exhibition, 2001
Brassel, Linda, 158n130
Breen, Marcus, 117, 233
Breynard, Shane, 238–243
BRG *see* Bitumen River Gallery (BRG); Bitumen River Gallery (BRG) exhibitions
Britain *see* United Kingdom
Broker, David, 15, 251
Brook, Donald, 6, 7, 32, 136
Brown, Elizabeth, 98
Brown, Geoffrey, 84
Brown, Jan, 7, 96
Brown, Karilyn, 82–83, 135, 167, 232–233
Brown, Steve, 69, 70
Buchanan, Meg, 79
Bull, Gordon, 229
Burke, Joseph, 35
Burn, Ian, 191
Butler, Roger, 66, 82, 124, 133n83, 150n118, 213
Byrne, Lisa, 15n39

CACSA *see* Contemporary Art Centre of South Australia (CACSA)
Café Boom Boom, 53
Cairns, Jim, 142

Callaghan, Michael, 167
campaign for free admission to ANG, 81–86, 117
Canberra, 17, 157
  accommodation, 22, 45
  art institution histories, 5–6
  arts community characteristics, 1–2, 150n117, 245–249, 252
    see also arts community
  arts funding *see* arts funding
  building costs, 45
  Centenary, 5–6
  'cultural fringe', 106, 107
  cultural performances in, 64, 65
  flexibility versus political orthodoxy, 131, 132, 150, 157, 160
  histories, 4–7
  local–national dichotomy, 2–3, 16, 17–21, 36–37, 41, 47–48, 62, 65–66, 71–72, 102–103, 193
  national capital construct, 19–21, 62, 64
  Pascoe's experience of, 62–65 *see also* Pascoe, Timothy, 1985 report on arts funding
  physical, social and economic divide, 45, 106–107
  planning responsibilities, 91
  population, 12–13, 19, 21–25, 47, 74, 106, 139, 247
  public artworks, 34–36, 227–228
  regional centre, 36, 39, 50–51
  social issues, 22, 23–24, 74
  social services for women and children, 22–25, 140, 146
  sociopolitical duality, 17–21, 36, 41
  see also Australian Capital Territory
Canberra Art Club, 26
Canberra Arts Marketing, 98
Canberra Brasilia exhibition, 2001, 238–243, *241*, *243*

Canberra Brickworks Precinct, 78–79
Canberra Children's Choir, 75
Canberra College of Advanced Education (CCAE), 55, 214
Canberra Community Arts Front (CCAF), 50, 53, 56n22, 60–61, 72, 75
Canberra Contemporary Art Space (CCAS), 4, 96, 150n117, *177*, 252
   administration, 202, 203–204
   administrative difficulties, 194–195, 199–200
   aims, 175, 195, 200
   Barney and, 15, 187, 201–212, 228–243
   Board, 188–189, 201–202
   directors (gender/list of), 15, 17
   see also Barney *above*; Smith *below*; Virgo *below*; *and* Broker, David; Runnegar, Brenda
   director's role, 172, 189
   establishment, 1, 9, 163, 173–174
   focus change under Smith, 191, 193, 195–196, 198, 200–201
   funding, 9, 175, 232, 234–235, 251
   gender representation in exhibitions, 13, 15
   international artist exchange, 238–243
   opening, 175
   premises, 96, *177*, 179, 180, 203, 251, 252
   significance of, 243
   Smith and, 185, 189–201
   Virgo and, 163, 174–181, 188, 224, 232
Canberra Contemporary Art Space (CCAS) exhibitions, 176–181, 187, 191–204
   film, 206
   Indigenous art, 204, 213, 217, 235–237
   performance art, 144, *145*, 204, *205*, 206–212, *207*
   tattooing, 225–232, *227*, *230*
   travelling exhibitions, 179, 191, 204, 227–232, 234–243
   see also minority exhibitions at BRG/CCAS
Canberra Critics Circle, 73, 97
Canberra Dance Ensemble, 60n39
Canberra Development Board, 56
Canberra Institute of the Arts, 166n11
Canberra Mothercraft Society, 22, *23*
Canberra Museum and Gallery (CMAG), 5, 6, 50, 101, 150n117, 172, 249
Canberra Opera, 56n22, 60n39, 61, 68, 75
Canberra Photographic Society, 26
Canberra Repertory Society, 29, 41, 42, 60n39
Canberra School of Art (CSA), 5, 7, 11, 51, 55
   in ADB discussion paper (1984), 59
   Art Forum program, 166, 220
   Bauhaus vision, 7, 48, 125
   BRG and, 106, 107, 108, 125, 166–167, 175
   EASS and, 77–78
   establishment, 20
   Gallery, 175n42, 203, 235, 237
   graduates, 11–12, 48, 57, 72, 77–80, 107, 117, 195
   Pascoe on, 67
   performance art in Sculpture Workshop, 204, 250
   premises, 6, 7
   printmaking cultures, 79–80, 131–133
   staff, 30, 48, 59, 125–126, 131–133, 136–137
   student gender, 14

student intake (1978), 132
women artists/teachers, 15, 82, 126, 131–135, 142, 146, 148–150, 152, 166n11, 180
workshops, 30, 44, 48, 77, 125–126
see also The Australian National University: School of Art; Canberra Technical College art school; Emerging Artist Support Scheme (EASS)
Canberra School of Music, 51, 166n11
Canberra Stereo Public Radio, 60n39, 75
Canberra Symphony Orchestra (CSO), 3n2, 3n3, 52, 56n22, 60n39, 75
Canberra Technical College art school, 5, 6–7, 26, 28 see also Canberra School of Art (CSA)
Canberra Theatre Centre (CTC), 32–33, 38n78, 41, 55, 60n39, 107, 249
 performances in 1974/75, 64
Canberra Theatre Gallery, 33, 107
Canberra Theatre Trust, 3n2, 41, 42
Canberra Times
 arts memorial advertisement, 68, *69*, 70
 awards sponsored by, 97, 180
 support for the arts, 41, 97
Canberra Women's Liberation (CWL), 24, 25, 109, 138, 139–140, 146n108
Canberra Youth Theatre (CYT), 49, 56n22, 60n39, 61, 70, 107
CAOA see Contemporary Art Organisations Australia (CAOA)
Capital Art Patrons' Organisation (CAPO), 53, 71, 72, 73–77, 78
Cardew, Gaynor, 78, 172n33, 174, 179
Caruana, Wally, 215

casino premium, 49, 71, 89, 92–93, 98–99, 102
CAST see Contemporary Art Space Tasmania (CAST)
CAT see Contemporary Art Tasmania (CAT)
Cattapan, Jon, 87
Causes exhibition, 1984, 232, 234
CCAE see Canberra College of Advanced Education
CCAF see Canberra Community Arts Front (CCAF)
CCAS see Canberra Contemporary Art Space (CCAS); Canberra Contemporary Art Space (CCAS) exhibitions
CDF see ACT Community Development Fund (CDF)
CEMA see Council for the Encouragement of Music and the Arts (CEMA)
Centenary of Canberra 2013, 5–6
Centre for Contemporary Photography, Melbourne, 10
Centre Gallery, 31
CEP see Community Employment Program (CEP)
Chameleon, Hobart, 10, 11–12, 234 see also Contemporary Art Tasmania (CAT)
Chapman, Christopher, 188, 190, 197–199
Chapman Gallery, 31
Charlesworth, JJ, 185
Chicago, Judy, 155
Chifley government, 49
Childers Group, The, 247, 248
Choreographic Centre, 65n51
Church, Julia, 13n32, 38n75, 165
 art student, 132, 146
 at/on BRG/Megalo, 111, 118, 144, 157
 community arts projects, 157n127, 218–219

Jill Posters member, 157, 158n130
on Morris, 148
prints by, *134*, 135, *147*, 148
Churcher, Betty, 5–6, 87, 251
Civic Permanent Art Award, 33
Civic Square, ACT, 33n60, 34, 93, 94, 100, 101
Clark, Deborah, 188, 200, 201, 226
Clark, Sir Kenneth, 34
Clark-Coolee, Bronwyn, 191
Cleghorn, Tom, 7
CMAG *see* Canberra Museum and Gallery (CMAG)
Cockatoo Workshop, Launceston, 234
collectives, 11–12, 43–44, 50, 165, 181–183, 187 *see also* Bitumen River Gallery (BRG); contemporary art spaces; Earthworks Poster Company/Collective; Jill Posters collective, Melbourne; Megalo
Collings, Joseph, 26
commercial galleries, 28–32, 54, 60, 81, 215
Commonwealth Art Advisory Board, 37, 81
Commonwealth government *see* federal government
Communist Party of Australia Marxist Leninist (CPAML), 128–130
community arts, 49–53, 67, 170
after self-government, 94–95
Binns and, 148–149
BRG projects, 217–219
community-focused cultural initiatives, 40–41, 43–44, 50, 92–103
critical support factors, absence of, 17, 48
exhibition spaces, 54
memorial advertisement, 68, *69*, 70
needs and government responses, 53–62
regional networks, 50–51
review of funding *see* Pascoe, Timothy, 1985 report on arts funding
rise and funding, 49–53
see also arts community
community arts organisations, 49–53, 59, 107
arts centres, 50, 56, 57, 60, 102
arts worker responses to Pascoe report, 68–71
lobbying, 57–58, 60–61, 247–248
recommendations to ADB, 55–56, 59–60
see also arts precincts; contemporary art spaces
Community Arts Program, 56n27, 67
community consultation, 90, 93–94, 99, 103, 248
Community Development Fund *see* ACT Community Development Fund (CDF)
Community Employment Program (CEP), 43n7, 52–53, 70n63, 170
community groups, 57 *see also* community arts organisations
Community Youth Support Scheme (CYSS), 43, 107, 111, 217 *see also* Jobless Action
community-focused cultural initiatives, 40–41, 43–44, 50, 92–103 *see also* community arts
contemporary art, 105–110, 124, 165–166
exhibitions, 112–117, 120–124
funding cuts, 247, 249
NGA temporary exhibition spaces, 86–87, 251–252 *see also* contemporary art spaces

Contemporary Art Centre of South
    Australia (CACSA), 9, 10
Contemporary Art Organisations
    Australia (CAOA), 9–10, 166n9
  gender representation in member
      exhibitions, 14–15
Contemporary Art Society (Australia),
    84
Contemporary Art Space Tasmania
    (CAST), 10, 15n38 *see also*
    Contemporary Art Tasmania
    (CAT)
Contemporary Art Space Working
    Group, 174 *see also* Bitumen River
    Gallery (BRG)
contemporary art spaces, 6–7, 9–12,
    117, 118, 163
  allocation of, 12, 57, 58, 60
  artist-run collectives, 11–12,
      43–44, 50, 105–106, 165,
      181–183, 187
  curatorial role and practice,
      185–188
  de Medici on, 195, 225
  federal government funding
      policy, 250
  funded art spaces, 9, 165,
      170–175, 250
  identities and institutionalisation,
      106n2, 187–188, 224–225
  lack of, 11, 17, 48, 57, 77, 78
  significance of, 250
  see also art galleries; arts precincts;
      Bitumen River Gallery (BRG);
      Canberra Contemporary Art
      Space (CCAS); community
      arts organisations; exhibition
      venues; Megalo; studio spaces
Contemporary Art Spaces
    Association, 166 *see also*
    Contemporary Art Organisations
    Australia (CAOA)
Contemporary Art Tasmania (CAT),
    9–10, 11

Convey, Sylvia, 172n33, 174
Coombs, HC 'Nugget', 6, 7n21,
    37n72, 38
  HC Coombs Creative Arts
      Fellowship, 120, 214
Cosgrove, Nick, 132, 233
Costigan, Paul, 174, 179
Costin, Warwick, 82
Council for the Encouragement of
    Music and the Arts (CEMA), 28,
    38n75, 39–40
  ACT branch, 40–41
countercultural movement, 13, 33,
    142, 144
the CoUNTess, 14–15
Cousins, Kerry-Anne, 73, 192,
    193–195, 236
Coward, Dan, 82, 83
Cowley, Jim, 136n90
CPMAL *see* Communist Party
    of Australia Marxist Leninist
    (CPAML)
Craft ACT/Craft Council of the
    ACT, 3n3, 27–28, 53, 60n39, 67,
    75, 101, 252n7
Croft, Brenda L, 216
Cruz, Maria, 191
CSA *see* Canberra School of Art
    (CSA)
CSO *see* Canberra Symphony
    Orchestra (CSO)
CTC *see* Canberra Theatre Centre
    (CTC)
Cullen, Gregor, 167
cultural capital term, 98
cultural councils *see* arts funding
    bodies *and specific organisations*;
    ACT Arts Development Board
    (ADB); ACT Cultural Council;
    Australia Council for the
    Arts (from 1973); Australian
    Council for the Arts (1967–73);
    Commonwealth Art Advisory
    Board; Cultural Facilities
    Corporation, ACT

cultural cringe, 195–196
Cultural Facilities Corporation, ACT, 101, 249 *see also* ACT Cultural Council
'cultural fringe', 106, 107
cultural infrastructure, 49, 89, 92–103, 248–249 *see also* arts precincts; community arts organisations
cultural workers *see* arts workers
Cummins, Bob, 226
curatorial role and practice, 185–187, 191, 196–197, 243
Currong Apartments, 242, *243*
CWL *see* Canberra Women's Liberation (CWL)
cyberfeminism, 156
CYSS *see* Community Youth Support Scheme (CYSS)
CYT *see* Canberra Youth Theatre (CYT)

Dadswell, Lyndon, 7
Dare, Zana, 158n130
Darling, Gordon, 124
David Jones department store, 33
Davies, Fiona, 13n32
Davies, Huw, 174
Davila, Juan, 166, 220
Davis, John, 136n90
Dawkins, Simon, 55, 60
DCT *see* Department of the Capital Territory (DCT)
de Mar, Lola, 7
de Medici, eX, 13n32, 17, 171, 174, 176, *205*
   60 heads exhibition, 1997, 228–232, *230*
   art practice, 221–232
   BRG and, 172n33, 182, 219–220, 222, 224, 234
   CCAS and, 195, 222–225
   on contemporary art space purpose, 195, 225

   knife, 1985, 223n101, 224
   Pistol, 1985, 223–224, *223*
   relationship with Virgo, 224–225
   tattooing, 172n33, 225–232, *227*, *230*
de Stoop, Jane, 27n34
Deakin High School, 33
Debenham, Pam, 188
del Castillo, Mariana, 13n32
Denton, Mark, 111, 132, 164, 165, 166, 167, 218–219, 234
Department of Education, NSW, 6n19, 7n21
Department of Territories and Local Government (DTLG), 58, 70, 234
Department of the Capital Territory (DCT), 25, 41, 50, 54, 72, 110, 136n89
Department of the Interior, 6
Desmond, Michael, 86, 87
Deves, Jenny, 27n34
Dickens, Lynn, 179
Domestic contradictions: perceptions of the domestic sphere exhibition, 1987, 179
Doug Anthony All Stars, 73
Down to Earth ConFest, 33, 142
Downie, Chris, 12
Dowse, Sara, 97, 139n97
Dreamings: the art of Aboriginal Australia exhibition, 1988–90, 215
Dreamtime to machinetime exhibition, 1981, 120–123, *121*, 214–215
Drill Hall Gallery, 86–87, 251
DTLG *see* Department of Territories and Local Government (DTLG)
Durant, Mark Alice, 183

Earthworks Poster Company/ Collective, 82, 110, 148, 150n118, 213
East Space, 252
Eaton, Janenne, 180
Eaton, Pat, 140

education in the arts, Pascoe recommendations, 67 *see also* art schools
Eggert, Anna, 13n32, 188
Electric Tipi, 226
Elliot, Megan, 202, 213, 235, 237
Ellis, Ruth, 226
Elsie House, 25, 140n99
Emerging Artist Support Scheme (EASS), 71, 72, 77–78
emerging artists, 11–12, 33, 54–55, 76–78, 110, 170, 174–175, 195, 224–225 *see also* community arts; contemporary art
employment programs *see* job creation initiatives
Ender, Brigitte, 78
Ethos 1961 (Tom Bass), 34, 101
Ewington, Julie, 175–176, 179, 182, 203
exhibition catalogues, 191–194, 197, 198, 221, 229
exhibition venues, 32–33, 53–55
  lack of, 48, 77
  see also art galleries; contemporary art spaces; *and names of specific organisations:*
exhibitions *see* art galleries; Bitumen River Gallery (BRG) exhibitions; Canberra Contemporary Art Space (CCAS) exhibitions; performance art; travelling exhibitions
experimental art, 10n25, 66, 67, 136
  see also contemporary art
Experimental Art Foundation, Adelaide, 6n18, 10, 82, 106, 136, 166, 172, 174, 234

Fabyc, Deej, 157, 158n130, 182
Fantasia Galleries, 32, 148
Farnham, Ken, 41–42
Farquhar-Still, Geoff, 79n84
Faulkner, Sarah, 87

Federal Capital Advisory Committee (FCAC), 45
Federal Capital Commission (FCC), 22 *see also* National Capital Development Commission (NCDC)
federal government
  'arts' definition, 36, 42
  arts funding mechanisms, 37–38, 61 *see also* arts funding
  cultural institutions *see* national cultural institutions
  performing arts/flagship focus, 2–3, 17, 36–37, 42, 71–72
  public artworks responsibility, 34–36
  waning commitment to ACT community, 47–48, 61
  see also specific governments:; Chifley government; Fraser government; Holt government; Menzies government; Whitlam government
female artists *see* women artists
female-centric language, 155–156
femininity, and *Slut* poster, 150–161
feminism, 24–25, 49n2, 109, 129, 138–140
  and art, 80–81, *141*, 148–161, 179
  cyberfeminism, 156
  first-wave, 25, 138n96
  lipstick feminism, 155, 158
  second-wave, 138–139, 152, 153–157, 158, 161
  third-wave, 138–139, 152, 157, 161
  see also social activism; women's liberation movement
Ferguson, Andrew, 87
Ferguson, Mark, 70
Ferguson, Tim, 73

Festival of Creative Arts and
    Sciences, 33
*A first look: Philip Morris Arts Grant
    purchases 1983–1986* exhibition,
    1986, 87
The first Super Doreen show, 1982,
    146, 148
    poster, *147*
Fisher, John, 136n90
Fitzpatrick, Donal, 250
Flavin, Dan, 87
Flower, Cedric, 35
Fogwell, Dianne, 79, 133
Foley, Fiona, 216
Follett government (ACT), 91, 93, 96
Fooke, Maggie, 158n130
Fools Gallery Theatre Co, 49, 107
Ford, Paul, 110, 111, 117, 118, 122,
    132, 233
Fortune Theatre, 174n37
Foster, Hal, 143
The Foundry, 217, *218*
Francis, Ivor, 85
Frank, Dale, 187, 190, 196–201, *197*
Franklin, Annie, 179
Fraser government, 38, 43, 74, 146
Freeth, Gordon, 34
Frewin, Elizabeth, 174
Frith, Clifford, 127
From Dreamtime to machinetime
    exhibition, 1981, 120–123, *121*,
    214–215
Full flight project (1981–83), 149
funding *see* arts funding
fundraising
    CAPO, 53, 71, 72, 73–77, 78
    CCAS auction, 251

Gaha, Adrienne, 180
Gallegos, Elena, 222
galleries *see* art galleries
Gallery A (Canberra), 31
Gallery Fred, 79n84
Gallery Huntley, 29–30
Galloway, Maeve, 52
gambling revenue *see* casino premium
Garran, Robert (of *Muse* magazine), 72
Garran, Sir Robert, 39–40
Gascoigne, Rosalie, 32, 59, 123, 143,
    148, 191
gay themes, 220–221, 224
Gemes, Judo (Juno), 216
gender representation
    in administration, 15
    art students, 14
    in exhibitions, 13–15
George Paton Gallery, University
    of Melbourne, 10n25, 32n54,
    209n62, 233n129
Gerber, Matthys, 191
Gertrude Contemporary,
    Melbourne, 10
Gilbert, Christie, *205*
Goethe Institut, 55
    travelling exhibition, CCAS, 1994,
    224n103, 227–228, *227*
Goldfields Art Centre, Kalgoorlie, 231
Gollan, Daphne, 139n97
Gordon, Mark, 65n51
Gorman House Arts Centre, 22n9,
    50, 55, 57, 58, 60n39, 101, 133,
    174n37, 251 *see also* Canberra
    Contemporary Art Space (CCAS)
Gorton government, 85
government in the ACT *see* Australian
    Capital Territory; Australian
    Capital Territory Legislative
    Assembly; federal government
Grady, Ben, 51, 166, 171, 180
grants *see* arts funding
Grayson, Richard, 174, 186, 187
Great Britain *see* United Kingdom
Green, Erica, 15n39, 117, 172, 173,
    179
Griffin Centre, Civic, 57
Griffith Gallery, 32

Grishin, Sasha, 30, 31, 58, 164, 168, 220n92
   exhibition reviews, 87, 180, 191n20, 192–193, 219, 221
   on NGA entry fee, 83–84
   on Nickolls, 122, 123
Grounds, Marr, 136n90
Grove, Joy, 27n34

Hagerty, Marie, 79n84
Haley, Eileen, 109, 139n97
Hamilton, Ian, 136n90
Hamilton, Richard, 208
Hard Times publication, 116
Harrington, Tom, 79n84
Harrison, Stephen, 73
Haslem, John, 111
Hawker College Theatre, 102
Hayden, Bill, 37n72, 39
Haynes, Peter, 192–193
Healey, Ken, 78
Healey, Sue, 65n51
Helen Maxwell Gallery, 81 *see also* Maxwell, Helen
Henderson, Beryl, 25, 139, 139n97
Herbst, Adam, 226
Herel, Petr, 30
Higginbotham, Julie, 158n130, 233
Hinchliffe, Meredith, 27n34, 79
Historic Memorials Committee, 37
histories of Canberra, 4–7
Hobba, Leigh, 136n90
Hodgman, Michael, 83
Hoff, Ursula, 125
Holford, Sir William, 34
Holmes, Cherylynn, 13n32, 33, 139, 142–143, 146, 171
Holt, Beatrice, 22
Holt government, 64, 81, 85
Holyoake, Catriona, 13n32
   and Jill Posters collective, 157–160
   Slut poster, 1983, 138–139, 150–161, *151*

Honybun, Liz, 136n90
Hookey, Gordon, 235–237
Horridge, Naomi, 209
House, Matilda, 235
Human Veins Dance Theatre, 3n2, 3n3, 60n39, 61, 67, 69
   history and successors, 65n51
Humphries, Gary, 76

I am you: artists against violence, art for tolerance exhibition, 1994, 224n103, 227–228, *227*
I won't see you in paradise (slut) poster 1983, 138–139, 150–161, *151*
Iceberg Gallery, Melbourne, 232–233
The image of desire exhibition, 1985, 220–221
Indigenous art, 80, 190, 204, 212–217
   at BRG, 120–123, 212, 213–214, 215
   at CCAS, 213, 217, 235–237
   in commercial galleries, 29, 31, 81, 215
   in national and state galleries, 215
   research opportunities, 250
   Urban Indigenous art, 33, 120–123, 212, 214–217, 235
industrial relations and arts workers involvement, 126–131
Inside out: out of the mainstream: a group exhibition, 1994, 225–226
'Inside out', performance art season, 1998, *205–206*
Institute of Modern Art (IMA), Brisbane, 9, 10n24, 106, 231, 237n140
institutional galleries *see* art museums; national cultural institutions
International Women's Day, 25, 139n97, 140n99
International Women's Year, 139n97

Jigsaw Theatre Company, 49, 56n22, 75, 107
Jill Posters collective, Melbourne, 150–153, 157–161
   members, 158n130
job creation initiatives, 43–44, 52–53, 217–218 *see also* Community Employment Program (CEP); Community Youth Support Scheme (CYSS)
Jobless Action, 43–44, 52–53, 59, 107–110, 111
   BRG and, 9, 44, 143
   Megalo and, 9, 44, 53, 109–111, 143–144
   poster, *44*
John Curtin House, 33
Johnson, Di, 110
Jolly, Martyn, 188, 189
Jones, Bo, 11–12
Jones, Stephanie, 13n32
Jubelin, Narelle, 180

Kaleski, Sonja, 54
Kavanagh, Annie, 43, 52, 110
Keinholz, Edward, 87
Kelly, Deborah, 13n32
Kelly, Gail, 70
Kennedy, Brian, 85
Kennedy, Cate, 73
Kerr, David, 136n90
Kerr, Joan, 136, 137
King, Grahame, 125
Kingsland, Sir Richard, 6, 7n21, 51, 55, 58
Kingston Art Centre, 57, 58, 60, 78, 79
Kingston Arts Precinct, 100, 241n149, 252n7
Kleinert, Ingo, 136–138
Koehne, Jim, 70
Koori art '84 exhibition, Sydney, 1984, 120, 122–123, 215–216

Kosuth, Joseph, 87
Kristeva, Julia, 159

La Perouse Gallery, 32
Lang, Jill, 43
language, female-centric, 155–156
Larter, Pat, 136n90
Larter, Richard, 30
Lasseters Gallery, 32
Le Grand, Hendrieka, 28
Le Grand, Henri, 7, 28
Le Grand, Michael, 28
Lee, Lindy, 191, 192
Lendon, Nigel, 135
Lewis, Ruark, 191
libraries, 92, 93, 94, 101 *see also* National Library of Australia (NLA)
Lightworks: works of art using light as a medium exhibition, 1985–86, 86–87
Lindsay, Sir Darryl, 34, 81n87
Link Gallery, 33
Lippard, Lucy, 129–130, 135
lipstick feminism, 155, 158
literary arts, 40, 73, 94, 97, 101
Little, Colin, 110, 111, 122, 213, 214
Livingstone, Charles, 217
lobbying *see* advocacy for the arts
local government *see* Australian Capital Territory Legislative Assembly; Australian Capital Territory: self-government
local–national dichotomy, 2–3, 16, 17–21, 36–37, 41, 47–48, 62, 65–66, 71–72, 102–103, 193
   see also Australian Capital Territory; Canberra; federal government
Looby, Keith, 30

M16, 150n117, 252n7
Mackenzie Art Gallery, Regina, Saskatchewan, 190
MacPherson, Robert, 191

Macquarie Galleries Canberra, 31–32
Macquarie Galleries Sydney, 32
Madigan, Colin, 81
Magarey, Susan, 139n97
magazines *see Muse* magazine
Majura Women's Group, 5, 27, 50
Maloon, Terence, 87n110
Manderson, Roland, 110, 221
Martin, Mandy, 13n32, 17, 79, 108, 146, 219
   background and impacts, 125, 126–135, 152, 157
Maxwell, Helen, 15, 79, 80–81
McConchie, Barbara, 27n34
McDonald, Euan, 191
McDonald, Robert, 166
McFarlane, Jenny, 229
McGillick, Paul, 137
McKee, Paull, 206–212, *207*
McLean, Hawk, *205*
McQueen, Humphrey, 117, 131
McVeigh, Tom, 83, 84
Megalo, 5, 80, 144, 150n117, 246, 252n7
   archive, 2n1
   BRG and, 106, 108, 111–112
   directors, 179n49, 246
   establishment, 9, 58, 108–110, 143–144
   exhibition at CCAS, 179
   funding, 53, 110, 174n37
   funding, lobbying for, 60n39
   Jobless Action and, 44, 53, 109–110, 143
   posters, *44*, 112, *113–115*, 115–116, *121*, *141*, 213, *218*
   significance of, 108–109, 213, 246
Meikle, Ian, 97
Melbourne
   art scene, 156–161
   Canberra artists' exhibitions, 232–233
   Jill Posters collective, 150–153, 157–161

memorial notice for community arts, 68, *69*, 70
Menzies government, 2, 21, 34–35, 81–82
Meryl Tankard Company, 65n51
Meyer, Laura, 155
Mico, Domenic, 50, 70n63
Miles, Barbara, 158n130
minority exhibitions at BRG/CCAS, 212, 223
   Foundry clients' work, 217–218
   gay themes, 220–221, 224, 225
   Indigenous art, 120–123, 212–217, 235–237
   photocopy works, 180–181, 222–224, 231
   photography, 216–217
   posters, 212–213
   tattooing, 225–232
   work by children with disabilities, 218–219
Modjeska, Drusilla, 139n97
Moje, Klaus, 79, 168
Mollison, James, 82, 86, 123–124, 137
Moloney, Lindsay, 30
MONA, Hobart, 86n102
Monaro Camera Club, 26n26
Morosi, Junie, 142
Morris, Anne, 146, 148, 152
Morrow, David, 110, 111, 132
   Well, I've never heard of YOU either postcard, 112, *114*
Mortensen, Kevin, 136n90
Mothers' memories others' memories (MMOM) project (1979–81), 149
Moulen, Cassie, 132
Mundine, Djon, 216
Musa, Helen, 73, 97, 189, 190, 196
Muse magazine, 72–73, 75, 110, 116, 190, 194

NAA *see* National Archives of Australia (NAA)
Naii Ngarrambai Wanggirali Burrangiri Nangi Dyannai Ngurui (the lay of the land is how you know your country; when you look behind you, you can always see your tracks) installation, 1995, 213, 235–237, *236*
  artists, *237*
Narek Galleries, 32
national – local dichotomy *see* local–national dichotomy
National Archives of Australia (NAA), 4–5, 20
National Capital Authority (NCA), 91, 252
national capital construct *see under* Canberra
National Capital Development Commission (NCDC), 21, 31, 53–54, 56, 57–58, 125n54
  public artworks program, 34–36
  replacement bodies, 91
national cultural institutions, 4–5, 6, 20, 33, 48, 59, 64, 252 *see also* Australian War Memorial (AWM); National Archives of Australia (NAA); National Film and Sound Archive (NFSA); National Gallery of Australia (NGA); National Library of Australia (NLA); National Museum of Australia (NMA); National Portrait Gallery (NPG)
National Film and Sound Archive (NFSA), 20
National Gallery of Australia (NGA)
  benefit for local arts (perception of), 3, 33
  budget cuts, 87, 251, 252
  collection and acquisitions, 2n1, 37–38, 66, 124, 150, 213, 215, 220
  contemporary art exhibition spaces, 86–87, 251–252
  'free admission' campaign, 81–86
  opening, 20, 58, 64, 82
  Pascoe on, 3, 67
  role, 55, 59, 66, 67, 81n87
  senior staff, 82 *see also* Butler, Roger; Mollison, James; Thomas, Daniel
National Gallery of Victoria, 215
National Institute of Dramatic Arts, 39n81
National Jewish Centre, 33
National Library of Australia (NLA), 5, 20, 55, 84, 101
National Museum of Australia (NMA), 20
National Portrait Gallery (NPG), 20
Nauman, Bruce, 87
Navilly, Renald, *205*
NCA *see* National Capital Authority (NCA)
NCDC *see* National Capital Development Commission (NCDC)
New South Wales Council for the Encouragement of Music and the Arts (CEMA), 28, 38n75, 39–41
Newmarch, Annie, 127, 128–129, 179
NFSA *see* National Film and Sound Archive (NFSA)
NGA *see* National Gallery of Australia (NGA)
Nickolls, Trevor, 33, 120, 212–216
  Dreamtime to machinetime exhibition, 1981, 120–123, *121*, 214–215
Niemeyer, Oscar, 239, 240, 242
Nixon, John, 136n90
NLA *see* National Library of Australia (NLA)
NMA *see* National Museum of Australia (NMA)

Norrie, Susan, 191, 192
Northern Centre for Contemporary Art, Darwin, 10, 11
Nowhere utopia exhibition, 1987, 180–181, 182, 222–224, *223*, 232, 234
NPG *see* National Portrait Gallery (NPG)
nuclear disarmament campaign, 13, 154
Nundah Gallery, 28, 29

Off the beach event, 1985, 144, *145*
Old Tote Theatre, 41
Oltolgyi, Angelic, 179
Oops Multiarts, 49
Opera ACT, 3n2
Orr, Jillian, 136n90
Osborne, Ruth, 65n51
Our Place exhibition, 1981, 218–219
Overall, Sir John, 34–35
Oxley, Roslyn, 197

Page, Geoff, 58
Parr, Mike, 136n90
Pascoe, Timothy, 1985 report on arts funding, 48, 62–71
   author credentials, 62, 63–64, 102
   conclusions and recommendations, 3, 28, 66–67
   consequences, 169–170
   flawed methodology, 64–65, 89
   misconceptions, 3, 17, 67–68, 89, 102, 250
   responses to, 68–71, 169–170
   terms of reference, 61–62
Pastoral Gallery, 32
patrons of the arts
   CAPO, 53, 71, 72, 73–77, 78
   CCAS fundraising auction, 251
Peascod, Alan, 59

Penner, Marta, 239–243
performance art
   at CCAS, 204, *205*, 206–212, *207*, 250
   festivals, 136–138
   gallery-based immersion and audience interaction, 208–212
   research opportunities, 250
Performance Space, Sydney, 9, 10n24, 231
performing arts
   ACA ACT and, 40
   AETT and, 36–39
   after self-government, 94, 95, 99–100
   CAPO funding, 75
   community organisations, 49–50, 107
   events in Canberra, 64–65
   federal government focus on, 2–3, 17, 36–37, 41, 63
   primacy of, 48, 51–52, 59, 66, 69, 102
Perkins, Hetti, 216
Perth Institute of Contemporary Arts, 10
Phillips, Morgyn, 79
Photo Access, 150n117, 174n37, 203, 252n7
photocopy works, 124, 180–181, 222–224, 225, 231
Photofile (publication), 10
Piccinini, Patricia, *Skywhale*, 2013, 245, *246*
Pithie, Kristian, 31
Playhouse Gallery, 32
political activism, 126–130, 135, 139–140, 248 *see also* feminism; social activism
population of Canberra, 12–13, 19, 21–25, 47, 74, 106, 139, 247
Post-atomic card!: Working art!, colour postcard, 154, *154*

posters and poster making, 13, 15, 108–110, 124, 146, 212–213
   Bill posters appreciated exhibition, 112, *113–115*, 115–116, 212–213
   collections of, 2n1
   Jill Posters collective, 150–153, 157–161
   NGA acquisitions, 124, 150, 213
   political posters, 128–129, 131
   see also Megalo; prints and printmaking
Powell, Andrew, 233
Praxis, Perth, 106, 234 *see also* Perth Institute of Contemporary Arts
Prime cultural estate exhibition, 1986, 78–79
Print Council of Australia, 125–126
prints and printmaking, 15, 75, 79–80, 106, 108–110
   collections of, 2n1
   culture at CSA, 79–80, 131–133
   NGA acquisitions, 66, 124, 150, 213, 220
   skills development among unemployed, 44, 52–53
   see also Jill Posters collective, Melbourne; Megalo; posters and poster making; Studio One
Progressive Art Movement (PAM), 126, 128, 130
Prowse, Ruth, 29–30, 31
Pryor, Juilee, 166
public artworks, 34–36, 227–228
public housing built on Bauhaus principles, 125n54

QL2 Youth Dance Ensemble, 65n51
Quantum Leap Youth Choreographic Ensemble, 65n51
Quinn, Lucy, 6

Radford, Gail, 139n97
Radford, Ron, 251
radio programs, 50, 75, 196, 202–203
Radok, Stephanie, 164, 172n33, 174, 176, 233
Ramsay, Bob, 136n90
Ramsay, Gordon, 248
Rankine, Susan, 87
Ransome, Kay, 164
rape of women in war commemoration march, 1982, 140 poster, *141*
Rauschenberg, Robert, 87
Redback Graphix, 167
Redletter, 165
Reeves, Kate, 158n130
Refshauge, Richard, 100–101
Reid, Elizabeth, 139n97
Reid House, 49–50
research opportunities, 249–250
Rhodes, Linda, 158n130
Richardson, Elvis, 14–15
Riverside Gallery, 32
Roberts, Neil, 168–169, 174, 176, 191, 192
Robertson, Toni, 82, 83, 135, 148
Romantisystem exhibition, 1994, 191–196, 201
Rose, Jacqueline, 191, 192
Rubbo, Kiffy, 10n25, 32n54
Runnegar, Brenda, 13n32, 15n39, 188, 189, 201–202, 224, 226
Russell, Colin, 152–153, 233
Ryan, Julia, 25, 139n97
Ryan, Lyndall, 139–140
Ryan, Susan, 55

SA SOA *see* South Australian School of Art (SA SOA)
Saint, Paul, 191
Salon coda: the making of history exhibition, 1987, 176, *177*
Samuels, Jeffrey, 215
Sandeha, Veet, 174

Sandland, Bronwen, 13n32
  Beautiful home exhibition, 1998, 206–212, *207*
Sangster, Gary, 166
Santamaria, Catherine, 58, 61, 68
Satellite of love exhibition, 1994–95, 187, 190, 196–201, *197*
Savage, Lesley, 136n90
Saxton, Robert, 166
Schmeisser, Jorg, 30, 79, 83, 108, 125, 126, 131–133, 233n129
Scratching exhibition, 1994, 225, 226
screen-printing *see* prints and printmaking
Secombe, Erica, 13n32
Selby, Lois, 202
Select Committee on Cultural Activities and Facilities (ACT), 71, 89, 91, 93–97, 98, 100, 101, 102–103, 252n7
Select Committee on the Establishment of a Casino (ACT), 91, 92–93, 95
Sellbach, Udo, 7, 59, 125–126, 131, 137, 166n11
Serilus, Gaida, 110, 111, *121*, 122
Sever, Nancy, 87n110
Shead, Gary, 30
Shera, Geoff, 124
Sheridan, Noel, 82, 106n2, 136
Shiels, Julie, 157n127, 158n130
Simic, Anna, *205*
Simons, Anna, 31–32
Single Women's Shelter Collective, 146
Site specific city exhibition, 1987, 176, *178*
Skywhale, 2013, 245, *246*
Slut poster, 1983, 138–139, 150–161, *151*
Smith, Terry, 16, 117, 129–130, 136n90, 137, 166
Smith, Trevor, 238, 249
  background, 190
  at CCAS, 15, 17, 185, 189–202, 232, 235, 243
  exhibitions curated, 187, 191–201
  and Runnegar, 201–202
social activism, 2, 5, 13, 80–81, 106–109
  BRG exhibitions, 112, 115–116
  Jobless Action programs, 43–44, 108
  for women's services, 24–25, 140, 146
  see also arts community: activism; Jobless Action; women's liberation movement
social services for women and children, 22–25, 140, 146
Solander Gallery, 28–29
South Australia, political and industrial events, 126–130
South Australian School of Art (SA SOA), 125, 126, 127, 129, 164, 203
'Space for Artists' campaign, 57
Spain, Mark, 79n84
Splinters (theatre collective), 79n84, 226
Spring Music Festival, 41
St John the Baptist Church, Reid, 55
Stagecoach, 60n39
Stagecoach Theatre School, 53
Standing Committee on Planning, Development and Infrastructure (ACT), 89, 91, 98–100, 102, 103
Stanhope government (ACT), 227
Stanton, Susan, 30
Strathnairn homestead, 50
Street Theatre, 95, 99, 100, 102
Studio Nundah, 28, 29
Studio One, 75, 79–80, 174n37
studio spaces, 78–79, 96
  allocation of, 12, 57, 58, 60
  lack of, 11, 17, 48, 57, 77, 78
  see also contemporary art spaces
Sugden, Greg, 171
Sunday in the Park, 50, 72
Super Doreen, 1982, 146, *147*, 148

Sutherland, Peter, 50
Swen, Hiroe, 32
Szeeman, Harald, 185

Tate Gallery response to user-pays principle, 85
tattooing, 225–232, *227*, *230*
Taubman, Wendy, 69–70
Taylor, Ben, 133
Taylor, Michael, 59
Temin, Kathy, 191
theatre *see* performing arts
Theatre ACT, 3n3, 56n22, 60n39, 67, 68, 69, 75
Thomas, Daniel, 82, 137, 175, 185
Thomas, Rover, 123
Thorp, Richard, 74
Thor's Hammer, 79n84
Through Art Unity Theatre (TAU), 70, 169
Thursday Group, 27
Tin Sheds art workshop, 110, 148
Tipping, Richard, 136n90
Tjampitjinpa, Dinny Nolan, 120
Tobias, Lin, 158n130
Tobin, Julia, 158n130
Toora Single Women's Shelter, 146
Toora Women Inc, 5
travelling exhibitions, 33, 40, 201
    Binns', 149
    BRG, 166, 172, 222–223, 232–234, 243
    CCAS, 179, 191, 204, 227–232, 234–243
    international, 204, 215, 227–228, 231, 237–243
travelling performances in Canberra, 64–65
Tremblay, Theo, 80
Trendall, Arthur, 35
Trevillian, Annie, 179
Trevor Nickolls: from Dreamtime to machinetime exhibition *see under* Nickolls, Trevor

Trezzi, Nicola, 186
True bird grit (book, 1982), 133, *134*, 135
Trust Ballet Company, 39n81
Truth rules OK? exhibition, 1984, 168
Truth rules II exhibition, 1986, 172
Tuckson, Tony, 215
Tuffin's Music Studios, 33
Tuggeranong, ACT, 50, 56
    Arts Centre, 102, 218n85
Tully, Peter, 87
Twigg, Tony, 136n90

Underhill, Nancy, 84
United Kingdom
    alternative arts movement, 51
    arts funding models and policies, 2, 38n75
    Council for the Encouragement of Music and the Arts (CEMA), 39
    feminism movement, 138n96
    user-pays pricing at art museums, 85
United States
    arts funding models and policies, 2, 38n75
    feminism movement, 138n96, 139
University of Melbourne George Paton Gallery, 10n25, 32n54, 209n62, 233n129
Unsworth, Ken, 136n90
UP Front Theatre, 70n63
Urban Indigenous art, 33, 120–123, 212, 214–217, 235
Urban tribalwear and beyond exhibition, 1991, 87
Ure, Richard, 125n54
Uren, Tom, 55, 60, 61
user-pays pricing, 81–86

Vandermark, Peter, 79
Vanduren, Margaret, 27n34

Vaskess, Stuart, 79n84, 226
Vaughan, Gerard, 252
Vignando, Catrina, 27n34
Virgo, Anne
    at ACG, 163, 166, 171, 172, 173–174, 180
    at BRG, 15n39, 17, 70, 117, 163, 164–172, 181, 183, 224
    on BRG, 172, 173–174, 181, 182
    at CCAS, 15n39, 17, 163, 174–181, 188, 224, 232
    relationship with de Medici, 224–225
    teaching at CSA, 166n11
Virtual reality exhibition, 1994–95, 187, 196–197
Vis-a-Vis Dance Canberra, 65n51
visual arts, 2–3, 33, 48–49, 65, 71
    CAPO funding, 75, 77
    federal government funding, 37–38, 42
    funding after ACT self-government, 96–103, 247–249
    funding cuts, 247
    Pascoe report, 66–68, 89, 250
    versus primacy of performing arts, 36–37, 59, 71, 102
    user-pays pricing, 81–86
    see also art galleries; community arts; exhibition venues; posters and poster making; prints and printmaking; studio spaces
Visual Arts Board (VAB) of Australia Council *see under* Australia Council for the Arts (from 1973)
VNS Matrix, 156

Waaka, Mereana Otene, 235
Wadlington, Helen, 78
Wage Pause Program, 52–53, 57
Wallace, Daphne, 216
Wallace-Crabbe, Robin, 7, 59
Waller, Ruth, 13n32, 188, 191
Walsh, David, 86n102
Walters, Donald, 136n90
Walters, Kath, 132, 157, 158n130, 165
Ward, Biff, 109, 139–140
Warden, Ian, 83, 84
Warren, Joyce (Joy), 28–29, 31
Warren, Robert (Bob), 28–29
Watson, Jenny, 30
Watt, Alan, 59
Watt, David, 188, 204
Wawrzyńczak, Anni Doyle, 13n32
Webb, Julian, 43, 52–53, 107, 110–111, 116
Wednesday Group, 27
Wells, Di, 132, 157n128
Wesley Centre, 32
Whaley, George, 55
Whitehead, James, 78
Whitlam, Gough, 25, 85
Whitlam government, 25, 42–43, 74, 85, 140, 142, 195
Wicks, Arthur, 136n90, 176
    Mobile observatory, 1987, *178*
Williams, Darcy, 31
Williams, David, 77, 91, 96, 98
Wilson, Carole, 153, 158, 160
Winston, Denis, 35
Wolfe, Ross, 173, 232
women
    artists *see* women artists
    Australian Women's archive project, 5
    Canberra population, 22, 24–25
    female-centric language, 155–156
    influence on arts scene, 3–4, 12–15, 28–31, 138–150
    social activism, 2, 5, 13, 24–25, 140 *see also* feminism
women against rape march, 1982, 140, *141*
Women and Arts Festival 1982, 146
Women and Children's Committee, 22

women artists, 10n25, 80–81
    art student gender statistics, 14
    at CSA, 15, 126, 131–135, 142, 146, 148–150, 152, 166n11, 180
    exhibition statistics, 13–15
    gallery for (aGOG), 15, 79, 80–81, 225–226
    see also names of individual artists
Women's Art Movement, 10n25, 148, 149
Women's Art Register, 10n25, 146
Women's Electoral Lobby (WEL) ACT, 139n97, 140
women's groups, 3–4, 5, 27, 50
women's liberation movement, 13, 24–25, 139–140, 155 *see also* Canberra Women's Liberation (CWL); feminism; social activism
women's refuges, 2, 5, 24, 25, 140, 146
women's services, 22–25, 140, 146
Women's Theatre Workshop, 50
Wood, Bill, 76n78, 91, 92, 93–96, 252n7
Woodrow, Carol, 49, 65
Woodward, Joe, 107n6
Work saints exhibition, 1986, 172n33, 222
Wrigley, Derek, 27n34

Yarralumla Brickworks, 78–79
Yarralumla Marine Centre, 33
YMCA, 33
Young Elizabethan Theatre Players, 39n81

www.ingramcontent.com/pod-product-compliance
Lightning Source LLC
Chambersburg PA
CBHW040519220526
45473CB00013B/2921